THE POPE'S CABINET

JOHAN ICKX

The Pope's Cabinet

Pius XII's Secret War for Saving Jews

SOPHIA INSTITUTE PRESS
Manchester, New Hampshire

EWTN Publishing, Inc.
5817 Old Leeds Road, Irondale, AL 35210

Distributed by Sophia Institute Press, Box 5284, Manchester, NH 03108.

paperback ISBN 978-1-64413-858-8

ebook ISBN 978-1-64413-859-5

Library of Congress Control Number: 2022039461

To Herbert † and Adelinde Hoischen-Scheirle,
the German grandparents in Rome of
Annelies, Charlotte, and Catharina

Foreword by the Editor

ELECTED AS POPE Pius XII on March 2, 1939, Eugenio Pacelli left a controversial legacy. Lauded after the Second World War as the savior of Rome and of many Jews, Pius XII was later on criticized for his passivity during the Holocaust and became known as the "Pope of Silence," a negative image popularized by the 1963 play *The Deputy* by the German playwright Rolf Hochhuth, which was later adapted as the film *Amen* by Costa-Gavras.

Beyond the polemic that started years after the war, questions remain: What did Pope Pius XII know about the atrocities committed during the war, and when was he informed of them? Did the Holy See do everything in its power to help the victims of Nazi barbarity?

On March 2, 2020, by decision of Pope Francis, the Vatican archives of the Pius XII pontificate were opened for researchers, allowing the veil to finally be lifted on the position of the pope and the Catholic Church in the face of Nazism.

No one is better acquainted with the archives of Pius XII than Johan Ickx, director of the Historical Archive of the Secretariat of State to the Vatican, which preserves the political and diplomatic treasure of the Holy See's foreign policy. In this labyrinth of classified documents, all his expertise was needed to make sense of the files and pinpoint the pope's actions and convictions within them. Johan Ickx's experience over more than twenty years at the heart of different archives of the Vatican and in Rome meant that he was uniquely qualified to undertake the monumental task of analyzing the more than one and a half million documents on the war and the afterwar period already available for research and immersing the reader in this fascinating story.

In this extraordinary work, which does not claim to be exhaustive, history is told through the human stories that reveal the divergent attitudes held at the heart of the Vatican. Johan Ickx takes the reader into the mysterious world of the Roman Curia and Vatican diplomacy, in which information of a confidential, diplomatic nature is often communicated in language that would otherwise be incomprehensible to the uninitiated. He brings to life the Cabinet, the circle of intimates around Pius XII, from which all the decisions of the Sovereign Pontiff emanated and which alone was authorized to speak in his name.

During the Second World War, the whole world sought assistance from the Vatican. Many people pinned their hopes on the papacy. Drawing on previously unpublished documents (letters, photographs, drawings, newspaper articles), Johan Ickx paid special attention in his investigations to the Cabinet's approach to the Jews amid the terror of the Nazis and the Holocaust. The book includes a moving list of names selected from the thousands of anonymous individuals who were directly assisted by Pius XII and "his Cabinet."

Each chapter begins with "A Tale of …" and gives the reader an inside look at the office of Pius XII and its interactions with the outside world. Taking his inspiration from Italian literature, and in particular from the *Decameron* by Giovanni Boccaccio, Johan Ickx has breathed life into the hundreds of thousands of documents read, analyzed, and cross-checked, many of which led down blind alleys. The point of departure for every chapter is the daily life of the Cabinet and the bustling activity of the State Secretariat of the Vatican, in particular its Ministry of Foreign Affairs in wartime. In creating this work of a lifetime, Johan Ickx has had access to documents that no other eyes have seen.

Rarely does an editor have the opportunity to publish a work of such great historical value, a work that is a milestone in the search for the truth about the role of the Church in the face of absolute evil.

Contents

THE POPE'S CABINET

Introduction

ON JANUARY 24, 2020, for the first time in our lives, my wife and I set foot in the New World. The permanent observer of the Holy See to the United Nations and the Pave the Way Foundation had invited me to New York, along with a group of fine scholars, and had asked me, on the occasion of the International Holocaust Remembrance Day at the United Nations, to give a lecture on Pius XII and the Jews of Rome. In the dining room of our hotel, the television news informed us on a loop of the growing concern over the COVID-19 situation in America.

Almost a year before, Pope Francis had announced the opening of all the archives of the Vatican for Pius XII's pontificate, prompting many friends and colleagues to encourage me to write a book. Truth be told, the thought had been on my mind for some time. The pandemic and ensuing lockdown gave it a decisive boost.

As coincidences go, in Germany, Rolf Hochhuth died during the pandemic lockdown. Hochhuth was the author of the well-known theater play *Der Stellvertreter* (*The Deputy*). The play, engineered and funded by the Soviet Secret Service, had been staged in 1963 in Berlin and translated into almost all European languages. Its message spread like a lethal virus and damned in less than a few months the memory of the work of Pius XII during World War II. The seductive antagonism shown in the play, although nothing more than a theatrical invention, contributed to making it a "historical forgery." It has to be said: it remains a most stubborn artifact of the Soviet Secret Service's production market.

The action of Pius XII during World War II, which had been praised and honored by the highest-ranking politicians and Jewish personalities worldwide immediately after the war, was damned in less than a few months. The play's "accusation of the silence(s)" regarding Pius XII, already present in the Soviet and Socialist press since the early days of the Cold War, was now injected in the Western world's public opinion. It has stuck and has been exploited ever since and for a variety of reasons. For the next generations, the tone was set.

In January 1964, at the end of his first international visit to Jordan and Israel, Pope Paul VI responded to the accusations made against Pius XII, coming close to provoking a diplomatic incident. Basing his stance on the first principle that every historian has a moral duty to follow, he said, "History, not the artificial manipulation of the facts and their preconceived interpretation as operated in the 'Deputy,' will claim the truth about Pius XII's action during the last war against the criminal excesses of the Nazi regime, and will demonstrate how vigilant, assiduous, selfless and courageous it was, in the real context of the facts and conditions of those years."[1]

For the record, Pope Paul VI had been an active participant and a daily witness of the Vatican's diplomacy during the Second World War. From December 1937 onwards, he had been the substitute of the Secretariat of State while Eugenio Pacelli, the future Pope Pius XII, was the secretary of state. Of the man he had come to know over two decades he said later on:

> Under the calm and gentle aspect and under an always chosen and
> moderate language … is revealed a noble and strong temperament,
> capable of assuming positions of great fortitude and fearless risk. It is
> not true that he was insensitive and isolated. Instead, he was very fine
> and very sensitive. He loved solitude, because the richness of his spirit
> and his extraordinary ability to think and work sought precisely to avoid
> unnecessary distractions and superfluous leisures; but he was not a
> stranger to life, or indifferent to surrounding people and events, and he
> indeed sought to always be informed of everything and to participate,
> up to internal suffering, in the passion of history, in which he felt a part.[2]

---

[1] Tommaso. Toschi, Giovanni Battista Montini (Arcivescovo di Milano), *Discori e scritti milanesi* (1954–1963), Istituto Paolo VI, Brescia, p. 5843.
[2] Tommaso. Toschi, Giovanni Battista Montini (Arcivescovo di Milano), *Discori e scritti milanesi* (1954–1963), Istituto Paolo VI, Brescia, p. 5844.

Not surprisingly, it was Pope Paul VI who commissioned four Jesuits — Pierre Blet, Robert A. Graham, Angelo Martini, and Bernhard Schneider — to respond to the infamous accusations with an edition of the diplomatic-political documentation of the Holy See. The ensuing *Actes et documents du Saint-Siège relatifs à la Seconde Guerre Mondiale* would not receive a better fate than Pius XII himself, and it was attacked for its incompleteness immediately after its publication. Recently the four Jesuits have even been accused, on the basis of false conjectures and conspiracy theories, of having deliberately concealed some documents.[3]

Where and when did Pius XII come into my life? Before going to Rome, I studied philosophy, religious sciences, and theology at the Catholic University of Leuven in Belgium. An interest for the Italian Renaissance — and a particular fascination for the Neoplatonic circles at the Medici court in Florence — took me to Rome in 1988 where I started studying ecclesiastical history at the Jesuit Pontifical Gregorian University. It must have been in the 1990s that a very good friend of our family brought with him to Rome a gift — a book published in Paris in 1964 by Alexis Curvers titled *Pie XII, Le pape outragé* (Pius XII, the outraged pope). Reading it upended all the views I held on Pius XII and his reputation. It set a lingering intuition that would grow over the years. Then the book *Pie XII et la Seconde Guerre Mondiale d'après les archives du Vatican*, which was published in 1997 by one of my Jesuit professors, Fr. Pierre Blet, would do the rest. In 2000, I started working at the Holy See in the Archives of the Congregation for the Doctrine of Faith, the Archives of the Roman Inquisition and the Congregation of the Index. Five years later, I was appointed archivist of the Historical Archive of the Tribunal of the Apostolic Penitentiary and had the pleasure of preparing this outstanding documental collection for its opening to the public in the new study room of the Cancelleria Palace. In 2010, I was called in to manage the Historical Archive of the Section for Relations with States and International Organizations of the Secretariat of State, which is equivalent to a foreign ministry at the service of the pope. To get the whole picture on my connections with Pius XII, one element should still be added: from 2000 until 2018, I was also the archivist of the Pontifical Institute Santa Maria dell'Anima, which, besides preserving exceptional treasures on the history of Rome, maintains the

[3] Hubert Wolf e.a., *Der Papst, der wusste und schwieg. Dokumente aus den gerade geöffneten Archiven des Vatikans zeigen, dass Papst Pius XII. Persönlich über den Holocaust informiert war — und dass Akten unterschlagen wurden*, in *Die Zeit*, April 23, 2020, p. 13–14.

thousands of documents of Msgr. Alois Hudal, the controversial Austrian rector of that institution in Rome during World War II.

For archivists and historians, documents often provoke what John Keats called "a joy forever." Today still, I get shivers down my spine every time I enter the vast archival repository and run my hands over these documents. After all those years, I never grow tired of it. But the documents preserved in the Historical Archive of the Secretariat of State beat all records in uniqueness: thanks to the universality of the Catholic Church, they offer an extensive reflection of the history of every nation in the world.

Some earlier studies in particular — such as those by Pierre Blet, Ronald J. Rychlak, the Italian professor of Parma, Alessandro Duce, and Michael Hesemann — put a milestone in the study of Pius XII's activity during the war, and opened, as far as it was possible at the time, the window on the activity of the Section for Relations with States and International Organizations of the Secretariat of State, but could not penetrate the individual sphere of the characters of the Cabinet.[4] In fact, the story remained incomplete and meager: as a basic source, the *Actes et documents* gave only access to the official correspondence. Where were the actors that playwright Rolf Hochhuth once presented on the theater scene? What really happened behind the curtains of official diplomacy in the Vatican? What of the people and activities that were not at all covered nor even mentioned in Hochhuth's theater play?

Would it even be possible to return faithfully to history, stripped of the tinsel of this comic illusion? I believe in giving the lead to the genuine original documents, letting them do the talking and, by doing so, bringing to life those who wrote, inspired, and preserved them. Once they get their real voices back, their unaffected intentions and integrity, avoiding the pollution created by subsequent literature, would it be possible to transform the actors into real characters, making them move not on the stage but in their actual context consisting of offices and rooms, presidents' suites in capital cities, basilicas in Rome, or the Apostolic Palace in the Vatican? If so, the real play can begin.

---

[4] Pierre Blet, *Pie XII et la Seconde Guerre Mondiale*, Cinisello Balsamo, 1999; Ronald J. Rychlak, *Hitler, the War and The Pope*, Huntington, 2000; Alessandro Duce, *La Santa Sede e la questione ebraica (1933-1945)*, Roma, 2006; Michael Hesemann, *Der Papst und der Holocaust. Pius XII. und die geheimen Akten im Vatikan*, Stuttgart, 2018.

To fulfill that aim, I have dug into the gigantic Historical Archive of the Section for Relations with States and International Organizations, and limiting myself to these only, I have made a personal selection among the previously undisclosed material, fully aware that further historical evidence may still be discovered in other Vatican archives and elsewhere.

The opening of the archives of the Holy See related to the pontificate of Pius XII could bring to life these "real actors," but how do you deal with the millions of documents at hand? I let myself be inspired by a writer far more gifted and talented, so much as to be considered one of the "three crowns" of Italian literature, together with Dante and Petrarch. In 1348, the Black Death spread with particular strength over Italy and the whole of Europe. Desperate people sought "quarantine." So did the ten young storytellers brought to life by Giovanni Boccaccio in his brilliant *Decameron*. These youngsters, secluded in a countryside villa to escape the pestilence, take turns sharing unique narratives with their friends. As I have been, for more than thirty years, in a self-chosen "exile in Italy" and living as a *fiammingo a Roma*, "a Fleming in Rome," the theme of being distanced from home is familiar to me. Therefore, it felt natural to find inspiration in this masterpiece of Italian literature. Is it not coincidence that the recent pandemic has forced us — family, friends, and colleagues — to a self-imposed isolation? And, although not quite as young as Boccaccio's raconteurs, I was keen to borrow their lyre and tell these tales and short stories as I would narrate them to one of my good friends.

This explains my choice of presenting these fragments of our recent history through an unusual genre, that of the "narratives," or "Tales" and "Short Stories" as the chapters in my book are called. This choice has consequences: indeed, tales and short stories do not have to respond to any chronological obligation, and at the same time, they lend themselves to approaching a theme from various angles in different situations. My Tales cover a specific topic, whereas my Short Stories present a "life experience" of Jews, baptized or not, who ask Pius XII for help. Where the Tales are based on the most various archival sources preserved in the Historical Archive of the Section for Relations with States and International Organizations of the Secretariat of State, the Short Stories take their inspiration from the "Ebrei Files" — which I would dare to call a kind of "Pacelli's list." This specific archival series is a compendium of almost all the Jews, baptized or not, that were, in their different individual circumstances, as much as possible taken care of by

the Cabinet.[5] Read the book as if you were listening to Mussorgsky's musical suite
Pictures at an Exhibition, but keep in mind that all the characters, conversations,
and situations correspond to historical reality.

Inevitably, my Tales and Short Stories will fall short of the immense reality
and the sometimes-startling facts and anecdotes the documents of the Historical
Archive of the Secretariat of State are preserving. But then the book you have in
your hands is not meant to be a classic history textbook. Its only intention is to
revive the actors of the Cabinet, but this time based on archival sources, without,
as far as possible, contamination of postwar literature and scholarly interpretations. Once and for all, I wanted the stark naked documents to dictate the rules,
the rhythm, and the content.

These stories open the door to the corridors and salons of the Vatican's Ministry
of Foreign Affairs and its embassies, the nunciatures. The reader will discover how
these devout, dedicated people worked and proceeded daily in the service of the
pope and in defense of Christian principles, more often than not "without making noise." They give you, the reader, a chance to enter, observe, and browse with
me through these outstanding political, diplomatic, and historical documents, a
privilege normally reserved only to academic scholars.

Walking and glancing together through the Historical Archive of the Secretariat
of State, you will witness how the pope set up a web of escape routes that smuggled
people out of danger, and oversaw a network of priests operating across Europe
with one aim, to save lives wherever they could. To my knowledge, always very
limited, the Secretariat of State in the Vatican is the only ministry of foreign affairs in the world with an appropriate office and a complete international network
dedicated to rescue persecuted people during the Second World War. Today, the
Ebrei Files are proof of that. Here, newly revealed documents will shine new light
on Pope Pacelli's far-reaching influence and the labyrinthine network of relationships he relied upon to cast influence across Nazi-occupied Europe. More than
anything else, they will acquaint us with the Cabinet, his inner circle of trusted

---

[5] Recently, at the behest of Pope Francis, this peculiar archival series was given free
access to the public on the Internet: https://www.vatican.va/roman_curia/secre-
tariat_state/sezione-rapporti-stati/archivio-storico/serie-ebrei/serie-ebrei_it.html.
This decision will certainly also enhance the research on the Holocaust victims by
cross-research on the many digital collections of Yad Vashem, Holocaust museums,
and Holocaust research centers across the world.

collaborators, who, with their own characters, qualities, and flaws — sometimes costly to his agenda — carried his action.

Pius XII's and his Cabinet's unseen documents will provide a counterpoint to the false narrative previously accepted by many. No one lives a perfect life, not even the greatest nor most beloved and revered saints, but we all deserve to be remembered in truth. This book will reveal a man struggling to uphold the weight of office, the ideals of the Church, and the teachings of Christ at a time when many might reasonably be called to question the existence of God at all.

Notice for the Reader

THE DOCUMENTS CITED in this book are all preserved in Vatican City, Historical Archive of the Secretariat of State — Section for Relations with States and International Organizations (ASRS). In particular, unless otherwise indicated, they are part of the archival fund *Congregation for Extraordinary Ecclesiastical Affairs* (AA.EE.SS.), Pius XII, part I or II.

At the end of this book the reader will also find the biographies of the main figures of the Roman Curia at the time of Pius XII, as well as a glossary explaining the technical terms used throughout the text.

All photos come from the Historical Archive of the Secretariat of State — Section for Relations with States and International Organizations (ASRS): "Copyright © Archivio Storico — Sezione per i Rapporti con gli Stati e con le Organizzazioni Internazionali — Segreteria di Stato."

The Cabinet
The Jews of Pius XII

The Pope: **Pius XII** (in life: Eugenio Pacelli)
The Cardinal: His Eminence Cardinal **Luigi Maglione**, Secretary of State
The Secretary: His Excellence Msgr. **Domenico Tardini**,
Secretary for Extraordinary Ecclesiastical Affairs
The Substitute: Msgr. **Giovanni Battista Montini**, Substitute
for Ordinary Affairs and Secretary of the Code
*Undersecretary for Extraordinary Ecclesiastical
Affairs*: Msgr. **Giuseppe Malusardi**

The Staff
Msgr. Giulio Barbetta, *Minutes-taker,* "*Desk Officer*"
Msgr. Angelo Dell'Acqua, Counselor of Nunciature, "*Desk Officer*"
Msgr. Giuseppe Di Meglio, *Uditore di Nunziatura di 1a Classe,* "*Desk Officer*"
Msgr. Antonio Samorè, *Uditore di Nunziatura di 2a Classe,* "*Desk Officer*"
Msgr. Pietro Sigismondi, *Uditore di Nunziatura di 2° Classe,* "*Desk Officer*"
Msgr. Armando Lombardi, *Uditore di Nunziatura di 2° Classe,* "*Desk Officer*"
Msgr. Corrado Bafile, *Segretario di Nunziatura di 1° Classe,* "*Desk Officer*"

External actors: Msgr. Bernardini, Msgr. Burzio, Msgr. Cassulo,
Msgr. Hurley, Msgr. Orsenigo, Carlo Pacelli, Msgr. Roncalli, Msgr.
Rotta, Msgr. Valeri, Sr. Slachta, Fr. Musters, and many more…

1

A Tale of Two Fools, Many Missing
Maidens, and a Go-Between

Berghof Villa, Obersalzberg, Bavarian Alps — July 28, 1940

THE ALPINE SLOPES were summer green, scattered with brightly colored wildflowers. The pine-scented air was thick with bird songs. In the deep, forested countryside, a secluded wooden and stone villa sat framed by a dramatic mountain backdrop.

In this serene, idyllic location, four politicians and their aides sat in deep discussion, coffee cups strewn around the table, shirtsleeves rolled up. Yet the discussion engaged was anything but serene. In fact, their conversation was about to plunge another European country into crisis and preempt one of the darkest and most violent periods of World War II.

President Jozef Tiso of Slovakia, who was a Catholic priest, and his prime minister, Vojtech Lázar "Béla" Tuka, were on an official visit to meet both Hitler and the German foreign minister, Joachim von Ribbentrop. During those mountain talks a new pact was born. Slovak politics opposed to the Nazis, and those that were more neutral, was now of the past. The supporters of National Socialism had boldly risen to the forefront.

Article from Grenzbote *announcing that Durčansky is replaced by Tuka as Minister of Foreign Affairs.*[6]

6   ASRS, AA.EE.SS., Cecoslovacchia 164, f. 13, "Grenzbote. Deutsches Tagblatt für die Karpaten Länder," July 30, 1940.

Slovakia's minister of foreign affairs, Ferdinand Ďurčanský, was a Nazi critic, and due to his anti-Nazi views, he had been excluded from these talks. Once the Slovak media broke the news about the meeting at the forest villa, Ďurčanský had no option but to resign. And in a sign of the power grab to come by Tiso's inner circle, his portfolio was taken over by Tuka, who assumed both roles — that of prime minister and of foreign affairs minister.

The Holy See's representative in the country was the chargé d'affaires, Msgr. Giuseppe Burzio. A very dutiful official, Burzio collected together the most reliable information he could regarding this critical turning point for Slovakia — newspaper reports, insider information, and anecdotes. In doing so, he began a series of highly detailed, critically important reports that he would provide to Rome.

One of these earliest reports was written on August 7, 1940,[7] but due to the painfully slow communications of war-torn Europe, it did not reach the Cabinet until nine days later. Briefing Secretary of State Cardinal Maglione in detail, Burzio shared disturbing information about the nomination of Nazi sympathizers Msgr. Ján Vojtaššák, the bishop of Spiš, and two other clerics as members to the State Council, Slovakia's highest legislative body. It might seem surprising to some, but in Slovakia at that time, the presence of clergy in government was a normal thing. In fact, it was such a deeply rooted tradition that even the president was a priest. But adopting an administration that was closely allied to the Nazis was unprecedented and steered the country toward dark, uncharted waters. With bishops and clergy across Europe risking their lives to actively oppose the Nazis, this schizophrenic situation created deep cracks within the Church.

And it created a serious quandary for the Holy See.

Msgr. Burzio made the point that usually these posts by nomination were "honorary positions"; however, "in the actual circumstances they could bring with them a certain political and moral responsibility."[8] And the responsibility had clearly been taken on by dangerous men.

In spite of Burzio's reports, Rome was by this time aware of this troubling circumstance. In mid-August, Msgr. Vojtaššák had already written in personally, requesting for

---

[7]   ASRS, AA.EE.SS., Cecoslovacchia 164, f. 5ʳ, letter of Msgr. Burzio to Card. Maglione, Bratislava, August 7, 1940.

[8]   ASRS, AA.EE.SS., Cecoslovacchia 164, f. 5ʳ, letter of Msgr. Burzio to Card. Maglione, Bratislava, August 7, 1940.

benestare (permission) to take up the post.[9] Cardinal Maglione was rendered speechless at Vojtaššák's actions. He scrawled across Burzio's report, posing the terse question "*Quid agendum?*—What should one do?" before handing the report to Pius XII.

Here the Historical Archive offers a unique insight into Pius XII's position toward a bishop who clearly turned his back on the tenets of his Christian faith, those of charity and justice, by collaborating with the Nazis. During the audience that took place on August 20, 1940, with the pope, Msgr. Tardini, secretary of the Cabinet, wrote visible in neat pencil script, referring to the state of mind of Pius XII, "The Holy Father does not see all this without worries." [10]

And so Rome's response to Burzio's report was unequivocal: "Make it clear in a delicate way to the Bishop of Scepusio, that the Holy See does not see without worries that clerics, especially in the given circumstances, take up posts that have political and moral responsibilities."[11]

The language is, as usual, carefully diplomatic. But by using the Holy Father's sentence "does not see without worries" and Burzio's own language about "political and moral responsibilities," they make it very clear they do not support Vojtaššák taking up the post. Burzio passed on the letter to Vojtaššák, telling him personally, "It was not opportune to accept institutional and governmental posts."[12]

However, in the meantime, on August 13, Vojtaššák had written another official letter to Pope Pius XII, this time with a personal "humble request" for permission, deliberately downplaying his role as "only an honorary post."[13] He made no mention that the members of the council of state were continually called to vote in favor of concrete measures against the Jews. This letter arrived on Burzio's desk and was then transmitted to Rome on August 21, the same day as the dissuasive answer of Rome to Vojtaššák's first request.

[9] ASRS, AA.EE.SS., Cecoslovacchia 164, f. 18, letter of Msgr. Vojtaššák to Pope Pius XII, August 13, 1940.
[10] ASRS, AA.EE.SS., Cecoslovacchia 164, f. 5, handwritten note of Msgr. Tardini, August 20, 1940.
[11] ASRS, AA.EE.SS., Cecoslovacchia 164, 7^r, draft of telegram of Card. Maglione to Msgr. Burzio, August 21, 1940.
[12] ASRS, AA.EE.SS., Cecoslovacchia 164, f. 17, letter of Msgr. Burzio to Card. Maglione, August 21, 1940.
[13] ASRS, AA.EE.SS., Cecoslovacchia 164, f. 18, letter of Msgr. Vojtaššák to Pope Pius XII, August 13, 1940. Arrived in Rome only after August 21, probably towards the end of that month.

What Rome didn't know was that a week before writing his second letter, Vojtaššák had already, arrogantly and without permission from the Holy See, accepted the post. He had taken his oath as a member of the council of state on August 6. His "humble request" to the pope was presented after he had already made his decision. In short, he was lying. This behavior can be interpreted as a well-pondered attempt of Vojtaššák and his accomplices to put the Vatican in a corner and obtain a written consent that would have surely been considered a trophy and put to good use by Nazis and Fascists.

As soon as the Holy Father had made clear on August 21 that "it wasn't opportune that Priests accept official charge," Msgr. Vojtaššák should at least have willingly renounced the post in humble obedience.

But what can be done when it's discovered that your own people are cheating on you? Such a realization must have been both infuriating and dismaying to the Holy See. Since Vojtaššák had already taken up the post, the Holy See had no choice but to accept it as a fait accompli. Therefore, the response on September 9, 1940, was polite but curt: "His Holiness let know that he does not oppose Mons. Vojtaššák's acceptance of his nomination as a member to the State Council."[14]

The language used here cries for clarification. The usual wording of the pope when he accepts a request is "*nulla osta*" (no objection). Rather, in his answer to Vojtaššák, the pope chooses to reply that he "does not oppose" ("but neither approves," in the diplomatic language) the acceptance of his appointment.

As things stand, the Holy See cannot interfere in the hierarchy or governance of another country. In addition, the old Code of Canon Law stipulated that assignments of priests to public offices were the prerogative of the local episcopacy, not of the Roman Pontiff or his dicasteries.[15] There can be little doubt that many within the Holy See wished they could have interfered in this alarming state of affairs, but that isn't how it works.

The curt but significant wording of the reply was intentionally designed so it would not compromise the Holy See. And by referencing Vojtaššák alone, they were careful not to create a precedent that any other Nazi-sympathizing priests might try to use later.

[14] ASRS, AA.EE.SS., Cecoslovacchia 164, f. 19, handwritten note from Maglione.
[15] The 1917 Pio-Benedictine Code of Canon Law in English translation, San Francisco, 2001, 70–71 (Canon 139, §3 and §4).

Later that week the chargé d'affaires in Bratislava, Msgr. Burzio, reported to Rome again,[16] this time with his own analysis on the consequences of President Tiso's official visit to Hitler. It was Burzio's belief that the Nazis courted Tiso because they had been displeased with the Slovak government overall, especially with former foreign minister Ďurčanský, who had tried to retain Slovak independence and limit anti-Semitic measures. Burzio wrote: "The Nazi leadership accused Signor Ďurčanský of trying to protect the Jews and some saw this as the real reason for his downfall." But now with Ďurčanský gone, Burzio had a very troubling prediction — that "very soon vehement measures" would be taken against the Jews.[17]

His acute political summation went on to explain that the new Slovak government was also determined to purge any pro-Russian propaganda. Anyone suspected of being a Communist sympathizer would be considered criminal under new laws, laws designed to both scare the populace and create a convenient excuse for arresting political opponents. For some in Rome this tough line on Communism was good news. For others, it was unsettling.

Burzio's dark calculations were correct, though the government crackdown did not start with the Jews but with politically motivated nationalism, beginning with measures against Seventh-day Adventists and Protestants. Although Slovakia is predominantly Catholic, in Burzio's opinion these new restrictions weren't really about religion. Rather, they were inspired and put in place by *Odium Cechorum*,[18] a hatred toward Slovak citizens of Czech background, who had a more religiously diverse Protestant population.

Burzio's incisive analysis posed a question: "How long will the political convictions of and, especially, his conscience as a priest, allow Tiso to walk arm in arm with his National Socialist masters?" He was convinced, perhaps wishful thinking on his part, that Tiso might be playing a strategic game, "hoping to save that which could be saved, and that the application of the Nazi-methods would not be driven to extreme consequences." But in a foreshadowing of the terror to come, he stated, "Only later on will one be able to judge if his calculations were right."[19]

---

[16] ASRS, AA.EE.SS., Cecoslovacchia 164, f. 10ᵛ, report from Msgr. Burzio, July 31, 1940.

[17] ASRS, AA.EE.SS., Cecoslovacchia 164, f. 10ᵛ, report from Msgr. Burzio, July 31, 1940.

[18] ASRS, AA.EE.SS., Cecoslovacchia 164, f. 26, report from Msgr. Burzio, Bratislava, January 15, 1941.

[19] ASRS, AA.EE.SS., Cecoslovacchia 164, f. 36ᵛ, report from Msgr. Burzio, Bratislava, September 5, 1940.

Burzio correctly determined that what Germany wanted most from Slovakia was not ideological but economical, and it was rooted in Slovak's thriving industrial base. As such, Jewish-owned businesses were the next target. Burzio reported how shops and businesses owned by Jewish citizens were forced to post clearly visible signs, stating "Jewish enterprise" or "Jewish store." Avenues that had once been pleasant places to Slovakians to stroll and shop were now marred by the hateful, visible stamp of Nazi prejudice. Burzio stated that "one remains stunned by the fact that the whole economical life of the country was in hands of the Jews, and that a few restrictive laws against this predominance is not such a bad idea." He continued: "Unfortunately the measures that are taken are crossing the limits of justice and tend to block the Jews completely out of the economic and social life of the country. All of this not for the benefit of the Slovaks, but for that of the Germans whose hands will receive all the sources of income and wealth that were once in the hands of the Jews."[20] He then listed the most restrictive measures taken against the Jewish population: "The closing of all (Jewish) public locales; prohibition to have Christian housemaids under 40 years of age; denouncement and registration of all houses and goods; interdiction to attend middle and high schools, also to organise or open such schools for themselves so that from now on the education of Jewish youngsters will end at elementary school level." The banning of Jewish children from middle and high schools had immediately caused "inconveniencies for the ecclesiastical authorities, because if this law-set would be applied thoroughly, many children of Jewish origin but of Catholic faith, would have to leave their Catholic elementary schools to attend Jewish elementary schools. And those children already in middle and high school will have to interrupt their education."[21]

Burzio then issued a dire warning to Rome, revealing that even harsher, crueler measures would soon be announced, "in the matter of matrimonial legislation." The danger of the State interfering in the sacrament of Matrimony was something that greatly concerned the Holy See. That a State would meddle in and attempt to restrict or even destroy something that was a holy bond between two people was a slap in the face of the Catholic Faith. Burzio hoped that Slovak bishops would take "a common and strong line against" any laws concerning interracial marriage. But he

---

[20] ASRS, AA.EE.SS., Cecoslovacchia 164, f. 36^v, report from Msgr. Burzio, Bratislava, September 5, 1940.

[21] ASRS, AA.EE.SS., Cecoslovacchia 164, f. 37^r, report from Msgr. Burzio, Bratislava, September 5, 1940.

was also well aware that since the clergy was divided between Nazis sympathizers and opponents, this was unlikely.

We know that Burzio's report was read with concern by Pius XII, because Maglione wrote back to Burzio, instructing him to continue informing Rome of these troubling developments, especially regarding the attitude of the bishops in Slovakia and "the steps those Bishops would take to preserve the rights not only of the Catholic youth, including those of non-Aryan heritage, for an education conforming to their faith."[22] Maglione's words made it clear that these instructions came directly from the Holy Father himself. For me, this is additional evidence that proves a person's race had no distinction for Pius XII.

*

*   *

Slovakia's descent into terror continued apace. On October 8, 1940, President Tiso gave a public speech to a group of twenty thousand Catholic pilgrims near the town of Žilina, in northern Slovakia, justifying the government's anti-Semitic measures.[23] Tiso boldly proclaimed that in ancient times the Jews had very good leaders, and then he falsely subverted one of the teachings of Moses by claiming Moses ordered all Jews to give back their earnings every fifty years.[24] In reality, what Moses had preached was that all earnings that had been gained unjustly should be returned to the original owner. Tiso might well have known this, yet he deliberately twisted the meaning of the teaching. In doing so, he wished to prove that the Jews were required by their religion to give back to Slovakia. In his speech he proclaimed that this was clear and certain evidence that the Jewish people had forgotten their own teachings. In consequence, he argued, it was wrong of them to complain that, for example, their radios had been taken away. Tiso's speech was just getting started with its twisted hatred. He continued: "It is not right that they criticise, in name of Christian principles, the fact that their stores and commercial licences are taken away from them. They were only compelled to give back that which they once took from the Christians. It is not right that they complain of being excluded from the state schools, while their motto has always been that of

---

[22] ASRS, AA.EE.SS., Cecoslovacchia 164, f. 39^r, draft of a dispatch signed by Card. Maglione, written by the hand of Msgr. Samorè, *minutante* (sent on October 5).

[23] ASRS, AA.EE.SS., Cecoslovacchia 164, ff. 41$^{r/v}$, speech of Msgr. Tiso.

[24] The Holy Bible, Leviticus 25.

working just a little and earn a lot."[25] This pure, unadulterated racism, spewing forth like toxic waste from the mouth of a priest, is undeniably shocking. A full transcript of Tiso's speech was hand-delivered to the office in Rome on October 8, 1940.[26] On October 10, Pius XII read it.

The Cabinet has noted, along with the date the transcript was received, the name of the source from which it came. As I researched the hundreds of Slovakia documents, I noticed that on several occasions this same source reappeared, on quite a regular basis. The Cabinet's pencil marks say "passed by Commendatore Babuscio," the only identifying element on these documents. Without it, we'd have no idea how these documents found their way to the secretary of state and then to the pope's desk.

Who was the mysterious Commendatore Babuscio? My old Jesuit professor and eminent historian Fr. Pierre Blet[27] depicts Francesco Babuscio Rizzo as an Italian government diplomat. At the outbreak of World War II, his official title was counselor of the embassy of Italy to the Holy See, part of the Italian government's foreign affairs team. His title meant he was regularly meeting the Holy See in an official capacity. But what is surprising here is it seems he was also passing on intelligence intended for his government. It is additionally interesting to note that the documents he passed on are not stamped or marked as officially from the Italian foreign ministry. They are blank, aside from his name noted by the office. This could suggest this brave and helpful man in the shadows was acting in a personal rather than official capacity. It is also possible that his superior, the Italian ambassador, was behind it. But these seemingly clandestine actions certainly would not have been authorized higher up in Mussolini's Fascist administration. And who knows what might have happened to Babuscio Rizzo had he been found out by that administration, given the Fascists' affinity for cruel retaliations? What his motives were, and who else may have been behind his actions, is something that merits further investigation. We do know that Babuscio was a friend and confidant of Cabinet Secretary Tardini, and that on a separate occasion — as Fr. Blet already pointed out — he warned the Vatican of planned anti-Church measures by Mussolini.

[25] ASRS, AA.EE.SS., Cecoslovacchia, 164, ff. 41$^{r/v}$, speech of Msgr. Tiso.

[26] ASRS, AA.EE.SS., Cecoslovacchia, 164, ff. 41$^{r/v}$, speech of Msgr. Tiso.

[27] Pierre Blet, *Pie XII et la Seconde Guerre mondiale d'après les archives du Vatican*, Paris, 2005, p. 122; p. 146; p. 237.

On August 28, 1940, Babuscio Rizzo passed along three additional tran-scripts — a copy of an Italian government memo about the Slovakian policy on "Religious churches and sects," a transcript of a speech by Slovakian prime minister Tuka, and a newspaper report on a different speech, "Measures on the Jews," by Sano Mach, the minister of internal affairs.[28]

Both Tuka's and Sano Mach's speeches reveal just how quickly the country was descending into violent, savage anti-Semitism. In one particular speech given by Prime Minister Tuka on August 24, 1940, he made it brutally clear how things would progress regarding Jews in Slovakia:

Photo of the salute to Tuka during the national anthem after his maiden speech.[29]

> The Jew is irreconcilable with National Socialism, because the Jews
> are either capitalists or communists. And that's why we have to
> radically resolve the Jewish question. We don't want to kill the Jews,

[28] ASRS, AA.EE.SS., Cecoslovacchia 164, ff. 55–59, typewritten reports passed over by Comm. Francesco Babuscio Rizzo, October 28, 1940; f. 61, typewritten informa-tion passed over by the Italian embassy, November 28, 1941; ff. 64–68, typewritten report passed over by the Italian embassy, January 1941.

[29] ASRS, AA.EE.SS., Cecoslovacchia 164, f. 81 (*Slowakische Rundschau* 2 (1941) 4, p. 16).

but in Slovakia we cannot allow the Jewish capital to broaden its tentacles more and more. We can no longer support the fact that our economic and commercial life is poisoned by the Jewish spirit, and we cannot permit our literature and arts to remain under their influence. They say that the Jews are indispensable for affairs of life and therefore they should be tolerated. This is not true at all. We can go on without the Jews and therefore I don't want to hear of their indispensability.[30]

A day later, Sano Mach gave a speech entitled "Measures on the Jews," which took a similarly ominous tone.

Amid all this, tensions continued to grow in the Slovakian episcopacy between those who supported Tiso and the Nazis, and those who found their views and declarations intolerable. One of Tiso's highest-profile supporters, a canon by the name Koerper, held multiple public roles — deputy of the parliament, chaplain of the Hlinka Guard (the militia maintained by the Slovak People's Party from 1938 to 1945, also called the president's guard), and official at the Ministry of Public Instruction. He was the target of a strident attack in the *Katolicke Noviny*, the influential, weekly Catholic journal of Slovakia, sponsored by the bishops. The published statement accused Koerper of immorally profiting from his public positions.[31] Although he was one of Tiso's key allies, the National Socialists hung him out to dry, using the fallout as a convenient excuse to get rid of not only Koerper but also any other Catholics serving within the public sector.

Chargé d'Affaires Msgr. Burzio saw all of this coming. He pointed out in his latest dispatch that it was inevitable the National Socialists would eventually rid themselves of any and all Catholics — even the ones on their side who claimed the same racial ideology.

Once again, the Cabinet was provided firsthand information on the situation by the embassy of Italy to the Holy See through Commendatore Babuscio. Without hesitation, he shared reports on the Slovak situation: "It is not easy to reconcile National Socialism with the principles of Hlinka (Catholic based principles) and

---

[30] ASRS, AA.EE.SS., Cecoslovacchia 164, f. 58, typewritten reports passed over by Comm. Francesco Babuscio Rizzo, October 28, 1940.

[31] ASRS, AA.EE.SS., Cecoslovacchia 164, f. 65, typewritten report passed over by the Italian embassy [Babuscio], January 1941.

to apply them to a country in which the church, the religion and the Priests have always had a prominent role. ... The protection of Nazi Germany is not something that one can receive in part: it is a system that organizes the life of a nation into the finest details. One accepts all of it or one doesn't at all."[32]

On January 21, 1941, things in Slovakia escalated even more. Tuka announced his fourteen-point program of Slovak National Socialism. The term was a smoke-screen to make it appear as if the country was acting independently, that it was not as extreme as the Nazis and was not intending to, in Tuka's own words, "eliminate the Jews." But, of course, the ruthless President Tiso was lying to the public, as events went on to prove.

A copy of Tuka's fourteen-point program, which was published in the Nazi-friendly *Slowakische Rundschau*, arrived at the offices of the Cabinet. Someone, maybe Cardinal Maglione himself, underlined points thirteen and fourteen in red pencil. Thirteen stated:

> As basis of all moral life religion is protected by the State. And the ministers of God will be paid by the State. The income of the Priests should, following the basic principles of social justice, be divided among all the ministers of a religion. The Slovak clergy were always the central warriors of Slovak nationalism. The Slovak priests had always a Slovak heart and what they proved in the past they prove also today and will prove it also in the future.

The significant wording here is "in the future." It is a deliberate poisoning of the old ideals of Slovak nationalism and softening of the new ideals and brutality of Nazism. Under the new Slovak order, religion might be protected but only if it behaved itself and stayed in line.

Point fourteen was far less about political gaming. Its simple, cruel intent was quite clear: "Finally resolve the Jewish question."[33]

The methods Nazism used to co-opt Slovak nationalism (and some of the Slovak Church) is evidenced in the archives from detailed transcriptions of German newspapers sent in by the chargé d'affaires, Msgr. Burzio. In one report, he quoted from an article in the *Völkischer Beobachter*, the official newspaper of the National

---

[32] ASRS, AA.EE.SS., Cecoslovacchia 164, f. 67, typewritten report passed over by the Italian embassy [Babuscio], February 1, 1941 (p. 4).

[33] ASRS, AA.EE.SS., Cecoslovacchia 164, f. 75, *Slowakische Rundschau* 2 (1941) 4, p. 5.

Socialist Party in Berlin. Burzio underlined key phrases: "The religious problem in Slovakia is an element far more important and heavier than in other Slavic countries where state and confessional membership coincide.... The young nationalism of Slovakia will have to, if it wants or not, cope with this problem."[34] Entitled "Not All the Ways Lead to Rome," the article was also reproduced in other newspapers.

The Reich propaganda machine intended to create a situation that coerced or pushed Slovak politicians and even its society into accepting the false claim that Nazism was the same as their version of nationalism. Yet to embrace that meant giving up religious conscience. Sadly, several Slovak priests followed that lead and tore apart from Rome — as suggested by the newspaper article.

On the other hand, the *Katolicke Noviny*, the Slovak Catholic weekly, remained steadfastly and courageously critical of the Nazis. Articles they published told of the growing divisions amongst the population and warned that Nazism was a false prophecy: "Probably, for the best publicity they will put on display a priest or even two or three that have turned their back and have drifted far away from the shores of the Church into a sea of malcontent and unease. But that priest will no longer be a real servant of God but an apostate and a renegade as one will see immediately by his works."[35] But the new Slovak "nationalization" continued to spread, rapidly and seemingly unfettered, like a disease without a cure. An article in the *Gardista*, a Slovak National Socialist–supporting newspaper, lamented that "many Jewish enterprises that should have been liquidated a long time ago have been able to escape the measures of the government, thanks to the protection of high-ranking people."[36] By "high-ranking people," the writer was referring to Nazi-opposing bishops and clergy.

In his report, Burzio quoted a report from a different newspaper, the *Slovak*. The piece was entitled "Preparations for the Transfer of All Hebrews Out of Europe," and it read in part: "The government has dismantled all Jewish enterprises and organizations ... and instead a Jewish Plant, with nine sections, has been organised. This central plant started its activities a few days ago, and already there are 144 employees working there. One foresees that their number will increase to 250. Every

[34] ASRS, AA.EE.SS., Cecoslovacchia 164, ff. 85–86, "Der Grenzbote," February 16, 1941 (cites the "Völkischer Beobachter") and f. 92, "Der Grenzbote," February 22, 1941.

[35] ASRS, AA.EE.SS., Cecoslovacchia 164, f. 88, "Katolicke Noviny," February 16, 1941.

[36] ASRS, AA.EE.SS., Cecoslovacchia 164, f. 94, "Slovak" (= paper of Hlinka's party), February 2, 1941; "Gardist" (Slovak national socialist paper), February 21, 1941.

Jew living in Slovakia has to become a member of that central plant, and in doing so will become legitimatised." In real terms, this shocking development meant all Jews in Slovakia had to leave their homes in villages and towns across Slovakia to go live and work in the new plant, the Central. Apparently, these independent, productive Jewish Slovakians were to be reduced to slaves in the service of the Nazis. And this action was a direct result — the physical embodiment — of Tiso's speech subverting Moses. The article continued:

> The Central should serve as a training house where every Jew can learn a manual job or craft, that will be of utility in his new home-land. One estimates that, after the war, the Jews will be dislodged out of Europe in two or three years. The costs for this colonisation should be paid by the single states in proportion to the Jews living on their territory. In Slovakia such a cost would be about 40 or 50 thousand coronas. The total number of Jews present in Slovakia is currently 85,000. If the costs would be too excessive for the State, the rich Jews should contribute to help their poorer brothers.[37]

This chilling text presented the real intentions of the Slovak government. Reading this, it's clear they had only one thing in mind. They first would use the Jews as slave labor and then would expel them from Slovakia all together.

Back in Rome, Fr. Wladimir Ledóchowski, the superior general of the Jesuits, briefed the Cabinet on the contents of the telegram Tiso had sent to Hitler on the Fuhrer's fifty-second birthday. A clearer, more devoted declaration of love to the *Reichskanzler*[38] and his Nazi program would be hard to find. Tiso wrote: "The time of your fifty-second birthday coincides with another important day in the battle for the future of our nations, with the victory of Your Excellency's armies. I beg you to accept my most sincere wishes and dedication, in order that God continues to bless the German army that is fighting for the just cause."[39] Prime Minister Tuka also sent a birthday telegram in which he assured the Fuhrer "of my fidelity and my firm belief in our vital work."

---

[37] ASRS, AA.EE.SS., Cecoslovacchia 164, f. 94, typewritten copy of article taken out of "Slovak," February 21, 1941.

[38] Chancellor of the Third Reich.

[39] ASRS, AA.EE.SS., Cecoslovacchia 164, ff. 97–98, typewrittten copy of the message of Tiso to Hitler (taken out of "Slovak," April 20, 1941, p. 3).

Not long after this, a Msgr. Ferencik, who served as both a Catholic priest and deputy of the Slovak parliament, wrote yet another article in lavish praise of Hitler. This was far beyond the pale and all too much for Pius XII. Having been forced to swallow the blatant disobedience of Vojtaššák and other members of the Slovak clergy for joining the National Socialist government against his opinion, the pope was not going to stand for it again. He annulled Msgr. Ferencik's name from the list of domestic prelates of His Holiness.[40] It was a blunt message to other Slovak clergy that such public support for the Nazis was absolutely unacceptable and would not be tolerated.

New eyewitness reports began coming into the Cabinet from Slovakia. One, in particular, was from the Jesuit provincial of the town of Hriňová.[41] The Jesuit described the country as a "Nazi colony with 75 per cent of the industry in Nazi hands. Trains carrying 500 wagons of flour disappeared, we don't know where. While in the country we eat only black bread. And in the capital, there has been no bread for the past three days." He also reported that Slovakia had "to give hospitality to 10,000 juvenile Germans (Hitler Youth), to whom it is forbidden to go into a church even if they were educated as 'believers in god.' These young guys are insolent. While marching they have to sing the following refrain: 'Jesus was a son of a Jew and his mother was Maria Kohn.'" The Maria Kohn referred to was the Jewish resistance hero, Marianne Cohn. The Jesuit continued with his report:

> In the Nazi schools Christ is presented as a despicable Jew and the German Propaganda Counsellor holds conferences on how one can paralyse and destroy the influence of the Church. Prime Minister Tuka takes the Holy Communion every day but has become a blind instrument of the Nazis. Valuable people are now less involved in public life and offices, all this while apostate priests, freemasons and other obscure individuals take over command on the public sphere, earning exorbitant loans that exceed 40,000 coronas a month. The entering in the war of Slovakia has excited the population a lot, given that it was a priest declaring that war.[42]

[40] ASRS, AA.EE.SS., Cecoslovacchia 164, f. 101.
[41] ASRS, AA.EE.SS., Cecoslovacchia 164, f. 109; f. 112.
[42] ASRS, AA.EE.SS., Cecoslovacchia 164, ff. 113–114.

That last observation had already been made in one of Burzio's reports. The informant laid bare not only the climate of dread but the clear disgust many Catholics felt toward Tuka and others who continued to practice the sacraments but were clearly aligned with the Nazis.

*

*   *

The summer of 1941 ended. September arrived. The situation grew ever worse. Catholic journals were confiscated, and journalists were arrested, journalists such as the redactor-in-chief of *Katolicke Noviny*. These newsmen and reporters were imprisoned and brutally interrogated, all on orders from Berlin.[43] The media censorship was very severe, intended to terrorize Catholic journalists. And order came that, in the future, the wordings of the press would have to change. For example, terms such as *neopaganism* or *neopagan spirit* had to be replaced with other words like *worldly spirit*. Quoting paragraphs from encyclicals was forbidden, especially those that referred to modern human errors.[44] Also banned were the allocutions of the Holy Father, especially those in which he referred to the unity of humankind or allusions to injustice, for the Nazis certainly could not allow anything to be published that ran counter to their views of a "master race." The Catholic press had been, until that point, the only way left to get messages from Rome or words of Pius XII disseminated to the public. Now it became dangerously impossible.

The Cabinet was informed of these fierce new changes and restrictions. Immediately they sought interesting articles that could be sent over to Msgr. Burzio to be published in Slovakia. Burzio was ordered to try and find ways to continue media coverage of the pope's words in Slovakia, and to keep the secretary of state informed as to his success and what effect it had. They advised him to make full use of his diplomatic status should Tiso's government put him in difficulty or danger. This aggression toward the Roman Catholic Church seemed to parallel the ever-growing inhumane hatred of the Jews.

[43] ASRS, AA.EE.SS., Cecoslovacchia 164, f. 123, "L'eco della parola del Santo Padre nel popolo Slovacco" (October 1941).
[44] ASRS, AA.EE.SS., Cecoslovacchia 164, f. 123, "L'eco della parola del Santo Padre nel popolo Slovacco" (October 1941).

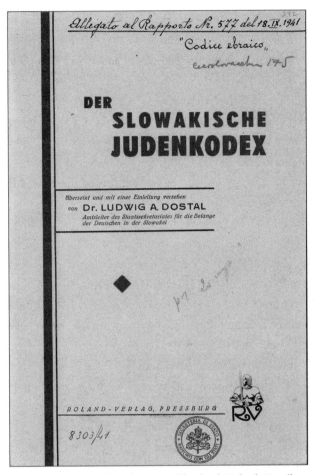

Published version in German language of the Slovak Codex for Jews.[45]

During that month of September 1941, Burzio transmitted to the Cabinet a detailed report on the publication of the Judenkodex, the new Slovak Codex for Jews.[46] The pope's chargé d'affaires pointed out the many nearly identical points of the earlier Nürnberg Laws, which emanated in Nazi Germany, coincidentally or not, in the very same month of September six years earlier.[47] There was only

[45] ASRS, AA.EE.SS., Cecoslovacchia 175, f. 242.

[46] ASRS, AA.EE.SS., Cecoslovacchia 175, ff. 238–241ᵛ, report from Msgr. Burzio to Card. Maglione, September 18, 1941.

[47] The Nürnberg Laws, as they came to be known, were race-based measures depriving Jews of rights. They were designed by Adolf Hitler and approved by the Nazi Party at a convention in Nürnberg on September 15, 1935.

one slight difference. That difference dealt with the consideration by the Slovak Codex of the "half-Jew," identified as someone married to a Christian. Where the Nürnberg Laws made no distinction, the Slovak Judenkodex considered someone Jewish only if they had married a non-Jew after April 20, 1939.

On the same morning the proclamation of the codex was announced in the press, Chargé d'Affaires Burzio made an official visit to President Tiso. Msgr. Burzio could only lament about the codex, pointing out his profound disagreement with it.[48]

Immediately after the Slovak Codex for Jews was announced, the massacres began. Various horrific eyewitness reports confirmed these atrocities to Rome throughout late 1941 into the spring of 1942.[49]

On March 20, 1942, Msgr. Burzio transmitted a plea from the rabbi of Budapest to intervene with the Slovak government in favor of Jews who were destined to be deported to Galicia, in Polish-occupied territory.[50] In the same week, on March 24, the rabbi of Budapest visited Angelo Rotta, the nuncio in Hungary, where he implored the nuncio to ask the pope to intervene again with the Slovak government. This time, it was on behalf of thousands of young Slovak girls of Jewish race who had been forcibly trafficked to the front to become prostitutes for German soldiers.[51]

The news about the trafficked girls landed on Pope Pius XII's desk. Surely his heart cried out for these innocent children of God, for he gave immediate instruction to Cardinal Maglione to call the Slovakian ambassador to the Holy See, "to interest him in the matter and ask him to intervene with his government."[52] Maglione, knowing the critical and timely importance of this order, executed it immediately on the morning of March 25. Then, at 7:55 a.m., an urgent cable came in from Burzio, relaying a rumor that the government had suspended new Jewish deportations due to the Holy See's intervention. However, in that same cable, he reported the devastating information that "last night a lot of Jewish women between 16 and 25

[48] ASRS, AA.EE.SS., Cecoslovacchia 175, f. 241.
[49] ASRS, AA.EE.SS., Cecoslovacchia 175, f. 471, report of Msgr. Burzio to Card. Maglione, March 11, 1942. Burzio cites details of an atrocity committed by the SS in occupied Russia, where the Jews in a little village were loaded onto trucks, driven outside the village, and massacred by machine gun.
[50] ASRS, AA.EE.SS., Cecoslovacchia, 175, ff. 405$^{r/v}$, letter of Msgr. Rotta to Card. Maglione, March 20, 1942.
[51] ASRS, AA.EE.SS., Cecoslovacchia, 175, f. 411, cable of Msgr. Rotta to the Secretariat of State, March 24, 1942, at 6:14 p.m.
[52] ASRS, AA.EE.SS., Cecoslovacchia 175, f. 413, internal note "*Ex Aud. SS.mi 24 marzo 1942.*"

years old were taken away from their families, and, one thinks, will be destined to prostitution at the Russian front."[53] Now things began moving fast and furious at the highest levels of the Secretariat of State. *Minutante* Msgr. Dell'Acqua had to stand by, returning empty-handed to his office, while the higher echelons took the matter in their own hands. He noted: "His Excellency Reverend Monsignor Tardini says to me that His Eminence has already summoned with urgence the Slovak Minister to the Holy See." And so Cardinal Maglione, receiving the Slovak ambassador Sidor in his office that very same day, signed the content of what we should consider a short but "to the point" diplomatic conversation:[54] "I called the Minister and I prayed him to intervene immediately with his Government, so that it would stop an unnecessary horror."[55]

The next cable was sent by Burzio on the evening of March 25 but did not arrive in the Apostolic Palace until 9:30 a.m. the next day. This cable made perfectly clear that the pope's pleas had fallen on deaf ears. Burzio had heard from his sources at the Slovakian Ministry of Foreign Affairs that the Slovak government had announced "a deportation is underway of about 10,000 men and women as a first contingent."[56]

Around the same time, although it is difficult to say if before or after the meeting of Maglione and the Slovak ambassador Sidor, the British ambassador to the Holy See, D'Arcy Osborne, told of troubling intelligence received by the British. It stated that ninety thousand Jews were scheduled to be forcibly moved from Slovakia to a ghetto in Poland. D'Arcy Osborne wrote: "I have been instructed by my government to inform your Eminence and ask if the Holy See believes there is some way to lessen this inhumane measure of German inspiration." [57]

But of course, there was little chance. The Cabinet was fully aware of this yet gave it a try anyway. They summoned the Slovak ambassador to the Holy See and demanded that he intervene immediately with his government to prevent "such sad actuations."

[53] ASRS, AA.EE.SS., Cecoslovacchia, 175, f. 412, cable of Msgr. Burzio, March 25, 1942.
[54] ASRS, AA.EE.SS., Cecoslovacchia 175, f. 414, internal note "25th of March 1942 (Ore 12.30)."
[55] ASRS, AA.EE.SS., Cecoslovacchia 175, f. 413, internal note "Ex Aud. SS.mi 24 marzo 1942," handwriting of Card. Maglione.
[56] ASRS, AA.EE.SS., Cecoslovacchia, 175, f. 416, cable of Msgr. Burzio (sent March 25 at 6:10 p.m.; received: March 26 at 9:30 a.m.).
[57] ASRS, AA.EE.SS., Cecoslovacchia, 175, f. 415, letter of Osborne to Card. Maglione, March 25, 1942.

Senior Vatican officials are well known in public diplomatic circumstances for not losing their tempers, an important quality for someone in such an important position. Yet inside, Tardini was boiling. After Pius XII and Cardinal Secretary of State Maglione discussed the Slovak situation on March 27, the pope had ordered that an immediate telegram be sent to Chargé d'Affaires Burzio with instructions to "tell him of the *steps* made here and charge him to personally make a *step* regarding Tiso." With his typical Roman sense of realism, Tardini could not help but explode, once again making clear his disgust toward President Tiso. Between brackets he noted: "I don't know if the *steps* will succeed in stopping ... the *fools*! And the *fools* are two: Tuka who is acting, and Tiso — a priest — who let these things happen!"[58]

May these attempts at intervention by Rome have actually made things worse, as had been the case in other countries such as Poland? A new eyewitness report sent in by Nuncio Rotta of Budapest one month later certainly points in that direction. The report suggested that the deportations had been stepped up a degree. The eyewitness described thirty cattle wagons packed with desperate, terrified young Jewish maidens departing toward the German border. This transport, with unknown destination, was apparently organized by the Nazi-SS.[59]

The eyewitness to this atrocity was a young Hungarian woman named Anna Végh. She worked for a charity committee helping Jews and was one of Nuncio Rotta's trusted sources. Anna spoke of a second contingent of fifty cattle wagons, this time filled with Jewish men. The wagons departed from Žilina, probably in the direction of Poland. Then yet another thousand young girls were deported to an "unknown destination."[60] For each Jew deported, Slovakia had paid Germany 500 reichsmark (about $2,000 today).

But, rather naïvely or perhaps with wishful thinking, Anna wrote that "President Tiso was highly moved by the intervention of the Holy Father.... It affected his health." Tardini, justifiably cynical, found this to be darkly amusing. Unable to hide his personal dislike of the Slovakian president, Tardini wittily noted, in Roman

---

[58] ASRS, AA.EE.SS., Cecoslovacchia, 175, f. 417, internal note of Msgr. Tardini, March 27, 1942.

[59] ASRS, AA.EE.SS., Cecoslovacchia, 175, f. 465, report from Msgr. Rotta to Card. Maglione, April 17, 1942.

[60] ASRS, AA.EE.SS., Cecoslovacchia, 175, f. 465, report from Msgr. Rotta to Card. Maglione, April 17, 1942.

slang, that Tiso "does not look as if his health has been affected — in photographs he looks always rather ... *paffutello* [chubby]."[61]

A few days later, a letter arrived at the Cabinet from the leaders of the World Jewish Congress and the Jewish Agency for Palestine. It thanked the Holy See for their efforts with the Slovak government. In the midst of the war, Jewish leaders continued to put their hope in the pope and his team, a team that had a great deal of perseverance and took many actions. But it was also a team that had come up against what seemed to be the impenetrable wall of the totalitarian regimes and had lost a lot of the political toughness and ability to change what was happening in Europe.

*

* *

The devastating storm of deportations did not slow down, as Burzio's next report informed. He wrote how the Slovak government had prepared new mass deportation plans in secrecy with the German authorities. But keeping such a big operation hidden was impossible. All the details, including the planned date, had been leaked to the media, creating a public outcry. This opposition backed the government into a corner. Burzio reported that Minister Mach was forced to give a speech denying the government was acting under German orders. Mach said: "Slovakia assumed before the entire world full responsibility for its actions, and also declared expressly that there had been no pressure at all from Germany."[62]

Burzio was justly furious. He denounced some of the Slovakian episcopacy for their guilt and their part in enabling all this. During the parliamentary sessions in which deportation decisions were taken, Msgr. Vojtaššák, the bishop who had disobeyed Pius XII by taking up a government post against his express wishes, "stood passively instead of standing up against this inhumane project." Vojtaššák was also reported to have told another priest that it would have been better if the ecclesiastical authorities had stayed out of this question, "not creating obstacles for the government and the President." In the same conversation,

---

[61] ASRS, AA.EE.SS., Cecoslovacchia, 175, f. 465, report from Msgr. Rotta to Card. Maglione, April 17, 1942.
[62] ASRS, AA.EE.SS., Cecoslovacchia 175, ff. 445–447ʳ, report from Msgr. Burzio to Card. Maglione "About deportations of Jews," March 31, 1942.

Vojtaššák had also called the Jews the *"worst enemies of Slovakia."* Burzio's post didn't hide his disgust: "Vojtaššák is a great chauvinist. Of my part I am completely convinced of that."[63]

He then referred to another episode between Vojtaššák and Bishop Sapieha of Poland, which revealed Vojtaššák's ultra-nationalistic intolerance. The Polish bishop had tried to intervene on behalf of some Polish-born priests, who had been unfairly driven out of their Slovakian parishes. "I heard Vojtaššák answering — *humanitas nostra esset fere peccaminosa* — (our humanity towards these priests was almost sinful)."

Even as Burzio attempted to express it with ever-veiled diplomatic words, he made it clear that he found Vojtaššák's anti-Semitism blatantly obvious: "Of such a man you cannot pretend that he would have tenderness towards the Jews."[64] But, as Burzio was keen to point out, there were still voices of dissent within the Slovak clergy, such as Msgr. Carsky, the bishop of Presov, "who sees it clearly." Carsky had spoken up, saying: "If we remain passive now that they are taking away the girls of the Jews, what will we do when they start taking the girls of our people?"[65]

The plight of the missing Jewish girls remained firmly on the Cabinet's agenda. The nightmare image of innocents being rounded up, thrown into wagons, and taken away to be raped and abused at the hands of Nazi soldiers was unbearable. And the raids that had started on March 25 continued unabated each night, executed by Slovakian Hlinka guards. Through cross-checked sources it seems that after these young women were stolen away from their families

> the girls were put in an industry-plant called "Patronka," in the neighbourhood of Bratislava. There they were searched, spoiled of all their belongings (suitcases, purses, rings, earrings, pencils, food...) and personal documents and they were given a simple serial number. If someone protest[ed] or lament[ed], she [was] brutally beaten with "calci and bastonate" [kicking with the feet and hitting with

---

[63] ASRS, AA.EE.SS., Cecoslovacchia 175, ff. 445ᵛ–446ʳ, letter of Msgr. Burzio to Card. Maglione, March 31, 1942.

[64] ASRS, AA.EE.SS., Cecoslovacchia 175, f. 446ʳ, letter of Msgr. Burzio to Card. Maglione, March 31, 1942.

[65] ASRS, AA.EE.SS., Cecoslovacchia 175, f. 446ʳ, letter of Msgr. Burzio to Card. Maglione, March 31, 1942.

sticks]. And this infamy was executed by the men of the lowest order, ... under the direction of an inspector of the Reich.[66]

In addition to the kidnapping of the Jewish girls, Burzio also reported the violent raids on Jewish homes, and consequently the desperate escape of thousands of Jews into Hungary. But those poor, frantic, fleeing people simply ran into the arms of the Nazis on the other side of the border.

As Maglione sat at his desk, moved and gravely frustrated, he prepared an answer to Msgr. Burzio, adding: "The news that was gently transmitted can only provoke sadness in the heart of the Holy See."[67]

There had been thousands of individual requests for "presidential grace," or mercy, from President Tiso. Msgr. Burzio explained: "The only hope for these Jews is to obtain from the President of the Republic [Tiso] the grace of 'discrimination.' Thousands and thousands of pleas are now under examination by the President's secretary. In the first place are those of Jews of Christian religion.... As I was assured, a large number of dispenses have already been given out."[68]

Huge volumes of information continued to arrive. The charity worker Anna Végh wrote from Budapest: "In that very moment, on the 11th of April 1942, about 8,500 persons were already deported. The government's plan is to reach a number of 20,000 by the end of the week."[69] On April 11, the British ambassador to the Holy See, D'Arcy Osborne, checked in with Cardinal Maglione to ask again "if the Holy See has intervened in favor of the Slovak Jews." Maglione's handwritten notes of that conversation are evidence of that: "I have answered him with a yes. Osborne was also already briefed about steps that were previously taken. I also insisted again to the Slovak minister to the Holy See."[70]

This much is true. Sidor, the Slovak representative to the Holy See, came to see Maglione on that same day. During their meeting, held in the Apostolic Palace, Sidor

[66] ASRS, AA.EE.SS., Cecoslovacchia 175, f. 446ᵛ, letter of Msgr. Burzio to Card. Maglione, March 31, 1942.
[67] ASRS, AA.EE.SS., Cecoslovacchia 175, f. 496, draft of dispatch to Msgr. Burzio, March 21, 1942.
[68] ASRS, AA.EE.SS., Cecoslovacchia 175, ff. 490ʳ/ᵛ, report from Msgr. Burzio, April 9, 1942.
[69] ASRS, AA.EE.SS., Cecoslovacchia 175, f. 468, report from eyewitness (1942), sent by Msgr. Rotta.
[70] ASRS, AA.EE.SS., Cecoslovacchia 175, f. 424, handwritten notes of Card. Maglione, April 11, 1942.

told of his recent visit to Bratislava, where he personally met with President Tiso and Prime Minister Tuka. They had discussed the measures taken toward the Jews. The diplomat claimed to Maglione "that President Tiso had assured him he had interceded to soften the measures. And that he had conceded to several baptized Jews the exemptions or dispensations that were in his power to grant." And Prime Minister Tuka had allegedly said that he hadn't yet responded to the various messages and appeals from the Holy See because he intended to "give a verbal explanation with certain explanations to the Holy Father and to the Secretary of State at a later date."[71]

Maglione didn't buy any of this obvious flimflam from the Slovak side. He noted:

> Sidor tried, (without convincing me) to give me some justifications on the mass-deportations of the Jews. Several times I took the occasion to formulate the point of view of the Holy See, and then expressed myself with force against the recent treatment of the hundreds of girls who were taken away from their families and destined to be lost forever to the abyss. I told him that such acts are an eyesore for a catholic country.[72]
>
> Sidor then, tried to say — always without convincing me — that those poor girls were only destined to honest work elsewhere. I answered that, even if this was so, it would be anyway a sad thing, because it is always inhuman to separate girls and youngsters from their families against their wishes. And to work where, without any assistance they are exposed to the worst dangers. I told him that what had been reported to me was not as he said. The destination of these poor girls was quite different! I asked him to let his government know of our conversation.[73]

Sadly, this is where the trail of the abducted girls goes cold. The horrors that befell them were surely appalling. The Cabinet now had no doubt that Tiso's government had reached a murderous point of no return.

[71] ASRS, AA.EE.SS., Cecoslovacchia 175, ff. 435–436ᵛ, handwritten notes of Card. Maglione of the meeting with Ambassador Sidor, April 11, 1942.

[72] ASRS, AA.EE.SS., Cecoslovacchia, 175, f. 436, handwritten notes of Card. Maglione of the meeting with Ambassador Sidor, April 11, 1942.

[73] ASRS, AA.EE.SS., Cecoslovacchia, 175, f. 436ᵛ, handwritten notes of Card. Maglione of the meeting with Ambassador Sidor, April 11, 1942.

An anonymous, undated report came in stating that "at 12:00 this morning journalists of the Allied countries and other media convened in the Prime Minister's office with Minister Mach, for a press conference on the question of the Hebrews on Slovakia. And particularly in relation to the discordant voices that run through the population in Slovakia."

That the Slovakian government chose to give a press conference to proudly proclaim their perceived right to murder hundreds of thousands is utterly astounding. Mach told the assembled reporters "to resolve the Jewish question in a totalitarian way has to lead to the exclusion of all the Jews in Slovak public life.... The decision to 'transfer the Jews' is being now applied practically, while numerous trains have left already Slovakia, and others will follow until the last Jew of Slovakia is gone. The definitive decision of the Jewish Problem for Slovakia had been taken by the council of State."[74] In the margin, someone in the Cabinet marked this paragraph with a cross, underlining and emphasizing the shocking importance of it. The shadow of Vojtaššák loomed large over all of it; he sat on the council of state as these final measures were agreed.

Maglione received a full copy of the speech, which was handed over by the loyal go-between, Commendatore Babuscio Rizzo of the Italian embassy.[75]

Minister Mach also noted that "baptisms that were given by certain clerics would no longer be taken into account. Baptized or not, all the Jews shall have to leave.... Jews that were fugitives in Hungary should be given back to the Slovak government, for this an agreement is on its way to the Hungarian government."[76]

The Nazi noose was tightening. There was clearly no escape anymore. Those gravely unfortunate souls who were trapped in Slovakia would be deported. Those who escaped would be handed back. Mach continued:

> I am informed about the Sanatoria and hospitals, that are filled with Jewish men and women: they claim imaginary diseases in the hope of escaping the law. A commission of medical doctors will visit all these "temporarily" sick people and will decide on

[74] ASRS, AA.EE.SS., Cecoslovacchia, 175, f. 454, typewritten report handed over by Comm. Babuscio, May 8, 1942.
[75] ASRS, AA.EE.SS., Cecoslovacchia 175, f. 454, transcript of speech handed over by Comm. Babuscio, dated May 1942.
[76] ASRS, AA.EE.SS., Cecoslovacchia 175, f. 455, transcript of speech handed over by Comm. Babuscio, dated May 1942.

their fate. . . . Jews that are irreplaceable will be examined by a
special commission that will then decide on temporary permits
with periodical revisions, until one will find an Aryan element
to replace the Jew.[77]

Tiso's government was probably the most sophisticated executers of the Nazi doctrine, and it did so without any attempt of propagandizing or soft-soaping. Even
the Nazis themselves attempted at times to cover up and trick the international
community. But in Slovakia, the political class of that time acted with a brazen
public openness, even a pride, at their vile actions. The Slovak press conference
made waves across a mostly horrified Europe. But in Fascist Italy, the newspaper
Corriere della Sera headline sounded: "Full Power of the Slovak Government for
Expulsion of the Jews."[78]

Messages and letters continued to fly in to the secretary of state, including a
new eyewitness report from an ordinary civilian, a businessman from Germany:
"Finding myself for business reasons for a week in Budapest, I was asked to bring
these facts to your knowledge." Not mentioning the identity of his sources, he
reported that:

The Jews, who, for obvious reasons, are trying to get into Hungary
are being given back to the border authorities from where they came
from. This happens as a consequence of German pressure. These
Jews are interned in concentration camps where there is no food,
sanitation or medical services. Therefore, a lot of these unfortunate
people die. The Red Cross of Hungary has tried to intervene, but
their authorization was refused.[79]

This offered yet another confirmation that the Nazis did not allow any interference
in their persecution and extermination activities, not by the Red Cross, and even
less so by the Holy See.

---

[77] ASRS, AA.EE.SS., Cecoslovacchia 175, f. 455, transcript of speech handed over by
Comm. Babuscio, dated May 1942.
[78] ASRS, AA.EE.SS., Cecoslovacchia 175, f. 498, newspaper article of *Piccolo* of Trieste,
March 17, 1942; f. 499, newspaper article of *Corriere della Sera*, March 17, 1942.
[79] ASRS, AA.EE.SS., Cecoslovacchia, 175, ff. 460–462ᵛ, eyewitness report sent with a
letter from cardinal archbishop of Genoa, Card. Boetto, S.J. (the initials signify Boetto
was a Jesuit), April 16, 1942.

This eyewitness then revealed something the Cabinet already knew, the tragic story of the girls. He continued: "Another fact, even worse, happened in Slovakia where thousands of young Jewish women were brought to other places, I don't know exactly where, to be given 'as food' for the soldiers."[80] The eyewitness declared to be of Aryan race and was moved by his "humanitarian sentiments to communicate all this." His sincere report on the case of the Jewish girls is a reminder there were German citizens who, although part of the wider machine, were opposed to Nazi brutality.

In Slovakia, a few active senior bishops continued to speak out. They prepared a collective letter on the Jewish question to be published in the *Katolicke Noviny*. The state censor first refused its publication. Later on, however, the censor told the bishops that if they made certain changes to the text that would soften or change the meaning of it, they could publish it. Yet to print a censored version would mean the letter would lose the strong criticism of the government that the bishops had intended. They boldly refused to publish a propaganda-amended version and, disobeying the censor, published their original text.[81]

On July 6, British ambassador D'Arcy Osborne made his appearance once more, asking again if the Holy See had been able to intervene in favor of the deportation of the Jews in Slovakia, and if so, with what result?[82] *Minutante* Msgr. Dell'Acqua was given the job of replying. He noted that he was suspicious of the British diplomat's repeated questioning. D'Arcy Osborne had already been informed personally several times by Cardinal Secretary of State Maglione that the pope had interceded more than once. It seemed to Dell'Acqua that with this new letter, D'Arcy Osborne was trying to get a written document out of the secretary of state on this subject, something Dell'Acqua considered "*assai delicato*" (most delicate), and he feared the British might use that for Allied propaganda. Dell'Acqua suggested to his superiors that it would be convenient to repeat orally to D'Arcy Osborne that the Holy See has made several moves in this regard, "without obtaining great … results."[83]

---

[80] ASRS, AA.EE.SS., Cecoslovacchia 175, f. 462, eyewitness report sent with a letter from cardinal archbishop of Genoa, Card. Boetto, S.J. (the initials signify Boetto was a Jesuit), April 16, 1942.

[81] ASRS, AA.EE.SS., Cecoslovacchia 175, ff. 474–475, report of Msgr. Burzio to Card. Maglione, April 27, 1942.

[82] ASRS, AA.EE.SS., Cecoslovacchia 175, f. 427, letter of Osborne to Card. Maglione, July 6, 1942.

[83] ASRS, AA.EE.SS., Cecoslovacchia, 175, f. 430, typewritten internal note of Msgr. Dell'Acqua, "Ebrei in Slovacchia."

Tardini agreed to that. But after having heard Pius XII on this, he gave Dell'Acqua his okay to prepare a written response, referencing the latest protest letter by the Slovak bishops. Tardini noted his own thoughts in a nota bene: "The disaster is that the president of the Slovaks is a priest. That the Holy See cannot stop Hitler, we all can understand. But that it cannot halt a priest, who can understand that?"[84]

Cabinet Secretary Tardini, as readers do to this day, struggled with a critical question: Why could the Holy See not stop a murderous priest? He wrangled with the apparent incapacity of the Holy See to interfere in matters of local bishops and their political choices. And, of course, the German propaganda machine did its utmost to ensure the Church looked bad. The helping hand of the Italian commendatore, Francesco Babuscio, delivered a new text from a radio message by Minister Mach in which he tried to sell the idea that Catholic Slovaks in the end came to approve, even if only in an indirect way, the "solution" of the question of the Jews currently in place.[85]

On May 15, 1942, Mach's new constitutional law came into being. All Jews would be deported from Slovak territory. An exception was made for only two groups: those who had become members of a Christian confession before March 14, 1939, and those who had a valid matrimonial contract with a non-Jewish partner prior to September 10, 1941.

Although this could be seen as a slight concession compared to Mach's earlier press conference, it also invalidated all the baptismal certificates the Church, as in other countries, had given out over the past three years in an attempt to save lives.

The chargé d'affaires, Msgr. Burzio, was utterly dismayed. He told of his disgust that "some priests who were deputies in Parliament voted in favor of this law, others abstained, but not one of them dared vote against it."[86] In Pius XII's inner circle, it provoked the same consternation. Cardinal Maglione wrote back to Burzio: "The Holy See has learned of the new heavy measures adopted by the Slovak government against the non-Aryans with utter dismay. And this is even worse because it

---

[84] ASRS, AA.EE.SS., Cecoslovacchia 175, f. 431, handwritten note of Msgr. Tardini, July 13, 1942.

[85] ASRS, AA.EE.SS., Cecoslovacchia 175, f. 502, typewritten report "dall'Ambasciata d'Italia," June 12, 1942.

[86] ASRS, AA.EE.SS., Cecoslovacchia 175, f. 504[r/v], report from Msgr. Burzio to Card. Maglione, May 23, 1942.

seems from what you are saying is that the new law would be emanated with the participation of some priests, deputies of that parliament."[87] While they were clearly distraught, there was still very little the Cabinet could do to punish the offenders. For a non-Catholic, it might be difficult to understand that the possibilities of the hierarchy in Rome to intervene in matters concerning local hierarchies are limited. According to the Catholic canon, priesthood is a sacrament emanating from the Holy Spirit, not a job, and inviolable as such.

Priests in politics — always a nasty problem for the Church, as it was then for Pius XII and continues to be so up to our days. Msgr. Tardini could never be at ease with the presence of priests in politics, and so we find him in 1945 once more well aware of the eventual scandal and at the same time regretting the impotence to intervene in this pressing issue: "Are there not too many priests in places of great political responsibility now? Is this not a danger for the Church? On the other hand, can it be generally prohibited? What should be required is that these priests would be 'good ones.' Otherwise! ... Therefore an instruction to the Ordinaries [local bishops and archbishops] might perhaps be appropriate in order they would give out such permits only to worthy priests."[88]

Commendatore Babuscio passed on an Italian intelligence report telling how the continued presence of a handful of Jews, mostly those who had been pardoned by Tiso (even though, as later on Msgr. Burzio would affirm, those dispenses had been few and their concession subject of huge corruption of the entourage of the president[89]) or baptized as Catholic, was still too much for the Nazis:

> Preoccupied by the number of these privileged Jews the National Socialist circles broke their silence, and once more took on an extremely aggressive anti-Semitic stance, denouncing to the public numerous cases of corruption of falsification of baptism certificates, of sabotage and violation of dispositions made by the commissariat for food distribution; of subversive activity against the Slovak people,

---

[87] ASRS, AA.EE.SS., Cecoslovacchia 175, f. 508, draft of letter of Card. Maglione to Msgr. Burzio, June 19, 1942.
[88] ASRS, AA.EE.SS., Ungheria 125, f. 130ʳ.
[89] ASRS, AA.EE.SS., Cecoslovacchia 175, f. 636, letter of Msgr. Burzio to Card. Maglione, March 7, 1943.

of anti-state propaganda and dredging up the past of these Jews and
their accomplices or their Aryan protectors.[90]

The Italian intelligence report quoted the Slovak press: "The most dangerous Jews
would be exactly those who made it possible to escape deportation using their relations and astuteness or with the corrupt system preferred by them." According to
the report, "this thesis is repeated in newspapers, on radio broadcasts and in the
Slovak popular party press.... The government has the firm intention to resolve
to 'the last drop the Jewish question.'"[91] The author of this intelligence analysis
claimed that the Slovak government saw recent baptismal certificates as part of
that "corruption," and suggested "a re-examination of all the baptism certificates
and work permits given out to Jews and, in case of falsification, no punishment
but immediate deportation."[92]

It seems insane and defies belief that the idea of deportation to a concentration
camp was not considered a punishment. It is interesting to note, too, that the official
government line never even hinted that the Jews were destined for extermination.
Tiso's government talked only in public about resolving the "Jewish Problem,"
by taking them out of Slovakian society, leaving open what the future for those
deported people would be. Once out of Slovakia, the government could cynically
claim it was no longer their problem and leave it to their German masters from there.

At the start of 1943, more bad news came to the Cabinet by way of Nuncio
Rotta in Hungary. He disclosed that twenty thousand Jews remaining in Slovakia,
many of them baptized Catholic, were now to be deported. It seems the exemption
for those baptized before 1939 had been cruelly brief.

Individuals begged the pope to help. Sr. Margherita Slachta, a Hungarian nun and
personal confidant of Pius XII, made a special trip to Rome[93] to try to rescue those
final twenty thousand Slovak Jews. She handed over several reports she herself had
written. In one of these she said: "Minister Mach has said that in two months, this
means March and April 1943, the complete deportation of all Jews that remained

[90] ASRS, AA.EE.SS., Cecoslovacchia 175, f. 599, report passed on by Comm. Babuscio,
September 29, 1942.
[91] ASRS, AA.EE.SS., Cecoslovacchia 175, f. 562, report passed on by Comm. Babuscio,
September 29, 1942.
[92] ASRS, AA.EE.SS., Cecoslovacchia 175, f. 562, report passed on by Comm. Babuscio,
September 29, 1942.
[93] She lived in Via Giulia 1. Cfr. ASRS, AA.EE.SS., Cecoslovacchia 175, f. 596.

in Slovakia had to be executed. These count a number of 20,000; half of them are Christians."[94] On the sister's report, a hopeless Tardini made a note: "We've already interested ourselves to the case in Slovakia. Is that true? What can one do?"[95] Now it was the desk officer Msgr. Giuseppe Di Meglio who wrote underneath: "Today a dispatch signed by the Cardinal was sent out to Msgr. Burzio, who is charged with intervening on behalf of the 20,000 Slovaks."[96] The details Sr. Slachta gave on the deportation of twenty thousand Jews was echoed in a report from Burzio in late February.[97] However, a next report at the beginning of March 1943 did not lend solid evidence to the nun's claim that the Jews would have been executed, and the Slovakian authorities did not give any specific details on it.[98] Still, the Cabinet was able to determine the clear intentions of the Slovak government as expressed in a discourse of Minister Mach: "One of our duties, considering we have eliminated 80 percent of the Jews, is that of closing the game with those who are left over. All of us know very well what the presence of those 20,000 Jews means."[99] This time, the Catholic bishops did not stand still. In February, they had written a joint letter to the government in defense of those baptized Jews, playing on the national Slovak Catholic sentiment and the prerogatives of the Catholic Church in the country.[100]

The pope was immediately alarmed by these grave tidings, and at the end of an audience he issued an order "to interest Monsignor Burzio."[101] According to Di Meglio, Tardini, and Maglione, it was high time to intervene. Burzio, as the pope's representative in Slovakia, was ordered to do all he could: "If what the news report

[94] ASRS, AA.EE.SS., Cecoslovacchia 175, f. 386, internal note by Msgr. Di Meglio, March 8, 1943; and in particular f. 593, internal note, March 5, 1943; ff. 599–603, letter and report from Sr. Slachta, March 22, 1943; ff. 606–610, report on "concrete facts of the pogrom," March 8, 1943.

[95] ASRS, AA.EE.SS., Cecoslovacchia 175, f. 593, internal note, March 5, 1943.

[96] ASRS, AA.EE.SS., Cecoslovacchia 175, f. 593, internal note, March 5, 1943.

[97] ASRS, AA.EE.SS., Cecoslovacchia 175, f. 583, report from Msgr. Burzio to Card. Maglione, February 26, 1943.

[98] ASRS, AA.EE.SS., Cecoslovacchia 175, f. 636, report of Msgr. Burzio to Card. Maglione, March 7, 1943.

[99] ASRS, AA.EE.SS., Cecoslovacchia 175, f. 637, copy with text of the discourse of Minister Mach, February 7, 1943.

[100] ASRS, AA.EE.SS., Cecoslovacchia 175, ff. 638–639, copy of the letter of the Slovakian bishops to the Slovak government, February 17, 1943.

[101] ASRS, AA.EE.SS., Cecoslovacchia 175, f. 583, report from Msgr. Burzio to Card. Maglione, February 26, 1943.

are indeed reality, I beg Your Excellency to be willing to make rigorously every effort in dealing with that government in order that so many unhappy people will be spared from such a hard fate."[102] The chargé d'affaires knew exactly what to do. Burzio met with Tuka, the Slovakian prime minister of foreign affairs, and wrote in his report as follows:

> So, I thought the moment had come to execute the instructions given by Your Eminence, with Dispaccio 1376/43 of 6 March, and that is to take steps to get in touch with the Government, in order that the Jews still living in Slovakia would be spared from the hard fate of deportation. So, I asked for an Audience with the Minister of Foreign Affairs. It was given to me on the 7th of March at 11 am.

With a taste of bitter disgust, Msgr. Burzio then set the general tone of his report:

> There is nothing more unpleasant and humiliating than having a conversation with this character, whom others call the sphinx, others the maniac, the other cynical Pharisee. When I exposed the subject of my visit to him, his manner visibly altered and he said, annoyed: "Monsignor, I do not understand what the Vatican has to do with the Jews of Slovakia. You have to let the Holy See know that I reject this move." I did not react to the impolite and vulgar answer and pointed out to him that the Holy See did not meddle and did not intend to meddle in the internal things of Slovakia. I asked him to consider the move, which I take on behalf of the Holy See,[103] as dictated solely by reasons of humanity and Christian charity; I added that it did not seem inappropriate to me to speak of human and Christian sentiments to the leaders of a state, which, according to the words of its own constitution, "brings together on the basis of *natural law* all the moral and economic forces of the people in a *Christian* and national community."
>
> "The state is not and cannot be Christian!" — declared Dr. Tuka — "There is no article of the Constitution that declares

---

[102] ASRS, AA.EE.SS., Cecoslovacchia 175, f. 585, draft of letter of Card. Maglione to Msgr. Burzio, March 6, 1943.

[103] ASRS, AA.EE.SS., Cecoslovacchia 175, f. 650.

Slovakia a Christian state. And then, when it comes to Jews, it is vain to invoke principles of Christianity and humanity. I don't understand why you want to prevent me from carrying out my mission, which is to get rid of Slovakia of this plague, from this gang of evildoers and gangsters."

I remarked to the Minister that it was unfair to consider and to treat the thousands of innocent women and children who were part of last year's deportations as evildoers.

"When it comes to rules of importance and scope for a nation, the government cannot react timidly. Jews are an associative race, and cannot be assimilated; they are pernicious and deleterious elements, which must be eradicated and removed without regard. But in short, tell me, Monsignor, if the Church or the Holy See ever protested, when our Slovak people, brutalized and reduced to misery by the Jewish exploiters, were forced to emigrate en masse to the Americas? And why didn't they protest when the Italian and German peoples of Tyrol were exchanged and in other similar cases? Even the Bishops and the Slovak clergy have meddled beyond need in this affair and take the defenses of the Jews; this shows that the Jewish element is still very influential in Slovakia and is one more reason to end it once and for all."[104]

Msgr. Burzio then sat back and uttered calmly: "Your Excellency is, without a doubt, aware of the sad news about the atrocious fate of the Jews deported to Poland and Ukraine. The whole world talks about it. Admitting for a moment that a state can disregard the norms of natural law and the dictates of Christianity, it does not seem to me that it can, for its own prestige and for the future good of its nation, be disinterested in international opinion and the judgment of history."

To which Tuka replied:

I have no direct information to authorize me to believe such rumors, spread by Jewish propaganda. However, it is my intention to send a commission to inquire about the presence of the Jews deported from Slovakia. If these reports of atrocities were true, I would not

[104] ASRS, AA.EE.SS., Cecoslovacchia 175, f. 650ᵛ.

allow one more Jew to cross the Slovak border. You have mentioned the judgment of history: if history speaks one day of present-day Slovakia, it will remember that there was a good and courageous man at the head of the government, who had the strength to free his country from the greatest of scourges. As for international opinion, we know that it is divided into two currents: one does not worry me and the other does not interest me, because it is directed or influenced by Jewish propaganda.

Burzio then noted, "He had the impudence to add that even the Vatican is not entirely immune from this influence." And with the sinking realization that talking to Tuka was no better than talking to a wall, Burzio continued:

Is it worthwhile that I go on to report to Your Eminence the continuation of my conversation with a demented person? Nor is it to be hoped that with this superman, arguments addressed to his conscience would be efficient. He prevents them and repeats what he already has said to me at that point, that I would beware to even touch that point: "I know what is good and what is bad; I am a convinced and practicing Catholic; I attend Holy Mass every day[105] and I receive Holy Communion very frequently. And I am calm about my actions; for me the supreme spiritual authority, more than the Bishops, more than the Church, is my conscience and my confessor."

I asked Mr. Tuka one last question: "Being this the opinion rather than a current belief, can I at least communicate to the Holy See that the deportation of Jews from Slovakia does not take place on the initiative of the Slovak Government, but rather under external pressure?"

The Minister responded: "I assure you on my honor as a Christian, that it is our will and our initiative. This, yes, it is true, that I was offered the possibility of realizing my plan and I, for sure, did not refuse it."

He added then "that Jews baptized before the statutory deadline will not be deported; likewise, those useful to the State and those who have obtained exemption

[105] ASRS, AA.EE.SS., Cecoslovacchia 175, f. 651.

will not be removed. That, however, regarding the latter, the concessions will have to be reviewed, because many documents have been falsified and there has been no small amount of corruption."

Burzio continued:

> Afterwards, he still wanted to underline his absolute conviction, "that to free Slovakia from the 'Jewish plague' there is no other means than forced and mass deportation." I observed that for the offenders there are laws, courts, convictions and prisons, but that it is the primordial and inviolable right of everyone not to be punished without prior judgment or for the crimes of others. He replied: "Prison is not enough; prison does not improve anyone; also believe me that I have experienced this for nine years."[106]
>
> Unwittingly, with this reply, Mr. Tuka said the greatest truth and the only sincere thing during the whole conversation. Finally, with real relief, I could leave, accompanied by Tuka's parting words, which summarize the outcome of the meeting: "As a Vatican official, you have done your duty and I will do mine; we will remain friends, but the Jews will leave."

Burzio then concluded:

> However, the move has produced some good effects. The first to react was Tiso, the President of the Republic who, when informed of the meeting, called and expressed his regret for the attitude and response of the Foreign Minister. He also made some confidential statements, of which however he begged me not to communicate in writing but possibly only by voice.
>
> This morning, the Minister of Cults sent a representative to the Apostolic Nunciature. The representative informed me that Dr. Tuka reported yesterday on the meeting of the Council of Ministers about the conversation he had with me and that all Ministers

---

[106] After the founding of Czechoslovakia in late 1918, Tuka, at the time a law professor, joined the autonomist Slovak People's Party. In 1928, he was charged with espionage and high treason, found guilty and sentenced to fifteen years' imprisonment. He served about nine years.

protested, considering the intervention of the Holy See to be an honor for Slovakia. He also told me that the Council of Ministers immediately decided that the deportation of the 4,000 Jews for which the Ministry of the Interior had already given the relative dispositions was suspended; that baptized Jews will no longer be deported whatever the date of baptism; and that as far as other Jews are concerned, discernment must be carried out and only those elements truly harmful to the state must be removed. I hope the facts will confirm this information.[107]

*

*　*

With a heavy heart, Cabinet Secretary Tardini sat in his office in April 1943, pondering the words he would use in the umpteenth official note to the Slovakian ambassador to the Holy See. He must have been exhausted, both mentally and spiritually, knowing the importance of the matter yet also well aware of the obstacles that continued to stand in the way. He reflected on the whole terrible issue, making the following personal notes for himself:

(1) The Jewish question is one of humanity. The persecutions to which the Jews in Germany and in the occupied countries are submitted … or subdued are an offense to justice, to charity, to humanity. The same brutal treatment is also extended to baptized Jews. Thus, the Catholic Church has complete justification to intervene, and in the name of the divine right as well as in the name of the natural law.

(2) In Slovakia the head of State is a priest. Hence, the scandal is bigger, and as equally big is the danger that the responsibility could be poured onto the Catholic Church itself. For this motive it would seem opportune for the Holy See to once more raise its protest, repeating — in a clearer way — that which was explained already a year ago in a diplomatic note to his Excellence Sidor.

(3) Since, especially during this last period, the heads of the Jewish people have addressed the Holy See in order to implore for help, it

---

[107] ASRS, AA.EE.SS., Cecoslovacchia 175, f. 652.

would not be out of place to make this diplomatic note of the Holy See in a discreet way known to the public (the fact of its transmission, the content of the document, more than the text itself).

This is to show to the world that the Holy See fulfils its obligations of charity, not to gain the sympathy of the Jews in case they would one day be among the victors. (Given that the Jewish people — as far as one can see in the future — will never be close … friends of the Holy See and of the Catholic Church.)

But that will render the work of charity more victorious.[108]

Tardini's words are both realistic and, at the same time, prophetic. They make clear that the Catholic Church was not intervening to curry favor but was doing so solely on the basis of Christian charity. He was aware that at times throughout history the relationship between the Jews and the Catholic Church had been rather difficult. But he firmly believed this past history should not have any impact on the charitable actions of the Holy See.

A day later, on April 8, 1943, Tardini once more took his personal annotations and thoughts to discuss the Slovak dossier with the pope. During this audience, Pope Pius XII decided that there should be another well-prepared *note verbale* to present to the Slovak government.[109] The favorable outcome of this *note verbale* (in my opinion, a masterpiece of written diplomacy), and the fate of those twenty thousand people whose lives were at risk, is history.

---

[108] ASRS, AA.EE.SS., Cecoslovacchia 175, ff. 643$^{r/v}$, handwritten notes of Msgr. Tardini, April 7, 1943.

[109] ASRS, AA.EE.SS., Cecoslovacchia 175, f. 643, handwritten notes on the decision of Pius XII, April 8, 1943.

2

Short Story of People on the Run
and Their Silent Saviors

THE EVENTS DEPICTED in the documents of the Historical Archive of the
Secretariat of State reflect the daily work of the Holy See during wartime, particularly its diplomatic and high politics negotiations with the rest of the world. It is
therefore surprising, in that serious Cabinetcratic environment, to find testimonies
of the slow, detailed, and meticulous work of actors behind the scenes — from the
grassroots level up to the highest authorities across the globe — striving to save
individuals and creating the possibilities to do so. Running into such evidentiary
material might be, in my modest opinion, unique in the context of archival material
of a "foreign ministry." I will try to bring it to light here for the first time.

More specifically, this story will deal with the archival "Ebrei" (Jews) series (also
referred to as the Ebrei Files in this book), a collection of hundreds and hundreds
of files and tenfold number of documents. Each of them usually represents a family
or a group of individuals. Each tells a story of people in need, those who have written to the pope themselves or those who were referred to him by intermediaries.

The study of these Ebrei Files will be interesting not only for scholars and
professional historians, and for experts in Holocaust research, but also for those
involved in the work of identifying the lost and genealogical research.

For unknown reasons, the existence of the Ebrei Files was kept secret until
now. A portion of their content, dated up until 1939, was revealed by the historian
Robert Aleksander Maryks, as a result of his research on the Jesuit archives in

Rome. However, he did not have access to the original files of the Secretariat of State and certainly not those of the World War II years, and probably also therefore erroneously supposed that the matter of the aid to Jews by the Secretariat of State concerned only Catholic baptized Jews, as the title of his book suggests.[110]

How exactly did this Ebrei series, with its hundreds of files, come to be?

All the other archival series of the Historical Archive of the Secretariat of State are named after and relate to specific countries — for instance, Russia, England, Peru, and Argentina. These series are organic, developed and filed chronologically with a Cabinetcratic, administrative logic. In the context of the Historical Archive, the composition of the Ebrei Files is therefore quite anomalous, insofar as it contains an ancient nucleus of files gathered during the wartime years by the Cabinet, to which files coming from other archival series were later on added. We can attest to this because documents contained in it have often been taken out from different series already existing and inserted in this new one, and with a last intervention, the files were ordered alphabetically by their family names, starting with the anonymous.[111]

We can better understand the existence of the Ebrei Files if we take into account an important decision taken at the highest level of the Secretariat of State at the beginning of World War II. This decision made the First Section (Foreign Affairs), or as we call it, the Cabinet, headed by Tardini, responsible for dealing with "all issues regarding non-Aryans." As the First Section handled existing key relationships with foreign diplomats and governments, they could use those contacts and connections to obtain help for refugees and for people looking for an exit. The responsibility for grants and direct financial aid to Jews and other people in difficulty was given to the Second Section (General Affairs), headed by substitute Montini. Cardinal Maglione was in overall charge of both sections.[112] It can't be excluded that the other section disposed of its own register or file system, which

---

[110] Aleksander Maryks, *Pouring Jewish Water into Fascist Wine: Untold Stories of (Catholic) Jews from the Archive of Mussolini's Jesuit Pietro Tacchi Venturi*, Leiden, 2012.

[111] There was an original nucleus of sampled documents on *Ebrei* (Jews) but this was later on enlarged by the archivist, who added additional personal files on cases taken from other archival series, mostly out of the series Italia 1054 and Stati Ecclesiastici 575. These two series probably already contained material only on the saving of Jews from the very start of the war. The cases were then enlisted into the *Ebrei* files in alphabetical order and prepared for consultation in fascicles containing from one to twenty-five cases each.

[112] ASRS, AA.EE.SS., Ebrei 162, f. 40.

would mean that other archives of the Holy See, as for instance the Apostolic Archives, preserve similar material regarding the Jews.

The existence of this particular archival series is tangible proof of the interest shown for people who, for reason of racial laws, were no longer considered common citizens, whether they were Jews or baptized Jews. As one can presume, there are undoubtedly countless other stories of requests for assistance for those categorized as Jews that are yet to be found between thousands of documents in other archival series, such as Hungary, Slovakia, Poland, the Netherlands, and more.

The Ebrei Files count approximately twenty-eight hundred requests for interventions or help. Most come from refugees themselves; some come from good-hearted people interceding for them. Some are from individuals, while others come from married couples, entire families, or groups. The series reflects a glimpse of the destiny of more than four thousand Jews, some who practiced the Jewish faith, but the majority of whom were Christians of Jewish lineage. It is easy to understand why this is so. From a juridical and diplomatic point of view — and Nazi Germany knew how to play this out — the Holy See was only authorized to intervene on behalf of Catholics around the world.

The bulk of requests span the years between 1938 and 1944.[113] These six years represent a period of intense activity in the Apostolic Palace in Rome, landing an average of about two requests for help a day on their desks, with a peak period in the years 1939–1942, when an average of about five requests for help a day were handled.

With the agonizingly slow communications of wartime, requests often came in too late to save a life. By the time the written plea reached the Holy See, the person could have already been captured, deported to a concentration camp, or even killed. This explains why some dossiers were opened and closed without any outcome. In other cases, the solicitor for help could have found an acceptable resolution through other sources in the meantime. Another possibility is that in certain sensitive cases, no traces were left by the staff of Pius XII as they proceeded to help someone.

Many people will assume that only baptized individuals were eligible for help from Rome, given that the Cabinet was working for the pope, head of the Catholic

---

[113] Rarely a file does go beyond 1944. It is the case with two newspaper articles on the Baptism of Zolli, the chief rabbi of Rome, and his wife. Their presence in the series might explain that the office considered this Baptism as related to the activity of Pius XII in saving Jews. ASRS, AA.EE.SS., Ebrei 170, ff. 33–34b.

Church. The Nazis and their accomplices would certainly have assumed so, though
there came the time when they would no longer take Christian Baptism into consideration and the Jewish ancestry of a person would become the only factor for
deportation and a death sentence. Yet the Ebrei Files show that the efforts and intentions were to try and save every single human being, regardless of color or creed.

One should recall here that the Nazis and Fascists made an initial distinction
between Jews. For them, a first group consisted of the Jews who practiced the
Jewish faith. From the beginning, those were target number one for deportation.

The second group consisted of Jews who had converted to Christianity. In
this group, the distinction was drawn between those who had converted a long
time before the war and those who did so just before the war or during the first
years of the war. The hopes of both these groups of Christian converts to escape
deportation were soon shattered due to the continually changing and ever more
aggressive anti-Jewish laws. One should also note that Nazi Germany was not the
only country with racial policies in place. Some countries that offered passports
and visa to Pius XII, to be granted by him personally, specified that those documents were to be issued exclusively to Christian-baptized Jews, and they had to
have been baptized since a certain date. This clause was probably also included to
avoid diplomatic incidents or tensions with Germany and its allies. Such was the
case for Albert Katz. He contacted the nunciature of France in July 1941 with a
request for immigration to Brazil. He had been baptized only a year before. At his
first glimpse of Katz's file, Tardini wrote down the irrevocable verdict — "impossible" — and added, "Also recently the Embassy [of Brazil] has declared not be able
to make any exception."[114] A similar case was that of the Hungarian family of Oscar
and Ghisela Lakatos. In 1941, they were recommended by the ecclesiastical consul
of the Hungarian delegation to the Holy See in Rome. The consul wrote directly
to the desk officer Msgr. Dell'Acqua, saying: "The family cannot continue their
life in Hungary. They are composed of four groups of couples. The parents Oscar
and Ghisela and their two daughters were baptized. This baptism was suggested
by me. They have deposited their assets in Switzerland and the money is transfer-
able to other countries."[115] The file tells us further on that "the documents on the
Lakatos couple Oscar and Ghisela were seen by the embassy of Brazil to the Holy

[114] ASRS, AA.EE.SS., Ebrei 68, f. 11.
[115] ASRS, AA.EE.SS., Ebrei 75, ff. 19–27.

See." We can assume from this that the Brazilian embassy was likely to issue a visa. However, it is not known whether or not the extended family managed to escape.

A third group of Jews considered, from 1941 onwards, appropriate for deportation by the Nazis consisted of Christians of Jewish lineage: they themselves were baptized at birth but one or more of their parents or grandparents were Jewish. That was sufficient to put those persons in the crosshairs of Nazi and Fascist terrorism during the war.

Unfortunately, it's not always clear from the files if there was a positive result or not regarding a particular case. The actions taken by the Holy See such as obtaining visas and other measures are noted evidently, but we often don't learn what then became of the person or persons or if they reached their final destination.

Then there were heartbreaking instances in which the Cabinet, often the Secretary of State Cardinal Maglione himself, was explicit on the fact that an intervention could have nothing but a negative outcome. One such case was that of Mr. Herbert Jorysz, a Jew from Breslau (now Wrocław, the historic capital of Lower Silesia, attached to Poland in 1945). Mr. Jorysz's request came in on Christmas Day of 1938.[116] He wrote on behalf of his whole family, pleading with the Holy See to intervene with the German government to obtain permission for their emigration. The family had been stripped of citizenship, and "there are special difficulties because they are without passports." The Cabinet noted: "A disastrous case." And yet, despite all this, the staff of Pius XII would always try. An immediate dispatch was issued to Nuncio Orsenigo in Berlin, but as one can imagine, the outcome was not likely a positive one.

In other cases, the Cabinet had to admit to itself that due to the ever-extending Nazi occupation in Europe, it was increasingly impossible to intervene on behalf of the persecuted, particularly when the requests came from non-baptized Jews. The frontline between Russia and Germany became an invisible but formidable wall, which made whole swaths of Europe impenetrable. In some of these oppressed regions, the Catholic clergy and laypeople, who might have been able and willing to help the refugees, had all been wiped out themselves.

A good example of the growing frustration Pius XII's staff felt at not being able to help the persecuted appears as comments noted in two letters, both of which were written in Yiddish and had arrived from Poland. The letters came with a request for intervention of the Holy See to immigrate to Palestine. On the first

[116] ASRS, AA.EE.SS., Ebrei 66, ff. 24–26.

letter Tardini noted, "What can one do anymore by now?" and on the other, which was written on July 20, 1939, but had not reached the Cabinet until October 18, Dell'Acqua wrote a similar discouraged comment: "As things are as they are now in Poland, there is nothing to do."[117]

Letter from H. Kusowicki from Poland in Yiddish, July 20, 1939.[118]

[117] ASRS, AA.EE.SS., Ebrei 74, ff. 66–67.
[118] ASRS, AA.EE.SS., Ebrei 74, f. 67.

In between the thousands of requests, sometimes — but very rarely — one encounters letters from other non-Jewish persons facing adversity. These rare cases made their appeals with the same urgency, the same hope and desire, to emigrate, to get the proper protection, or to get news of family members who had disappeared.

Such was the case of Mr. Anton Kalicinski, an Austrian Catholic. We learn from his file that on his mother's side he was nephew of Msgr. Ferdinand Pawlikowski, the prince-bishop of Graz-Seckau in Austria. In the 1930s, Anton had been an active member of Catholic organizations as well as a member of the Patriotic Front, the Fascist Austrian party.[119] With the annexation of Austria by Germany, the Patriotic Front was dissolved in 1938. Anton's journalistic activities for the *Volksblatt*, a Catholic newspaper in Graz, caught the Nazis' critical attention, thus throwing Anton into immediate peril. This Austrian nationalist became a victim of religious persecution by the Nazis. Desperate and knowing the consequences of remaining where he was, he knew he needed to act quickly. He took refuge in Rome where he was hidden by Catholic supporters. He asked the Holy See for three things: "a recommendation letter to the English and the French to overcome the international control, a recommendation for a Brazilian visa as soon as possible and the money for the transit from Genoa for Rio and Lages in Brazil." Anton was lucky. He had four well-connected churchmen in Rome to support his plea.[120] But the best thing that happened for him was the recommendation of the bishop of Lages in Brazil, a Franciscan, who offered to take Anton with him personally to South America.[121] We can only imagine the relief he felt when such good news reached him. The situation was similar for the music composer, Sergei Koufferoff, an orthodox Christian. After the outbreak of the war, Sergei encountered trouble in his attempt to pass the border of France. The reason for this was simply that he was of Russian nationality. Cardinal Giovanni Battista Nasalli, archbishop of Bologna — clarifying that he did not know the man personally but that fact would not stop him from promoting Koufferoff's case — notified Msgr. Dell'Acqua of the situation. That same week Cardinal Maglione wrote Nuncio Msgr. Valerio Valeri in France, asking for his intervention on behalf of the seventy-six-year-old composer.[122]

[119] Leaders of Austrian Patriotic Party were Engelbert Dollfuss and Kurt Alois von Schuschnigg. Dollfuss was killed in 1934.

[120] ASRS, AA.EE.SS., Ebrei 67, f. 65. The three of the four churchmen were Msgr. Alois Hudal, the rector of Santa Maria dell'Anima, the Jesuit father Robert Leiber, the private secretary of Pius XII, and Card. Sibilia.

[121] ASRS, AA.EE.SS., Ebrei 67, f. 62.

[122] ASRS, AA.EE.SS., Ebrei 167, ff. 2–10ᵛ.

A Jewish Pole named Erica Kadisch sent a plea to the Holy See in September 1942, trying to investigate the fate of her parents, Richard and Elsa Sarne, as well as her (unnamed) sister in Poland. The last time she had heard of her family was in 1941 when they had been arrested and imprisoned in the concentration camp of Izbica, near Lublin.[123] Erica lived in Rome at Piazza Siculi 2. She had been baptized in 1939, most likely when faced with the Fascist discrimination laws in Italy. In 1941 she graduated in medicine from Rome's La Sapienza University. Tardini wrote on her file: "Mgr dell'Acqua: can we do something? (Kadisch)."[124]

Dell'Acqua's internal investigation tells us that the Secretariat of State had previously put 500 lire (about 320 euros) at Erica's disposal to send to her parents and had already tried to obtain the permission for a transfer of her Jewish family members to Italy. Unfortunately, it had proved pointless. At the end of July 1941, Erica sent the money to the *Judenrat*, a local Jewish committee in Izbica, asking them to pass it on to her family in the concentration camp. She received devastating word back that neither her sister nor her parents were still there anymore. She had no further trace of them. They seemed to have vanished into the Nazi black hole without a trace. It is at that exact moment, in 1942, that she asked the Holy See once more for help finding out what had happened to them. The Cabinet wrote to Nuncio Orsenigo in Berlin on Erica's behalf requesting "any secure news on her parents and sister who a short time ago were still in the concentration camp in Izbica."[125] Erica's file in the Historical Archive of the Secretariat of State doesn't include any news regarding her family past that point. There is no record indicating they were found. We can only guess at the family's ultimate tragic fate. But there is reason to speculate Erica herself survived. Internet records show there was an Erika Kadisch, widow of Zumaglini, who died in a hospital in Genoa, Italy, on September 28, 2012, at the age of ninety-seven.[126] Our Erica, the student in medicine in Rome in 1941, was born on February 14, 1915, exactly ninety-seven years before. Could this have been the same Erica?

The Ebrei Files prove beyond doubt that Pius XII and his staff did everything they could to also offer assistance to those practicing the Jewish faith. Many times,

[123] ASRS, AA.EE.SS., Ebrei 67, f. 6.

[124] ASRS, AA.EE.SS., Ebrei 67, f. 7.

[125] ASRS, AA.EE.SS., Ebrei 67, f. 6. An interesting detail is also that Monsignor Dell'Acqua, probably for safety reasons, suggests to use a mediator and to send any communication through a certain Miss Evelina Borgognini, living in Via Piave 29 in Rome.

[126] See: http://vercellioggi.it/dett_necrologio.asp?id=226&.

however, these sincere and concentrated efforts were in vain, due to external obstacles. Such is the case of Else Katz, a Jewish mother of four children who asked for help immigrating to Palestine. On February 9, 1940, she wrote from Breslau, a Nazi-occupied Polish city:

> Your Holiness,
>
> I ask you humbly to apologize, when I allow myself to present the following request:
>
> I am a German Jew [Roman Catholic grandparents]. My husband has participated in the World War and died from the consequences of his heavy injuries — shot through the lungs — after unendless suffer in 1920. My sons, Max, Otto, Johannes, Dietrich as also the daughter in law Anna and Grandson Michael reside since years in Palestina.
>
> I am in possession of a consular certificate that I allege in photo-copy that, due to the War situation, was not added anymore to my passport.
>
> I have to fear that this certificate will expire. — I referred the matter already to the Offices of Palestina in Berlin, Genf and Trieste, for the last one in Via del Monte 7, but without any result.
>
> Your Holiness has already helped so many of my fellow-believers and now a mother, with the only wish to join her children, is asking very urgently for help.
>
> Maybe it would be possible for your Holiness, to provide me a "royal certificate" of the English king [Palestine was at the time a British mandate].
>
> After all the efforts of me and my sons to obtain my emigration failed, is the last remaining beam of hope the intercession of your Holiness.
>
> War widow Else Katz[127]

Msgr. Dell'Acqua immediately prepared a dispatch to Msgr. Orsenigo, papal nuncio in Germany, to let him know that "the Holy See was quite sad not being able to provide her (Mrs. Katz) the requested documents. In fact, the immigration to Palestine is regulated by mandatory provisions of and the English authorities are not likely to dispensate."[128]

---

[127] ASRS, AA.EE.SS., Ebrei 68, ff. 15–16.
[128] ASRS, AA.EE.SS., Ebrei 68, ff. 18$^{r/v}$.

Sometimes the requests created difficulties for the Holy See on different levels, which in some instances dealt with issues of morality. Such was the case of Lilly Weiss, a Catholic Jew from Paris. She was a divorced woman living with her fiancé and working in a theater company. Lilly approached many sources for help, including the auxiliary bishop of Paris, who in turn referred her to a Benedictine monk named Dom Odo von Württemberg, director of the Catholic aid for refugees in Switzerland. It seems likely that Dom von Württemberg had heard that the Brazilian embassy had put up to three thousand visas at the Holy See's disposal, and so he wrote directly to the embassy on Lilly's behalf.[129] But the file shows that the ambassador there told him to "first submit everything to the Secretariat of State of his Holiness." This reveals how the procedures worked: an embassy to the Holy See would not accept a request for a visa without the direct instruction from the Secretariat of State; though the passports were offered by the Brazilian government, they were at disposal of Pius XII personally.

Lilly and her fiancé made similar requests to other consulates but encountered the same Cabinetcratic delays. Once their file reached the Holy See itself, the Cabinet tasked the nuncio in Paris to investigate their case. This was standard procedure. But it seems the nuncio had reasons to doubt the morality of Lilly and her fiancé, writing to Rome that "they are not worthy to be helped." Such verdict may sound harsh. But the fear of embarrassment that would put at risk other passport requests was legitimate. As we have already witnessed, in other cases the Brazilian government blandly refused to give out the passports and sometimes even threatened to withdraw them due to "abuse" of it (for non-Catholics) by the Holy See. We know that this report and Lilly's letter were kept for a while by Pius XII.[130] In April 1940, as all this was underway, Lilly was arrested by the Vichy State for making "defeatist discourses against France" and sent to a concentration camp. A few weeks later, on June 5, 1940, a new request came in on Lilly's behalf. This time it was sent by another go-between who asked for a visa for Brazil "for these Catholics of Hebrew race that are resident in Limoges in France." From this request we gather more details about Lilly's artistic company and, for the times, her quite unusual living situation before her life was threatened. Lilly herself was forty years old and had a son. She lived with her theater company colleague, sixty-eight-year-old Mathilde

---

[129] ASRS, AA.EE.SS., Ebrei 162, f. 104.
[130] ASRS, AA.EE.SS., Ebrei 162, f. 108a.

Hermann, who had a daughter, and with her thirty-four-year-old fiancé, a man named Max Kundergraber. All five of them were now requesting visas.

The first request had made no mention of there being five people. This was often the case — people wrote to the Holy See without giving the full picture. And without such complete and honest picture, any visa application was bound to fail and to put in danger the future credibility of the Holy See. That is why nuncios were often asked to fully assess all cases. Unfortunately, these investigations frequently took a great deal of time, and time was not something fleeing refugees had. The final note on Lilly's file is a sentence written by Msgr. Dell'Acqua, which states: "It would be good to take in consideration what was written by the Nuncio in France in regard of these persons." By that he meant that her civil status — and what was seen as her questionable moral choices — could cause a lot of trouble for many others. Lilly's file ends there.[131]

On other occasions requests came in from within Rome itself, especially toward the end of the war. Such was a letter from an Italian woman named Ines Stame. She wrote in November 1943, one month after the raid on the ghetto of Rome, during which 1,259 Jews were captured by the Gestapo and 1,023 were immediately deported to Auschwitz. Only sixteen of those unfortunate souls survived. Ines, when she appealed to Pius XII, must have been in mortal dread out of fears that her family would be rounded up next. Her words appear jumbled, written in haste, as if she is in shock. As well she might have been, given that her comfortable and seemingly safe life had just been thrown upside down. Ines explained that she was married to an Aryan and that she and her family were Catholic. However, her mother, who had died fifty years earlier, was Jewish — hence her classification as such.[132]

She wrote:

> To the most beloved Holy Father, our highest pontiff.
>
> In the most horrifying and desperate moment in which all the most barbaric and inhumane horrors disturb my mind. As a terrorised mother, the most horrible of the infamies still comes. And makes me even or really directly mad with fright: A next injustice, *deportation*!
>
> To be deported at age 64 and in the middle of the innumerable, innocent victims, I Catholic since I was child, married in a Christian

[131] ASRS, AA.EE.SS., Ebrei 162, ff. 92–108b.
[132] ASRS, AA.EE.SS., Ebrei 143, ff. 12–15.

union in 1907 with an Aryan from a very Catholic family and mother of two adorable creatures, Gabriella and Rafaello [*sic*], to whom I gave the name of the two divine archangels in order that they would be forever accompanied and protected in their lives by them!

Gabriella, 36 years old, a heavenly mother also she was raised and educated in the most sane moral and Christian principles; And so my Rafaello from when he was very little, was half boarded in the first class of the San Guiseppe [school] in Piazza Di Spagna where he was for 7 years completing his studies in the institute of De Merode.

Everything in my house was Catholic and pure devotion, including me as a Dama of San Vincenzo[133] since several years in the Parish of Santa Maria delle Grazie in the zone of Trionfale.

I express in the most pained way of my faith and of my beneficence my uninterrupted prayers and novenas, the profound faith in the good God, have conceded me "numerous unexpected graces" of the Madonna delle Grazie, for which prodigious Saint Rita pleaded for me more than once.

While anxiousness and tears and pain were accompanying still since three years my life for the faraway destination in Croatia of my Rafaello, he has been lost for months and months. 8 days or so when all my hopes were abandoning me ... the Madonna delle Grazie brought back all of a sudden in my house my treasure Rafaello safe and sound, even if he had to overcome the innumerable dangers of 18 days of travel.

The joy and the tranquillity turned back to me immensely ... but very soon the nightmare and torment of the racial tragedy that appeared has thrown all my family in the most terrifying desperation, all given my belonging to the Israelite religion of my Mother Eriastina, dead for 50 years!!

The most recent and very cruel racial laws struck us inexorably. In all this exasperation, one only soft beam of light is reilluminating in some moment the complete darkness of my terror: it is the figure of the sweetest, the most pure, of our beloved Pontiff. And

---

[133] The San Vincenzo charitable works were organized by the Catholic Church worldwide.

I see his hand raised in a sign of benediction and encouragement, and of help! And is to the angelic pontiff that I dare to recourse on my knees, clutching myself with all my forces at this unique divine anchor of salvation.

Holy Father have mercy on my two kids, of whom they want to rip away and torture the old mother. Please save me Holy Father, receive me where it is possible, me taking refuge temporarily in your "intangible Vatican city" or in an institute of sisters, wherever, in any case. Do not leave me in the hands of these horrible executioners.[134]

Ines joined to her letter a personal recommendation from a Msgr. Brugnola. The archives show that her request was discussed with the pope on November 21, 1943, and that Pius XII charged the office to see what Msgr. Dell'Acqua could possibly do. A day later, Dell'Acqua explained that he told Msgr. Brugnola it was "not possible for her to come into the Vatican. But maybe one could try the sisters of Maria Bambina or the Sisters dell'Addolorata. Brugnola thanked for the suggestions and said he was about to do his part. He would go to these Sisters talking with them and have Ines sheltered and taken in for some days at least." The archives don't show if the religious sisters agreed and then received Ines and her children in time to save their lives. However, it is plausible because they did so for many others.

The existence of the Ebrei Files raises some questions. Why was this activity of the Holy See kept secret until now? Why did the Holy See not use this as evidence in defense against the unjust attacks against Pius XII, attacks that accused him of being a Nazi sympathizer? The stories encapsulated in the files are testament to just some of the millions of lives torn apart by racist violence. They include row upon row of photographs, faces, histories, families and loved ones lost. Their very existence in the Secretariat of State's Historical Archive also sheds new light on another hidden story, that of Pius XII's courageous, compassionate, and active silence.

---

[134] ASRS, AA.EE.SS., Ebrei 143, ff. 13–14ᵛ.

3

A Tale of Two Children of the Light

New York — February 17, 1940

As he sailed for his post on "the Rex" at noon today, Mr. Taylor added that he "believed a useful purpose would be served by coordination of the efforts of the two great leaders."[135]

THIS SHORT AND simple press release by the National Catholic Welfare Conference heralded an unprecedented new era of diplomatic relations between the United States of America and the Holy See. President Franklin Roosevelt had appointed his close friend Myron Taylor as his special personal envoy to the Vatican.

Prior to this, diplomatic relations between the largely Protestant United States and the Holy See had been tricky. They were established for the first time in 1784, with what was more of a commercial type of agreement to open the Italian ports of Civitavecchia and Ancona to American vessels. However, in 1867 the American mission came to an official end "but through no fault or action of the Holy See. The American Congress simply refused to continue the appropriation of the American mission."[136]

[135] ASRS, AA.EE.SS., America 259, f. 10, National Catholic Welfare Conference (NCWC) Press Department release.
[136] ASRS, AA.EE.SS., Extracta, America 237, f. 41.

But during the late 1930s, as the buildup to war increased, calls had been grow-ing for a restoration of relations. In 1939, a year before Myron Taylor's appoint-ment, American congressman Emanuel Celler wrote: "In my opinion, the action of our Government was somewhat hasty and ill-advised, and was not reciprocal regarding the good-will that the Papal See had always manifested towards our government and people. I believe the time has now come when these diplomatic relations, groundlessly severed, should be restored. That restoration would be a clarion call to the civilized peoples of the world that religious and personal liber-ties are inherent in our Democracy."[137]

And indeed, in the week before Christmas 1939, the president announced of the restored relations by personal telegram, referring to the pope as "a good and an old friend."[138]

This much was true. The two men had formed an extraordinary friendship when they met in 1936 when Pacelli, then cardinal secretary of state, traveled on a pastoral visit to America. He and Roosevelt instantly hit it off, forming a friend-ship both personal and strategic that would last long after Pacelli's election as pope.

Another opportunity for Pacelli to meet with an American political repre-sentative occurred in March 1939, during the ceremonies by which he acceded to the papal throne. At that time, he met with Joseph P. Kennedy, father of John and Robert Kennedy. Joseph Kennedy was at the time serving as ambassador for the United States to Great Britain: "Mr. Kennedy's presence served to emphasize the very friendly relations that have always existed between our Government and the Holy See."

Roosevelt and Pacelli became regular pen pals, and their written communica-tions continued into the years during which Pacelli served as pope. Their joint letters were published after the war as part of Myron Taylor's memoirs.[139] Their correspondence reveals not only a genuine affection for each other but also shows

[137] ASRS, AA.EE.SS., Exctracta, America 237, f. 42.

[138] ASRS, AA.EE.SS., Extracta, America 237, ff. 69b–73, telegram of President Roosevelt of December 23, 1939. The letter of Roosevelt with the same text is also preserved in: Extracta, America 237, ff. 91–95. The text was integrally published in the Vatican's newspaper *L'Osservatore Romano* of December 26–27, 1939.

[139] Myron C. Taylor, *Pope Pius XII and Roosevelt: Wartime Correspondence between Presi-dent Roosevelt and Pope Pius XII*, New York, 1947. For the documentation conserved in the afterwar period on this publication in various languages, see: ASRS, AA.EE. SS., America 301D.

that both men felt keenly the unique historical responsibility the other one had. What comes across most is a desire to support one another morally from a distance, whilst pushing for their common goal — the defense of civilization against barbarism. That one man was head of the Catholic Church and the other the Protestant leader of the "free world" makes their close friendship unexpected. But it also helps explain why Roosevelt chose Taylor to take up the sensitive role as his Vatican envoy. Aside from being an old friend of the president, Taylor was a successful industry leader, having been both chairman and chief executive of the United States Steel Corporation. To send him was very much a personal decision by the president, and one that didn't go down well with large sections of the government and the U.S. media. The Vatican was not beloved by many Americans, especially not the powerful Protestant lobby, as was reported by the apostolic delegate[140] and the press in Fascist Italy, such as the newspaper *Il Messagero*, which headlined "The American Protestants against the Resumption of Relations with the Vatican."[141]

The Historical Archive of the Secretariat of State can now shed further light on this unique friendship between the president and the pope. Its documents also reveal that others in their own administrations were not always happy to follow their respective shared agendas, including those in the Cabinet. Within the walls of the Apostolic Palace the intimate nature of the relationship was seen as a risk to the Holy See's political impartiality. There were fears that with such a relationship the American government would attempt to impose its own agenda on the Holy See.

And on the other side of the Atlantic, the published correspondence shows that Roosevelt would personally have given in to the pope's desire for the United States to accept more refugees but failed to do so when faced with the reluctance of his administration to raise the set quotas.

As he set sail for Rome, Myron Taylor gave this statement to the National Catholic Welfare Conference (NCWC):[142]

> President Roosevelt has asked me to proceed to Italy to serve as
> his personal representative to Pope Pius XII who has agreed to

[140] ASRS, AA.EE.SS., Extracta, America 237, f. 225ᵛ, Report from Msgr. Cicognani of January 18, 1940.
[141] ASRS, AA.EE.SS., Extracta, America 237, f. 174, article of *Il Messagero* of January 28, 1940 ("I protestanti americani contro la ripresa di relazioni con il Vaticano").
[142] ASRS, AA.EE.SS., America 259, f. 10, National Catholic Welfare Conference (NCWC) Press Department release.

receive me in this capacity. We shall explore every possibility regarding what the representative might do to assist in furthering his
desire and that of the United States for the reestablishment of peace
upon the foundation of freedom and independence for all nations.
Not only has his Holiness shown his profound interest in any step
which might lead toward this goal, but his declarations on behalf of
suffering humanity, regardless of race or creed, have led us in this
country to believe that a useful purpose might be served through
some coordination of effort.

This is a great and critical moment in world history, and I am
determined to do my utmost to assist in avoiding further suffering.[143]

For the newly appointed diplomat there was no doubt that Pius XII had made clear
"declarations on behalf of suffering humanity, regardless of race and creed." In simple
terms, that means Taylor was convinced the pope had spoken up for all people
in need, especially the Jews. That the American government was "determined" to
"assist in avoiding further suffering" is evidence they saw a close collaboration with
the Holy See as a means to do so. If the U.S. president or his administration had even
the minimum of suspicion that Pius XII displayed a modicum of sympathy toward
Hitler or Nazi ideology, they would never have proposed a diplomatic relationship with him. Those who believe the myths and criticism that swirl around Pius
XII to this day should reflect on that. But friendship between pope and president
aside, the thawing of diplomatic relations had also been many years in the making.

With a striking similarity, in 1914, when Pacelli was minister of foreign affairs
of the Holy See, the British government sent, also for the first time in centuries, a
diplomatic representative to the Vatican. Before World War II there had been at
least two attempts at dialogue between the Vatican and the United States, but both
times the talks broke down. Probably also because of "a more general American
mentality, one not ready to welcome recognition of the Vatican due to a persist-
ing Anti-Catholic prejudice."[144] In those days, many in the Catholic Church saw
Protestants as heretics and viewed the pope's initiative as extremely subversive.

---

[143] ASRS, AA.EE.SS., America 259, f. 10, National Catholic Welfare Conference
(NCWC) Press Department release.

[144] Cristina Rossi, *Santa Sede e Stati Uniti (1932–1939)*, Roma, 2017, p. 122 and p. 173
(= Mappamondi, 21).

Of additional concern was the fact that Taylor's title of "special personal envoy" instead of the usual "state ambassador" bypassed the usual rules of engagement and diplomatic norms.

The Historical Archive of the Secretariat of State contain a consistent number of original letters from Roosevelt to Pius XII (including typewritten transcriptions and photocopies). One, in Roosevelt's elegant prose, stands out in particular. He wrote it just hours after Taylor's appointment was confirmed:

> I am entrusting this special mission to Mr Taylor who is a very old friend of mine, and in whom I repose the utmost confidence. His humanitarian efforts on behalf of those whom political disruption has rendered homeless are well known to Your Holiness.
>
> I shall be happy to feel that he may be the channel of communications for any views you and I may wish to exchange in the interests of concord among the peoples of the world.
>
> I am asking Mr Taylor to convey my cordial greetings to you, my old and good friend. And my sincere hope that the common ideals of religion and humanity itself can have united expression for the reestablishment of a more permanent peace on the foundations of freedom and an assurance of life and integrity of all nations under God.
>
> Cordially your friend
>
> (Sd.) Franklin D. Roosevelt[145]

What leaps off the page of his letter is that, despite their positions as world leaders, this was simply two men talking person to person, two men who genuinely liked each other. It reads like an extension of any particular conversations they might have had in person when they first met. But it can't be overstated how surprising it is, given their respective positions, to see both men transcend the theoretical and dogmatical basis of their own religious convictions to find a common ground. For

[145] ASRS, AA.EE.SS., America 259, f. 17, two different copies produced by the Cabinet of the letter from President Roosevelt to Pius XII, February 14, 1940, f. 15; f. 16. A copy of the handwritten letter at ff. 17–18. The original is preserved in the Archives of the Secretariat of State, Section for General Affairs. It was already published by Myron C. Taylor, *Wartime Correspondence between President Roosevelt and Pope Pius XII*, New York, 1947, p. 31.

both, God was the source of life and human integrity. Today, that thinking doesn't sound so unusual. But in the 1930s and 1940s this was quite radical theology for both Protestants and Catholics.

This also puts Pius XII in a hitherto unknown light, showing him ahead of the curve in his ecumenical thinking. My view is that this paved the way for some of the major changes that the Second Vatican Council sanctioned in the 1960s on dialogue between the Christian creeds.

*

*   *

After docking in Rome, Myron Taylor, accompanied by his wife, Anabel, moved into a beautifully frescoed Renaissance villa with large fragrant gardens on the outskirts of Rome. Once settled in, his first port of call was to make a personal visit to Cardinal Secretary of State Maglione.

Maglione wanted to ensure that all meetings and briefings with the new envoy went smoothly. To that end, he charged an intelligent and vibrant young American priest by the name of Joseph P. Hurley as Taylor's main liaison, interpreter, and point of contact. Hurley was the first American to hold official office within the Vatican.

Hurley kept meticulous and richly detailed notes of all of Taylor's discussions and movements. Due to these accurate reports, kept in the Historical Archive, we have a full picture of Taylor's day-to-day activities in Rome as well as the frantic diplomatic activity that ensued. Hurley's minutes contain details of a conversation between Taylor and Cardinal Maglione, on March 8, 1940.[146] Taylor tells how, just before his departure from Washington, President Roosevelt gave him a memo about an anti-Semitic movement active in the cities of Brooklyn, Baltimore, and Detroit. This movement was promoted by the controversial priest Fr. Charles Coughlin, a radio presenter and an outspoken anti-Semite — he was a 1930s version of a modern-day shock jock. Taylor made the point that Coughlin was supported by many Catholics in those cities, and he feared this would create anti-Catholic sentiment unless Coughlin was reined in. Maglione asked Taylor to leave him some background on Coughlin's anti-Semitic activities, with a firm promise to follow it up.

Hurley's detailed minutes tell us that at the same initial meeting, Taylor brought up the fate of three hundred Jewish Polish refugees currently stuck in Trieste, Italy. These refugees sought travel permits to enter Palestine, which was still under British

---

[146] ASRS, AA.EE.SS., America 259, ff. 29–30.

protectorate. With a heavy sigh Maglione replied that "the refugee issue has become much more difficult since the outbreak of war." The cardinal was pointedly making reference to the fact that very few countries, America included, were willing to take in more refugees. The U.S. diplomat responded in quite a wily way, saying, "I know the problem is more one for the British government, but I wanted to bring it to the attention of the Holy See."[147]

Why is it Taylor even bothered to ask about refugees who wanted British permits while the United States was refusing to increase their own quotas? This could read as a cynical way of appearing to be concerned for refugees without having to take actual action. From his reply, it seems this was not lost on the cardinal.

After a long and wide-ranging meeting, Taylor took his leave but not before inviting Cardinal Maglione for a group dinner, along with all the other ambassadors accredited to the Holy See, with the "aim of enhancing cooperation." Taylor was certainly hitting the ground running. The ever-serious cardinal gladly accepted but preferred lunch to a dinner.

And as good as his word, the very next day Maglione, during an audience with the pope, raised in person the topic of the rogue priest turned radio presenter, Fr. Coughlin. Internal memos of their conversation reveal the pope was clearly angered, expressing "especially the desire that Coughlin be called to order."[148]

Pius XII referred to Coughlin as "an element of disorder," whose radio messages "do nothing else than take advantage of the malaise of certain classes to excite passions. The decent people don't follow him, only those who have disorderly tendencies."[149]

In those packed first few days, U.S. Special Envoy Taylor worked tirelessly. He hosted daily lunches and dinners either in his villa or in one of Rome's many restaurants, bringing together ambassadors, diplomats, and key international players.

Yet the diplomat who set sail for Rome truly hoping it would be possible to prevent further escalation of war was quickly disabused of his optimism. He confided in Maglione that the encounters left him deeply pessimistic: "I have the keen impression that for the moment almost all of them are convinced that there is nothing that can be done as far as it concerns a step forward in favor of peace."[150]

[147] ASRS, AA.EE.SS., America 259, ff. 29–30.

[148] ASRS, AA.EE.SS., America 259, f. 129.

[149] ASRS, AA.EE.SS., America 259, f. 129.

[150] ASRS, AA.EE.SS., America 259, f. 34 (Hurley's minutes, March 15, 1940).

But despite the fact that the Pact of Steel, the military and political alliance between Italy and Germany, was signed a year earlier on May 22, 1939, Special Envoy Taylor somehow still appeared naïvely convinced that Italy's role in the war could be limited. He asked Maglione: "In the case there isn't anything to do in this very moment, how can President Roosevelt be of help to keep Italy away from the danger of being dragged into war on the German side?"

Hurley's minutes also tell of an interesting anecdote during dinner at the Belgian embassy to the Holy See: Taylor had a long conversation with André François-Poncet, the French ambassador to Italy.[151] At some point during the evening, perhaps over glasses of fine Italian wine, François-Poncet told Hurley that "the French government is ready to negotiate with the Italians on all pending questions between the two countries, and that there exists no insurmountable difficulties except the Tunisian question. For the rest the French are disposed to share with the Italians in full disclosure."[152] With this revelation, Taylor concluded that the Allied countries "are prepared to make important concessions to prevent the participation in the war of Italy besides Germany."[153]

This conversation is proof that as late as April 1940 the Allies were still trying to make concessions where they could to avoid the escalation of an all-out world war.

By the end of March, the determined Taylor was still wining and dining his away around Rome, and putting his idealistic strategies into place with the suggestion (apparently made by President Roosevelt) to convene a conference of the prime ministers of France, Italy, England, and Germany. Taylor suggested that "such a conference might take place on a ship near the Azores with Roosevelt present as representative of the neutrals. Before convoking the conference, President Roosevelt would seek the approval and support of His Holiness, the neutral Powers and Protestant Churches."[154]

It is of note that Roosevelt wanted the support of the major churches before going ahead with the proposed plan. Taylor makes clear "the plan is in an embryo stage, poising to ask the opinion of the Sovereign Pontiff on the advisability of the plan" during a scheduled audience the next day. But Taylor does also let slip that

---

[151] ASRS, AA.EE.SS., America 259, f. 39 (Hurley's minutes, April 24, 1940).

[152] Tunisia was disputed territory between France and Italy, later becoming the North African frontline.

[153] ASRS, AA.EE.SS., America 259, f. 39.

[154] ASRS, AA.EE.SS., America 259, f. 131, minutes of meeting between Maglione and Taylor, March 28, 1940.

he personally doesn't think much of Roosevelt's idea, going so far as to say, "The present is not the time to convoke such a conference."

In these frantic days the salons of Rome truly were a twisted web of international negotiations. The Holy See, despite its strict policy of impartiality, was inevitably caught up in it.

Hurley, the young American priest whose language skills had suddenly thrust him into this new world, was struggling to comprehend all he was hearing and seeing. On April 24, 1940, Hurley detailed his own private conversations with Special Envoy Taylor in an internal report for his superiors (speaking about himself in the third person):

> Taylor in a conversation with Hurley suggested the possibility that the United States might be obligated to enter in war, if Japan, in response to an expansion of the conflict zone in Europe, would decide to do good to disturb the status quo in the Pacific. This intervention would result in the United States finding themselves associated with the Allies in the European war. It was the opinion of competent generals in America that such an intervention should limit itself to naval operations.[155]

Taylor's words prophesied the bombing of Pearl Harbor. This is startling because it revealed that a possible U.S. plan to provoke a naval conflict with Japan as an excuse to enter the war and side with the Allies existed as early as March 1940. That Taylor trusted Hurley enough to have such frank conversations with him outside of any formal meetings suggests the two men formed something of a friendship, sharing similar views.

The young Hurley was fiercely intelligent but was also considered a bit of a combative character. He applied to the United States Military Academy at West Point but was not admitted due to a conflict regarding his place of residence. He then joined the priesthood. Failing to join the army had been something of a lifelong disappointment, but now to be witness to history in the making and to be party to these high-level diplomatic discussions was both exciting and an honor for him. The precision of his minutes suggests he was keeping not only official notes but a personal diary for himself too.

[155] ASRS, AA.EE.SS., America 259, f. 40.

Away from the increasingly frantic diplomatic efforts taking place in Rome, Myron Taylor's own appointment continued to be debated in the U.S. media, with many commentators firmly speaking out against it. Some American Catholic bishops, however, became involved in a campaign to win over hearts and minds about it. In an open letter to the editor of the *New York Times*, James H. Ryan, the bishop of Omaha in Nebraska, wrote a spirited defense of the newly created direct diplomatic relations between the Vatican and the United States:[156]

> The conflict has now entered its final stages and threatens to become one of the great battles in the history of human freedom. The Nazi and fascist ideologies, with their increasing emphasis on racism, have thrown down the gauntlet to Catholicism, which, because of its belief in the oneness of mankind, cannot capitulate to the new theories without sacrificing a fundamental tenet of a creed which is as old as Christianity itself. The democracies and the Catholic Church are one in their opposition to totalitarian philosophies, a fact made clear by statements of the late Pope Pius XI and proclaimed as the policy of the newly elected Pius XII in the first encyclical he addressed to the world. On whose standards victory, in this contest, shall perch ultimately, no man knows.

The letter was in direct response to recent statements from the Methodist Church, which was "unalterably opposed" to the establishment of relations between the United States and the Vatican.

In a different piece of the same "hearts and minds" campaign, New York judge John F. O'Brien, an expert in international law, was quoted on the NCWC News Service. He saw the Vatican, with its impartiality, as the only body that is capable of being able to communicate with all sides:[157]

> The situation in Europe has become one of great peril to religion with "great protestant nations" being conquered one by one. Is it not important to America to have diplomatic relations with the oldest institution — international in scope and impartial in interest — as the World Court in the League of Nations had hoped to be, but far

[156] ASRS, AA.EE.SS., America 259, f. 46, letter dated May 6, 1940 (*New York Times*).
[157] ASRS, AA.EE.SS., America 259, f. 48.

exceeding it in nobility of purpose, antiquity, character, stability
and enjoying the confidence of all nations?

The Catholic Church has constantly maintained throughout the
ages that man in his person possesses a dignity and a personality
and inalienable supranational rights conferred upon him by God.

That the Vatican was both impartial and supranational is key to understanding why,
leaving his personal friendship with Pius XII aside, Roosevelt saw the sensible
political strategy in restoring relations. The League of Nations had floundered
badly after World War I with both Germany and Italy leaving it. There was no
other international body, bar the Vatican, that had relationships with all the different warring sides of Europe.

Roosevelt truly believed Taylor's presence in Rome could make a difference
and prevent further escalation of conflict.

But fate had other plans.

*

* *

The energetic Myron Taylor had worked nonstop during the three months he'd
been in Rome. But in June 1940 he was taken seriously ill, with complications
from an earlier gall bladder operation.[158] A distraught Hurley telephoned Cardinal
Maglione to report that "Taylor is in a clinic and tomorrow morning will undergo
an operation. There are no high hopes that he will be able to survive his illness."[159]

The Cabinet prayed hard for Taylor's survival. The American was friendly and
affable, and despite any professional misgivings, everyone there had grown to like
him on a personal level. Taylor survived the surgery. But he remained too sick to
continue his mission.

A month after he was taken suddenly ill, a bitterly disappointed Taylor sat in
the garden of his villa. The fragrant scent of summer flowers filled the air as he put
ink to paper in a letter of regret to Foreign Minister Tardini: "I have been prevented
from illness from continuing my most agreeable meetings with you. I am not able
to come to the Vatican again to call on you before my departure for America. But I
want you to realise how thoroughly I appreciate the co-operative spirit displayed

[158] ASRS, AA.EE.SS., America 259, f. 137, internal note of Hurley of June 6, 1940.
[159] ASRS, AA.EE.SS., America 259, f. 49, internal memo, June 25, 1940.

by you and all your associates on my behalf during the last months." With no way to say goodbye in person, Tardini telegrammed back his own "heartfelt thanks."[160]

It seems bitter irony that Taylor's departure came in the same week as the news that Italy had fully entered the war. This was the very event Taylor had worked so hard to prevent.[161] Benjamin Welles, the U.S. ambassador to the Italian government, took over Taylor's role in the interim, with the help of Harold Tittmann — the general consul in Geneva and attaché to the mission of Taylor.[162] Both men assumed the task left behind by Taylor, and they put all their efforts into keeping up the diplomatic head of steam that had been created during Taylor's tenure. But try as they did, that momentum simply faded away.

Nevertheless, the friendship between the pope and the president continued, as did their personal correspondence. In a letter dated October 1, 1940, Roosevelt writes:

> Particular note has been taken of the assurance of your Holiness' continuing efforts to find the way to a peace which bears promise not only of permanency, but also of freedom from perpetual alarm and opportunity for the spiritual and material improvement of humanity. It's imperative that this search shall not be abandoned, no matter how deep the shadow of the present strife may be.... The whole world needs you in its search for peace and goodwill.[163]

He signs off with "very deep personal good wishes."

Inside the Cabinet, however, there was growing disquiet. A tiny scrap of paper is hidden in the archives. On it is Tardini's scrawl. In his usual sarcastic tone, he noted: "It's alright that Mr Taylor is only the *personal* representative of Roosevelt. It's alright also that the relations between Roosevelt and his Holiness are *personal* (non-official): *But* a little piece of paper like that ... *micragnoso* [miserable] — sent to the Pope. It seems to me a little bit too much."[164] Tardini's anger stemmed from the fact that he saw the personal relationship developing so informally, outside official lines and the usual norms. He could just about accept Taylor as special envoy, but having a president treating the pope as a friendly, informal pen pal? For

---

[160] ASRS, AA.EE.SS., American 259, f. 52, telegram from Tardini, August 23, 1940.

[161] ASRS, AA.EE.SS., America 259, f. 138, note of Hurley of June 7, 1940.

[162] ASRS, AA.EE.SS., America 259, f. 143, notes of Hurley, August 19, 1940.

[163] ASRS, AA.EE.SS., America 259, f. 57, letter from Roosevelt, October 1, 1940.

[164] ASRS, AA.EE.SS., America 259, f. 59, handwritten note of Tardini, November 4, 1940.

him, this was crossing the line. But perhaps that unique relationship also reveals something about the pressure and loneliness of both papal and presidential roles, that they sought solace in their correspondence with each other.

The letters between the two continued. The following year, on March 3, 1941, a newly reelected Roosevelt writes: "I take this occasion ... to reiterate the hope that through friendly association between the seekers of light and the seekers of peace everywhere a firm basis of lasting concord between man and nations can be established throughout the world once again. Only when the principles of Christianity and the right of all peoples to live free from the threat of external aggression are established can that peace which your Holiness and I both so ardently desire be found."[165] As I read these letters, I am continually struck by how a Catholic pope and a Protestant president saw themselves as so closely spiritually connected. In Roosevelt's view they were both children of the light, taking side against evil. It was a relationship of trust, respect, and mutual understanding.

But from that same intense period, one of the fiercest future critics of Pius XII's policy of impartiality would emerge: Joseph Hurley. The passionate young man who had been caught up in the world of war diplomacy couldn't understand why the pontiff took the positions he did. His genuine frustration at a perceived failure on the part of Pius XII to speak out would be repeated loudly and widely by Hurley immediately after the war. Hurley's impetuous criticisms could be seen as a precursor of Rolf Hochhuth, the author of the theater play *The Deputy*, thanks to which the same criticisms are shared by many others still today. Of Pius XII's closest inner circle in the Cabinet at that time, no others made similar criticisms. What Hurley perceived as a lack of action by Pius XII remains an exception among the key players who were there. This passionate young man who wished to be a soldier before becoming a priest would go on to publish his personal diaries and become one of Pius XII's greatest detractors.

But what, specifically, did Hurley believe was the pope's primary failing? He felt that Pius XII did not do enough to speak out publicly against Hitler. In the book *Vatican Secret Diplomacy: Joseph P. Hurley and Pope Pius XII* (Yale University Press, 2008) by Jesuit author Charles R. Gallagher, Hurley is quoted as saying:

> A pope faced by clear and present evil had to provide unambiguous moral guidance to those who looked to him for leadership. He

---

[165] ASRS, AA.EE.SS., America 259, f. 70, copy of the letter from Roosevelt, March 3, 1941.

had to decide on the facts without evasion and condemn that evil
in the most explicit language. Confronted by mass murder on an
unprecedented scale, the natural human reaction is one of disbelief
and denial. Only when a pontiff — the supreme moral authority on
Earth — spoke out in the plainest terms could lesser folk grasp the
realities of the situation and do their moral duty as Christians.[166]

The roots of Hurley's discontent may be more personal and can be traced back
to the days of Myron Taylor's departure. Just two months after the ailing special
envoy Taylor returned to the United States, Hurley left Rome for Florida, becoming bishop of St. Augustine. Within the Holy See, Hurley had been increasingly
seen as a loose cannon with an impulsive temper. After Taylor's departure he was
given a role on *L'Osservatore Romano* but used it to publish anti-Fascist and pro-
Allied material, something the Cabinet saw as very risky and putting the agenda
of impartiality at risk — an agenda Hurley did not agree with. And so, Hurley
was in effect "promoted out" of Rome, although there are some historians who
argue that his appointment was made in order for him to remain in contact with
the ailing Taylor.[167]

In a review of Gallagher's book on Hurley, Andrew Palmer offers a more complex analysis:

The debate about the policy of Pope Pius XII towards the Axis
dictators remains hard to resolve. For Hurley, the issue was clear.
The Pope's ambivalence dismayed him. In the Papal Secretariat of
State earlier in the 1930s, he had gladly implemented the robust
opposition of Pope Pius XI to the developing fascist threat. When
Pius XII was elected in 1939 Papal policy became more nuanced,
reflecting his conviction that communism posed the more serious
menace. Hurley, too, was devoutly anti-communist but continued to
perceive the fascists as the more immediate danger, and he resolved

[166] Charles R. Gallagher, *Vatican Secret Diplomacy: Joseph P. Hurley and Pope Pius XII*, New Haven & London, 2008.
[167] Raymond Cohen, *Charles R. Gallagher, S.J., Vatican Secret Diplomacy: Joseph P. Hurley and Pope Pius XII* (New Haven and London, 2008) in *Studies in Jewish-Christian Relations* 4 (2009)(1) (see: https://ejournals.bc.edu/index.php/scjr/article/view/1530/1384).

to act accordingly. He saw propagandist opportunities in the relative independence of the Vatican daily *L'Osservatore Romano*. With clandestine briefing from the US embassy to Italy, and later their newly accredited mission to the Holy See, Hurley arranged for the traditionally staid newspaper to carry outspoken anti-fascist and pro-allied material, earning personal thanks from President Roosevelt. Pius XII reacted by "promoting" Hurley out of Rome in 1940 to the backwater diocese of St. Augustine, Florida.[168]

The words "clandestine briefing" here are a slight exaggeration. Hurley was at the heart of the diplomatic discussions by decision of Cardinal Secretary of State Maglione, the papal number two. That could not have happened had Pius XII and Cardinal Maglione not trusted Hurley.

It's worth noting that, much later after the war, Hurley returned to the fold as a nuncio in the Balkans. The smoke and mirrors of politics in that region shocked him, changing his views somewhat. There he came to understand that diplomacy is never quite as simple as it might first appear. Perhaps he also found a new appreciation of just what a difficult tightrope Pius XII had to walk during World War II.

By 1941, Myron Taylor had recovered from his illness. In September of that year, he returned to Rome for a private audience with the pope but wrote ahead to say that he planned on bringing with him three other U.S. government officials. That this was turning into an official diplomatic visit dressed up by the U.S. administration as a personal audience for Taylor invoked Tardini's anger. He noted:

> Taylor, the personal representative of the President is arriving with Mr. Williams, secret envoy of Roosevelt; and with him the gentlemen Stafford and West apparently for a private and personal visit to the Holy Father. I ask myself: Why all this ... deluge of ... Americans? What will the Italian government say, when it is already preoccupied by the arrival of Taylor? Could they not do things with a little bit less publicity?
>
> These Americans, that in reality are already at war with the Axis (in fact, Roosevelt in his discourses says clearly that he wants to

[168] Andrew Palmer, Rec. *Vatican Secret Diplomacy: Joseph P. Hurley and Pope Pius XII*, by Charles R. Gallagher, (New Haven, CT: Yale University Press, 2008), in *Cold War History* 10 (2010) 1, p. 140.

strike down totalitarianism) — should understand that the Holy See is in a very delicate situation, superior to the political and military conflict, but not indifferent towards the doctrinal errors and the practical consequences against the Church.[169]

In the end Taylor came alone. So it was with a degree of satisfaction that Tardini later annotated the bottom of the same document with the words "these gentlemen in the end did not come."

And on the question raised by Tardini on "What will the Italian government say?" Tardini already knew the answer. Because at eleven o'clock that same morning, the Italian ambassador, Mr. Attolico, had learned through the Italian media of Taylor's planned return and immediately beat a path to Tardini's door to "express his worries about the return of Mr. Taylor, as it was announced in the newspapers." The Italian government feared that Roosevelt was using Taylor to align the Holy See with the British, Americans, and Russians.

Tardini's notes of his conversation with the Italian ambassador go some way in revealing just how difficult it was for the Holy See to retain its official policy of impartiality when all parties involved tried to use them to score points against their enemies. He wrote what came to his mind: "The Ambassador ... addressed an issue to me ... suggesting it would be better for us to speak out against Bolshevism? Especially since the war against Russia will be long and hard.... Wouldn't it be better for the Italian people, who are opposed to Bolshevism, to hear some word from the Holy See to that effect?"[170]

It's obvious the ambassador was trying to influence the Holy See to assist with their propaganda against the Soviets by asking the pope to take a stand against Bolshevism. The wily Tardini didn't fall for it: "I answered the ambassador that the attitude of the Holy See towards Bolshevism did not need to be explained again. The Holy See has rebuked, condemned, anathematized Bolshevism with all its errors. To all that has been said, nothing is to be added and nothing is to be removed. The Holy See has pronounced itself very clearly. Tempore non suspecto."[171]

---

[169] ASRS, AA.EE.SS., America 273, f. 20.

[170] ASRS, AA.EE.SS., America 273, f. 24.

[171] The phrase *tempore non suspecto* literally means "time without suspicion." In a legal sense, the term refers to information obtained at a moment of time when the person giving the information has nothing to lose by telling the truth.

Tardini, determined to make his personal views known to the ambassador, said: "Now, on my behalf ... I would be delighted to see Communism defeated. It is the worst enemy of the Church, but it is not the only one. Nazism has carried out, and is still doing so, a real and genuine persecution of the Church. So, the Swastika is not ... exactly the cross of the crusades. And yet, precisely the Germans (not Mussolini) *have* been the first to talk about ... a crusade [against Communism]."[172] Tardini is quite openly, and bravely, condemning Nazism in front of the Italian ambassador. Attolico didn't give up. He pushed again for the pope to reaffirm the doctrinal position of the Catholic Church regarding Bolshevism. Tardini, keeping true to his stance, observed that "if the Holy See would make a public reminder of the errors and horrors of communism, it could not ... forget the aberrations and the persecutions of Nazism."

The discussion continued, growing more heated by the minute. The atmosphere in the room was tense. Ambassador Attolico fired back by pointing out that "in Moscow religious practice is forbidden whereas in Berlin it is not." At that point, Tardini shut the conversation down, stating: "Rumour has it that in a not far away future Germany wants to get to the same point, and even to go beyond that."[173]

The handwritten notes of this conversation were delivered to Pius XII in his private apartments. The pope read it all, digested it, and after due consideration shared his own thoughts, agreeing with Tardini that "since His Excellency Attolico has come back from [his last visit to] Berlin, the religious situation in Germany had gotten worse."

But Ambassador Attolico and the Italian government as a whole were still concerned by Myron Taylor's return. Tardini noted: "I calmed him by saying that this temporary and brief return has no ... overwhelming significance. One should not forget that Mr. Taylor is very much a friend of President Roosevelt: he is his personal representative to the Holy Father: he has a great veneration and a heart-warming connection (for a Protestant) with the venerated person of His Holiness. And, also, he has to settle some of his personal interests in Italy."[174]

By this time Taylor was, of course, a good friend of Tardini's. But ever the consummate diplomat, Tardini is able to mask his personal feelings and thoughts on the Americans when dealing with the Italians. We also learn from Tardini's

[172] ASRS, AA.EE.SS., America 273, ff. 24^v–25^r.
[173] ASRS, AA.EE.SS., America 273, f. 26^r.
[174] ASRS, AA.EE.SS., America 273, f. 26^v.

neat records that Taylor used his brief return to oversee and settle some personal affairs, donating his lovely house, the fifteenth-century Palmieri villa in Fiesole near Florence, to the Holy See and offering it up as a cultural space in which visiting American students could stay.

In September 1941 Taylor had an exhaustive schedule that he was determined to keep. He met several times with Msgr. Tardini, had two long conversations with Cardinal Maglione on September 10 and 11 and three separate private audiences with Pius XII on September 11, 16, and 21. All this was prior to leaving the country on September 22 and heading onwards to Great Britain.[175] The talks held within the Apostolic Palace created a major foundation for the agenda of Taylor's trip to London. It's remarkably clear that the Holy See and the Americans and the Allies had much in common to discuss.

During one of the first September meetings Taylor had with Maglione in the cardinal's office, Taylor said that "in the US everyone — without any exception — is convinced that Hitler will lose the war ... and there is in the United States unanimous desire to stay out of the war unless (1) Hitler would provoke the war with whatever incident (2) the Allies (England etc.) would be at risk of a defeat, which would mean the end of Christian civilization."

And there, where his Italian counterpart had argued for a papal statement against Communism, Taylor urged the Holy See for a public declaration against Nazism: "The moment is now for the Holy See to speak out, while in the States one is waiting for an explicit declaration, because there are only two personalities who can still speak for the triumph of justice: the Pope and the President of the United States." Maglione and Taylor sat and debated this for so long the hot tea they had been served earlier went quite cold. But for Maglione, Taylor's words made it all too transparent that the United States wanted to pull the Holy See in to help influence their military and political agenda, just as the Italians had tried to do. He noted: "It seems that the aim of the mission of Taylor was this and not another: induce his Holiness to endorse the Anglo-American declaration."[176]

While talking a week later to Tardini, Taylor also discussed the likelihood of the eventuality of the United States entering the war alongside Great Britain

[175] ASRS, AA.EE.SS., America 273, f. 11; ff. 34–48.
[176] ASRS, AA.EE.SS., America 273, ff. 38ᵛ–39, handwritten report of meeting with Taylor by Card. Maglione, September 10, 1941. The Anglo-American declaration was issued by both countries against the German invasions of Europe.

and the Allies. Tardini could see no good coming from such an escalation, saying sadly: "This will make the war an unendless and difficult one." "Long and difficult," agreed Taylor.

With some careful consideration, Tardini then proposed a hypothetical question:

> Let's suppose the survival of communism and the defeat of Nazism, one would find a Europe in the following conditions. All countries (the Balkans, the Latin and Germanic ones) would be on their knees. Communism would be triumphant and would invade every nation. We would have in continental Europe a new enormous militarist power (because communism has clearly shown the know-how and desire to arm itself), aggressive as Nazism (because it is known that communism tends to diffuse itself everywhere).
>
> Has the USA realised this eventuality? How will they prevent it? And, not preventing it, would the USA not find itself faced with, in a few years, another enemy, maybe stronger and much more dangerous than the same Hitler?
>
> Taylor remained surprised by my interrogation. It seemed almost that he never thought of this. And he asked me: "Do you think?" I answered him: "I am convinced of it."
>
> This time Mr. Taylor stood still and did not add a word nor explain anything.[177]

Tardini's words prophesied the future Cold War between the United States and the Soviet Union, particularly Soviet expansionism.

And no sooner had Taylor departed Rome on September 22 than Italian ambassador Attolico came rushing back to meet with Tardini. And Tardini, once again, calmed the waters, noting: "The Ambassador wants to write a rather extended report for his Government and is very worried. It seems I allayed the fears that Taylor's return has caused. A fear, apparently, that the unexpected visit of Mr. Taylor was a pre-announcement of America entering in the war."[178] That had not been the purpose of the visit, but of course as Taylor had predicted, it was not long before America did indeed enter the war.

[177] ASRS, AA.EE.SS., America 273, f. 56, handwritten report of meeting with Taylor by Msgr. Tardini, September 16, 1941; f. 59.
[178] ASRS, AA.EE.SS., America 273, f. 51.

A different hot diplomatic issue that came up repeatedly during Taylor's September 1941 audiences with the pontiff was the possible bombing of Rome by the British.

Taylor told Tardini that the British had declared, "for the umpteenth time," that if the Axis (Germany, Italy, and later on Japan) would bomb Athens or Cairo, the English would also bomb Rome as revenge. Tardini wrote in his very detailed notes that

> Taylor explains to me that "Cairo ... is the holy city for the Muslims as Rome is for the Catholics." He told me also the exact number of mosques that Cairo has (I don't remember how many ...). Now — adds Mr. Taylor — in the last few days the Axis has bombed the suburbs of Cairo, and thus ... England would like to avoid bombing Rome. But to do so, it would be necessary that the Axis does not bomb the city of Cairo. It is such a simple thing, abstain oneself of bombarding Cairo!

Tardini's sardonic humor at these games of wartime politics is always evident. He told Taylor he would pass on the comments on Cairo to the Italian ambassador regarding what was said about the bombing of Cairo. But, he added, "I cannot tell it the Germans, because they would possibly take it maybe as an argument *to* bombard Cairo."

And as Tardini continued: "That the Holy See puts the question in another light. Vatican City is situated in the middle of Rome and furthermore there are buildings, institutions and artistic works that are not Italian, but pontifical. How could the Pope keep silent if one of these buildings would be attacked? And would not such an eventual protest to be avoided, precisely given the good relationship which exists between the Holy See and England?"[179] Taylor promised to raise the issue with President Roosevelt.

As he prepared to leave Rome, Taylor received from the hands of Pius XII a personal letter for President Roosevelt, a letter in which the pope recalled the miserable human conditions of the many persecuted, deported, and homeless:

> In these tragic circumstances We are endeavoring, with all the forces at Our disposal, to bring material and spiritual comfort to countless

[179] ASRS, AA.EE.SS., America 273, ff. 54–55.

thousands who are numbered amongst the innocent and helpless victims. We would like, on this occasion, to express to Your Excellency Our cordial appreciation of the magnificent assistance the American people have given, and continue to offer, in this mission of mercy. They are, indeed, demonstrating once again a charitable understanding of the needs of their suffering fellowmen and a noble desire to alleviate their misery.[180]

Draft of personal letter from Pope Pius XII to Franklin Roosevelt, President of the United States of America.[181]

[180] ASRS, AA.EE.SS., America 273, f. 132, draft of personal letter of Pope Pius XII to President Roosevelt [handed over by Pius XII to Taylor on September 21, 1941].
[181] ASRS, AA.EE.SS., America 273, f. 131.

The risk of Rome's destruction had hung over the city like a dark cloud ever since the onset of the war, when the British threatened Italy with air raids on the capital if Italy entered the war alongside Nazi Germany.[182] That had only been averted after Pius XII asked the French and the British to respect, "in case of war, the city of Rome."[183] The issue then came up again in October 1940 during a private audience with the British envoy D'Arcy Osborne[184] when Pius XII "prayed him to ask the Government in London to abstain from air attacks on Rome. It is the diocese of the Pope: rich with ancient monuments and historical memories of universal importance."[185]

A month later, in November 1940, a telegram came to the Cabinet from Athens, requesting that the pope intervene in order to safeguard the Greek capital, which the Italians were threatening to bomb.[186] Tardini was charged by Pius XII to convene with both British envoy D'Arcy Osborne and Italian ambassador Attolico to "obtain the desired result."[187]

But the British government in London didn't appreciate the intervention and took a hard line with the Holy See. In an aide-mémoire they laid out their view on the matter:

> Given that Italian pilots had taken part in the bombardment of London, we have to reserve the liberty of action against Rome. The efforts of the Vatican to intervene are regrettable, not only because this government has not the slightest intention to let itself be influenced by [those efforts], but also because the intervention of the Vatican in favor of the city of Rome (to be distinguished from the City of the Vatican) cannot but give origin to the bad impression that the Pope would like to intervene to protect the Italian State and the fascist government against the consequences of their own … bombing of London.…

---

[182] ASRS, AA.EE.SS., Volumi Bianchi 1, f. 25, transcription by Card. Maglione of the Giornale d'Italia of June 9, 1940.

[183] ASRS, AA.EE.SS., Volumi Bianchi 1, f. 26; ff. 29–44, words of Pope Pius XII expressed during the audience of June 10, 1940.

[184] The British did not have a full ambassador to the Vatican at this time, but a legation situated on Vatican territory, although at times within the archives, D'Arcy Osborne, the British legate, is sometimes referred to as ambassador in the correspondence.

[185] ASRS, AA.EE.SS., Volumi Bianchi 1, f. 53, handwritten notes of Tardini (audience with Osborne, October 6, 1941).

[186] ASRS, AA.EE.SS., Volumi Bianchi 1, f. 59.

[187] ASRS, AA.EE.SS., Volumi Bianchi 1, f. 62.

And it should be said — en passant — that it troubled London a great deal that the Pope did not publicly condemn the German bombardment, sustained several times by the Italian aviation of the Anglican sanctuaries, like the St. Paul's Cathedral and Westminster Abbey in London, and the Abbeys of Canterbury and Coventry etc. etc.[188]

Tardini and D'Arcy Osborne met to discuss this matter. Tardini's notes detail the tense conversation:

(1) that the English Government, irritated by the *real* bombardments of the Germans and ... the *verbal* ones of Mussolini, feels itself pushed to bomb Rome, is *comprehensible*.

(2) that it reprimands the Pope for taking interest in the favor of Rome — which is the diocese of which he is the pastor — is *incomprehensible*.

(3) that it accuses the Pope of looking to favor, in this way, the fascist Government is inadmissible, and very false.[189]

On point three, Tardini notes that British envoy D'Arcy Osborne merely replied "that he did not have any thoughts about that."

This clearly angered Tardini. He threw down the gauntlet, telling D'Arcy Osborne: "If you want to do a thing that helps Mussolini and damages you, come then and bombard Rome."

Tardini also sternly reminded the envoy that the Vatican gave hospitality to numerous non-Italian ecclesiastical institutions and pontifical institutions (basilicas, seminars, dicasteries, palaces). D'Arcy Osborne retorted with a bit of classic British sarcasm: "But if a Bishop allows a bandit to set foot in his diocese ..."[190] To me, D'Arcy Osborne's quip is more than a little rich considering that he and the British delegation were also generously hosted on Vatican property.

---

[188] ASRS, AA.EE.SS., Volumi Bianchi 1, ff. 81–82, aide-mémoire of the British Legation to the Holy See, December 5, 1940.

[189] ASRS, AA.EE.SS., Volumi Bianchi 1, ff. 84–89: handwritten report of the meeting with the British legate to the Holy See, December 1940.

[190] ASRS, AA.EE.SS., Volumi Bianchi 1, ff. 90–91, personal notes of Tardini.

This row between the British and the Holy See didn't go away. D'Arcy Osborne reported some new intelligence his government had allegedly received: "The Italian Government is keeping ready equipment and munition that looked to be of British origin, with which it could hit the Vatican, in case the Royal Air Force would come to Rome. This way, they could naturally blame the English for any such bombardment and 'prove' that it was perpetrated by the English."[191] Tardini was suspicious of this, noting: "What do the British want? To find a reason, whatever reason, to bomb Rome."[192]

Returning to his office, Tardini dropped into his chair and began pondering. Then, all of a sudden, he grasped some blank sheets of paper from his desk drawer and unscrewed his pen, the mightiest weapon he owned. The minutes began to fly by, then the hours. The sheets were stained by the uninterrupted flood of his writing as the pope's minister of foreign affairs worked to recall the facts and comments of the last days and, in doing so, constructed his own personal analysis of it all: "The Holy See (even more, the Pope himself) did intervene in favor of Rome, holy city, diocese of the Pope, where so many artifacts, monuments and history and pontifical institutions are gathered. The English government does not ... show sensibility in front of such arguments, for to that government (as for all ... Anglicans) London counts more than Rome. If the former is bombarded, they don't see any reason to not also bomb the latter."

With the threatening tone of D'Arcy Osborne's words still reverberating in his ears and mind, he wrote: "But there is also the other side to this: when Italy sent its pilots over the Channel, the English government reserved itself explicitly *the right* to bomb Rome. Not much later these Italian pilots turned back to their homeland ... without having caused too much damage to London.... Then started the war between Italy and Greece. And the British government said: if the Italians bomb Athens, then the English Air Force will bomb Rome.... The Italians had ... the good sense not to bomb Athens."

The continuous and almost childish insistence of the British if-then logic and their threat over Rome was becoming crystal clear. In telegraphic style, Tardini jotted down:

[191] ASRS, AA.EE.SS., Volumi Bianchi 1, f. 93.
[192] ASRS, AA.EE.SS., Volumi Bianchi 1, f. 105, handwritten notes of Msgr. Tardini, March 25, 1941.

But now war between Germany and Greece is at stake. England tells
the Holy See, in the hope we would transmit the message to Italy,
and through Italy to Germany: "If the Germans bomb Athens, the
Royal Air Force will bomb Rome." When some days ago the Minister of Great Britain expressed to me the idea (I thought it was his
personal idea!) that the English would have to bomb Rome if the
Germans bombed Athens, I remained ... stunned and said to him:
"What has Rome to do with it when the Germans bomb ... Athens?"

And the Minister explained to me that, as the Germans are allies
of the Italians, and the English are allies of Athens. ... To which I
observed that this reasoning was a little unconvincing, unless one
wanted to find whatever reason to bomb Rome.

Tardini certainly understood what a growing danger for the Vatican this was shaping up to be:

> Now suppose that the Germans — specialists in destroying cit-
> ies — bomb Athens and that, consequently, the English bomb
> Rome: what will happen? The Italians will blame the English for
> it. These last ones will blame the Germans and the Germans will
> blame the Greeks ... and will return to bomb Athens again. Then,
> for vengeance, the English will return to bomb Rome. And between
> so much litigants, what will the Holy See experience? Maybe ruins
> and destruction of churches and basilicas ... and of Vatican City?

Weary but driven on by his need to give his conclusion to this whole war affair,
Tardini wrote:

> When I imagine that the Holy See — by initiative of the English
> Government — passing along information through the mediation
> of Italy, to the Germans that if they will bomb Athens then the
> English will bomb Rome, I ask myself if this intervention would
> spare the city of Rome or rather attract a bombardment? They would
> spare the city:
>> If the Germans had particular regards for the famous city of Athens
>> If the Germans really wanted what is best for Italy
>> If the Germans were well disposed towards the Holy See

If the Germans had any interest to not push the British to acts
of barbarism

But who can respond yes to all these ifs?[193]

Tardini's analysis makes two clear points — firstly, that the British were trying to use
the Holy See to send Germany a message. Secondly, that there was no way Germany,
the "specialist in destroying cities," would follow any basic rules of diplomacy anymore,
so it could not be trusted in any diplomatic negotiations on potential bombardments.
The answer to the four ifs were all obvious nos. At last, Tardini stood up from his
desk, leaving the sheets of paper with his private thoughts for others, like us, to read
in the future. Taking his coat and his black hat, he turned back to the turmoil of his
daily life, reflecting on how the Americans in all this could possibly make a difference.

*

*   *

In August 1941 Harold Tittmann, the U.S. chargé d'affaires who had taken over
Myron Taylor's role, came to say goodbye to Tardini. Tittmann was on his way to
Geneva in Switzerland, where he was to pick up his wife and children, who would
come join him in Rome. Tardini, never one to miss the opportunity for a touch of
sardonic humor, teased him: "Attention for the bombing!" He continued:

> I show myself worried while saying our relationship with England
> is good. But if any institution or pontifical basilica was touched,
> the Pope should protest. The Catholics of the entire world would
> suffer … and … Mr. Tittmann seems also worried (I think more
> for his daughters than for the basilicas), and he asks me if he is
> allowed to transmit all this to his government in order that they
> might intervene with the British. … I authorize him to do so (And
> there was no other reason why I've let him call to come to me).[194]

Tardini being Tardini, his quip had been entirely deliberate of course, as had been
his engineering of the meeting to say goodbye to Tittmann. Tardini truly was the
cleverest of diplomats at finding seemingly innocent ways to ensure the Holy See's
wishes or intentions were passed on informally, without it becoming an official act.

---

[193] ASRS, AA.EE.SS., Volumi Bianchi I, f. 106ᵛ.
[194] ASRS, AA.EE.SS., Volumi Bianchi 1, f. 117ᵛ, handwritten notes of Tardini.

*

* *

During the same time of Myron Taylor's brief return to Rome in September of 1941, the issue of bombing had reared its head again with the BBC reporting an imminent bombardment by the Royal Air Force. [195]

In a diplomatic note to Taylor the Holy See made its position unequivocally clear:

> The Secretariat of State has pointed out to Mr. Osborne and to Mr. Tittmann that if the State of Vatican City, or any of the basilicas, churches or pontifical buildings institutions in Rome (and they are very numerous and of very great historical and artistic importance) were to be hit, the Holy See could not remain silent. Nor would it be good that, with cordial relations existing between the Holy See and England, anything should happen to modify or disturb those relations.

Taylor promised to transmit this to President Roosevelt.[196]

And Pius XII raised the subject in person during an audience, speaking to Myron Taylor and saying that "if any pontifical buildings would be touched the Pope could not remain silent." Taylor's reply was curt: "This would be unfortunate."[197]

Yet the threats continued; the British were unequivocal: "The Prime Minister [Churchill] does not see why one should have regard towards Rome from the moment it became the capital of the Fascist Government."[198]

Pius XII, fully expecting the English to bomb at any time, gave the order for every word spoken and record written on the subject to be organized and filed. Msgr. Sigismondi was charged with the task.[199] The result of Sigismondi's work is an archival series known as "the white volumes," containing all the important documentation on the interventions of the Holy See on the saving of Rome from 1939 until 1945.

The details of these diplomatic conversations, unknown until today, can now be revealed in their entirety. And still it went on. On November 23, 1941, a strictly

---

[195] ASRS, AA.EE.SS., Volumi Bianchi 1, f. 146, handwritten notes of Tardini: "Secondo Radio Londra del 24 agosto."

[196] ASRS, AA.EE.SS., Volumi Bianchi 1, f. 147.

[197] ASRS, AA.EE.SS., America 273, f. 98.

[198] ASRS, AA.EE.SS., Volumi Bianchi 1, f. 151, internal note on a meeting between Msgr. Montini and Osborne, September 27, 1941.

[199] ASRS, AA.EE.SS., Volumi Bianchi 1, f. 152, internal note of October 2, 1941.

confidential *note verbale*[200] came in to the Secretariat of State from the American government: "In a telegram sent from Lisbon on the 1st of October, following his return from London and just before his departure for the United States onboard the 'Clipper,' His Excellence Mister Myron Taylor made known that it was his impression that Rome would not have been bombed by English airplanes, as long as Cairo would not be bombed [again] by the Axis."

The U.S. note continues: "Mister Taylor adds again, however, that it is his personal view that it would be prudent if the Italians would abstain from flying over London." The British were showing restraint but did not appear to be backing down on their bargaining over this, as further correspondence in the Archives over the following months demonstrates.[201]

Four years later, at the end of the war, Tardini, for reasons unknown, sat at his desk, once again poring over this last document, and scribbled the following observation: "Taylor departed from Rome to Lisbon. Then from Lisbon he went to London, where he talked with that government about the bombing of Rome."[202] One could be forgiven for thinking that, with this annotation, Tardini wanted to ensure that those who came after him would know that Taylor's mission to London was directly connected to the Holy See's interventions to prevent the destruction of Rome — along with all the treasures, art, and history contained in the Eternal City.

*

*   *

Toward the end of the Second World War, on May 26, 1944, the same Tardini and Tittmann would officially meet again in the antechambers of the Secretariat of State at 11:15 a.m. On the agenda of their meeting was nothing less than the issue of Jewish persecution, the Americans having called on the Holy See again to make a public statement against Hitler. Tardini, for once not sarcastic or sardonic, noted:

> I say to him:
> That the Holy See is always interested in the aid to Jewish persecuted. Pius XI started and Pius XII continued and continues in these charitable works.

---

[200] ASRS, AA.EE.SS., America 273, f. 99.
[201] ASRS, AA.EE.SS., Volumi Bianchi 1, ff. 175ss.
[202] ASRS, AA.EE.SS., America 273, f. 99.

> Hints and suggestions from the American Government will always be welcome. But the actions of the Holy See, if it can be parallel to that of the U.S. it should be however, for various reasons, independent of it.[203]

This meeting, held during the final days of the war, is key to unfolding all that happened in the wartime years between the United States and the Holy See. What I see is the Holy See once again reminding the Americans that we work with you, but please respect that we work separately.

The president and the pope were both convinced that as "children of the light" they had a common mission in the defeat of the forces of evil. Their correspondence, together with Hurley's detailed minutes, shows their cohesive efforts to prevent the war escalating and their joint disgust and horror of the Nazi persecutions. Where they did not agree was on how a papal pronouncement against Hitler should take place. The Americans urged for one repeatedly throughout the war, keeping their eyes closed to the need of the Holy See to maintain its complete impartiality. Many people don't understand why the Holy See didn't do what America had asked and issue a statement. But perhaps the careful art of diplomatic conversations detailed in this chapter goes some way to explaining why the Holy See had to be careful not to fall into diplomatic traps set by any other nation, traps that could harm their impartiality — and thus their ability to communicate with, and influence, all sides. Even if that country shared their values. Furthermore, it had to avoid compromising its networks and the courageous individuals engaged in life-saving operations.

The Holy See doesn't have armies or the ability to impose economic sanctions on another country. All it has are the quiet corridors and salons of the Vatican where diplomats come and go. And the ability to whisper in certain ears whenever possible.

That is soft diplomacy at its hardest.

[203] ASRS, AA.EE.SS., America 274, f. 29.

4

A Tale of "Good That Makes No Noise"

1940. THE AUTUMN air in Bucharest was unusually cold and dreary, and it matched the miserable situation facing Nuncio Cassulo. For a month or more he had been struggling with the age-old question concerning the Transylvanian dispute between Romanians and Hungarians. This question should have recently been finalized by the Vienna arbitration signed on August 30, 1940. However, the agreement, if one can call it that (for want of a better word — the Romanian ambassador reported Romania had to sign it or lose its independency[204]), created a worse situation for both Romania and Hungary.[205] Instead of resolving, it heightened the tensions.

In mid-October, Cardinal Maglione, the secretary of state, had asked Nuncio Cassulo to verify news received in Rome about the "Hungarian harassment of Romanians."[206] The following day, Msgr. Cassulo finished his report, which dealt with the "very difficult situation which in some places have taken on a truly tragic character," because "the acts of embezzlement and atrocity committed by the Hungarian people, militias, and authorities have been many, almost regularly and very serious."[207] The nuncio's report was for both the clergy and the Romanian

---

[204] ASRS, AA.EE.SS., Romania 142A, f. 644.

[205] ASRS, AA.EE.SS., Romania 142A, f. 646.

[206] ASRS, AA.EE.SS., Romania 142A, ff. 457^r–463^v, report of Msgr. Cassulo to Card. Maglione, October 15, 1940.

[207] ASRS, AA.EE.SS., Romania 142A, f. 458^r, report of Msgr. Cassulo to Card. Maglione, October 15, 1940.

population located in the area. It covered some acts of blatant cruelty, including an episode in which members of the clergy together with "100 other people and more, after being locked in prison, were passed through the streets of the city among the dismayed crowd and driven to the station and put on a freight train, shamelessly. I don't describe the details of the journey nor the material and moral discomfort in which they found themselves exposed."[208] No, this time he didn't include infinite descriptions but instead attached a photo of a train, which was very likely *that* train.[209]

Departure of a freight train deporting Romanians from Transylvania.[210]

It was a most striking photo, thought Cassulo, because on the one hand it was of perfect aesthetic composition, yet on the other hand it spoke — with the strength of more than a thousand words — of mass expulsions. It spoke silently yet vividly

[208] ASRS, AA.EE.SS., Romania 142A, f. 458ᵛ, report of Msgr. Cassulo to Card. Maglione, October 15, 1940. This account is that of the apostolic nuncio Msgr. Cassulo. For the sake of completeness, it would be opportune to take also a look to the reports that had been sent by the apostolic nuncio Msgr. Rotta in Budapest, reporting other elements of the ongoing clash and tensions.
[209] ASRS, AA.EE.SS., Romania 142A, f. 461ᵛ, report of Msgr. Cassulo to Card. Maglione, October 15, 1940.
[210] ASRS, AA.EE.SS., Romania 142A, f. 461ᵛ.

of people suddenly forced to abandon everything and to be packed like cattle on a train for destinations "unknown." Yes, it is merely a train. But its image cannot help but evoke thoughts of other trains, such as those deporting the Jews in the whole of Europe. This persecution of the Jews had long troubled Msgr. Cassulo, and it remained a thorn to his heart in the autumn of 1940.

A month later, on November 15, 1940, Cassulo sat to make notes in his diary. He racked his brain, recalling the facts of a particularly disturbing situation that all began thus:

> After an intimate feast for the King at the Belgian legation ... various subjects came up during a discussion, subjects that caught the interest of the Archbishop [Cisar]. One in particular dealt with the baptism of young Belgians who are departing, as well as the baptism of an entire Jewish family that once lived in Iran. For the first, the parents would need to give their consent and take seriously their children's Christian education. For the Hebrew family, a statement would be required affirming that there was a proper instruction.

As he wrote in his diary, "I begged the archbishop to prepare a memoire for me which I would present to the head of the Government about the baptized school-children from Jewish families."[211]

A few weeks later, Nuncio Cassulo added,

> A Madame Manoli came back with a young Hebrew girl who wanted to be baptized. I told them about the response I received from Rome and we agreed that Father Mantica [the parish priest of the Italian Catholic church] would take care of the matter. After Madame Manoli and the girl were gone, Father Clemente Koren dropped by with a family of converted Jews: five brothers with their aunt. The instruction received in school and the direction given by their aunt, who is already catholic, were the means grace has used to introduce the family to the Catholic faith. And since I, in these difficult moments for the Jews, have wanted, at Father Clemente's request, to give them a visa at their baptismal act, they had come to thank me and receive my blessing. They also offered me a bouquet

[211] ASRS, AA.EE.SS., Romania 186, vol. 28, pp. 509–510.

of carnations. After giving them paternal warnings, I invited them to visit the chapel. The flowers were placed before the tabernacle as an act of thanksgiving. They left very happy after having received the blessing.[212]

On December 9, 1940, Nuncio Cassulo sat down and picked up where he had left off in his diary: "After the walk, around 6 p.m., I received Father Mantica and we had a talk about the young Hebrew girl, Mihalovici, who sought to be baptized.... The work of the nuncio is no other than facilitating that of the archbishop, and so I told Father Mantica to ask Msgr. Durcovici to come by the Nunciature in order to organize the steps to take"[213] regarding the girl's Baptism. Msgr. Durcovici was the vicar-general of Bucharest, and Cassulo considered him to be "very competent in civil and church law matters."[214] One day later, Cassulo continued, "Msgr. Durcovici came by and I communicated all that had been done. We agreed to proceed, with the necessary caution and prudence, with the intention to interpret in the best way the mind of the church whose only aim is for the good of the souls."[215]

Msgr. Cassulo acted quickly on this matter, and the very next day he "made a visit to Msgr. Archbishop Canon Schubert [a member of the cathedral chapter] was also there, and we talked about the procedures they have in order to admit neophytes to be baptized."[216] The days that followed were incredibly demanding, and the cases that continued to present themselves to him were of the most diverse nature: "Canon Schubert was here with me. Having reviewed the documents concerning the baptism of the Mihalovici, we decided on the procedure to follow and we brought in the young girl who wants to be baptized. She was advised to agree that her father would be asked for his 'beneplacet,' his pleases."[217] And then "F[ather] Mantica recommended to me a young woman named [Ravina] Feingold." I sent her, along with a note from me, to the ambassador of Turkey in order for him to facilitate her passage to Palestine. She is a Catholic converted, most fervent. She

---

[212] ASRS, AA.EE.SS., Romania 186, vol. 28, pp. 558–559.

[213] ASRS, AA.EE.SS., Romania 186, vol. 28, p. 560.

[214] ASRS, AA.EE.SS., Romania 149, ff. 40ʳ–49ᵛ, report from Msgr. Cassulo to Card. Maglione; object was: "Transition of Jews to another cult," March 31, 1941.

[215] ASRS, AA.EE.SS., Romania 186, vol. 27, p. 560.

[216] ASRS, AA.EE.SS., Romania 186, vol. 27, p. 565b.

[217] ASRS, AA.EE.SS., Romania 186, vol. 27, p. 572.

would not like to go together with her family, who are all Jews, to Bessarabia, where it is difficult to practice catholic religion."[218] The following day, Cassulo received once more "missis Ravina Feingold who wants to go to Palestine. I encouraged her, but I think I could not do more for her."[219]

*

*   *

As of December 1940, the problems related to the legal status of the Jews had become a daily concern: "The lawyer Eugenio Kappler reminded me once again of the situation regarding students from Jewish families who cannot frequent catholic schools. I told him that I'm dealing with this matter and that one hopes to be able to give him a response in a short time."[220] Yet most of all Msgr. Cassulo remained troubled by the scenes in the streets of Bucharest, as he noted in his diary:

> Passing through the popular neighborhoods, where especially the Jews live, I have seen the acts of vandalism committed by the rebels. Many stores are devastated, set fire to and destroyed. One says that the victims are numerous, but it is difficult, in this moment, to know exactly the number and I believe one will never know. These are the consequences of a trend that has been going on for years. If abuses and other inconveniencies had over the time accumulated to the detriment of the nation, it would have been wise to develop a solution gradually without provoking hate against the people.[221]

The social and juridical questions concerning the Jews quickly became an increasingly complex and delicate problem for the nuncio. On February 20, 1941, thanks to his intervention, the Romanian government passed a decree-law that changed a provision that had been recently issued against Jews. This provision was related to Catholic schools and education.[222] General Ion Antonescu personally informed Msgr. Cassulo in writing that he had signed this decree, "by virtue of which Christian students will have the opportunity to attend, without discrimination of ethnic

---

[218] ASRS, AA.EE.SS., Romania 186, vol. 27, p. 578.

[219] ASRS, AA.EE.SS., Romania 186, vol. 27, p. 578.

[220] ASRS, AA.EE.SS., Romania 186, vol. 27, p. 582.

[221] ASRS, AA.EE.SS., Romania 186, vol. 28, pp. 81b–82.

[222] ASRS, AA.EE.SS., Romania 149, ff. 22ʳ–35ᵛ (the decree-law of February 20, 1941, on f. 31ʳ).

origin, the confessional schools of Christian religion."[223] But Cassulo hardly had time to celebrate the positive step that had just been obtained, for just a month later, on March 21, 1941, the Romanian government passed a law with decidedly negative implications both for the conversion of the Jews and for the freedom of the Catholic religion in general.[224] The new norm infringed some principles sanctioned by the Concordate between the Holy See and Romania aimed at ensuring exactly the free exercise of the Catholic religion.[225] With this new law, an article was introduced in the legal system on religions, through which, as summarized by the vicar-general Msgr. Durcovici,

> from now on the people of mosaic religion or the Jews, will be considered by civil law as always being of mosaic faith, even if they were baptized, which would be contrary to the truth as well as to the Concordat, because they will be no longer considered as Catholic faithful, what they in reality are ... and it's true, the law does not explicitly forbid the baptism of Jews, but not allowing anymore to Jews the civil right to change religion and on the other hand prohibiting to insert in the registers of baptism persons that do not have first fulfilled the civil formalities of this transition ... will automatically do incur the catholic priest into the penalty.[226]

[223] ASRS, AA.EE.SS., Romania 149, ff. 29ʳ, 61ʳ, typewritten copies of the letter of Gen. Ion Antonescu to Msgr. Cassulo, February 21, 1941.

[224] The contents of the decree-law of March 21, 1941, are reported in detail and with analysis in a "Votum" (a typewritten evaluation of and opinion on a problem) of April 5, 1941, by Msgr. Durcovici (ASRS, AA.EE.SS., Romania 149, ff. 39ʳ–49ᵛ, in part. ff. 42ʳ–46ʳ) and in a handwritten internal report of April 2, 1941 [sic, although one mentions also the votum of Msgr. Durcovici] of Msgr. Barbetta (ASRS, AA.EE. SS., Romania 149, ff. 55ʳ–56ᵛ).

[225] The Historical Archives preserve the official documentation relating to the signing, ratification, and subsequent interpretations of the Concordat between the Holy See and the Kingdom of Romania, signed on May 10, 1927, and ratified on July 7, 1929. In addition, a conspicuous position with the heading: "New negotiations for the Concordat between the Holy See and Romania (1921–1936)," consisting of eighteen bound files and a miscellaneous volume, collects various types of documentation (reports, letters, notes, minutes with revisions, opinions, etc.) as evidence of the long process of critical study, amendment, and negotiations leading up to the definitive drafting of the official act (ASRS, AA.EE.SS., IV period, Pos. 35 P.O.).

[226] ASRS, AA.EE.SS., Romania 149, f. 44ʳ (cit. the votum of Msgr. Durcovici).

Msgr. Barbetta, the *minutante* of the Cabinet to whom the case was assigned, defined this act carried out by the Romanian government with few but eloquently chosen words: "There is no doubt that it is a serious attack on the freedom of the Catholic Church in Romania, although, as the Nuncio [Cassulo] was told, and the Nuncio believed it all, nobody intended to do wrong."[227] This is an interesting last comment because it highlights a mistake (in diplomatic language we call it "a lightness") made — though we are not told whether by naïveté, negligence, or otherwise — by Cassulo.

At the end of that month, on March 26, 1941,[228] and acting in his capacity as dean of the diplomatic corps, Cassulo presented himself "at 12 a.m. . . . at the Ministry of Foreign Affairs. Minister [George] Cretziano [the minister of cults] welcomed me with the usual goodness and I had an hour conversation with him." Many questions related to churches, the Romanian college in Rome, and religious orders were on the agenda. But one particular question stood out as the most critical: "The Decree of interdiction for the Jews, prohibiting a conversion from one religion to another under the threat of severe punishment and also for those who try to help this conversion. . . . The minister has taken note of everything, we have summarized the whole conversation, and agreed that he would report on every single item."[229] It seems that his visit had no immediate result for converted Jews as such but may have helped other persecuted Christians. He reported in April that "after my intervention with the government, the Armenian Catholics were no longer harassed." But regarding the Jews there were no comments.[230] From the report of March 31, in which Cassulo conveyed to Cardinal Maglione the specifics of the interview he'd had with Minister Cretziano, we learn that the latter "declared that the Ministry of Foreign Affairs had had no part in this provision of the law."[231]

As if the objective political difficulties of the moment were not enough, it seems that the nunciature, in the course of its diplomatic duties, was continuously torn between the Ministry of Foreign Affairs and the Ministry of Cults, as their

[227] ASRS, AA.EE.SS., Romania 149, f. 55ʳ, handwritten internal report of Msgr. Barbetta.

[228] In his report to his superiors, Cassulo writes that he made this visit on March 25 (ASRS, AA.EE.SS., Romania 149, ff. 40ʳ–49ᵛ, report from Cassulo to Card. Maglione; item: "Passage of Jews to another cult," March 31, 1941).

[229] ASRS, AA.EE.SS., Romania 186, vol. 28, pp. 219ss.

[230] ASRS, AA.EE.SS., Romania 186, vol. 28, p. 242.

[231] ASRS, AA.EE.SS., Romania 149, ff. 40ʳ–49ᵛ (cit. from f. 40ʳ), report from Msgr. Cassulo to Card. Maglione on "Transition of Jews to another cult," March 31, 1941.

responsibilities over some matters that directly touched the Holy See overlapped. In a mid-April nuncio's report, in fact, we read: "The difficulties, Your Eminence, which have occurred so far, rather than from the Ministry of Foreign Affairs, have almost always come from the Ministry of Cults. In a note of last March, I complained to Minister Cretziano [sic] and, just yesterday, he told me that he had considered my findings and that he had made known to the Ministry of Cults the opportunity to recognize the efforts of the Nuncio aimed at the common good."[232]

This same mid-April report is interesting not so much for its content but rather for the notes added to it by attentive readers in the Secretariat of State. In particular, two notes that with few words — and no words at all for one of them — express a significant judgment on the personality of the nuncio. Where Cassulo wrote that he had not met Minister Cretziano for the last two weeks "due to my health being somewhat shaken by excessive work and also by the present serious concerns," someone in the Cabinet — almost certainly Secretary Tardini — underlined with a blue pencil the words "excessive work" and put a large exclamation mark in the margin, as if to shout, "This is the height! What excessive work?" Did Cassulo have a lazy nature? In the corridors of the Secretariat of State it seems that he was not known for his zeal and perspicacity. The text of the nuncio continued as follows: "Thank God, I have now recovered and have therefore been able to go to the Ministry of Foreign Affairs both to present Easter greetings and to keep up to date on current issues, which I have seen going on quite well." Another pencil, probably in the hand of the desk officer Msgr. Barbetta, underlined the words "which I have seen going on quite well." There was also a second line drawn under the words "going on" and written in the margin was "Have a good trip!" This is a comment imbued with laconic sarcasm, apparently aimed at pointing out the fact that the questions to which the nuncio referred were serious (the decree-law that was going to harm the rights of the Holy See had been passed less than a month before!), and yet he was slow to act. This showed a tendency of Cassulo to underestimate the situation that had already been highlighted by Barbetta in the former note of April 2, which included the words "and the Nuncio believed it all."[233]

Continuing to browse the papers produced by the Cabinet that tell us about the delicate legal issue, we come to an inevitable question: Did Cassulo possess

[232] ASRS, AA.EE.SS., Romania 149, ff. 51ʳ–54ᵛ, report from Msgr. Cassulo to Card. Maglione on "Visit to Minister Cretziano," April 14, 1941 (cit. from f. 54ʳ).
[233] See above, p. 101.

the necessary energy and astuteness required for his tasks? On May 12, 1941, he produced a new report for his superior that featured a document from Minister Cretziano regarding the conversion of the Jews.[234] Nuncio Cassulo introduced this document as follows:

> The response we have now received is quite satisfactory. It is the consequence of the repeated steps taken by Msgr. Nunzio [i.e., by himself] to the Ministry of Foreign Affairs where the delicacy and importance of the question perhaps touched, unwittingly, the Decree-Law of last March 18 [sic].[235] I say this because, after the observations were made, General Antonescu studied the matter and I now see with pleasure that the measure taken was not meant to constrain the freedom of the Church in Romania. Moreover, now more than ever, Your Eminence has in hand all the necessary documents to see if it is the case to take in account only the declaration now made, or if it would be necessary to ask for other assurances.[236]

However, Cassulo was wrong. And he was wrong on two points. The first mistake was this — it was not true that Cardinal Maglione had "in hand all the necessary documents," and that can be well understood by reading the encrypted telegram sent by Maglione to the nuncio on May 23: "Received Report N. 7418 [i.e., the one mentioned above] with letter from Minister Cretzianu. Since I do not know letter of Your Excellency No. 7348, I am not able to fully understand the Minister's answer." In other words, Cassulo had failed to send the contents of the letter with which he had addressed Cretziano in order to obtain the document he now provided in the annex. The cardinal's telegram continued: "Please, Your Excellency, make certain that Jews who have passed to Catholicism will enjoy rights guaranteed by the Concordat for Catholics in Romania: such as free profession Catholic religion, admission to Catholic schools, religious education, spiritual assistance in the army, hospitals, etc."[237]

[234] ASRS, AA.EE.SS., Romania 149, ff. 63ʳ–65ᵛ, report of Msgr. Cassulo to Card. Maglione, on "Transition of cult," May 12, 1941.

[235] It refers to the decree-law of March 21, 1941.

[236] ASRS, AA.EE.SS., Romania 149, ff. 63ʳ–65ᵛ, report of Msgr. Cassulo to Card. Maglione, on "Transition of cult," May 12, 1941 (cit. from ff. 63ʳ/ᵛ).

[237] ASRS, AA.EE.SS., Romania 149, f. 66ʳ, telegram in code from Card. Maglione to Msgr. Cassulo, May 23, 1941.

Why did Cardinal Maglione continue to press on this issue? To get an answer
to this, we need to read the document in question that was produced by Minister Cretziano. In it, he asserted (in French) that "the Decree-Law of March 21st
1941,[238] amending the Law for the general regime of the religions, does not bring
anything against the duly recognized rights of the Catholic Church in Romania.
Our authorities find no obstacle to Israelites converting to Catholicism, since
this change of religion has no effect on their marital status according to the laws
of our country."[239]

Here it is: the second serious mistake made by Cassulo appears obvious to us.
There is no need to exert any effort to understand it or explain it, both because
the text of Cretziano is so clear and because the *minutante* Msgr. Barbetta does
this for us by writing:

> Unfortunately, the letter from Minister Cretzianu does not reassure
> us: while, in fact, it seems to recognize the rights guaranteed to the
> Catholic Church in the Concordat, it also seems to deny Jews who
> have converted to Catholicism the civil rights that would flow to
> the faithful due to the fact that they now belonged to the Catholic
> Church. In other words, does the government intend to recognize
> baptized Jews as Catholics, or not? And how can Catholics assure
> for them both the freedom and exercise of worship, as well as spiri-
> tual assistance in the army, in hospitals, etc., admission to (at least)
> Catholic schools, religious education, etc.? If they can assure that,
> thank goodness: but the text of the Minister's reply to Msgr. Cas-
> sulo (who did not send the text of his letter to the Minister, and so
> ... ignotum per ignotum [unknown by unknown] ...) denies any
> [twice underlined!] civil rights."[240]

So why, one wonders, did the nuncio send Cretziano's document to his superiors,
calling it "satisfactory enough" and even bragging about his efforts to obtain it? Is
it possible that he did not realize the evident ambiguity of the text contained in the

---

[238] On the document figures the date of March 18, 1941.

[239] ASRS, AA.EE.SS., Romania 149, f. 64ʳ, copy of the letter of Minister Al. Cretziano
to Msgr. Cassulo, May 12, 1941.

[240] ASRS, AA.EE.SS., Romania 149, ff. 67ʳ/ᵛ, handwritten internal note of Msgr. Barbetta
on "Law of transitions of cult in Romania," May 20, 1941.

letter and therefore did not notice the double game just played by the minister? This conclusion appears strange. Yet it would seem so after reading the pages of his diary, which tell us of his meeting with Minister Cretziano just after the letter was produced.

The entry on Cassulo's diary for May 17, 1941, mentions he met the minister of cults[241] with whom he discussed eight points on the agenda. "I thanked the Minister for [his] written declaration about the transition of religion [conversion to Catholicism] by the Jews. I asked him if such a formal declaration of a Minister would on its own also be sufficient for the future, or if it would be a good idea to give the declaration the force and stability provided by a Decree of law." Msgr. Cassulo knew that a minister's letter didn't have the authority and the lasting power of a law.

> He answered that the letter he wrote was sufficient and in case of difficulties, the minister was ready to defend the decision he had made. A Decree of Law was also a possibility, but in that case, it would create difficulties for the government, for such a law would make it appear as if the government was against the Jews, even though the law helped them. And so giving it consideration, I thought it was better not to insist and to remain in agreement with Minister Cretziano.[242]

However, another possible explanation regarding Cassulo's decision would be that he found himself in a very critical situation. He knew that the extremist and racist wing of the Romanian government was gaining strength and intended to take political steps toward persecution of the Jews. For this reason, Cassulo did not want to be seen as asking "too much," which could risk the Catholic Church being deprived of all rights acquired in the country and, therefore, prevent them from being of help to the persecuted.

A much later report, dated 1944, dealt with a request for the protection of Jews in Transnistria. Cassulo wrote on that occasion:

> It seems to me therefore, unnecessary to take other steps with the Romanian government which, for its part, takes into benevolent consideration on every occasion the word of the Apostolic Nuncio

---

[241] "At 12 a.m. I was received by the Minister Cretziano." ASRS, AA.EE.SS., Romania 186, vol. 28, p. 357.

[242] ASRS, AA.EE.SS., Romania 186, vol. 28, pp. 357ss.

[i.e., himself], who by now is known by all as the highest and most effective protector of so many poor families who are in concentration camps or in need of assistance. Of course, we don't know everything. But it can be said that the Romanian government, on the whole, is giving thought to reconciling the dispositions taken with a sense of broad understanding, and the government would be more likely to do this if it didn't fear the reaction from those who were strongly opposed to favoring the Israelites. Your Eminence can therefore be assured that here we do everything possible in the desired sense.[243]

At this point, we could assume one of two things. Either Cassulo lacked resourcefulness, or he was afraid of aiming too high and risking losing everything. If, on the one hand, it is undeniable that some aspects of his behavior remain unclear, it is certain that, reading his diaries, he does not seem to have been a slacker. Above all, it emerges — as we will see later — that during the period of his nunciature many Jews were saved.

*
*   *

July 28, 1941. Cassulo wrote a new report to Cardinal Secretary of State Maglione, to inform him that he had carried out his instructions

> to ask the Romanian Government for further explanations and clarifications regarding the Decree-Law issued on the conversion of the Jews to the Catholic faith. With a special Note in which I pointed out the main points that affected the Concordat and the freedom of the Church ... and also on several occasions, verbally, I asked the Government if it would give more explanations and formal assurances on this matter.[244]

And this time the nuncio did not fail. A week before he had obtained a *note verbale* in which the Ministry of Foreign Affairs provided unambiguous explanations on the recent laws affecting Jews, affirming the rights recognized by the Concordat,

---

[243] ASRS, AA.EE.SS., Romania 149, ff. 79$^{r/v}$, report of Msgr. Cassulo to Card. Maglione, on "Jews in Transnistria," March 16, 1944.

[244] ASRS, AA.EE.SS., Romania 149, ff. 126$^{r/v}$, report from Msgr. Cassulo to Card. Maglione on "Education and religious instruction of baptized Jews," July 28, 1941.

including for Jews who had converted to the Catholic religion[245] — a *note verbale* that, as we will see later, would remain in the mind of Barbetta still for a long time.

July continued to be an extremely intense month for Cassulo. During that time, he informed Rome that General Antonescu, president of the Council of Ministers, had taken over command of the troops that were operating in Bucovina and in Bessarabia and transferred the vice presidency of the council ad interim to the minister of foreign affairs, Mihai Antonescu, one of the youngest personalities within the Romanian government.

The nuncio did not waste any time and went to visit him on July 25. He described his meeting:

> I had never met him before, but as he had been before the right-hand man of the President, he knew of me and of my relationship with the President.... The Minister told me that he was profoundly faithful and that he was well aware of the influence of the Catholic Church among the Nations and that he was working with the General to help orientate the Romanian Church towards the Church of Rome. The minister has a very sharp mind, a very marked religious sentiment and, even if he is young and, at his young age, he has been a professor of international rights at the University of Bucharest, Minister of Justice, and now he is also in charge of the Ministry of Propaganda.[246]

In August 1941, when Cassulo reported the military successes of the Romanian troops alongside the German ones, he also mentioned "the Jewish problem that is not resolved yet." According to Cassulo, the government witnessing the Jews giving a helping hand to the Communist Party as well as supporting the Soviets had resulted in a great deal of severe repressions.[247] "From time to time, I have been asked to intervene to mitigate the tension in particular cases, but I consider these matters quite delicate and only by approaching them with the sentiment of charity can one obtain some good result. The most important goal has been to obtain, on

---

[245] ASRS, AA.EE.SS., Romania 149, f. 127ʳ, *Note verbale* of the Romanian Ministry of Foreign Affairs to the apostolic nunciature, July 21, 1941.

[246] ASRS, AA.EE.SS., Romania 155, f. 79ᵛ, report from Msgr. Cassulo to Card. Maglione, July 28, 1941.

[247] ASRS, AA.EE.SS., Romania 155, f. 74ᵛ, report of Msgr. Cassulo to Card. Maglione, August 7, 1941.

the educational and religious level, the right for baptized Jews to benefit from the liberty conceded through the Concordate."[248]

Shortly after those written words, Cassulo had the opportunity to return to Rome and personally visit with Pius XII on September 6, 1941. Thanks to the notes in his personal diary, we can read his cheerful thoughts on that visit on that sunny morning in the Vatican: "Before entering the Courtyard of S. Damaso, the Swiss Guard stopped me and held me back. The Holy Father, who had gone out for his morning promenade, was on his way back to his apartments. Standing there I saw him passing by in a car. My appointment was scheduled at 10:30 a.m. Going up to the papal antichambres, I was welcomed with cordiality by all the household and personnel in service." It's obvious that Cassulo was thrilled to be headed back to the Eternal City. Like a soldier returning from a long and exhausting battle, he shared his joy at seeing and meeting his old fellow colleagues and the employees of the pope's palace. The visit felt like a long-awaited homecoming.

> The 'Cameriere Segreto Partecipante' Nasalli Rocca held me back quite some time and then the marquis Pacelli, who was on duty, also arrived. At the end of a conversation with this noble, good, most distinguished man, I was admitted to the august presence of His Holiness, who received me most paternally and embraced me. The Holy Father kept me for at least one hour listening with inter-est and goodness to the account made by me regarding what had happened in Romania from September 1939 onwards. We talked about all the important issues: the tragic death of minister Calinesco and his successors ... the invasion of Bessarabia and the north of Bucovina ... arbitration of Vienna, polish refugees, status catholi-cus and juridical personalities, abdication of king Charles, general Antonescu, the earthquake, German intervention, the message of the vice-president of the Council, and the Slavic-soviet danger.[249]

It seems a bit strange that after all he had been dealing with back in Romania, in his personal memories Cassulo made no mention of the problem regarding the baptized Jews, although this had been at the top of the list during his conversations

---

[248] ASRS, AA.EE.SS., Romania 155, ff. 74ᵛ–75, report of Msgr. Cassulo to Card. Maglione, August 7, 1941.

[249] ASRS, AA.EE.SS., Romania 186, vol. 29, p. 48.

with the Bucharest government. Why so? Did Nuncio Cassulo simply not report the topic in his diary, or did he not discuss it with the Holy Father? And if the latter would be the case, was the omission intentional or not? From what emerges from the monumental number of handwritten pages of the nuncio's diaries — an extremely detailed recollection of his daily work that includes his meetings and the essential points of each of his interviews — it seems doubtful that he simply forgot to mention such a relevant topic. It is more likely that the nuncio, being a diplomat, knew perfectly well what to say and what to avoid in order to have a good political outcome for his actions. Although these are personal diaries, he very rarely wrote notes that revealed his emotions. Rather, he stuck to noting the facts almost as if he were writing an official report. There can be little question that everything Cassulo had experienced, everything he had tried to accomplish, and every situation of human suffering that he had witnessed would have made a deep and indelible mark on his soul. He seemed to be a man who did, indeed, have the sense of Christian compassion that one would hope to find in a true and devoted member of the Catholic Church and a priest. And it is obvious that as a nuncio, when he put pen to paper, he was well aware that his diaries would one day end up in the archives of the Holy See and would be read by someone. This may be the reason he carefully avoided expressing potentially contentious opinions, sentiments, or compromising facts and actions. In any case, as the written narrative of his visit with the pope continues, we can read between the lines and catch a glimpse of some his feelings:

> At the end of our conversation, I thanked the Pope for sending the Holy objects for the chapel of the Nunciature. I could have taken the opportunity to continue our conversation on other things related to my mission, but all of a sudden the Maestro di camera, Mons. Di S. Elia, came in announcing the arrival of a group of German soldiers waiting to receive the benediction. The Holy Father, after some conversation gave benedictions to me and all my relatives, then he embraced me again and went to meet people who were waiting in the rooms aside the Sala Clementina.
>
> I left, passing amongst some German soldiers who were gathered in one of the rooms, and sought out the Secretary of State. There I conferred with the minutanti Mons. Samorè and with Mons. Sigismondi.

> Then I went down to the office of the Substitute, Mons. Montini. While
> I was with him, I was introduced to the English minister to the Holy See,
> Mr. Osborne, with whom I gladly shared memories of some persons
> I had known on the occasion of my missions in Egypt and in Canada.

This was typical talk between diplomats. "With Mons. Montini I talked about various items of the nunciature for which more time for explanation was indispensable. Having these additional things to talk over with me, he asked me to come back to him in the evening, around 7 p.m."

September is a grand time to be visiting in Rome. It still feels like summer, but something in the air hints that autumn is on its way. The ancient and the modern blend in perfect harmony, with so many sights to see. And Cassulo was able to partake of the treasure that was the city and have what might be called a busy but perfect holiday. He wrote that

> in the afternoon, at 3:30 pm, minister general Papp, the Romanian
> diplomat, came to S. Pantaleo and wanted to accompany me to visit
> the ruins of Ostia Antica. The new street that brings us to the sea, the
> monuments we visited, the new city that emerged right there on that
> "smiling" beach are truly Roman. By 18:00 o'clock we were back a S.
> Pantaleo, where I received the mother superior of the [Congregation
> of] Madre Pie. A quarter to 7 p.m. I returned to the Vatican where
> Msgr. Montini was already expecting me and with him I continued
> our conversation for another hour or so. Back at s. Pantaleo I found
> a visiting card of Minister Basilio Grigoreco who was there before to
> see me. I felt sorry not having been able to meet with him.[250]

*
* *

Joyful songs don't last long, and the holiday had to come to an end. Critical business could not be left undone. Cassulo returned to Bucharest on October 15, 1941. Once back, many Jewish families came to his office, pressing him to intervene with both General Ion Antonescu, the marshal-president, and Mihai Antonescu, the minister of foreign affairs. Cassulo arranged an audience that was held a week

---

[250] ASRS, AA.EE.SS., Romania 186, vol. 29, pp. 49–50.

later and was facilitated by Minister Mihai Antonescu and Ion Antonescu, the marshal.[251] There, he learned that the minister of cults had been replaced. In his report to Rome, he could not hide a bit of uneasiness:

> I was told that recently Alexander Cretziano had resigned, and called in to take his place was Minister Davidesco [sic].... Minister Cretziano has always been very respectful with the Nuncio [i.e., himself], coop- erating with him for solutions to the most difficult problems. A man of open mind, with a sharp ... intellect with which he brings to the most diverse problems a sense of balance and a desire to help appease, a man who is sorry when the desired aim remained unattainable.[252]

Regarding the new minister Davidescu, however, Cassulo wrote: "As to our many issues, I think he does not have that superiority that we noticed in Cretziano. He leans easily toward the dissenting majority, to which he belongs and is very attached. However, he treats me well and so I hope not to have difficulties in fulfilling my mission. I will talk, as I always have done, very clearly and to the point, determined to keep firm on the defence of the rights of the Catholic Church." The unusual esteem, bordering on fascina- tion, shown by Cassulo for Cretziano could explain why, at first, he remained blind and deaf to the double game of the minister concerning the decree-law of March 21, 1941.

In the months following his visit to the pope in Rome, Cassulo noted the numerous benefits obtained from the government in matters of conversion and baptism of Jews in the following months. He also acknowledged the *note verbale* of July 21, 1941, as being a safety net for many miserable people. And this, explained Cassulo, was a reason for the mass influx of baptisms since the end of November 1941. But by Christmastime of that same year, new circumstances and burning needs regarding the sacrament of Baptism caused Msgr. Cassulo to contact Rome again. This time, he asked for clear instructions from the Holy Office in the hope that canon law would be interpreted in the right way. For even if things had recently calmed down in Romania, the situation could easily turn around. Here was the situation behind his move: where initially one had been able to dedicate the ap- propriate amount of time for the Baptism preparation of single individuals, now

---

[251] ASRS, AA.EE.SS., Romania 155, f. 70, report from Msgr. Cassulo to Card. Maglione, October 29, 1941.

[252] ASRS, AA.EE.SS., Romania 155, f. 68ᵛ, report from Msgr. Cassulo to Card. Maglione, October 29, 1941.

"the extreme danger to which the Jews are exposed make it so they find themselves caught in a nightmare of a future without hope of saving themselves and possibly being taken away to concentration camps in far off regions. They present themselves to be baptized by the Church in large numbers, looking to be saved in that way or, at least, hoping for a less frightening treatment."[253]

One of the reasons this situation seemed to be growing out of hand was rumors that the Holy See, well aware of the danger to which the Jews were exposed, had given order to baptize in masses, without prior religious instruction and leaving such educational training till after the Baptism. Cassulo insisted that when he learned of this fake news, he refuted it immediately and categorically and kept strictly to the instructions formerly given him by Rome. Furthermore, he checked in person to see how these Baptisms were being handled, and "the parish priest in Bucharest confirmed that a preparation time schedule was respected and abuses were avoided."[254] Cassulo also met with Archbishop Msgr. Cisar, who "in times past had shown himself quite difficult on the item of the baptism of the Jews." The archbishop told him that in the past the preparation time for the Baptism of a Jew was normally six months. Now, given the pending situation, he had convened a meeting with his chapter of the archdiocese to see how they could manage the surge in number of requests for Baptism.

> From what I was able to understand, the decision would have been, more or less, the following: to give to those who present themselves to be baptized a brief instruction on the principle points of the catholic faith, and after that an examination of the family-status to see if they are in order with the marriage etc. After this they are admitted to baptism with the obligation to regularly attend the Church and to complete the broader, complete requirements in order to be admitted to the Holy Communion.

Msgr. Cassulo did not leave the matter to chance. While asking for an assessment of the whole delicate question by the Holy See, he concluded by offering some astute personal guidelines that, if endorsed by his superiors, would give individual priests scope for appreciation and the possibility therefore to continue, in conscience, to baptize Jews:

---

[253] ASRS, AA.EE.SS., Romania 149, f. 147^v, report from Msgr. Cassulo to Card. Maglione, December 22, 1941.

[254] ASRS, AA.EE.SS., Romania 149, f. 147^v, report from Msgr. Cassulo to Card. Maglione, December 22, 1941.

Truly, it is a new fact that these Jews, professionals, business men, present themselves before the Priest, disposed to be instructed regardless of the time of the day. It is clear that by motifs of human nature one cannot refuse, but it is also true that Providence serves itself with natural means to arrive at salvation. It is up to the Priest to judge case by case and see if, all well-considered, to proceed or not to proceed with a moral certainty for admission to the Catholic Church.[255]

*

*   *

September 1942 was coming to a close, with hints of slightly cooler October weather just around the corner. In his office in Rome, the desk officer Msgr. Barbetta pushed open the windows, took a deep breath in the early morning air, and then sat back down at his desk. He picked up his pen and began drafting an internal note for the Cabinet, a note that analyzed the racial laws in Romania. The issue was troubling, and it could certainly become worse.

Over in Bucharest, the nuncio, Msgr. Cassulo, had been laboring for months in his attempt to create some kind of effective barrier against the pernicious anti-Jewish laws of the government. It had been almost a year since the opposition of the Romanian government to the conversions of Jews and had become a central concern of the Cabinet. All of Cassulo's correspondence, the annotations in his diary, and Barbetta's notes in the Historical Archive are evidence of it. Months earlier, Barbetta had come to the conclusion that the Romanian law specialists considered Jewish conversion to Catholicism as an external matter, as an act of civil administration, that should respond to the police regulations. Their insensibility toward the Church's conduct in this matter was inevitable. In an attempt to have all the facts fresh in mind, Barbetta looked at what he had written on the issue back in November 1941. At the time, he had considered that after what the Cabinet had done and what the nuncio had undertaken "nothing else was to be done anymore." He stopped on the nuncio's concluding words where he had written that he "had said to Mr. Davidescu [the Head of Antonescu's military cabinet] that his mission consisted of reconciling the interests of the State with the rights of the Church." It's funny, thought Barbetta with a sad smile at the corners of his mouth, how I

---

[255] ASRS, AA.EE.SS., Romania 149, f. 149.

commentated months ago on that, saying: "The formula is beautiful, but it's not always possible to turn it into practice. In fact, here we are talking about abuses executed by the State that are ... irreconcilable."[256]

Now almost a year later, Barbetta was at his desk, having to deal with the same ongoing and disturbing matter. He put down his pen, rubbed his forehead, and reflected on the fact that, in spite of the Romanian government declaring they had no intention of infringing the rights of the Catholic religion as recognized by the Concordat, the application of the racial laws in Romania had created some — as they called it in diplomatic terms — "inconveniences." And recently that same government had adapted a new principle: "The change of religion does not mean change of Jewish origin." So therefore, from that point on, the Christian-baptized Jews and recently converted Jews were considered racially Jews.[257]

As Romanian Jews were stripped of their civil rights, the nuncio faced a great challenge. A huge responsibility sat squarely on his shoulders, that of pressing the government for an official declaration that would guarantee to the Jews who had converted to Catholicism the same rights as those of the non-Jewish Catholic citizens. These rights would include the freedom to take part in religious practices as well as the rights to a religious education and to spiritual assistance of any kind by means of Catholic priests — whether in the army, in hospitals, in prisons, and so forth, in accordance with the Concordat.

Barbetta recalled the *note verbale* in which, a year ago, on July 21, 1941, the Romanian government had assured Cassulo[258] that "the Jews who have converted to the catholic religion benefit in religious matter of all the rights recognized by the Concordate, in particular, of the right to religious education, the right to spiritual assistance by catholic priests, and also of the right of access to all primary and secondary catholic schools. Although not complete, this declaration was considered by the Nuncio and the bishops to be satisfactory." It would be tempting to assume that with this official promise in his pocket, the nuncio would be able to sleep well and without worry, certain that the converts would be protected. Yet such an assumption would be wrong.

[256] ASRS, AA.EE.SS., Romania 149, f. 225, internal note of Msgr. Barbetta, November 9, 1941.

[257] ASRS, AA.EE.SS., Romania 149, f. 218, handwritten note of Msgr. Barbetta.

[258] ASRS, AA.EE.SS., Romania 149, f. 127ʳ, *Note verbale* of the Romanian Ministry of Foreign Affairs to the apostolic nunciature, July 21, 1941, alleged to the report of Msgr. Cassulo to Card. Maglione on "Education and religious instruction of baptized Jews," July 28, 1941 (ff. 126ʳ/ᵛ).

In fact, the portion of the Romanian political establishment that wanted to prosecute the Jews had not yet decided to desist from its intent. It was evidently looking for another trick, hoping to catch some error in the clergy's actions on the matter of converting Jews. It did not escape Msgr. Barbetta's attentions that "at a distance of almost a year, that is on the 18th of April 1942, Minister Papp, the Ambassador to the Holy See, asked Cardinal Maglione [i.e., the secretary of state] to transmit to the Pope the plea of his government to … restrain the conversions of the Jews to Catholicism, while they [these conversions] were suspect or at least that they would be postponed till after the war."[259] The minister of the Romanian embassy to the Holy See met with Maglione and insisted the Holy Father would be given personally the formal plea from the government of Bucharest that "due to the enormous influx of requests for baptisms by Jews, in numbers too enormous and thus suspect, one suspends at least for a while (for example till the end of the war) the baptizing of Jews in the Church." In that meeting, Cardinal Maglione had responded to the Romanian diplomat that "the ecclesiastical authorities in Romania did everything possible not to let themselves be misled. To recommend them to be attentive and prudent in this respect seems, in my opinion, superfluous. However, to please the Government, one will tell the Nuncio to make the usual recommendation and with the necessary tactfulness: it is not customary to go beyond that."[260] As would be expected, Pope Pius XII was kept continuously abreast on the issue.

Msgr. Barbetta's internal note continued: "Cardinal Maglione, after having given clear clarifications on the strange presumption of the government, asked the Nuncio if he ever had run into an abuse in the interpretation of the rules given in this matter by the Holy Office." This is in line with the information that had come into the Cabinet a few months earlier, alerting that "the Jews, in mass, ask in Romania to become catholic; measures are taken on that issue by the Ecclesiastical authorities."[261]

Cardinal Maglione was somewhat surprised by the Romanian government's strange request but knew that competences on these doctrinal matters lay in other hands. He immediately sent an order "to transmit to the Holy Office the Nuncio's reports, but also to keep a copy of them on hand, and inform Msgr. Cassulo that his report has been transmitted to the Holy Office."[262]

[259] ASRS, AA.EE.SS., Romania 149, f. 218ᵛ, handwritten note of Msgr. Barbetta.

[260] ASRS, AA.EE.SS., Romania 149, f. 153.

[261] ASRS, AA.EE.SS., Romania 149, f. 146, cover of the report of Msgr. Cassulo to Card. Maglione, December 22, 1941.

[262] ASRS, AA.EE.SS., Romania 149, f. 146.

It took just a week to get a response from the Holy Office. The reply reaffirmed what was in its former response on this question, but specified certain elements:

> However, when it is indisputably established that baptism cannot be postponed without great difficulty until the completion of training, and when the priests' conscience is weighed down heavily due to this, they may baptise those, but only those, they know to be on the one hand well taught on the basic truths of faith that are indispensable to a Christian life, and on the other hand are sincerely willing to live a life according to the precepts of the Catholic faith and who will later complete catechism in order to be admitted to Holy Eucharistic Communion.[263]

When Cassulo had the opportunity to read this particular statement, he surely breathed a sigh of relief.

After giving his explanations on the rather odd request of the Romanian government — that of suspending Baptisms until after the war — Cardinal Maglione bluntly asked Cassulo if he had ever experienced or become aware of any abuse of the rules of Baptism as decreed by the Holy Office. Of course, the nuncio fully denied such a thing. He politely reminded Maglione of his own words when he once wrote that "in the spiritual field, one cannot put up obstacles when the conversion is work of the Divine grace. And this is the principle point of the discussion, from the first moment on, when the movement of the Jews towards the Church became greater."[264] To his defense, Cassulo argued: "In general the bishops and the priests all respected the given instructions, but some exceptions have been verified. I know that the archbishop of Bucharest had to intervene to clamp down on abuses committed by one or two oblivious priests who were too easy on admitting to the baptism individuals who were not always orderly prepared and moved by grace."[265]

Then he repeated the words he had written at the end of the previous year:

> It is a fact that offers a great deal on which to reflect. Important persons, professionals, business men alike want to be instructed in the Catholic

---

[263] ASRS, AA.EE.SS., Romania 149, f. 158ᵛ, copy of the letter of the Holy Office to Msgr. Cassulo, April 30, 1942.

[264] ASRS, AA.EE.SS., Romania 149, f. 161, letter of Msgr. Cassulo to Card. Maglione, May 24, 1942.

[265] ASRS, AA.EE.SS., Romania 149, ff. 161–161ᵛ, letter of Msgr. Cassulo to Card. Maglione, May 24, 1942.

faith. They leave their activities and interests at any moment of the day in order to get the religious instruction and preparation for the baptism.... When the Romanian government, in its high wisdom and compliance has given in to our insistence for the recognition of the rights of the Church, especially for those rights regarding education and religious assistance of the newly baptized, the Jews have felt supported and comforted. This has been very useful for the movement of conversions. It is true that many were not able to obtain it all, but the fact of being able to call oneself catholic is a great recommendation. When the occasion occurs, however, I will take in account what His Eminence has thought useful to point out.[266]

*

*   *

Cassulo had to keep things going on both sides. On June 19, 1942, when he was received by Minister Radu Davidescu, the mood was not very different from before. In his diaries he described that "having drawn the minister's attention to the condition of the converted Jews, especially those of Cernăuți [in Bukavina], he told me that the matter is very delicate and that, according to the government, the conversions of the moment are largely driven by material interests. In this regard, he recommended that the Catholic clergy has to be very cautious." Nuncio Cassulo went back home, and he did "not fail to ensure that the Catholic Church followed, as always, the strictest instructions on this important matter."[267] He would warn the clergy of this again and again.

The same was true when the Sisters of Notre Dame de Sion visited the nunciature on July 15, sisters to whom he had "given instructions on the admission of Jews to baptism so that no abuse occurs."[268] That evening, however, it seems a bit of trouble began for Msgr. Cassulo, because he noted in his diary that during her visit

Miss Nanu, a convert, and who appeared to me [Cassulo] a good practicing Catholic, asked me what I think about the current

[266] ASRS, AA.EE.SS., Romania 149, f. 161ᵛ, letter of Msgr. Cassulo to Card. Maglione, May 24, 1942.
[267] ASRS, AA.EE.SS., Romania 186, vol. 31, p. 5.
[268] ASRS, AA.EE.SS., Romania 186, vol. 31, p. 56.

conversion of the Jews. I replied that conversion must be a work
of divine grace and that, before admitting someone to baptism,
the church uses and keeps its attention on this very important
point. She understood, and warned me of abuses that, unfortunately, occur both by those who admit and instruct them as
well as by those who ask to join the Catholic Church for human
motives only.[269]

Was Miss Nanu's comment only a warning? Or was it also a threat? Could it be
that Catholics such as Miss Nanu, in particular those who had recently converted,
were showing intolerance toward their former coreligionists? Certainly, Cassulo
was perfectly aware of the dangerousness of the rumors that were circulating and
of which Miss Nanu had become a spokesperson. *"Le bien ne fait pas de bruit; le
bruit ne fait pas de bien"* — good makes no noise; noise does no good. Cassulo
would often write on the guard sheets of his diaries meaningful excerpts from
religious texts, aphorisms, maxims, and other quotations that he considered to
be particularly significant. Well, the St. Francis de Sales quote regarding noise
producing no good, which was transcribed at the end of one of his diaries, must
have sounded very appropriate to him on this occasion.[270]

Coincidence or not, Miss Nanu had barely left the nunciature when surprising things began to happen. During their personal visit to the nunciature in July
1942, Msgr. Durcovici, the vicar-general of the Archbishopric of Bucharest, along
with the parish priest of Barazia, told Msgr. Cassulo "that an inspector of the
Ministry of Cults and a police officer showed up to carry out an inspection of
the parish registers in order to find out the number of baptized Jews, their names,
the name of who baptized them, and also to see related documents." Cassulo
recommended that both priests "pay very close attention to such an important
and delicate matter," but at the same time he suggested for the priests "to use a
polite and friendly tone and to show the inspector courtesy, not giving in to the
injunction, and . . . await instructions."[271] Msgr. Durcovici wrote to Cassulo on July
17 with more details. "He brought an account of the facts on the investigation

[269] ASRS, AA.EE.SS., Romania 186, vol. 31, pp. 56–57.
[270] ASRS, AA.EE.SS., Romania 186, vol. 32, p. 601.
[271] ASRS, AA.EE.SS., Romania 186, vol. 31, p. 59.

that the Ministry of Cults intends to execute regarding the baptism conferred on the Jews. An answer will be given in days" reported Cassulo.[272]

The day after receiving the account from Msgr. Durcovici, Nuncio Cassulo arranged a meeting with Minister Davidescu, the recently appointed minister of cults. At half past noon, he sat face-to-face with him. The first item on the agenda was "the baptism of Jews."[273] They agreed, in order not to complicate things, that the inspections would not take place anymore, but instead a note on the baptized would be transmitted to the Ministry of Cults. The purpose was to respond to the recent and always more severe anti-Jewish laws.[274] Cassulo reported all these facts to Rome.[275]

Immediately following the meeting with Minister Davidescu, Cassulo explained to Msgr. Durcovici until what point one could make concessions to the Romanian authorities: a list of the names of the baptized could be passed on. Anything beyond that was unacceptable. The police inspector and his right hand were received by the archbishop himself, who in a courteous yet firm way made them understand that "in the matters of the sacraments the Catholic Church is completely free and that no government whatsoever can interfere in such issues, not even the police. I can concede that a note will be handed over with the names of the baptized who have also followed all canonical norms."[276] And thus, a list indicating only the names of Jews who had converted and had become members of Catholic Church was handed out.

*

*   *

Back in Rome, the desk officer, Msgr. Barbetta, was quite alarmed by the news of "a Police inspector verifying the parish registers of Bucharest to find names of the baptized Jews and of the *priests who baptized* them."[277] Fortunately, this interference

[272] ASRS, AA.EE.SS., Romania 186, vol. 31, p. 63.

[273] ASRS, AA.EE.SS., Romania 186, vol. 31, p. 67.

[274] ASRS, AA.EE.SS., Romania 149, f. 198^v, report of Msgr. Cassulo to Card. Maglione, July 28, 1942.

[275] ASRS, AA.EE.SS., Romania 149, f. 198^v, report of Msgr. Cassulo to Card. Maglione, July 28, 1942.

[276] ASRS, AA.EE.SS., Romania 186, f. 198^v, report of Msgr. Cassulo to Card. Maglione, July 28, 1942.

[277] ASRS, AA.EE.SS., Romania 149, f. 219, handwritten note of Msgr. Barbetta.

had been modified for courtesy reasons and, as we were told, from now on only a summary list of the baptized was provided to the intruders. At least for the time being.

But Barbetta hardly had to wait a few weeks for his uneasy feelings to be confirmed. Toward the end of August, worse tidings were coming in from Bucharest. The copy of the aide-mémoire of the Ministry of Cults now lying on his desk stated that

> regarding the research done by a Delegate of the Ministry of Cults in the [Baptism] registers of the General-Vicariate of Bucharest, the Ministry of Foreign Affairs has the honour to inform the Apostolic Nunciature that the competent authorities, given the actual situation, are not able to renounce the right to surveillance and control. In the present exceptional situation, and taken in account also the dispositions of the VI art. of the concordat, the Ministry of Foreign Affairs pleads with the Apostolic Nunciature to not interpret these measures of control already taken, or to be taken in the future, by *the competent authorities* ... as an attack by the State on the exercise of the catholic cult [*sic*] in Romania.[278]

Cassulo responded to the Ministry of Foreign Affairs within ten days with a *note verbale,* leaving an official response to the content of the aide-mémoire pending for the time being.[279] First Rome needed to tell him what to do.

Along with Msgr. Barbetta, we can ask ourselves what was meant by "the competent authorities." Were they the Romanian Ministry of Foreign Affairs or that of the Cults?[280] Barbetta had come to realize that these two Romanian authorities contradicted each other, and he feared that a showdown between the two could be at the expense of the Holy See's attempt to obtain favorable measures for the Jews.

It did not escape the Cabinet's attention that Nuncio Cassulo limited himself to declaring that the order had come from the Ministry of Cults and that the government thought that the Jews converted to Catholicism to evade the new laws. Barbetta asked himself,

---

[278] ASRS, AA.EE.SS., Romania 149, f. 203, copy of the aide-mémoire of the Ministry of Foreign Affairs to the apostolic nunciature in Bucharest, 22nd of August 1942.

[279] ASRS, AA.EE.SS., Romania 149, f. 204, *Note verbale* of the nunciature to the Ministry of Foreign Affairs, August 31, 1942.

[280] ASRS, AA.EE.SS., Romania 149, f. 219, handwritten note of Msgr. Barbetta, September 27, 1942.

Which laws is Msgr. Cassulo referring to? Civil rights, employment, commercial activity, the military.... The Jews are already
excluded from all those. And this while he [Cassulo] is saying
nothing about the essential points of the matter: what is the aim,
evident or concealed, of the investigation? What were the consequences of the government's first investigation? Why do they want
to know the names of those priests that baptized? What could be
the "future" measures?[281]

Barbetta suggested "to limit for the moment the response of the Holy See to an
official visit of the Nuncio in Bucharest to General Antonescu, during which he
will state clearly that the new measures do not fit with the Concordate and that
if those new measures were enacted, the Holy See would have no other option
but to protest against it. In the meanwhile, one should investigate the aim the
Government has in mind with the requisitions." Cardinal Maglione fully agreed
with this proposal.

In Bucharest, this certainly came as a big disappointment for Msgr. Cassulo.
For more than a year he had hoped that the previous agreements with the Ministry
of Foreign Affairs would have put a nail in the coffin on this sad chapter in the
history of Romania.

All of Cassulo's sweet illusions were overshadowed by an unexpected change of
the law regarding the Jews in Romania. Msgr. Barbetta received information that the
Romanian government was about to enact a law by which all the Jews of Transylvania would be deported to Transnistria and their houses occupied by Germans who
had lost their houses due to bombardments. Among those "Hungarians of Hebrew
race" there were also three to four thousand who had converted more than twenty
years ago to Catholicism. Tardini wrote: "The Nuncio promised to go and talk with
Antonescu: now these Jews would like the Holy See to support the Nuncio's work, in
order that at least the converted Jews would not be deported."[282] The "at least" could
sound as if Tardini was not interested in the fate of the other Jews. It is, instead, given
in by his awareness that interventions of Rome and the Catholic Church at this point

[281] ASRS, AA.EE.SS., Romania 149, f. 219ᵛ, handwritten note of Msgr. Barbetta, September 27, 1942.
[282] ASRS, AA.EE.SS., Romania 149, f. 215, internal note of Msgr. Barbetta, September
11, 1942.

could at most reach still only the baptized Jews. Tardini's blunt comment sounded
as a clear order to Barbetta: "Support the work of the Nuncio!"

And it was the nuncio in Switzerland, Msgr. Bernardini, who sounded a new
alarm bell in the autumn of 1942, transmitting to Rome a report given him by the
president of the Jewish community in Switzerland.[283] His troubling report warned
of possible similar restrictive measures in the near future by the governments of
Spain and Hungary. It confirmed the earlier report in Latin written by the Jews of
Čzernivci[284] and sent in by Cassulo. Ever the cautious and careful man, Cardinal
Maglione wanted all new or unknown elements in those reports to be checked.[285]
All those documents were passed on to Msgr. Bafile, the *minutante* colleague of Bar-
betta in charge of Switzerland, to execute the order. In describing the deportation
of 185,000 Jews in autumn of 1942 and the abuses Jews in Romania were suffering,
Bafile gave central importance to the recent compilation of the Statute of Jews.

This Statute of Jews divided the Jewish people into four categories. The first
group was labeled "more favored Jews" (ex-soldiers, decorated in war, etc.). The
second group were "descendants of mixed marriages, as well as baptized Jews,"
who would receive similar treatment as those from the first group. The third group
would be labeled the "tolerated Jews" — those who were born in the old Romanian
borders; these would be confined in the ghettos by the government. The fourth
group contained the most unfortunate of all, the "unwanted Jews," all residing in
the annexed territories (Bessarabia, Bucovina, and Transnistria); they would be
deported as soon as possible.[286] Bafile annotated the words of Nuncio Cassulo, "the
desperate situation explains how a certain kind of psychosis [*sic*] is found in the
rush to receive the baptism, in the hope to save oneself of deportation, through
mitigation by the State and the protection of the Church."[287] On November 8, 1942,
Tardini urged Msgr. Barbetta "to compare Bafile's outline of the situation with all
the other information already in possession."

[283] ASRS, AA.EE.SS., Romania 149, ff. 164–180, typewritten report on the situation
of the Jews in Romania [October 1942].

[284] ASRS, AA.EE.SS., Romania 149, f. 192–193ᵛ, typewrittten report of the Jews of
Čzernivci to Pope Pius XII, June 24, 1942 (arrived July 6, 1942).

[285] ASRS, AA.EE.SS., Romania 149, f. 191, handwritten note of Card. Maglione, October
31, 1942.

[286] ASRS, AA.EE.SS., Romania 149, f. 189ʳ/ᵛ, internal note of Msgr. Bafile, November
7, 1942.

[287] ASRS, AA.EE.SS., Romania 149, f. 189ᵛ, internal note of Msgr. Bafile, November 7, 1942.

*

* *

Maglione and Tardini went to work with all their energy, mobilizing the Cabinet on the Romanian issue with a focus on the baptized Jews. On December 11, 1942, Mr. Mihai Antonescu, minister of foreign affairs, declared officially that the Romanian government would never leave behind the principles of the Christian religion, be it out of respect to the divine law or out of respect for the commitments of the Concordat. So, in Romania, the Jews could convert to Catholicism and as such obtain the rights to spiritual help guaranteed by law to all Catholics. Among these were the rights to religious liberty, Catholic schools, religious assistance in the army, and more. At least, this was according to the Ministry of Foreign Affairs. Different, not to say completely contrary, was the reality made clear in a circular letter sent by the Ministry of Cults to the Latin archbishop of Bucharest. Nuncio Cassulo reacted strongly to that circular letter with a *note verbale* to the vice-minister president of Romania.[288]

As Barbetta had suspected, the issue of the "baptized Jews" had become a test of strength between the moderate and fundamentalist wings of the puppet Nazi government. But as he keenly observed a few weeks later in Rome, "The State ignores at the civil level this conversion [to Catholicism] of the individual, and eliminates the Jews from its offices, public charges, etc. of which by force of the racial laws they are excluded." Barbetta asked his superiors if it was allowed to transmit his internal report on the baptized Jews in Romania to Msgr. Arata, the assessor of the Congregation for the Oriental Churches.[289] Cardinal Maglione responded, "That's ok." Before closing the envelope, Barbetta sat back in his chair and peered out the window at the outside world, a world of struggles and successes, sadness and joys, terrors and liberations. And he was well aware that while he was just one man, he was a cog in the enormous and important machinery that strived to bring relief. He realized very clearly the difficulty of the situation over there in Romania. He changed the ink of his pen, and before putting the letter into the envelope on February 13, 1943, he added with a different ink this conclusion: "The Holy See has,

[288] ASRS, AA.EE.SS., Romania 149, f. 254, copy of the *note verbale* of Msgr. Cassulo to Minister Antonesco, February 5, 1943.
[289] ASRS, AA.EE.SS., Romania 149, f. 245, internal note of Msgr. Barbetta, February 12, 1943.

on several occasions, attempted to intervene in favor of the baptized Jews in order that the application of the racial laws would have been alleviated in their favor."[290]

*

*   *

"Over there in Romania," late in the evening on that same day, Msgr. Cassulo arrived at the Ministry of Foreign Affairs for an official visit to the minister of foreign affairs and vice president of the Council of Ministers. Cassulo had written a short *note verbale* expressing his displeasure and surprise, requesting that the minister reexamine his former notes and responses; he also asked for an assuring word given the fact that the Holy See had considered the case closed. Now, sitting in front of Minister Mihai Antonescu, Cassulo described how the minister took up his phone and called his colleague at the Ministry of Education and Cults, Minister Petrovici. When the latter was told over the telephone about the circular letter that was sent earlier by his own ministry to the archbishop of Bucharest, "it seemed" — so reports Cassulo to Rome — "he came from heaven and he had known nothing about it.... Now, we agreed that the next day Minister Petrovici would write to me with assurance that the document had been withdrawn, and that the directives of the government on the question remained those decided earlier by the Council of Ministers, conform to the agreements taken between the government and Monsignor Apostolic Nuncio." When they touched on the aid for the Jews who had been transported to Transnistria, "Minister Antonescu responded that he, himself, had already given it some thought and that he did not intend to make a persecutor of himself, even if he had to act to conduct everything to perfection."[291] Once again, Cassulo had defused the situation.

At this point, Cassulo seemed convinced that the response given by Minister Antonescu in December had received the *"benestare"* — the blessing — of the Holy See.[292] This was a slightly exaggerated expectation by the nuncio, one that did not escape Barbetta's attention. Barbetta stated in his internal note that "in our response we said that the declarations of Minister Antonescu, in which he had stated that regarding the Jewish question the Romanian government would have

[290] ASRS, AA.EE.SS., Romania 149, f. 246^v, internal note of Msgr. Barbetta, February 13, 1943.

[291] ASRS, AA.EE.SS., Romania 149, f. 249^v, report of Msgr. Cassulo to Card. Maglione, February 14, 1943.

[292] ASRS, AA.EE.SS., Romania 149, f. 249, report of Msgr. Cassulo to Card. Maglione, February 14, 1943.

respect for the Christian principles, we noted that the Divine law and stipulations of the Concordate 'did honor' the Minister. We also said that one had to remain vigilant because it was important for words to turn into facts."[293] At the words "did honor the Minister," Tardini commented to Barbetta: "You see, Barbetta, when you write to Msgr. Cassulo, one must be very cautious also . . . regarding the honor!" In addition, Cardinal Maglione also spent a few words to explain this awkward and rough statement of Barbetta: "With Msgr. Cassulo one never knows where one will end up. Therefore I asked for the precedents on this case. Now, what to do?"[294]

Tardini's note is a perfect example of his well-known comments seasoned with pungent Roman sarcasm, which in this case — as often happens — leaves today's reader with an open question: What did the secretary of the Congregation for Extraordinary Ecclesiastical Affairs mean exactly by the word play on "honor"? Think back also to the quite suspicious question of Cardinal Maglione on the correct procedure regarding the Baptisms to Cassulo and the exaggeration of Msgr. Cassulo in having interpreted the response of the Holy See as an approval as mentioned by Barbetta at the beginning of the text. The most logical explanation is that the nuncio, in order to help as many Jews in Romania as possible, used cunning in an attempt to overcome political obstacles by turning Cabinetcracy to his own advantage, carefully weighing the words he used in the correspondence with his superiors and his Romanian interlocutors so that, in the meantime, the rescue mechanism based on Baptisms would not be stopped.

The fact that in Cassulo's diaries the concept that "conversion, more than a human thing, is divine work"[295] is cited by him more than once goes to support the interpretation proposed here. It seems as if one can read between the lines the favorable disposition of Cassulo toward the mass Baptisms of Jews that raised considerable problems for the Romanian government. Yet the nuncio, well aware that *scripta manent* (written words remain), never explicitly expressed himself in this sense, writing, rather, that it was a duty to abide by the rules issued by the Holy Office.

*

*   *

[293] ASRS, AA.EE.SS., Romania 149, f. 257, internal note of Msgr. Barbetta, March 4, 1943.
[294] ASRS, AA.EE.SS., Romania 149, f. 257, internal note of Msgr. Barbetta, March 4, 1943.
[295] ASRS, AA.EE.SS., Romania 186, vol. 31, p. 61.

In any case, through the joint efforts of Cassulo, Barbetta, Tardini, and Maglione during the mandate of Pius XII, some positive results for the Jews surely had been realized, given the gratitude expressed in person by the chief rabbi of Bucharest, Dr. Safran, during the spring of the following year. During the first week of March 1943, Dr. Safran paid a visit to the nunciature in Romania. The purpose of the visit was to present the greetings and best wishes from his community on the occasion of the anniversary of the Holy Father's election to the pontificate. Msgr. Cassulo notes that

> Grateful for the protection that His Holiness has granted and grants to his co-religionists, he [Dr. Safran] has asked me to convey to the Holy Father the expression of their gratitude. When questioned about the condition of civil internees, the Rabbi immediately understood that I had interpreted his desire to discuss the matter. In fact, he gave me a memo relating to many poor … orphans for whom he requested the kind attention of the Holy See and the Romanian government. A small photograph taken on the spot showed me the bleak condition of so many miserable people. I prayed that Dr. Safran keep me posted with a short report on the adult deportees in order to know the places where they are concentrated. Dr. Safran left me warmly grateful and moved.[296]

Even so, dark clouds still lingered on the horizon. For only two days later,

> back at the nunciature, I received Dr. Safran, the great Rabbi of Bucharest who gave me a second memorandum on the non-Aryan civilian deportees in Transnistria. It was recommended that action would be taken regarding the Romanian government in order to prevent foreign elements from exciting the local population and causing them to rage against the Jews. Illegal and even public posters were displayed throughout the city and it is feared that this month actions will move from threats to deeds. Having taken note of what has been shared with me, I continue to recommend that his community cooperate, calmly and peacefully, for the good of the country, remaining faithful to the law and divine commandments.[297]

[296] ASRS, AA.EE.SS., Romania 186, vol. 32, p. 3.
[297] ASRS, AA.EE.SS., Romania 186, vol. 32, pp. 9–10.

The situation was intensifying. Not a week later "after lunch, at sixteen, Msgr. Schubert came to me on behalf of a group of Jews of Austrian origin who are under threat to leave Romania by April. I promised to take care of it."[298]

> Later, Dr. Safran, the Rabbi of Bucharest visited again. He told me of the increasing difficulties. The Romanian government has conceded that a considerable number of Jewish children can pass through here and go to Palestine, but it appears that the German authorities are opposing it. Three children, traveling with others, were already stopped at the Bulgarian-Turkish border.... Rabbi Safran advised me to write to the Apostolic Delegate of Sofia to protect them in some way.[299]

The anecdotes in the nuncio's diaries show a persistent mutual understanding and respect between the two men, the rabbi and the nuncio. And Cassulo, in his turn, gave some useful instruction: "I advised him to write me a letter with all the data relating to the pitiful case. After assuring him that the Holy Father and his Nuncio make every effort to improve the condition of the Jews, especially of the deportees and that the Romanian government welcomes our proposals, Dr. Safran left my office, very grateful for the paternal treatment used towards his fellow citizens."[300]

Some of the positive effects of the work of the Holy See were noticed beyond the Romanian borders. On April 8, 1943, Nuncio Bernardini in Bern, Switzerland, transmitted to the Cabinet reports on the situation of the Jews in Poland, Romania, and Transnistria, reports that had been sent to him by Dr. A. Silberschein, the president of the "Committee for Assistance to the Jewish Population Affected by War." He added the comment, "In that [report] on Romania, one affirms that for a while the situation got better, probably in the aftermath of the steps taken by the Vatican."[301] And in Bucharest on April 11, "around eleven o'clock, Msgr. [Angelo] Prinetto, brought good news from Msgr. Roncalli and Msgr. Mazzoli."[302] One can only guess that behind these cryptic words of "good news" was the hidden message that they had succeeded in guiding some Jews, children or adults, toward freedom

[298] ASRS, AA.EE.SS., Romania 186, vol. 32, pp. 126a–127.
[299] ASRS, AA.EE.SS., Romania 186, vol. 32, p. 128.
[300] ASRS, AA.EE.SS., Romania 186, vol. 32, pp. 128–129.
[301] ASRS, AA.EE.SS., Romania 149, f. 267, letter of Msgr. Bernardini to Card. Maglione, April 8, 1943.
[302] ASRS, AA.EE.SS., Romania 186, vol. 32, p. 136.

and salvation. To learn more about that, one should listen to and read the words of the chief rabbi of Bucharest.

Newspaper interview of the chief rabbi of Bucharest, Dr. A. Safran.[303]

[303] ASRS, AA.EE.SS., Romania 149, f. 90.

In 1944, he declared: "Message of His Eminence the Great Rabbi of Romania Dr. Alexandre Safran, addressed to the Jews of everywhere, by the willingness of the representatives of the foreign press in Bucharest."[304] After he expressed his gratitude to King Michael I (the last king of Romania) for saving his life and that of many others, he posed the following question:

> But thinking back on a past so recent, on the chains of oppression that still seem so fresh, how can we consider it all over without thinking, with profound recognition, of our benefactors? My permanent contact with His Excellency the Apostolic Nuncio, the Dean of the Diplomatic Corps of Bucharest, and the pairing of my soul with his, have been decisive for the fate of our poor Community. In the house of this High Prelate, before his good heart I poured my warm tears, much as a distressed father would, for my Community that struggled feverishly between life and death. I cannot forget the drama of our interviews and the emotion shown by his Excellence during our interviews during autumn two years ago when the deportation of the Jews arrested in the country was decided. The intervention of His Excellence that followed these interviews managed to circumvent a total misfortune.[305]

And a bit later, in a newspaper interview of September 27, 1944, Safran attested:

> Among other interventions done in favor of my countrymen, there is the one I made to the Apostolic Nuncio, through whose understanding and kindness I sought the happy result of my efforts. A Jewish philosopher taught us that thankfulness is the memory of the heart. I must say that in the painful situation in which we found ourselves, after having carried out all the means and tried all possible ways to help my compatriots, I had nothing left but to entrust myself to the benevolence of Msgr. Apostolic Nuncio. In the serious dangers of those moments, His Excellency was unable to offer an appointment and so, ignoring all the protocol rules, I went to him unexpectedly in the evening. And with each subsequent visit, he received me

[304] ASRS, AA.EE.SS., Romania 149, ff. 92–96.
[305] ASRS, AA.EE.SS., Romania 149, f. 94.

with a big heart full of compassionate interest. His Excellency's interventions were decisive in the face of the perils to which our very existence was exposed. When our situation seemed desperate, his prodigious intervention raised us up from our unhappiness.

For two years, on dreadful days when the deportations of Romanian Jews outside Romania were already established and the deported were punished with compulsory labour, the high moral authority of Msgr. Nunzio has saved us. With God's help, he has worked to ensure that deportations would no longer take place. I will not forget the moving talks I had with His Excellency in those days. His words of encouragement always accompanied me even after he dismissed me.

Then he further explained Cassulo's efforts in detail:

His Excellency has begun the legal action for the relief to the Jews deported to Transnistria: he has always dealt with this painful matter in every detail. He visited Transnistria, entering the concentration camps and distributing considerable relief. The condition of the orphans has been close to his good heart all this time. He actively sought to repatriate all the Jews from Transnistria, but he took a special interest in orphans as would a loving father. With great satisfaction he communicated that he had obtained the approval for the orphans to leave for the Holy Land! I confess that it was a gift from God to have been able to bring such a great spirit closer to us in the current circumstances.[306]

The documents of the Historical Archive tell us further that Cassulo, for this operation in favor of the Jews in Transnistria, could largely count on the support of his colleague in Istanbul, Nuncio Angelo Giuseppe Roncalli. For on direct request of Isaac Herzog, chief rabbi of Jerusalem, in favor of fifty-five thousand Jews in Transnistria, the Cabinet orchestrated another safety line between the pope's nuncios in Bucharest and Istanbul.[307] Roncalli, after a private visit with the chief rabbi at

---

[306] ASRS, AA.EE.SS., Romania 149, f. 89, translation of an interview of Chief Rabbi Safran published in the newspaper *Mantuira* of September 27, 1944.

[307] ASRS, AA.EE.SS., Romania 149, ff. 70–76.

the nunciature of Istanbul, informed Cardinal Maglione by cable as follows: "It seems that a beneficial action could be done.... The Bucharest government could provide it immediately or at least permit them to evacuate."[308]

These are true signs that, in the darkest moments of human history, apostolic nuncios and apostolic delegates of Pius XII, all over the world, were operating for the good and fighting against evil. Evidently, those who managed to obtain the best results in pursuing the good worked in the service of others with humility, as Cassulo himself seems to tell us still today through his beloved "memorabilia" of quotations and maxims: "Nobody is richer, more powerful and freer than the one who knows how to leave himself and all things and put himself in last place."[309] Their actions, like drops sculpting the rock one chip at a time, moved in local politics with skill and cunning, and without "making noise," given that — as Cassulo reminded us — "*Le bien ne fait pas de bruit; le bruit ne fait pas de bien.*"[310]

---

[308] ASRS, AA.EE.SS., Romania 149, f. 75, cable of Nuncio Roncalli to Card. Maglione, February 28, 1944, at 8:00 p.m.

[309] ASRS, AA.EE.SS., Romania 186, vol. 30, p. 1f.

[310] An approximate translation is as follows: "Good makes no noise; noise does no good."

5

A Short Story of a Very Pitiful Case

ABBAZIA. TODAY THIS lovely Croatian coastal town is known as the thriving resort of Opatija, located on the Adriatic Sea. Its nineteenth-century houses and wide, blossom-fragranced boulevards hum with the energy of tourism. The picturesque Učka mountain range that rises behind the town offers biking and hiking trails for adventurous souls.

But the town has suffered through its share of political and social darkness. At the end of World War I, large portions of Croatia (formerly known as Dalmatia and then part of the Austro-Hungarian Empire) were annexed by Italy. From 1922 onward, the population was subject to a forced policy of Italianization imposed by the Fascist government of Mussolini. The heartless policy was intended to force cultural and ethnic assimilation among the local populace. Croatian society was to be crushed in favor of an Italian one. Only Italian speakers were permitted to hold positions of power within civil life, and Italian was the only language taught in schools. It was an internal, cruel suppression.

By 1939, the wider brutality of rising Fascism in greater Europe had reached Abbazia. Boatloads of refugees were arriving in droves.

These cold, exhausted, and fearful refugees included the Ferenczy family. Maria Gerda Ferenczy, her husband Oskar, and their eighteen-year-old daughter, Manon Gertrude, arrived in the Italian-annexed town of Abbazia that very year. This Austrian family was, like thousands of others of Jewish descent, on the run for their lives. Their once affluent lifestyle in tatters, all that remained were each other and the few small belongings they could carry in a suitcase. Their hearts would certainly have been filled with dread as to what had caused them to flee Austria, wondering if at some time in the future they might find some semblance of security.

A file on the Ferenczy family, preserved among thousands of other family files in the Historical Archive of the Secretariat of State, contains part of their life story. The Ferenczy file is surprisingly detailed, for which we have the highly literate Maria Gerda herself to thank, as she wrote regularly to the pope and members of the Cabinet. The official file is titled "Signora Gerda Maria Ferenczy — Israelita."

It is true the family was of Jewish heritage, but that's not how they identified themselves. Both Maria Gerda's and Oskar's families had been practicing Catholics for at least three generations. Both husband and wife had been baptized into the Catholic Faith at birth, and Maria Gerda studied at the elementary Catholic school of Notre Dame de Sion, very likely the one in Vienna. She described her family as "Catholics coming from Austria, ... who are now suffering only because the grandparents lived their lives without being baptized."[311]

But in those dark days of 1939, the Nazis and their racist supporters didn't care how generations of families lived their day-to-day lives, what they believed, or how they prayed. The Nazis and their ilk looked through a very specific, twisted lens in order to decide who was or was not a worthy human being. And that lens was focused only on genetic heritage.

Maria Gerda, who referred to herself as a "successful author and journalist," had watched as her family fell victim to growing anti-Semitic laws and chose to get out of Austria while they still could. The final straw came when her daughter Manon, a star pupil, had been taken out of school in her final year because Jews were no longer allowed a public education. After leaving Austria, the family initially found shelter in Zagreb, Croatia's capital.

Maria Gerda wrote that in Zagreb the "charitable Bishop Dr. Stepinac, with most generous way eked out our lives, until in May 1939 the local authorities in Zagreb converted to the same Nazi ideology. And all non-Aryans regardless of their religious denomination were expelled and handed over at the Italian border."[312] At this point, the family had to move from Zagreb to Abbazia. From that moment on, the family lived in abject fear, surviving day to day. The clothes on their backs, their wedding rings, every single possession they had left was sold so they could eat.

[311] ASRS, AA.EE.SS., Ebrei 37, f. 10.
[312] ASRS, AA.EE.SS., Ebrei 37, f. 10ᵛ.

One day — as she described it — she was on her knees before the Madonna following Holy Communion, wrecked with desperation and despair. But suddenly she had a moment of enlightenment, a revelation that she should open her "very heavy loaded heart to His Holiness Pope Pius XII and to ask him to strengthen me with advice on finding the strength to remain upright: I thought that, even if the whole world abandons me, the Holy Father cannot leave his tormented daughter unheard, the Holy Father will help us in order to have eternal salvation."[313] In her first letter to the pope, she confided that right before this powerful revelation, she had come from selling her treasured Bible in order to be able to buy bread.

Maria Gerda's first letter, dated November 16, 1939, explains that in Austria her family had been well-off and "respected people." Oskar had served as an army officer, later taking on a banking career and obtaining the position of director of the Wiener Grossbank. Together, Maria Gerda and Oskar had raised their daughter, Manon, "in a devout and humble way." But Manon "had been ripped out of school in the middle of her studies, and after the last years, the family suffered such poverty that, if God would not think about a miracle, we will soon be homeless."[314] She wrote that in Abbazia there was a handful of charity committees set up to help practicing Jews but that Christian Jews such as her family were "completely abandoned." This would have been both a cultural and personal shock to the family, being treated as the lowest of the low and having no one in the community who cared about their welfare. "Both myself and my daughter show damage of health. All the efforts we made to get passports to cross the ocean failed. Now we have put our only confidence in the grace of God. Without a miracle, there is no longer a way out."[315] At this point she signed off, enclosing a letter of personal recommendation given to the family by the Catholic Committee for Refugees of Zagreb, dated September 4, 1939. That committee had existed under the protection of the archbishop of Zagreb, Aloysius Stepinac. The letter was given to her by his personal secretary, Franjo Šeper, who many years later would become cardinal and prefect of the Congregation of the Holy Office. The letter of recommendation stated that the Ferenczy family had lived under the committee's protection and prayed whatever authority read it to please take their case into consideration. Maria Gerda had kept this precious letter safe for months, certain that at some point it would prove to be valuable.

[313] ASRS, AA.EE.SS., Ebrei 37, f. 11.
[314] ASRS, AA.EE.SS., Ebrei 37, ff. 10ᵛ–11ʳ.
[315] ASRS, AA.EE.SS., Ebrei 37, f. 11.

Not only did Maria Gerda's letter to the pope make its way to the desk of her intended recipient Pius XII, but he presumably read it personally and took it to heart. An internal memo, dated November 20, 1939, reads: "The family Ferenczy, non-Aryan, catholic (father, mother and 18-year-old daughter), refugees in Abbazia implore the H. Father to help her. A very pitiful case."

At the bottom of the memo, a suggestion followed: "Maybe a subsidy?"[316] Msgr. Dell'Acqua was given the task of dealing with this "very pitiful case." His superior, Cardinal Secretary of State Maglione, however, was quite uncertain about what to do next. He pointed out that Maria Gerda had not expressed a clear wish as to what kind of help she wanted from them.

Letter of recommendation from the Catholic Refugee Committee of Zagreb issued to the Ferenczy family.[317]

[316] ASRS, AA.EE.SS., Ebrei 37, f. 9bis.
[317] ASRS, AA.EE.SS., Ebrei 37, f. 12.

So, on November 22, two days after the pope had given order to follow up on the case, a dispatch signed by Maglione was sent to the bishop of the Diocese of Fiume, Msgr. Ugo Camozzo, with an instruction "to inquire on the type of help that could possibly be given to this family."[318]

No response was forthcoming.

On December 20, 1939, one month later, an increasingly desperate Maria Gerda Ferenczy again wrote to Pius XII. She told him that the family had asked permission to leave for Abyssinia (now known as Ethiopia), but as they did not possess the proper visas, she had been warned that if they risked travel there, they would be expelled at the border and handed over to the German authorities. There truly could be no worse fate than that.

After this warning she had sought additional information from the German consulate. She claimed that they made it clear in no uncertain terms that if the family did indeed attempt this travel, they would be arrested at the border and deported to a concentration camp in Poland. Maria Gerda's letter is one of the earliest pieces of evidence in the Historical Archive showing when the Vatican was informed of deportations to Poland. It is also of interest to note that the German consulate was willing to tell the family this.

Maria Gerda declared a "great faith in God, thanks to whom we get the strength to bear this terrible distress. It was again this morning as I was kneeling before the Holy Virgin, that the Holy Mother pointed again towards the feet of his Holiness the pope." She plead the pope for "mercy for his faithful children," begging him to make it possible for them to stay longer on the Italian territory until their immigration to Abyssinia or to another destination could be organized, in order to avoid "the hell of the German concentration camp."[319]

The urgency of Maria Gerda's request was noted by Pius XII and his staff, because the lines in her letter above are annotated in the left margin with sharp red pencil marks. And there, written on a little scrap of paper, is a synthesis of what Maria Gerda asked for: "Supplicates the Holy Father to have for herself and her family (husband and daughter) the permit to stay in Italy until they have the possibility to emigrate to Ethiopia or elsewhere. She is aware, by turning back to Germany they would all be deported to Poland."

[318] ASRS, AA.EE.SS., Ebrei 37, f. 13.
[319] ASRS, AA.EE.SS., Ebrei 37, ff. 14–15.

Immediately, Msgr. Dell'Acqua was instructed to prepare another dispatch to Bishop Ugo Camozzo of Fiume. It had been a full month since the bishop had been asked about this matter, and for some unknown reason he had failed to answer. He was now given firm orders to intervene with the Italian authorities with the aim of obtaining a permit for extended stay for the Ferenczy family.[320]

Internal note summarizing Maria Gerda Ferenczy's request to Pius XII.[321]

[320] ASRS, AA.EE.SS., Ebrei 37, f. 16.
[321] ASRS, AA.EE.SS., Ebrei 37, f. 13bis.

The dispatch made clear to Bishop Camozzo that there could be no excuse. It also informed him that the Secretariat of State was aware that, since December 15, all Italian prefectures had been authorized to allow German and Polish Jews, living on Italian soil, to remain until they found a new place to live. The draft of the dispatch to Bishop Camozzo, signed by Cardinal Maglione, bears a last-minute addition from Dell'Acqua. He wrote, "In consideration of this it seems superfluous, at least for now, for an intervention by the Holy See as was indicated, because ... the family Ferenczy, of Viennese origin will be able to benefit from this new disposition."[322] Bishop Camozzo should have shared the content of the letter with the Ferenczy family, who still lived in Abbazia in the guesthouse *Eremitaggio*.

The Cabinet sent out these very clear instructions on New Year's Eve of 1939. The year ended. 1940 began. Winter held the world in its chilly embrace but then at last gave way to spring. Yet the arrival of spring did not bring good tidings. Europe descended into further chaos and violence. But still no reply from Bishop Camozzo. Why he was so reticent remains unclear.

Then, at the end of April, a new letter addressed to the pope arrived. Again, Maria Gerda asked Pius XII to help her and her family immigrate to somewhere, anywhere. She wrote:

> Thanks to the "holysome" intervention of your Holiness, Emigrants were left in peace to live their miserable lives under the Italian sun during the first months of this year. But, today, on the 20th of April 1940, it was communicated that due to political complications the old dreadful ghost of the persecutions would rear its head again. They say that the moment Italy will give up its neutrality, they will put us over the border at the Brenner mountain pass.[323]

The Brenner Pass, the mountain border between Italy and Austria, had been annexed by Germany since the Anschluss — the incorporation of Austria within the German Reich — and was now a dreaded highway to Hell for refugees. Maria Gerda was all too painfully aware of this. She informed the pope that her family had tried constantly to get visas for Belgium, France, Portugal, and Switzerland, but without

[322] ASRS, AA.EE.SS., Ebrei 37, f. 16.
[323] ASRS, AA.EE.SS., Ebrei 37, ff. 7$^{r/v}$–8^r.

success. What poor Maria Gerda may not have known while stuck in Abbazia was how the situation for refugees had also rapidly deteriorated in these countries.

It is clear from the Historical Archive that the Cabinet kept a watchful eye on her case, as proves a July 1 internal note by the substitute Msgr. Montini that referenced the case.[324]

*

*   *

But more bad news was yet to come. Oskar was arrested with the accusation of being non-Aryan. A terrified Maria Gerda wrote that her husband had been taken to Torretta di Fiume, a detention center. Msgr. Dell'Acqua immediately prepared another letter, this time to Fr. Tacchi Venturi, at the Piazza del Gesù in Rome. [325] Tacchi Venturi was very well connected, known to have direct access to Mussolini and the official circles around him.

Dell'Acqua made it clear to Tacchi Venturi that Oskar Ferenczy's wife had directly implored the Holy Father for help. Dell'Acqua asked Fr. Tacchi Venturi if he could arrange a permit that would at the very least allow a priest to visit Oskar in the detention center in order to transfer messages to him from his wife as well as to comfort him with Holy Communion.

Venturi did as he was asked. He sent a letter to the chief of police in Rome stating that orders had been given to the Prefecture of Fiume that would allow a priest to visit a Mr. Francesco Oskar Ferenczy. The information was relayed to the Cabinet on July 19.[326]

As chance would have it, the head of the Office for Foreigners at the Questura of Fiume at the time was a man named Giovanni Palatucci. No one knew then that Palatucci, who is today a national hero in Italy, was part of the resistance. He bravely signed and falsified as many papers as he could for Jews across the area, helping these people escape. He was later caught, arrested, and deported to Dachau where he was murdered.

Some weeks later, on August 7, a letter from Maria Gerda arrived by express post. Maria Gerda stated that the mother superior of the Sisters of Notre Dame de Sion in Trieste had informed her that the pope might have visas for Brazil. She

[324] ASRS, AA.EE.SS., Ebrei 37, f. 17.
[325] ASRS, AA.EE.SS., Ebrei 37, f. 18.
[326] ASRS, AA.EE.SS., Ebrei 37, f. 20.

appealed to him, requesting visas "if I would be able to bring forward a certificate of my religion, signed by the Bishop Ugo Camozzo."

Ever the forward thinker and planner, Maria Gerda explained she had already posted "by express" the certificate to Msgr. Dell'Acqua. This was now a "matter of life and death for my husband" because "Oskar, although he survived all these hard times, has become very ill." Oskar's lungs had been left permanently damaged as a consequence of his four-year military service during the First World War. And now, "the absence of good fresh air and caring puts his life in danger." She hoped "to soon be in another part of the world with our child, to find liberation and salvation from the persecutions that for us as Christians by birth are *doubly hard to bear*."

Her letter to Msgr. Dell'Acqua is stamped in the Archives as having arrived in mid-August. The tone at the beginning of this letter was quite matter of fact and businesslike, asking "for the obtaining of a Visa for Brazil . . . highly urgent."[327] She also included a Baptism certificate from the Diocese of Fiume, which stated, "Mr. Oscar Ferenczi, his wife Maria Gerda and their daughter Manon, were baptized at birth in the catholic religion in Vienna."[328]

But quickly, the businesslike tone of her writing changed, revealing a growing depression and anxiety regarding her family's plight. She wrote:

> As a consequence of the race-laws we lost our complete fortune. And in those 2 years of emigration we drank the whole *cup of bitterness*. If we didn't have our faith, the profound belief and confidence in the Virgin Mary and her divine Son, we would not be alive anymore. The last 6 weeks drove us almost over the edge and my mind races in a panic from one problem to another. . . .
>
> *After receiving a Visa this will all be over*. And therefore, I beg you in the name of our Lord, give the order for the issuance of the Visa by *telegraph*, for each hour *passing holds the fate of* 3 faithful people who may be or no longer be. If possible, please, inform the Questura (Police Chief) of Fiume by telegraph.
>
> *You will save a family*.
>
> I pray to the Holy Virgin to give my plea wings, and that she blesses you with them.

[327] ASRS, AA.EE.SS., Ebrei 37, f. 23ᵛ.
[328] ASRS, AA.EE.SS., Ebrei 37, f. 25.

At the bottom of the letter, she added the names and dates of birth of herself and her family: "Franz Oscar Ferenczy 25 August 1889, Roman catholic, Maria Gerda, 29 March 1894, Vienna, Roman Catholic, Manon Gertrude Ferenczy 4/12 1920."[329]

During that long, tumultuous summer of 1940, the escalating war occupied every waking moment at the Cabinet as they dealt with crisis after crisis. But they did not give up on this family.

Immediately after Dell'Acqua received Maria Gerda's letter, an emergency subsidy of 800 lire (about $600) was transmitted to the Ferenczy family. The family's file in the Historical Archive shows that although Maria Gerda had directly requested the embassy of Brazil for visas, she had not received any.[330] Her frustration and anxiety had to be great at this point, having tried and tried to no avail. On August 12, the Brazilian consulate of Trieste informed Maria Gerda that the formalities for the concession of visas would begin only after the request was authorized by the Brazilian embassy to the Holy See.[331] The information she was given was as conflicting as it was confusing. But then Don Angelo Comoretti, a priest of the Diocese of Fiume, assured her that he had heard from Bishop Camozzo that the Brazilian embassy to the Holy See had already authorized the request.

Puzzled and uncertain as to what steps had actually been taken regarding her visa request, Maria Gerda wrote once more to Dell'Acqua on August 17 in the hope of clarifying the matter. When he heard that she had been told the embassy had approved her request, Dell'Acqua was most displeased. Because sadly, it was not true. In reality, the Holy See had only informed the bishop of Fiume that they "had interested the Brazilian Embassy"[332] to her request — not that it had been authorized. Internal notes reveal Msgr. Dell'Acqua feared that misleading information or false whispers could risk blocking or unravelling the whole case.

Yet on August 19, 1940, Cardinal Maglione was finally able to undersign a letter in which he stated that the embassy of Brazil to the Holy See had indeed authorized visas for the Ferenczys. He alerted Bishop Camozzo about this and instructed him to inform Maria Gerda at once.[333]

[329] ASRS, AA.EE.SS., Ebrei 37, f. 24ᵛ.
[330] ASRS, AA.EE.SS., Ebrei 37, f. 31.
[331] ASRS, AA.EE.SS., Ebrei 37, f. 33.
[332] ASRS, AA.EE.SS., Ebrei 37, f. 32, handwritten note of Dell'Acqua in the margin.
[333] ASRS, AA.EE.SS., Ebrei 37, f. 34, draft of letter of Card. Maglione to Msgr. Camozza.

Finally, the family could seek a new life on the other side of the world. They set sail on a boat, the aptly named *Cape of Good Hope*, and headed out across the wide Atlantic. All was well that ended well.

Or so it seemed.

Almost one year later, in July 1941, an urgent telegram sent by the *Cape of Good Hope*'s chaplain arrived in the office: "*Polizia RioJaneiro respinge sbarco Oskar Ferenzi Non Riconosce Visto Intervenite Urgentissimo Per Mezzo Nunciatur Presso Polizia RioJaneiro Ferenczi Rimane a Bordo Cabo Esperanza*" It was signed: "Capellano."[334]

It translates as "The police of Rio de Janeiro rejects the arrival on land of Oskar Ferenczy. Doesn't recognize his visa. Most urgent intervention is asked by means of the nunciature to the police of Rio de Janeiro. Ferenczi remains on board of the boat *Cabo de Esperanza*."

The agony of Maria Gerda and her family is impossible to imagine. Brazil was almost within touching distance. No doubt they could look out from the ship and see the shore of what they saw as their promised land, and yet they were stranded at sea as surely as they'd been stranded on land back in Italy. Just when they thought they would be safe, once again they were not.

The Cabinet sprang into action. A cable was sent immediately, confirming the validity of the visas. In pencil underneath the cable Tardini scrawls a little message of hope: "That it goes well!"[335]

This time it did.

On the evening of July 29, 1941, Maria Gerda, Oskar, and Manon Ferenczy set foot on Brazilian soil. Their future was uncertain, but this family of three was together and alive.[336]

*
*   *

The case of Maria Gerda, Oskar, and Manon Ferenczy offers a great deal to consider. It is obvious that Christian-baptized Jews found themselves literally caught and crushed between their two identities. As racial discrimination laws intensified, there was no longer a differentiation between baptized or non-baptized Jews. The laws only considered, with detached coldness, race and Jewish descent.

[334] ASRS, AA.EE.SS., Ebrei 37, f. 36.
[335] ASRS, AA.EE.SS., Ebrei 37, f. 36.
[336] ASRS, AA.EE.SS., Ebrei 37, f. 38, cable of the apostolic nunciature, July 30, 1941.

Gerda herself revealed this clearly and repeatedly in her letters to Pope Pius XII. Wherever the family sought solace they found only fundamental intolerance toward them, from Vienna and Zagreb to Abbazia and Fiume, and even on their arrival on the shores of Rio de Janeiro. And when it wasn't racial laws that hindered them, there were numerous Cabinetcratic quagmires. Another detail of the story is interesting. When Camozzo, the bishop of Fiume, failed to respond immediately to the first dispatch of the secretary of state, the Cabinet got quite frustrated and with a second dispatch urged the bishop to act.

Also interesting is the continued story of the prefecture and the related Questura of Fiume. I mentioned above that in those days the head of the Cabinet for Foreigners of the Questura was Giovanni Palatucci. He is a martyr of Dachau and a known resistance hero who has been remembered with a tree at Yad Vashem, the World Holocaust Remembrance Center in Jerusalem. The archives preserve a postwar newspaper article on Giovanni Palatucci.

Published in the *Jerusalem Post* of Thursday, July 17, 1952, it reads:

> Ramat Gan Street Named After Priest
>
> RAMAT GAN, Wednesday — A street near Tel Binyamin is to be named after an Italian priest who was instrumental in saving the lives of many Jews during the war and who was later deported to Dachau camp and murdered there. The priest was Dr. Giovanni Palatucci. The street will be named "Rehov Hapodim" (Dr. Giovanni Palatucci). Hapodim means "The Redeemers."[337]

The journalist made an error by identifying Giovanni Palatucci as a priest. He was a police official and an ordinary Catholic. Perhaps the confusion occurred because Giovanni was the nephew of another Palatucci, the Franciscan bishop of Salerno, also famous for his help and assistance to Jews.

In the case of Maria Gerda and her family, it is easy to envision a successful, behind-the-scenes line of action taken on their behalf. Even if it seems that certain people did not have any direct contact with the family or between each other, the story suggests a large web of individuals who steadfastly took part. None would have been successful without the support of the others. All were driven by their common Christian inspiration.

[337] ASRS, AA.EE.SS., Palestina 44, f. 1.

Those who intervened for the family can be called heroes. But perhaps we can paraphrase George Orwell and say that some heroes are more hero than others. While Palatucci, of the Prefecture of Fiume, has a tree on the Yad Vashem hill, Pius XII doesn't. Instead, for decades his reputation has been tarnished as he has been painted a sympathizer of Hitler. But a woman named Maria Gerda most certainly knew this not to be so.

6

A Tale of Secret Informers

THE HORRIFIC, GROWING specter of Nazi terrorism had been threatening both Jews and Catholics for years. Yet no less frightening was the menace and insistent aggression of the Soviet Bolshevik army toward Catholics in those first years of World War II. The thousands of documents preserved in the Historical Archive of the Secretariat of State on these terrible circumstances of Soviet and Nazi occupation, in Poland in particular, are a testament to the constant concern it represented for Pius XII and the secretary of state. The Cabinet did not just sit and stare. The members were greatly troubled and determined to do all they could to alleviate or circumvent the horrors the occupations presented. What the Cabinet needed was reliable information. Therefore, in order to learn what was really happening in the now almost impenetrable East, an active network of trusted, and sometimes less trustworthy, informers was set up.

In October 1940, the Cabinet registered *ad futuram rei memoriam* (to serve as a permanent documentary record of a fact) that a man named Fr. Jerzy (George) Moskwa had had face-to-face discussions with Pius XII and Cardinal Secretary of State Maglione,[338] the prefect of the Congregation for the Oriental Churches, Cardinal Tisserant, Foreign Secretary Msgr. Tardini, and the substitute Montini. These intense discussions centered on the oppressive religious conditions under the Soviet government of Russia. Fr. Moskwa knew very well what he was talking

[338] ASRS, AA.EE.SS., Stati Ecclesiastici 688a, f. 44 (pro memoria), October 12, 1940.

about, as he had spent time undercover, dressing as an ordinary Russian and enduring the hardships of a Russian workman.

But who was Fr. Moskwa? He was born in Zurich, Switzerland, in 1910 and attended Kraków University. He graduated from the philosophy department in 1935, then continued his studies in the theology department of the Jesuit Gregorian University in Rome. There he graduated in 1939 and, at age twenty-nine, was ordained a priest of the Oriental (Eastern) Rite. A courageously pious man, Moskwa first served in Albertyn, outside Slonim (which was at that time part of Poland but is now in Belarus), where the Jesuits had their novitiate, and then became a professor and rector of the seminary in the Ukrainian city of Dubno. In December 1939 — during the Soviet occupation — he traveled to the city of L'viv (now in Ukraine, at the time part of Poland) with a false passport and secured a job at a petroleum depot of Neftegaz.

Moskwa lived in constant danger under the intense and constant scrutiny of Soviet officials, and so once back in Rome in October 1940, aside from the above-mentioned conversations, he appealed to the pope for a papal blessing for himself and his companions. In his appeal he also passed on the greetings of the Catholic metropolitan archbishop of Leopoli in Ukraine, Andrej Szeptykyi.

From the outset, Szeptykyi had taken a great interest in Moskwa's hidden mission, "very small for the moment, but with the help of God one hopes it will little by little grow larger."[339] However, securing the meetings in Rome with the pope and his collaborators would not take place without a hitch.

Earlier that year, at the end of January 1940, Moskwa had crossed the border into Poland using an Italian visa on a passport obtained through the mediation of the secretary of state.[340] Documents preserved in the Historical Archive tell us he returned to L'viv. Seven months later, in the late evening of August 23, 1940, the secretary of state in Rome received an urgent cable from Nuncio Angelo Rotta in Budapest saying that Moskwa was without a passport and urgently needed to speak with the Holy See in the name of Archbishop Andrej Szeptykyi. He also needed to receive instructions before "his return in Poland-Russia."[341]

[339] ASRS, AA.EE.SS., Stati Ecclesiastici 688a, f. 44 (pro memoria), October 12, 1940.
[340] ASRS, AA.EE.SS., Stati Ecclesiastici 688a, f. 62.
[341] ASRS, AA.EE.SS., Stati Ecclesiastici 688a, f. 74, message in code, Msgr. Rotta to Card. Maglione, from September 23, 1940.

Apparently, a few days earlier, on August 15, 1940, Moskwa had been arrested by Hungarian guards while attempting to cross the border illegally. Sent to prison in Budapest, he was able to alert others of his arrest through the prison chaplain, not only his fellow Jesuit fathers, as literature generally suggests,[342] but also the official channels of the Holy See, as we saw from Rotta's cable. Thanks to their joint intervention, he was released two months later.

But the difficulties facing Fr. Moskwa regarding a departure from Hungary and entry into Italy were immense. With the war in full expansion, it was far too dangerous and complicated to travel across Germany. He suggested an organized transit to Venice.[343] Diplomatic interventions were made on his behalf. On September 28, 1940, the Italian government's Ministry of Foreign Affairs informed the Cabinet that the "known" father has been given a permit to come to Rome by plane.[344]

Moskwa didn't arrive when expected. Uneasy about his continued absence, the substitute Montini sent a coded message back to Budapest on October 4 to ask if the "known" father could come to Rome or if it would be easier to send someone to Budapest to talk with him there. On October 5, 1940, however, Moskwa finally made it onto a plane and into Rome.[345]

Now safe in Rome in late autumn of 1940, Fr. Moskwa prepared an extended and secret report. During the face-to-face meetings, he told the secretary of state's office that "if His Holiness would deign to hear some information, then Father Moskwa would be most willing to volunteer it, with as much accuracy as possible."[346]

His secret report, some sixteen pages long, was submitted on December 28, 1940. He indeed offered an immense number of details, focusing on Church-related issues that covered the devastated religious situation under the Russian occupation of Poland, the religious situation in Russia itself, and some observations on the Red Army.[347] At that time in Ukraine and Poland, the Bolsheviks were aggressively targeting Catholics and Church institutions.

---

[342] University of Notre Dame, *Book of Remembrance, Biographies of Catholic Clergy and Laity Repressed in the Soviet Union (USSR) from 1918 to 1953* ().

[343] ASRS, AA.EE.SS., Stati Ecclesiastici 688a, f. 70 (message in code, from October 23, 1940; they changed the key of the code).

[344] ASRS, AA.EE.SS., Stati Ecclesiastici 688a, f. 67 (message in code, from September 28, 1940).

[345] ASRS, AA.EE.SS., Stati Ecclesiastici 688a, f. 65 (message in code, from October 5, 1940).

[346] ASRS, AA.EE.SS., Stati Ecclesiastici 688a, f. 44.

[347] ASRS, AA.EE.SS., Stati Ecclesiastici 688a, ff. 46–61.

But in spite of what appeared to be very solid credibility, Fr. Moskwa's efforts were not appreciated by everyone. Some fellow Jesuits in Rome threw a shadow of great doubts on the reliability of this information and on the trustworthiness of Fr. Moskwa himself. A letter that accompanied the report, sent from the Jesuit headquarters in Rome, attempted to undermine it. Handwritten comments on the bottom sneakily say: "P.S. Your Reverend Father knows very well F[ather] M[oskwa], and so you would also know very well that one should take his information *cum grano salis* [with a grain of salt]!" The last three words are underlined in red for maximum effect. PHOTO [348]

A letter expressing criticism of Fr. Moskwa.[348]

This sheds a troubling light on the atmosphere in some Church circles. They were underestimating just how bad the situation was in Europe by dismissing grassroots-level reports coming in from priests and religious fathers who wrote about church buildings being closed and devastated, of mass deportations of Catholics and so forth, as mere exaggerations. Or were his fellow Jesuits perhaps just envious?

Moskwa's report pulls no punches. He tells of over half a million Ukrainian citizens being deported under the Bolsheviks. Yet notwithstanding the relentless

[348] ASRS, AA.EE.SS., Stati Ecclesiastici 688a, f. 45.

anti-religious propaganda spread by the Russians, churches were nevertheless filled up with devout, dedicated people who prayed fervently.[349]

"A particular cruelty during these deportations," he cited,

> are the deportation of some students of the Santa Maria Magdalena school in Leopoli [L'viv]. Poor children that, on a day that they went to school as always were, without being able to communicate with their parents, put on camions, brought to the railway station, and then closed up in very cold wagons and deported. Now, it happens frequently that young girls on their arrival are forced to marry some local men. So is the case of a young niece of professor Wolańczyk of Leopoli [L'viv], a very delicate woman with university schooling, who was subjected to violence on her arrival after deportation and forced to marry a peasant cattle farmer. To avoid such disgrace, our deported youngsters frequently marry among themselves as early as the age of 14.[350]

Even though the Jesuits threw scorn on some of Moskwa's testimonies, it appears the Holy See took him seriously and wanted his mission to continue. To have such a daring man "in the trenches," so to speak, was exactly what they wanted and needed. Therefore, they asked him to return to the Soviet zone to proceed with his "pastoral ministry," which in reality would also serve as an undercover investigation.

For the Church hierarchy remaining in Poland the dangers continued to be grave. The Polish embassy to the Holy See reported in a confidential note regarding Archbishop Romuald Jałbrzykowski of Wilno:

> He was forced in the last few days to present himself to the Bolshevik Police Cabinet where he had to undergo numerous interrogations, and where he was menaced with the threat of deportation. This threat seemed so serious that Monsignor Jałbrzykowski went subsequent interrogations with a little suitcase in his hand, declaring to the Soviet authorities that he was prepared to be taken away at any instance. It seems the esteem of which the Archbishop of Wilno enjoys, not only by the Catholics but also by the Orthodox,

---

[349] ASRS, AA.EE.SS., Stati Ecclesiastici 688a, f. 52.
[350] ASRS, AA.EE.SS., Stati Ecclesiastici 688a, ff. 52–53.

the Jews, and even the Bolsheviks continues to grow. And that is one of the reasons that attract the difficulties to him from the Bolshevik authorities.[351]

Until the summer of 1941, Poland was divided into two occupied zones, one by the Soviets and the other by the Nazis, the second of which caused just as many worries for the Holy See. The secretary of state received supplementary information through the apostolic delegate in London. The pope's diplomat transmitted a "memo" written by the colonel chaplain of the Polish army, the Reverend Zygmunt Kaczyński, who wrote:

> Of recent months both the press and the wireless of Germany have been reporting abroad that there is no religious persecution in Germany, and that the Catholic Church both in the Reich, and also in the occupied countries enjoy complete freedom. That under the Nazis religious life is developing and growing more profound, that the Catholic clergy and laity have every facility in this regard.
>
> In fact, the Vatican wireless in its broadcasts on November 16th and 17th have denied all this, stressing the particularly "brutal" stance the German government takes toward the Church in Poland, yet German propaganda has not ceased to tell the world of the tolerance of the Nazi government.
>
> During the past few days the Polish Government has again received information from Poland of even more unusually harsh persecutions of well-known and eminent Catholics.[352]

He cited this case:

> Particularly terrible has been the fate of Wladyslaw Tempka, a lawyer in Cracow, and his wife Sofia, who were horribly beaten and have been imprisoned ever since. Recently we have received the news, that Mr. Tempka has been deported from Cracow to a concentration camp, while his wife Sofja, who is pregnant, is in the prison hospital in Cracow. Their two young children are left at home without

[351] ASRS, AA.EE.SS., Stati Ecclesiastici 688a, f. 92, confidential note of the Polish embassy to the Holy See to the secretary of state, March 27, 1941.
[352] ASRS, AA.EE.SS., Stati Ecclesiastici 688a, f. 24, account of Canon Zygmunt Kaczyński, January 28, 1941.

parents, care or means of existence. Mr. Tempka is known all over Poland as an outstanding and meritorious worker in the Catholic Action for which he worked and which for many years he served faithfully. He is known as an unusual[ly] kind and self-sacrificing man. Even after Poland had been occupied by the Germans troops, he sent the undersigned monetary sums for the poor priests and churches. The Catholic spirituality and laity in Poland grieve for the fate of M. Tempka and his wife, but in their fear of the present situation they cannot help them in the least.[353]

Kaczyński's report continued: "Therefore, through me they implore Your Excellency to be kind as to ask the Apostolic See to intervene with the German Government on behalf of the Tempkas that they may be restored to liberty and enabled to educate their children."

Raw fear hung over Poland. In public, people tended to avoid each other's gazes, moving quickly from one place to another, uncertain from one moment to the next as to the danger they might encounter from their ever-vigilant and cruel occupiers. Even as the sun rose and birds sang in the blue skies overhead, there was very little song in the hearts of the Poles. Many wanted desperately to help the distressed victims like Władysław and his wife, but they knew that speaking or acting out was akin to suicide. The brutal reality was that although the Soviet and Nazi ideologies were different, they wreaked the same terror. Both Poland and Ukraine experienced the cruelties of deportations and deprivation of every human need. Families found themselves without enough clothing, food, or medicines. Many parents wept behind their hands as they tried to keep a brave façade. Young children wept openly.

Kaczyński had no way of knowing that relations between the Holy See and the German embassy to the Holy See were already extremely tense. Requesting help at this time was like asking for sun on a rainy day. He shared individual cases, each of which reflected the reality faced by millions of Polish Catholic people suffering under Nazi occupation.

At the same time, I take the liberty of asking for the gracious intervention of the Apostolic See on behalf of 35 professors of the

---

[353] ASRS, AA.EE.SS., Stati Ecclesiastici 688a, ff. 24–25, account of Canon Zygmunt Kaczyński, January 28, 1941.

Cracow University, who have been detained and oppressed since last year in Concentration camps at Oranienburg and Dachau. Among them several who were particularly well known in Polish Catholic circles. Of these the following are held in Oranienburg: Aleksander Birkenmajer, Wladislaw Semkovic, Father Marian Michalski, Father Jan Salamucha, Jan Miodonski. Of the mentioned professors, Birkenmajer, Semkowicz and Miodonski were ill in that camp. In the concentration camp at Dachau, the flower of the younger generation of Cracow professors of sciences have been languishing for a year. Among them are the following who are especially esteemed in the Catholic world and are members of the Catholic Action: Kasimir Piwiarski: lecturer on modern Polish history in the Department of Philosophy of the Jagiellon University, Kazimierz Lepszy: lecturer on universal history in the Department of Philosophy of the Jagiellon University.[354]

The scale of terror at that time in Poland is difficult to imagine. Countless innocent people of all ages, from the youngest child to the elderly, faced the horrors of torment and slaughter, first by the Soviets and then by the Nazis. The president of the Polish Republic himself, Władysław Rackiewicz, wrote to Pius XII early April 1941 and depicted the dire situation clearly: "Eighteen months after the aggressors won over the last Polish regular detachments that fought for the liberty of their homeland, the people are now suffering a persecution without precedent in European history.... The picture is very simple: all the Institutions and the Polish national patrimony are systematically destroyed, this while millions of human beings are menaced with extermination."[355]

President of Poland Rackiewicz warned the pope that the Germans had publicly declared that the Holy See agreed wholeheartedly with their policy, presenting the pope as a leader who had no concern for democracy nor individual liberties. They were doing all they could to convince the Polish public that the pope viewed the German "new order" with confidence and benevolent interest. The newspaper articles in possession of the secretary of state were but a minor part of all that was

[354] ASRS, AA.EE.SS., Stati Ecclesiastici 688a, ff. 24–27.
[355] ASRS, AA.EE.SS., Stati Ecclesiastici 688a, f. 104, letter of President Rackiewicz to Pius XII, April 6, 1941.

published in the whole of Poland. And — so wrote President Rackiewicz — "one can ask himself how many oral declarations on the same subject are made by members of the German administration and generally by the Germans present in Poland, in short, what is the role of the *Fluesterpropaganda* [whisper propaganda], in which the Germans are excelling better than ever."[356] Of this ambiguous ideological tactical agenda of the Nazis in Poland, the whisper propaganda and disinformation spread by the Nazi-minded press as well as the campaign of blasphemous ridiculing of the Catholic Faith, the Cabinet was briefed and itself already aware.[357]

Photographs of a mock service by German SS sent by the Polish embassy to the Holy See to the Secretariat of State, May–June 1941. One of these photos was published in the Times on May 20, 1941.[358]

[356] ASRS, AA.EE.SS., Stati Ecclesiastici 688a, f. 107, letter of President Rackiewicz to Pius XII, April 6, 1941.

[357] ASRS, Stati Ecclesiatici 688a, f. 433, note of the Polish embassy to the Holy See on "Propagande antichretienne en Pologne," March 8, 1941.

[358] Stati Ecclesiatici 688a, f. 416 and ASRS, AA.EE.SS., Stati Ecclesiastici 688a, f. 621.

The Polish president's letter was immensely troubling and required a strong, well-crafted response. On June 25, 1941, after a preparation of three drafts and several insertions by the pope himself and members of the Cabinet, a solemn and private letter was sent to President Rackiewicz. In this remarkable document, Pius XII made an assurance that there would be aid for the people of Poland, whether they be under Nazi occupation, on the run, or in asylum abroad. The letter asserted:

> Obstacles and misinterpretations could neither change our attitude nor suspend nor slow down the activity which today occupies such a large place in our paternal apostolic ministry. We intend to pursue it with all the means at our disposal; and as long as the sufferings of Our sons last, We will not omit anything that can alleviate their pains and bring them some relief, while We will continue to lift up to God Our fervent, supplicating, persevering prayer. It is above all in that which Our heart has trust in; it gives us more nourishment than daily food; and that's why We are hopeful that divine mercy and the arm of the Most High will shorten the days of pain.[359]

The moves of the pope were carefully observed by the Germans, and they used their observations in an attempt to force him into narrow diplomatic shoes. In fact, in December of that year, they sent a telegram of complaint regarding the letters the pope has sent to the Polish bishops as well as the personal letter to the Polish president Rackiewicz. It was the counselor of the German embassy to the Holy See who transmitted this message. *Minutante* Msgr. Samorè responded that "the Holy Father in those pontifical letters, responded to tributes he received, and did not enter in political questions."[360]

Those in the office in Rome did their best to gather more information on the professors of the Krakow University, but, after a few days of searching, Msgr. Samorè had to note that he couldn't find any files on the university.[361]

The Nazis found an "easy" but wicked way to break the opposition to them by the Orthodox Church in the country. Looking at the photo published February

---

[359] ASRS, AA.EE.SS., Stati Ecclesiastici 688a, ff. 114$^{r/v}$, letter of Pius XII to President Rackiewicz, June 25, 1941.

[360] ASRS, AA.EE.SS., Stati Ecclesiastici 688a, f. 155, telegram of the embassy of Germany to the Holy See to the secretary of state, December 18, 1941.

[361] ASRS, AA.EE.SS., Stati Ecclesiastici 688a, f. 23.

13, 1941, in the German-made Polish newspaper *Krakauer Zeitung,* one could, even today, easily be seduced into thinking that the Orthodox patriarch and his eminent committee were well disposed toward the Nazi occupants. The photograph shows the patriarch during the reading of a public declaration of loyalty to the Nazis.

Die Ergebenheitserklärung des Bischofs Palladius

Der Chef des Distrikts Warschau, Gouverneur Dr. Fischer, nahm — wie bereits berichtet — im Auftrage des Generalgouverneurs die Ergebenheitserklärung des Bischofs Palladius der Diözese Krakau und Lemkenland der Orthodoxen Autokephalen Kirche entgegen   Aufn.: Bil

Newspaper article announcing Palladius, the Orthodox Bishop of Krakow's, declaration of loyalty to the Nazis.[362]

The comment under the picture mentions "a ceremony that took place in Krakow that put to an end the difficulties that the occupants faced from the Orthodox leaders in the country." The cutout of the newspaper came from the Polish embassy to the Holy See. This last excerpt revealed the pressure the Germans exercised upon the Orthodox metropolitan Waledyński: "He was arrested, renounced 'freely' to

[362] ASRS, AA.EE.SS., Stati Ecclesiastici 688a, f. 87.

his charge, was then freed, then arrested again, freed, and again arrested. Seeing his diocese had in the interval been occupied by Bishop Seraphim Lade, a puppet of the Nazis, Metropolite Waledyńsky finally submitted himself completely to the German authorities. The Nazis organized a very special ceremony in order to put in evidence his submission."[363] This was an easy way to crush the opposition and one with 100 percent certainty of success. Propaganda would do the rest.

Meanwhile, in February 1941, Nuncio Angelo Rotta in Hungary informed the Cabinet that Fr. Moskwa, using yet another Italian visa organized by the Secretariat of State, had been able to pass the border of Hungary and return to Russian-occupied Poland. The news was transmitted by a Hungarian Jesuit father who learned this from the person who had accompanied and helped Moskwa pass the frontier. Moskwa was headed for L'viv. From there he promised to give a sign of life to the nuncio in Budapest, confirming that his return had gone well.[364] Despite the constant dangers, Nuncio Rotta's informant operation gave tangible results. In mid-April of 1941, Nuncio Rotta sent Rome the message that the "Polish refugees in Hungary have established a clandestine radio with which they can communicate with (the Archbishop) of Leopoli [L'viv]."[365]

A few weeks later, on June 30, Rotta wrote again. This time he informed the secretary of state that Wilk-Wilkoslawski, a companion of Moskwa to whom we will come back, had bad news on Moskwa. "The Rev. P. Moskwa S.J. passed the russian-hungarian border but was arrested in Skole by the Russian authorities. From that moment on, nothing is known of him."[366]

Reports indicate that he was most probably sent to the L'viv prison, then transferred to the larger Kiev prison. Over the course of several months, he was tortured for information and intelligence. Knowing it was in his power to protect the Church, he steadfastly gave statements to his torturers that he had been recruited by Hungarian intelligence for espionage. And in spite of the ongoing, agonizing cruelties meted out to him, he never gave his real name — all in the hope he would be given the death sentence as a spy before the investigators discovered that he was

[363] ASRS, AA.EE.SS., Stati Ecclesiastici 688a, f. 78.
[364] ASRS, AA.EE.SS., Stati Ecclesiastici 688a, f. 62, report from Msgr. Rotta to Card. Maglione, February 3, 1941.
[365] ASRS, AA.EE.SS., Stati Ecclesiastici 688a, f. 309.
[366] ASRS, AA.EE.SS., Stati Ecclesiastici 688a, f. 38, report of Msgr. Rotta to Card. Maglione, June 30, 1941.

a priest. Had they learned that fact, there was a strong possibility that he would have been put on a public show trial or have put others in the Church in danger.

Sources outside of the Vatican reveal that on July 7, 1941, the brave and steadfast Fr. Moskwa was sentenced to death as an enemy of the people. On that same stagnant summer day, he was marched from his cell in Kiev Prison, stood up before his callous executioners, and shot. Did he say anything prior to his death, a prayer or perhaps a declaration against his murderers? Or did he remain stoically silent, determined that they would hear no more from him on this Earth?[367] There is no record. And with the death of Moskwa, it seems that the attempt for a secret information chain within occupied Poland and Bolshevik Russia would also have died. But this was not the case.

The Historical Archive contains more revelations about Fr. Moskwa, unknown until today, that would merit further investigation. However, Moskwa was not the only person to be acting at that time as a secret informant for Pius XII. There were others.

*

*   *

The original idea to set up a proper channel for contact with the Polish had first come approximately six months prior to Moskwa's capture and execution, on December 12, 1940. The plan had come through a memo sent to Maglione by Nuncio Rotta, which told of a Polish priest, Fr. Rzepko-Łaski. Rotta indicated that this priest was willing to offer his services for the transmission of secret correspondence from and to Poland, from the regions occupied by the Nazis as well as those occupied by the Soviets.

A first report, written in Latin by this new candidate "informer," was attached by the nuncio to his letter. It explained the great need for there to be an agent between Budapest and Poland. Of course, it would be neither official nor public, and yet it would be the most secure way to assure communication with Rome.[368] The nuncio also suggested his idea of a chain featuring a number of informers

---

[367] Sources: Osipova (1996), p. 185; Investigatory Matter G.I. Moskva, Archive Ts-GAOO (Ukraine); list compiled by R. Dzwonkowski, SAC; Madała, p. 111. University of Notre Dame, Book of Remembrance, Biographies of Catholic Clergy and Laity Repressed in the Soviet Union (USSR) from 1918 to 1953 (https://biographies.library.nd.edu/catalog/biography-1844).

[368] ASRS, AA.EE.SS., Stati Ecclesiastici 688a, f. 320.

transmitting information out of Poland.[369] It would start slowly and gradually expand once security could be guaranteed.[370]

Given the delicate nature of the whole operation, Cardinal Secretary of State Maglione was directly involved in the matter. In February he wrote to his staff, asking to explore the possibility. "This morning we talked about this project: would one have the goodness to give me any other relevant information."[371]

Unfortunately, during the investigation by the Cabinet, it turned out that the Society of Jesus had expelled Rzepko-Łaski in 1938.[372] One of the *minutante* reported the official reason for the Society of Jesus's decision as "not known."[373] Probably the Cabinet did some further investigation, but the preserved documentation in the Historical Archive remains silent on this regard. This created a major quandary for the Holy See. How could they have confidence in this potential informant? While the Holy See wrangled over this issue, they decided that a new candidate informer had to be found. This candidate was the Franciscan Fr. Peter Wilk-Wilkoslawski, who, at the beginning of 1941, had been assigned to the pastoral care of the deported Poles in Hungary.[374] These Poles, many of whom were Catholics, were very vulnerable and generally unwelcomed by the Hungarian populace.

And so Wilk-Wilkoslawski was charged with this responsibility on the recommendation of Fr. Ledóchowski, the superior general of the Jesuits.[375] In the end, it was agreed that Rzepko-Łaski, the priest who had left a "question mark" in the mind of the secretary of state, would work under him. Were they taking a chance with this decision?

In a letter to Nuncio Rotta, Cardinal Maglione instructed Rotta to warn Fr. Wilk-Wilkoslawski that he was to act with extreme caution and not place any final responsibility in the hands of Rzepko-Łaski. And, adding a letter to be delivered to the archbishop of Leopoli, he made it clear that, if possible, Fr. Moskwa should take with him or at least learn the content of the letter so he could deliver it verbally in person if necessary. In case Moskwa was no longer in Hungary, the letter could

[369] ASRS, AA.EE.SS., Stati Ecclesiastici 688a, f. 315.
[370] ASRS, AA.EE.SS., Stati Ecclesiastici 688a, f. 315ᵛ.
[371] ASRS, AA.EE.SS., Stati Ecclesiastici 688a, f. 316.
[372] ASRS, AA.EE.SS., Stati Ecclesiastici 688a, f. 324, note of Msgr. Mario Brini, December 21, 1940.
[373] ASRS, AA.EE.SS., Stati Ecclesiastici 688a, f. 324.
[374] ASRS, AA.EE.SS., Stati Ecclesiastici 688a, f. 310.
[375] ASRS, AA.EE.SS., Stati Ecclesiastici 688a, ff. 312–313.

be delivered by Wilk-Wilkoslawski. It seems there was a kind of hierarchy between the agents, with Moskwa as the most trustworthy for Rome.

Immediately, Wilk-Wilkoslawski proved himself to be incredibly useful. In a long report in Latin, he referred to Pius XII's encyclical *Summi pontificatus*, which had been written in 1939. In this writing, the pope exposed the dire consequences of the crisis of faith and the diffusion of anti-Christian ideologies, and he exhorted the Polish nation to face their persecution. Wilk-Wilkoslawski stated that the encyclical had been altered by the Germans. Where originally the pope's message lamented the invasion of Poland, condemning — indirectly, of course — Nazi totalitarianism, the text forged by the German propaganda services had become a message directed to the German soldiers and evoked the greatness of the German nation. It also falsely indoctrinated the Polish population with the view that Nazi ideology matched that of the Holy Father.[376] This was mere fake news that even today some people believe might be true. Evidently, Nazi propaganda worked very well.

Other sources of information on Russia, the Soviets, and occupied Poland found their way to the Holy See. A good example is the remarkable collection of documents that arrived in two suitcases from Salzburg in September 1946, belonging to Msgr. Antonio Kwiatkowski. The first suitcase contained various documents, correspondence, projection plates, and personal notes that never reached the Historical Archive.[377] The second one contained thousands of important, highly classified documents of the People's Commissariat for Internal Affairs, the N.K.V.D. — instructions for the intelligence service, methods and procedures for arrests, extort confessions, and transport and deportation of political prisoners. Photos of all these original documents are now preserved in the Archives, creating what could be regarded as a true "spy collection," surely worthy of further study.

However, not a great deal is known about Msgr. Kwiatkowski. The few biographical documents preserved in the suitcase collection reveal that he was in Romania in 1939, where he traveled through Vatra Dornei in the Bucovina region during the month of September[378] and ended up in Calimanesti, a southern Romanian town. There, he was employed by the military administration of the

---

[376] ASRS, AA.EE.SS., Stati Ecclesiastici 688a, ff. 241–242, report from Fr. Petrus Wilk-Wilkoslawski, O.F.M., January 7, 1941.

[377] "In the Archives only one suitcase arrived; maybe the one indicated as the second one." ASRS, AA.EE.SS., Extracta, Stati Ecclesiastici 474a, f. 613.

[378] ASRS, AA.EE.SS., Extracta, Stati Ecclesiastici 474a, f. 608.

Polish military that was fleeing the German invader. A leaflet of 1941 attests to his
activity in Rome, in service of the Polish broadcasting of Vatican Radio.[379] Msgr.
Kwiatkowski — as he wrote in May 1942 to Cardinal Maglione — had the intention of writing a comprehensive study on Communism for Pope Pius XII.[380] The
Holy See paid him a subsidy of 2,000 lire to permit him the acquisition of "necessary means to be able to continue my scientific researches on communism."[381] For
those investigations, however, he had to operate on dangerous Soviet-occupied
territory. Unfortunately, his end-of-the-war and postwar experiences remain not
only mysterious but also contradictory. It is possible that for some months in
1946 he was still living in Rome in the Polish Pontifical Institute at the Via Caval-
lini.[382] Nevertheless, the Cabinet noted in March 1947 that the suitcase arrived
in September 1946: "It is not to be excluded that Father K[wiatkowski], caught
by surprise by the Soviets after 1942, in Poland or in Germany, might have been
executed."[383] One could close the file of Msgr. Kwiatkowski here. Except that his
presumed death ultimately revealed itself as untrue.

I discovered a first source contradicting the alleged execution of Kwiatkowski
hidden in a file belonging to another archival series, namely that on Russia. It is an
article dated July 1, 1950, published in the Communist newspaper *Trybuna Ludu*
[the official paper of the Polish United Workers' Party], under the headline, "An
Agent of Hitler, Director of the Polish Broadcasting of the Vatican Radio." This article
reviewed a book, *The Vatican State* by Stefan Urbanski, in which the author referred
to Msgr. Antonio Kwiatkowski as "director of the transmission in Polish language
of the Vatican Radio" and described "how this person has expanded the American
imperialism, being at the same time one of the chief informants of the intelligence
service of the Vatican on Soviet Russia and countries of popular democracy."[384]

The article in the *Trybuna Ludu* offers an outline of Fr. Kwiatkowski's biography
to the readers:

---

[379] ASRS, AA.EE.SS., Extracta, Stati Ecclesiastici 474a, f. 610$^{r/v}$.

[380] ASRS, AA.EE.SS., Extracta, Stati Ecclesiastici 474a, f. 611, typewritten letter to Card.
     Maglione, May 30, 1942.

[381] ASRS, AA.EE.SS., Extracta, Stati Ecclesiastici 474a, f. 612, letter to Msgr. Montini,
     May 30, 1942.

[382] ASRS, AA.EE.SS., Stati Ecclesiastici 739, f. 109, handwritten note by Msgr. Giobbe
     [no date, probably 1946].

[383] ASRS, AA.EE.SS., Extracta, Stati Ecclesiastici 474a, f. 613.

[384] ASRS, AA.EE.SS., Russia 742, f. 265.

He ended his lyceum in Ostrog [now in Ukraine, then part of the Russian Empire] and Vilnius [now in Lithuania, then part of the Russian Empire] and seminar-studies in Petersburg in 1914 with a doctoral degree in theology. In 1914 he became vicar-parish priest in Moscow of the Church of St. Peter and Paul, at the same time teaching religion. He stayed in Moscow until 1917. In December 1917, he escaped to Charkow [now in Ukraine] where he accepted the responsibilities of chaplain and teacher of religion. On the 16th of March 1920, he was arrested by the Bolsheviks and was jailed for more than a year.

In 1921 — so we learn from the article — he established himself in Warsaw and traveled to Moscow as an expert member of the Polish delegation, taking part in the decisions on the Treaty of Riga establishing the new Russian-Polish border. "He went back to Moscow until 1925, collecting anti-communist material that he passed on to Pius XI, who granted him the title of prelate. He collated the material he gathered between the years 1925–1930."[385] Now his *journey* becomes even more interesting for us when the article reports that "in 1930, he founded an Institute for scientific studies on Bolshevism, published 15 books and started a review 'The battle against Bolshevism.' In 1936, he was in contact with the anti-Komintern [the special agency within the Propaganda Ministry under Joseph Goebbels], which he provided with material."

At this point, the biographical article takes a quite surprising twist:

> He took part in the International Conference of Heads of anti-Soviet intelligence services in Feldafing. He supplied material for the anti-Communist exhibition organized by Goebbels in Berlin, an event that toured all Nazi-occupied countries. In 1939, he left Poland, passing through Romania and traveled to Rome. He gathered and organized the material for a basic work on the history, the strategy, the tactics and influence of Bolshevism on the human psychology. He finished this work in 1943, departing for San Remo, where he compiled the data he brought with him from Rome.

Then follows the icing on the cake. Whereas the Cabinet was ignoring his fate, giving him up for dead, the Communist article continued: "In 1943 he moved

[385] ASRS, AA.EE.SS., Russia 742, f. 265.

to Berlin." The author of the article assures the reliability of his account when he states, "This description of his life was copied out from Kwiatkowski's personal file in the Gestapo archives."

Yet there is even more. The article continued in crescendo: "In 1944, when the last mice left the Hitlerian boat in flames, Kwiatkowski departed on command of the Gestapo to France with the aim to rally the French clergy. The contacts with France were facilitated by another German spy, Archbishop Msgr. Beaussart." Then came the apotheosis: "The undignified activity of Kwiatkowski was accompanied by the benedictions of Pope Pius XI and Pope Pius XII."[386] So in this case Kwiatkowski, the once-director of the Polish program on the Vatican Radio, would have been from 1943 onwards a "spy-collaborator" of the Gestapo, of the Nazis, or even of Hitler . . . with Pius XII himself giving him his blessing.

The Cabinet certainly was offended and disturbed by the implications of the *Trybuna Ludu* article. They perceived it as a pernicious piece of journalism crafted to link Pius XII, through its clergy, with top Nazi personalities. Neither did the article fit with information at their disposal. Almost two months prior to the article's publication in July 1950, the Catholic Committee for Refugees in New York had inquired on the person of Rev. Antonio Kwiatkowski, "who resides at 32, Hillmarton Road, n. 7, London, England. Before we take any action in this case, we are endeavouring to secure information concerning Father Kwiatkowski's activities in England and in Poland." The letter furthermore stated that Kwiatkowski was in poor health and the committee did "not wish to bring him to the United States unless his health permits it and he has the permission of His Ecclesiastical Superiors to do so."[387]

Minutante Luigi Poggi stated that "in the Archives there are no results on him." Surely this was an error. Could the archivist have completely forgotten the thousands of papers contained in the mysterious suitcase sent to Rome from Salisbury, just three years before? It's possible. However, Msgr. Poggi requested information from the Polish titular bishop Msgr. Gawlina, who had served as the rector of San Stanislao dei Polacchi, the Polish national church in Rome, since 1947.[388] Secretary Msgr. Tardini agreed that the request had to be sent,[389] and the response

[386] ASRS, AA.EE.SS., Russia 742, f. 266.
[387] ASRS, AA.EE.SS., Russia 742, f. 272, letter of Msgr. Emil N. Komora to Msgr. Tardini, May 11, 1950.
[388] ASRS, AA.EE.SS., Russia 742, f. 271.
[389] ASRS, AA.EE.SS., Russia 742, f. 272.

came quickly. Within a week, Msgr. Gawlina answered: "The Rev. Kwiatkowski of about 57 years old, belonged to the diocese of Mohilew and was an alumnus of the Roman-Catholic Ecclesiastical Academy of Petersburg. After the revolution of the year 1917 he lived a very eventful life in Soviet Russia." These details correspond with those of his early years and offer additional information on his presence in Romania. Gawlina stated: "The Polish government nominated him to membership of the Commission for the repatriation of documents and acts of Russia. In this occasion he garnered numerous merits towards the Holy See and Poland." On his becoming a prelate under Pius XI, more is revealed: "In 1922 he transmitted important historical documents about Moscow to the Holy See and was nominated 'Cameriere Segreto soprannumerario'" — that is, monsignor. Gawlina had spoken of Kwiatkowski's foundation of the anti-Communist institute in Warsavia, which was very well known by the subsequent apostolic nuncios in Poland: Lauri, Marmaggi, and Cortesi. So he continued: "In September 1939 he was evacuated from Poland together with the army and has taken with him numerous documents. During the war he lived in Rome and afterwards ... he went for good to England, where he is still today living in secret." In Gawlina's biographical sketch on Kwiatkowski, there was not a word about Germany nor Goebbels. Even in the last paragraph of his letter to Msgr. Tardini, Msgr. Gawlina admitted that he had recently obtained other information that caused him to revise his somewhat optimistic opinion on Kwiatkowski. Because he had come to know that "since 1939 his title of monsignor was not renewed and actually he rarely celebrates mass, even if that last detail could be explained with his renal disease as well as his exaggerated tendency to hide himself."[390] Funny how the details on Goebbels and his and the pope's liaison with Nazism remain unsaid in the other biographical accounts. Historians shall be able to discover the truth.

Another anecdote needs to be mentioned here. In order to do so, we should go back to the beginnings of World War II. At the end of July 1940, a man by the name of "Count" Giovanni Malvezzi, an Italian layman with high sensibilities for the suffering population in Poland, had returned from a journey through that country, where he had been supervising the Italian industrial plants of the I.R.I. — the Institute for Italian Reconstruction, which was founded in 1933. In

---

[390] ASRS, AA.EE.SS., Polonia 742, f. 269, letter of Msgr. Gawlina to Msgr. Tardini, May 26, 1950.

his first report to Pope Pius XII, he described the situation in Poland as well as that of the Polish Church, depicting the Poles as "living under terror … of the Gestapo, the Sonderdienst, the Arbeitsdienst, the hunger and the winter. They are demoralized. Radio is forbidden. Leaflets and cyclostyle that are still around are ever more ruthlessly hunted by the Gestapo. All the art treasures and libraries are taken away."[391]

On September 30, 1940, the *minutante* Msgr. Giulio Barbetta, alerted the superiors of the Secretariat of State that Count Malvezzi was returning to Rome by way of Paris and Brussels, where he already had delivered some letters to the nunciatures of both countries, and that on his arrival in Rome "he would give a fuller explanation and maybe an envelope."[392]

Barbetta reminded his superiors that since his first report in July, Count Malvezzi had sent additional updates on Poland. Barbetta suggested a meeting with either Cardinal Secretary of State Maglione or with Foreign Secretary Tardini could be very beneficial.

It seemed clear that Malvezzi wanted to help the Church, and Tardini replied that "he would most gladly meet with him, even if I know nothing of the report that he made previously." Then he asked: "With whom had he spoken previously?"

Msgr. Barbetta explained that "it was Monsignor Montini who met with him the other time and handed over the report to the cardinal. Everything should be kept somewhere in the archives."[393]

Three reports sent by Malvezzi dated the summer of 1941 are now preserved in the Historical Archive.[394] But his activity continued throughout the war years.[395] Among these administrative files and correspondence, two of his activities in 1943 merit mention. First, he gave a long pro memoria to the secretary of state during a visit on March 26, 1943, at 9:15 a.m.[396] Second, while acting as a

---

[391] ASRS, AA.EE.SS., Polonia 207, f. 2, note of the secretary of state on the report from Count Malvezzi, August 1, 1940.

[392] ASRS, AA.EE.SS., Polonia 207, f. 12.

[393] ASRS, AA.EE.SS., Polonia 207, f. 12.

[394] Charged by the secretary of state to bring a letter to the bishop of Lodz, July 16, 1941; report with information on the situation of Poland, July 1941 (f. 366ss); another report on the situation in Poland, July 1941 (f. 355ss).

[395] An example of 1942 see: Polonia 216, f. 601 (September 27, 1942).

[396] ASRS, AA.EE.SS., Polonia 216, ff. 315–326, pro memoria presented by Sig. Malvezzi, March 24, 1943 (for another copy see: ibid., ff. 332–346).

go-between in June 1943, he assured the delivery of a gift of 40,000 zloty from Pius XII to Msgr. Andrej Szeptykyi, the Ruthenian metropolite of L'viv.[397] Apparently, Malvezzi and his efforts were important assets to the Holy See.

Yet long after the war, economist professor Paolo Leon shared a rather controversial episode with a journalist from the Italian newspaper *La Repubblica*:[398]

> In 1954, with other twenty-somethings we had founded the circle Esprit, the Catholic magazine of Emmanuel Mounier. One day we were called by Giovanni Malvezzi, IRI manager, who told us how, during a trip in 1942 to the countries occupied by the Nazis, a prelate told him that Jews could be freed in exchange for money, gold, or values. Returning to Rome, Malvezzi rushed to the Pope to explain the violence and the extermination, of which the Pope already knew, and urged the Pontiff to raise funds to free as many people as possible. Pius XII told him that the Church had no money. Malvezzi suggested selling part of the treasure of St. Peter; the Pope lost his temper and, shouting that the goods of the Church are sacred, chased him away. Malvezzi wanted us to understand that even the evil deeds of the Church do not make the mission less holy. But since then I have gradually lost faith and all esteem for that Pope.

Typewriters in the Apostolic Palace were surely in near-constant use during these demanding times. The noisy clattering of keys echoed off the walls as critical notes and documents were pounded out, sometimes at a frantic pace, in order to keep important people in Rome and elsewhere informed as well as to compile incoming data on matters of utmost urgency. Count Malvezzi's name continued to appear in a number of these reports. One typewritten note, probably composed by the *minutante* Msgr. Samorè, on January 23, 1941, summarized a recent handwritten report from Malvezzi. In that account, Malvezzi revealed that the situations in Lodz and Warsaw were continuing to erode and had become even worse on both the material and spiritual levels. Spiritual assistance for the faithful was most desperately needed. He pleaded for a secular priest to serve as an envoy, one who would

---

[397] ASRS, AA.EE.SS., Polonia 216, f. 288, letter of Msgr. Szeptykyi to Card. Maglione, L'viv, June 12, 1943.

[398] https://ricerca.repubblica.it/repubblica/archivio/repubblica/2008/11/08/dubbi-sulla-beatificazione-di-pio-xii.html.

take an interest in the spiritual fates of the Polish people by organizing religious activities and charitable assistance.

Samorè also urged "that in every way one should use as go-betweens reliable people who would not expose the Holy See, in order to send assistance in the form of money. To the objection made by the Holy See that it will never do illegal business, restraint is ineffective when people are starving of hunger and lose faith by shortcomings of material help. He would be always at disposal to carry whatever, even at his personal risk."

At this point Msgr. Samorè observed keenly that "maybe it is not unrelated to this pushy recommendation a wish to realize some of the Polish money that the 'Società Posnanski' (a textile enterprise that he [Malvezzi] administrates on behalf of the I.R.I.) has not yet been able to transfer abroad. He would like for that money, maybe 70,000 Zloty, to be given in beneficence; and here, without too much fuss, the Holy See would give him the equivalent amount in lire."[399]

The Holy See refused to agree to Giovanni Malvezzi's personal monetary bargaining during the war. Could this be the reason why Malvezzi would later share the episode in a totally different light, one of seeking money to help free Jews, and then invent the story of a furious and shouting Pius XII? Did he do this to ease his conscience?

Who can say? The continuous constructive and beneficial activities during the war, however, make the 1954 account look even more awkward if not suspicious.

Of informers behind the frontlines, on a mission for the pope or through their own fervent initiative, there were the good and the bad, the brave as well as those whose motives remain unclear. But one thing is for sure: often their fame and bravery became colored differently once the war was over.

---

[399] Stati Ecclesiastici 688a, f. 397.

7

A Tale of a Cup of Coffee and Doublespeak

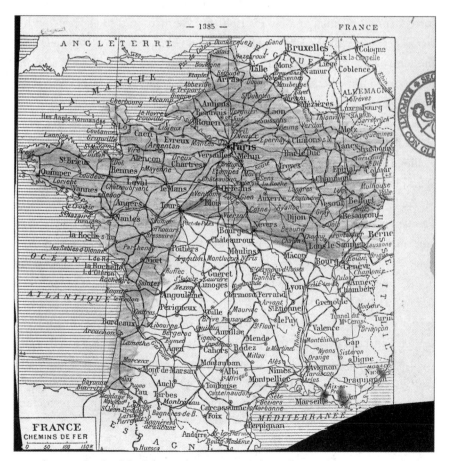

Map of France colored and divided in two by Monsignor Giulio Barbetta.

A RED-MARKED MAP[400] indicating the newly divided territory landed on the desk of Msgr. Giulio Barbetta. He made an internal note for himself, bemused that the spa town of Vichy, the capital of the new regime, was so small that his map of France did not even depict it. Barbetta was the *minutante* charged with recording and analyzing the changing political landscape of France following the German invasion in May 1940. A handwritten note of solemn denouncement, unsigned, accompanied the map: "The French Embassy has the honour of bringing to the attention of His Eminence the Cardinal Secretary of State, the conditions of the armistice that was imposed on France after the victory of Germany. These conditions constitute a flagrant abuse of force. They are without precedent in history."[401]

France was seen as a critical prize to power-hungry Germany. In fact, after the surrender of the Dutch on May 15, 1940, the Germans immediately and with a vengeance turned their eye toward France. After Germany's humiliating defeat on the fields of France in World War I, the country represented something of a trophy to Hitler. To bring home the capital city of Paris would have a huge symbolism for the Nazis. Hitler himself also had a personal fascination with France. He was a great admirer of French architecture, in particular the Opéra Garnier in Paris.

In June, following the fall of Paris to Germany, eighty-four-year-old Marshal Philippe Pétain was made chief of Vichy France. Pétain was considered a national World War I hero, the man who had led France to victory at the Battle of Verdun.

And with that, a new political order was born, splitting France in two. Northern France, and the strategically important Atlantic coast, was under direct German control. Southern France, to the borders of the Mediterranean Sea, became the *zone libre* (free zone) of Vichy France, working in close collaboration with the Nazis. The Vichy state spread to the borders of Italy, which at that point in the war was a key German ally.

Pétain's strong authoritarian government declared itself as standing for protection of private property, social harmony, and public order. Conservative and right wing, Pétain and his key ministers believed France had been seduced and damaged by moral disorder and decay, arguing that to combat this the new government needed full executive and legislative power, a power without restriction.

---

[400] ASRS, AA.EE.SS., Francia 876, f. 464.

[401] ASRS, AA.EE.SS., Francia 876, f. 463ʳ, note from the embassy of France to Holy See, June 26, 1940.

Immediately, however, Berlin began interfering in Vichy policy and law, making it very clear that this government was merely a puppet regime.

*

*   *

By the end of 1939, the French Jewish population numbered 300,000, of which 200,000 resided in Paris. Numbers had swelled due to many refugees fleeing from neighboring Holland, Belgium, and Luxembourg into France. They continued to swell with the annexation of the historically disputed territory of Alsace-Lorraine, including the city of Strasbourg, by Germany in 1940, as the region's Jewish population was expelled and sought safety in French territory. The French colonies and overseas territories also included substantial Jewish communities — 200,000 in Morocco, 120,000 in Algeria, and 80,000 in Tunisia. Although the Nazis made most public their efforts to erase the Jews from Europe, it is to this day a little-known fact that deportations took place in those African colonies too.

Throughout the summer of 1941, there were widespread arrests and political assassinations in France. Thousands of Jews were arrested, people who had committed no crime whatsoever but who were seen as unworthy beings to the Nazis. Jews in Paris were afraid to leave their houses, and some even feared falling asleep in their own homes, believing that their doors would be broken down at some wee hour and they would be dragged away. And a year later, in the summer of 1942, the deportations began. Initially, only non-French Jewish refugees were the victims, violently rounded up and sent away. Later, however, this would expand to French Jews and other French citizens, including many Catholics.

In those early days of Vichy France, the French Church hierarchy called for the faithful to not take positions against the government. Pétain was still very much a glorious war hero.

*

*   *

On May 17, 1940, as each day brought the fast-paced German army closer to Paris, the papal nuncio in France, Valerio Valeri, sent a memo to Cardinal Maglione in Rome:

> Here we are at the culminant moment of the war. . . . The Diplomatic
> Corps, notwithstanding one or two exceptions, desires to leave

> Paris where the enemy will arrive in a few days. As far as my own concerns, I declared to the Minister of Foreign Affairs that I was ready to remain or to follow the government when this last one would leave Paris.... If your Eminence has some preference in this respect I would be thankful if he would express it to me.[402]

And while he described a solemn public prayer at the Paris cathedral of Notre Dame followed by a procession for the victory of the French armies and its allies "that defend the spiritual heritage of humanity against the coalition of all the powers of evil,"[403] the situation remained tense and uncertain in the days to come.

After due consideration, Maglione, considering it opportune to maintain correspondence, especially since no papal diplomatic representations in Belgium and Holland was allowed any more, decided that Nuncio Valeri and his counselor Msgr. Alfredo Pacini should follow the government to Vichy France. The move was not meant as an implicit recognition of the Vichy government by the Holy See nor ordered for diplomatico-political reasons as has often been said: documents reveal that the initial decision was made for simpler, more practical motives. This would leave the nunciature in Paris in the hands of two men — Msgr. Bertoli, as *uditore* at the second level in his diplomatic career, and the secretary.[404] A similar situation and decision had occurred with the invasion of Germany into Belgium during the First World War. In 1914, the nuncio in Belgium, also accredited to the Dutch government, followed the Belgian government in exile to the French town Le Havre, while the nunciature of Brussels was left in the hands of the *uditore*, and the second secretary was sent to Den Haag to preside there over the presence in the internunciature.

Pius XII was deeply troubled by the situation in France. However, he had no option but to maintain good diplomacy with the new government of Vichy. Incidentally, Pétain's strict moral agenda bore fruit and was popular with many Catholics. Catholic schools received official recognition and financial support from the State. Family was promoted by the government as the core of society. Public morality was now defended and sanctioned by law.

---

[402] ASRS, AA.EE.SS., Francia 857, f. 64.

[403] ASRS, AA.EE.SS., Francia 857, f. 67, newspaper article, *Le Temps* of May 20, 1940.

[404] ASRS, AA.EE.SS., Francia 857, f. 75, draft of cable of Card. Maglione to Msgr. Valeri, May 26, 1940; f. 72, draft of cable of Card. Maglione to Msgr. Valeri, May 27, 1940.

For those first few months under the control of the Vichy government, the Catholic Church was optimistic that it could work alongside ministers who shared many of their guiding principles. But as the war progressed, that hope rapidly faded and died, and the few advantages offered by the Pétain government were soon overshadowed by its sinister side.

*

* *

When the Nazis began to target the lower clergy, persecuting priests, friars, and monks, the government of Vichy turned a blind eye.[405] And the darkest side of the government of Vichy started revealing itself in the fall of 1940 with the first of what would become many anti-Semitic decrees, banning Jews from public service, putting restrictions on Jews taking up certain professions, and executing limitations and confiscation of property and industry. Jews who could prove adherence to another religion were exempt, which included, for the moment, Christian Jews. At the same time, the Vichy government began a census of all Jewish people present on French territory.

In January 1941, *Minutante* Barbetta prepared a letter to Nuncio Valeri in Vichy regarding newspaper reports warning of proposed new laws on prenuptial examinations. The letter was prompted by an article from *Le Petit Dauphinois*, which read:

> One of the first preoccupations of Maréchal Pétain's government when it took power was — no need to reiterate it — to fight the dangers which were threatening the existence of our race itself. A healthy and vigorous young generation is, in fact, a certainty for the future of France. Certain countries have shown us at our expense, unfortunately, an example that we should not forget. The regulation of the selling of alcohol is one of the first healthy actions against the dangers of alcoholism. Other happy decisions will follow, and among them which can be announced is the health exam before marriage.[406]

Before composing the letter, Barbetta contacted Cardinal Maglione with notes for him to address, highlighted underneath in black ink: "This article is somewhat surprising. And

---

[405] ASRS, AA.EE.SS., Francia 880.
[406] ASRS, AA.EE.SS., Francia 892, f. 84, newspaper article, *Le Petit Dauphinois*, January 7, 1941.

a little bit enigmatic. That what is certain is that the pre-marital exam is by the example of Germany, Denmark etc, so will they want it to reach extreme consequences? For the time being it seems a draft law. Would it not be good to signal this to the Nuncio?"

Cardinal Maglione agreed. In red he wrote, "*Va Bene* [That's okay]."

Minutante Barbetta had been quietly alarmed regarding these premarital exams, which — as he had read in the newspaper — existed also in other countries like Germany, Denmark, seven states of the United States, Norway, Sweden, and Turkey. For clearly he believed them to be a pretext to racial discrimination, as had been the case in Germany. He saw through the pretense of the supposed health measures. And so, he drafted the letter to Nuncio Valeri. In return, he received reassurance from the nuncio that the law "has no basis in reality":

> My most reverend Eminence. In response to your dispatch of the 16th of this month. I didn't fail to get information about the intention of forcing youngsters to a medical examination before marriage. A similar communication was in the newspapers the 25th of this month but it was very brief and had no allusions on the situation regarding this in Germany. Yesterday I talked with one of these ministers who assured me that this morning he would discuss it with the Marshall Pétain. And the minister also said that we could stand easy and that nothing would have been done that would cause even the slightest harm to the doctrine or morals of the Church.[407]

The reassurances, which had been given to Valeri by an unnamed Vichy minister, are diplomatic, intended to reassure the Church nothing would be done to harm the Jewish people. But when read carefully, it is obvious the minister's response doesn't really answer the question of whether they intended to introduce the marriage laws or not.

In fact, toward the summer of 1941 the new laws on Aryanization were announced, including the systematic census of Jews in France.

Article 1 in the text of the new law of June 2, 1941, on the Jews stated: "Will be considered a Jew, He or she, belonging or not to any confession, which has at least three Grandparents of, or, two Grandparents only if his or her spouse has at least two Grandparents from the Jewish race."[408]

---

[407] ASRS, AA.EE.SS., Francia 892, f. 81, report from Msgr. Valeri to Card. Maglione, January 28, 1941.

[408] ASRS, AA.EE.SS., Francia 892, f. 232, Status of French Jews (law of June 2, 1941).

Someone in the office, maybe even the cardinal, marked this paragraph in red pencil. This development gravely concerned the Holy See because it showed a shift in the French disposition on Jews by labeling them as a race rather than a religion and thus worsening one step further the already painful situation of the Jews. From that moment on it made no difference what religion a person practiced; if their heritage was Jewish, they were regarded as Jewish. The Vatican protested vehemently against it, but to no avail, as the Historical Archive of the Secretariat of State show. In July 1941, the statutes on the Aryanization of both France and its colonies were passed.

Status of French Jews (law of June 2, 1941).[409]

---

[409] ASRS, AA.EE.SS., Francia 892, f. 230[r].

At the end of September, Nuncio Valeri sent another report to Rome, noting a specific, troubling exchange that occurred during a dinner of the diplomatic corps hosted by Marshal Pétain. At the time coffee was served, Marshal Pétain had approached him and, in the presence of the ambassadors of Brazil and Spain, bluntly raised the issue of the recent legislation on the Jews[410]: "He [Pétain] changed discourse on the new legislation of the Jews telling me he had recently received a letter from Léon Bérard, [the French ambassador to the Holy See] in which the latter [Bérard] affirmed that the Holy See, although considering some dispositions hard and a little bit inhuman, did on the whole not have any observations to make."

Nuncio Valeri, taken aback by this fabrication, made it clear that he did not believe it. Though anger coursed through his body, he calmly stirred the sugar in his coffee and responded to Marshal Pétain in straightforward terms. His report continued:

> I reacted quite vividly, and mostly because of the persons who were present. And I declared that the Holy See had already made clear its views on racism which is the basis of all dispositions taken towards the Jewish people. And that thereby Mister Bérard could not have expressed himself in such a simplistic way.
>
> Mr Marshall Pétain replied jokingly that maybe I wasn't in agreement with my superiors. And thus, he invited me to come and visit him so he could show me the letter from Mr Bérard and discuss the whole question. And in fact, I went there on the 26th [of September 1941] and the Marshall Pétain handed me over the letter so that I could read it. I took also a copy of it and I transmit it to Your Eminence for his information. As Your Eminence will note the pro-memoria of Bérard is quite more nuanced then that what the Marshall wanted me to believe.[411]

From Bérard's pro memoria it became clear to Nuncio Valeri that the French ambassador to the Holy See had used a theological ghostwriter to craft his memo outlining the Catholic position on the Jewish faith. Considering the style and

[410] ASRS, AA.EE.SS., Francia 892, f. 240, report from Msgr. Valeri to Card. Maglione, September 30, 1941.

[411] ASRS, AA.EE.SS., Francia 892, f. 240, report from Msgr. Valeri to Card. Maglione, September 30, 1941.

religious content of the memo, Valeri assumed it might have been written by Fr. Martin Stanislas Gillet, then master general of the Dominican order and living in Rome. Valeri continued:

> I gave him [Pétain] a little note with which I indicated the huge inconveniences that came out of the simplistic religious point of view of the said legislation, which, on the other hand, is also rather confusing.
>
> The Marshall replied to me that in substance he, too, deplored many of the dispositions that were taken against the Jews and that they were taken on the other side, under the pressure of the occupying forces. Anyway, notwithstanding his own desire, he didn't see how he could possibly revoke or modify these laws before the conclusion of peace.
>
> Of a slight indication regarding this, I should conclude that Marshall Pétain has contacted Mister Bérard to gather together some arguments that can be used in favor of eventual modification of this legislation.[412]

The nuncio reported here that Marshal Pétain suggested he himself wouldn't have introduced anti-Semitic laws but that he was forced to do so by Hitler. The marshal was lying, as historical studies have since proved, but Msgr. Valeri at the time had little reason to doubt it. And the nuncio saw it as a positive sign that Ambassador Bérard had been asked to provide some arguments to help modify the legislation, even if those efforts were in vain. Valeri seemed to be seeking chinks or gaps that might give him an opportunity to possibly prevent the legislation — or, if unable to do that, find ways to at least help water it down.

Both reports — the one commissioned to French Ambassador to the Holy See Léon Bérard, and the one that Pétain gave to Valeri — are preserved in the Historical Archive as a pair entitled "Attitude of the Holy See toward the racism problem." They offer some help in understanding why Marshal Pétain told Valeri that the Holy See was not in disagreement on the racial laws. In the first paragraph of his report, Ambassador Bérard writes that nothing had been said inside the Vatican that would suggest any criticism or disapproval of the proposed laws. He

---

[412] ASRS, AA.EE.SS., Francia 892, ff. 240ᵛ–241, report from Msgr. Valeri to Card. Maglione, September 30, 1941.

goes beyond that and reports that the papal authority had never seemed "[to be] dealing with or [to be] preoccupied with this part of the French politics."[413]

Just like Pétain had lied, so did Bérard. He tried to convince Pétain that the position of the Vatican toward racism was "very complex":

> I didn't have time to lay hands on documents regarding the statute of the Jews by the Italian fascists, because we don't have any direct official contacts with the Italian authorities. Therefore I will need more time if you also want that [information]. But I am able instead to deal with the principal subject of your letter of 7th of August: the position of the Holy See regarding the Jewish problem with an examination of the possible points of contradiction ... between the Church's teaching on this regard on one hand, and both the fascist and the French legislation on the other. There are a lot of differences and the material is very complex.[414]

Bérard's report assured Pétain that everything stated in his report had been double-checked by him during conversations with high-placed Catholic authorities in Rome. He then quoted the official position of the Church on racism:

> There is a fundamental, irrevocable, opposition between the doc-trine of the Church and the "racist theories." The Church, which is by definition universal, professes the unity of humankind. The one and only redeemer died for all men and the gospel addresses itself and will be announced to each creature. Each human being has an immortal soul assisted by the same grace and called to the same salvation of that all those alike. . . .
>
> All these propositions remain incompatible with the concept that uses the shape of the skull and the quality of blood, the apti-tudes and the vocation of peoples, and their religion, to establish finally a hierarchy of races, at the top of which appears a pure or royal race, that is called "Aryan."[415]

Bérard went on to quote from the encyclical *Mit brennender Sorge* (With burning concern) dated March 14, 1937. At the time this was written, Pope Pius XII was

[413] ASRS, AA.EE.SS., Francia 892, f. 212, mémoire de M. Bérard, September 2, 1941.
[414] ASRS, AA.EE.SS., Francia 892, f. 212, mémoire de M. Bérard, September 2, 1941.
[415] ASRS, AA.EE.SS., Francia 892, f. 213, mémoire de M. Bérard, September 2, 1941.

still Cardinal Eugenio Pacelli, the secretary of state. He compiled the text together with the German episcopacy. The encyclical, the first and only one issued in German language, was a bold and brave statement regarding racism and how the Catholic Church disapproved of it. It was secretly distributed over all the parishes of Germany, where it was read from the pulpits on the same Sunday. This enraged the Nazis, who would never tolerate criticism or challenges. Immediately after its publication and the reading from the pulpits, an enraged Hitler retaliated by burning copies of it. In May 1937, 1,100 priests were arrested and 304 were deported to Dachau three months later. Those events were sealed in Pacelli's memory. He knew that standing up to the Nazis in public could result in very heavy consequences for his fellow Catholics. Bérard quoted a section of that encyclical, which stated that "National Socialism 'is overthrowing and falsifying the order of all created things ordered by God.'"

Bérard then offered his own skewed analysis of the above: "Of this teaching on the racist ideas, one should not however deduct immediately that the Church is necessarily condemning each particular measure taken by this or another state against that what is called the Jewish race. The thinking of the Church on this issue has distinctions and nuances that one must acknowledge. And each issue must be considered separately."

At this point Bérard broke up his report with subheadings in order to keep it as simple and clear as possible for Pétain.

Under the heading "The Church, and the problem of anti-Semitism," he stated: "The principle that appears in first place, and the most important one, is that in the eyes of the Church a Jew who received valid baptism stops to be a Jew, and is absorbed into the flock of Christ."[416]

Bérard then invoked more general history of the Church, a history that reveals that while it often protected Jewish people against violence and injustice of their persecutors, it at the same time confined them in ghettos. He summarized for Pétain, in his own words, the doctrine of medieval Dominican Thomas Aquinas: "All oppressive policy against the Jews is prohibited, but he [Aquinas] recommends nothing less than taking measures to limit their actions in society and to restrain their influence.... This [legitimizes] forbidding them access of and to public functions. And it is also legitimate to not admit them in some cases to the

---

[416] ASRS, AA.EE.SS., Francia 892, ff. 215–216, mémoire de M. Bérard, September 2, 1941.

universities by way of numerus clausus and to liberal professions." In conclusion, he suggested that if one of the great Catholic thinkers also feared a Jewish presence in the public sphere, then this line of reasoning would not be so far removed from the Vichy government's own thinking. Notably, Bérard's report takes no notice of the changes in the Church's position on this issue since the medieval times in which Aquinas lived and wrote. Yes, Aquinas is part of the Catholic tradition, but tradition is always in flux. It is a continuous moving forward in time and with humanity. Bérard deliberately chose to ignore this context.

Bérard then went on to summarize arguments between the Holy See and the Fascist government of Italy around anti-Semitic laws, making the point to Marshal Pétain that he should expect to hear similar arguments raised in the case of France. Under the heading "The difficulties between the Holy See and Italy concerning the fascists' legislations on Jews," he claimed: "The measures adopted by the fascist government in Italy were not proceeded by any negotiation or agreement between the Holy See and the Italian state. The fascist law caused a lot of criticism from the Holy See. It is very useful to determine with precision the nature and the object of this opposition of divergences."[417]

Bérard explained that he was not in possession of the Italian documents but that "the clearest explanation of the Italian papers was given by people of the Vatican" to him. They explained that:

> The fascist law on Jews in Italy contains dispositions that touch the
> juridical rules or laws on martial union. It forbids ... the marriage
> between Italian Aryan subjects and individual persons of the Jewish
> race. The Church itself considers perfect not only the union between
> Catholics and converted Jews but also the union which is celebrated
> before a priest between Catholic and Jewish not converted. Notwith-
> standing, of course, the second one should have obtained the ecclesi-
> astical authorisation by dispensation. The innovation introduced in
> the Italian law has motivated strong disapproval from the Holy See.[418]

Throughout his report, Bérard disingenuously twisted parts of Catholic theology to tell Pétain what he knew he wanted to hear and to let him think that no one in

---

[417] ASRS, AA.EE.SS., Francia 892, f. 217, mémoire de M. Bérard, September 2, 1941.
[418] ASRS, AA.EE.SS., Francia 892, f. 217–218, mémoire de M. Bérard, September 2, 1941.

the Vatican would criticize his proposals. Nuncio Valeri, the diplomatic representative of the pope in France, did exactly the opposite, as did the French Cardinal Gerlier with his letter of protest.

The nuncio described a public scene a few days earlier: "Last Sunday during a visit by Marshall Pétain to the feast market in Lyon, Cardinal Gerlier gave Pétain a note [of protest] concerning the legislation on the Jews. He also gave him a letter on the same argument written by the Protestant Pastor Boegner, President of the Protestant Federation in France, who had asked the Cardinal to be their intermediary."[419]

Cardinal Gerlier, the *"primat des Gaules"* and archbishop of Lyon, was the highest representative of the Catholic Church in France at that time. That Gerlier was prepared to publicly criticize Marshal Pétain was a stunningly bold act. Furthermore, that he'd been asked to hand over a similar protest letter from the Protestant churches shows once again that the Jewish question and opposition laws often brought Christian churches closer to each other.

*

*   *

It was not until 1946, after the war ended and recriminations, anger, and disgust swept France during the "epuration," that the matter of Bérard's controversial report raised its head again. His report in full was splashed across the front page of *Le Monde Juif* as supposed "proof" of the Vatican's guilt and collusion with the racial laws and persecution. The headline screamed: "The Vatican Seen by Vichy." It was Msgr. Roncalli, former apostolic delegate in Turkey and Greece and in the meanwhile nuncio in Paris, who brought this to the attention of Cabinet Secretary Msgr. Tardini.[420]

While the article is damning, it is taken completely out of context. It doesn't explain that Bérard was a Vichy man. Nor does it refer to Nuncio Valeri's opposition.

Following the upheaval created by the article, the Cabinet commissioned an internal inquiry in 1946. The *minutante* Dell'Acqua recalled the events of 1941 as they had happened:

[419] ASRS, AA.EE.SS., Francia 892, f. 241, report from Msgr. Valeri, September 30, 1941.
[420] ASRS, AA.EE.SS., Francia 892, 207, letter of Msgr. G. B. Roncalli to Msgr. Tardini, Paris, October 25, 1946.

Article in Le Monde Juif (1946): "The Vatican Seen by Vichy."[421]

Ambassador Bérard is certainly not considered by the Jews to be [their] defender and protector. If my memory serves me well, some protests of the Holy See against the French racial laws didn't fail. If this would be true, then it would be good to prepare some article to be published in an Italian and French Catholic review and also in a newspaper for rectification. Excellency Valeri and Monsignor Barbetta (my predecessor in the office) that have dealt with this question could be more precise on it.[422]

Tardini noted in pencil with his usual sardonic air, "They should be!"[423] Then he ordered Msgr. Dell'Acqua to go back and talk with Valeri and Barbetta.

A long and detailed internal report, dated October 13, 1946, details Valeri's postwar recollection of the events: "In 1941 Marshall Pétain, during a cocktail event, and in presence of some ambassadors, went on as if the Vatican agreed with the government on the question of the measures taken against the Jews. I protested."[424]

[421] ASRS, AA.EE.SS., Francia 892, ff. 191ᵛ–203 (olim: Stati Ecclesiastici 575), article in Le Monde Juif (1946), 2.

[422] ASRS, AA.EE.SS., Francia 892, f. 224, internal note of Msgr. Dell'Acqua.

[423] ASRS, AA.EE.SS., Francia 892, f. 224, internal note of Msgr. Dell'Acqua.

[424] ASRS, AA.EE.SS., Francia 892, f. 189, handwritten note of Msgr. Valeri, November 7, 1946.

At the time of this inquiry, Bérard was seen as a traitor and Nazi collaborator in France. Although he had created confusion and misled Marshal Pétain on the true views of the Vatican on French racial laws, Bérard was still able to remain in Rome, safely holed up in his Vatican apartment, now as a refugee. He refused to leave the apartment of Santa Marta in order to return to France to face justice. Valeri explained: "Bérard remembers very well that he sent the report [on the Jewish question] and he seems to be reluctant to go back to France exactly for this motive.... Personally, I think that the fears of Bérard ... are too exaggerated."[425]

Whether Bérard's fears about returning to France were exaggerated or not, the Archives retain evidence of a continuing diplomatic row between the French government and the Holy See over the Vatican's sheltering of people the French believed were war criminals and collaborators. The government of France demanded that the Vatican hand over any such persons taking refuge.

A letter written in 1946 by Cardinal Tisserant, who had been newly promoted to the rank of cardinal bishop, to Jacques Maritain, the new postwar French ambassador to the Holy See, reveals this deep rift:

> I come to know that Your Excellency has given the order to banish from the institute on the 11th of this month the French refugees who have found asylum.... Your Excellency knows that I don't have any sympathy nor for collaborationism nor for Vichyism or Pétainism under whatever form they would be presented or labelled. But I also think, and I did say to Your Excellency, that we endorse compatriots that are landed in Italy, where crimes are not demonstrated that could justify a demand of extradition. One should see in those people brothers with a great need.[426]

What is interesting about this letter is that it is written by a Frenchman to a Frenchman and is indicative of some of the debate within France itself at that time around the attitudes toward collaborators.

Ambassador Jacques Maritain replied to the letter:

[425] ASRS, AA.EE.SS., Francia 892, f. 189ᵛ, handwritten note of Msgr. Valeri, November 7, 1946.
[426] ASRS, AA.EE.SS., Francia 910, f. 187, copy of a letter from Card. Tisserant, March 8, 1946.

My dear Eminence

I am anxious to respond in haste to your letter of 8 March. I don't believe that your Eminence was informed in full regarding all the elements of this situation.... It is quite clear that such an institution would not or should not offer shelter to men who are not refugees escaping from persecution but who should face the justice of their country for the errors they made against the nation. And that, if they are innocent, they should be able to justify themselves before their nation.

I ask your Eminence to accept the expression of my profound respect and devotion.

Jacques Maritain[427]

A different letter from Tisserant preserved in the Historical Archive, and which was addressed to Msgr. Tardini, made his position clear. Tisserant was an erudite man, a scholar of Byzantine churches, and a librarian. The heraldry of his letterhead, "from the orient and the west," displays this. He wrote:

Your Excellency does not ignore that for several months now there are also in Rome French refugees. The first of them came in November 1942 when the Germans occupied the Southern part of France. Italians, with a great sense of humanity, opened the frontiers to numerous groups of Jews. These were Jews who, in that time, were considered detrimental to France. They risked being handed over to the Germans by the government of Vichy, with well-known consequences.

Different French religious and ecclesial communities in Rome thought at that time that, notwithstanding the government's view, they should convene to help those French people.... In both the circumstances [during and after the war] those who accepted those refugees did not let the ambassador know, but our new ambassador His Excellency Maritain immediately made clear his disapproval of the act of charity by our fellow countrymen towards these present

[427] ASRS, AA.EE.SS., Francia 910, ff. 188[r/v], copy of a letter from Ambassador Maritain, March 11, 1946.

refugees. I have already discussed twice with him the question and I have let him know that I have encouraged with all my forces those who helped....

It happened then, at the beginning of this month, that H. tE. Maritain notified with a peremptory order that six or seven refugees living in San Luigi dei Francesi had to leave the house no later than the 11th of March. Considering that the pious institution was founded, not by the French Government, but by French curialists, to serve, in part, as an hospice for poor Frenchmen passing by in Rome, I believed it to be my duty to protest by a letter of 8th of March, of which I include a copy, as well as of the response that the Ambassador sent me on the 11th of March.... In his letter, Mr. Maritain, maintains a point of view as if these refugees are criminals, hunted by the French justice. Now, if this would be so why did he not proceed by means of the law and the international conventions, with a regular mandate for arrest?...

I beg your pardon for the extent of my exposition, and I ask you to accept the senses of my distinct and cordial respect/esteem.

Signed

Eugenio Card. Tisserant[428]

Tisserant's words here are quite straightforward. They are a sharp reminder that, only a few months earlier, the French government itself was on the wrong side.

On April 1, 1946, this letter, marked V. S. P., *Visto Santo Padre*, was read by Pius XII, the pope whose ideals of charity went beyond any ideological or political position.

---

[428] ASRS, AA.EE.SS., Francia 910 f. 186, letter of Card. Tisserant [to Msgr. Tardini] of March 27, 1946.

8

A Short Tale of Europe's Wasted Genius

IT WAS SOMEWHAT of a surprise to me to find the name of Paul Oskar Kristeller, the eminent Renaissance scholar known for being the primary author-ity on Renaissance philosophy and thought, listed in the Ebrei Files. Imagine my disappointment when I discovered that his dossier was almost empty, because his story is, without a doubt, a fascinating one.[429]

From his general biographies we know that Kristeller, born German, escaped from Italy to the United States. But the file in his name holds some extra secrets about the man. It contains a long, detailed, but undated curriculum vitae, which he personally typed out and addressed to the pope's administration. It gives us a keen insight into the life of a promising young Jewish scholar in Europe in the 1930s, and how his world changed brutally and irrevocably, giving him no choice but to leave the old continent. Here is what Oskar wrote to the Holy See about himself.[430]

> I was born May 22nd 1905 in Berlin, the son of the merchant Oskar
> Gräfenberg and his wife Alicen, nee Magnus. My father died in the
> same year and in 1911 my mother married the manufacturer Heinrich
> Kristeller, whose family name I assumed in 1919 with governmental

---

[429] ASRS, AA.EE.SS., Ebrei, 73, ff. 55ʳ–57ᵛ.

[430] The text was typewritten in English by Paul Oskar Kristeller himself. Final letters that are failing in the original were added. The author's inclusions for clarity are added in large brackets.

authorization. I attended the Mommsen-Gymnasium at Berlin-Char-lottenburg where I passed the final examination in Easter 1923. I then studied philosophy, history and mathematics in the universities of Heidelberg, Freiburg, Berlin and Marburg, especially under Profes-sors Heidegger, Ernst Hoffmann, Jaspers, Kroner and Rickert and I received the doctor's degree (Dr. Phil.) at Heidelberg in 1928 with the grade "magna cum laude" [great distinction]. I then studied classics at Berlin under Professors Deubner, Werner Jaeger, Maas, Eduard Norden, and passed the public examination in Greek, Latin and phi-losophy at Berlin in 1931 with the highest grade (mit Auszeichnung). In 1929 I published my doctoral dissertation about the conception of the soul in Plotinus' Ethics on which I had many favorable criticisms, especially in Germany. In October 1931 I began at Freiburg under professor Heidegger a study of platonism in th[e] Italian renaissance and prepared myself for the career of a university lecturer.

In 1932–1933 I received a research grant from the German Research Foundation (Notgemeinschaft der Deutschen Wissen-schaft) which permitted me to undertake my first researches in Italy.

The antisemitic legislation of the national-socialist government put a sudden end in 1933 to my career in Germany. I spent the year living with my parents and continued my studies privately. In 1934 I went to Italy and lived first in Rome where I made extensive research, with quite a bit being completed in the Vatican Library. From October 1934 to October 1935 I lived in Florence, where I was lecturer in German in the R[eale] Istituto Superiore di Magis-tero (now university department) and at the same time served as a teacher in a private German school.

In 1935 I held a research grant for three months from the Aca-demic Assistance Council in London (now Society for the protec-tion of Science and Learning). In November 1935 I became lecturer in German in the R[eale] Scuola Normale Superiore (which has the character of a university college) and in the University of Pisa and held this position for three years. In February 1937 I received from the University of Pisa an Italian doctoral diploma. In these last years I have continued my researches especially concerning the philosophy and literature of the Italian Renaissance and I published many essays in Italian periodicals and a critical edition of Marsilius Ficinus' unedited works in three volumes, under the auspices of the Scuola Normale Superiore and with a preface by Senator [Giovanni] Gentile. Other essays, other editions, and a monograph on Ficinus' philosophy are ready to be printed. Senator Gentile also invited me to join him in editing a new collection of humanistic texts. I have collected extensive unedited materials for the history of humanism and renaissance, gathered through my research in the manuscript collections of many libraries. I hope to publish these materials in the future.

Because of recent events I have lost my position which had been already confirmed for the next year. I must give up my researches and leave Italy in few months, almost without means and not being allowed to return to Germany.

Due to this situation I should like to go to America where I know many lernedmen [sic], and I hope to find there some position in a university, research institute, college, school or library. I have very good certificates concerning my scholarly and pedagogical activity from Germany (Hoffmann, Kroner, Cassirer, Eduard Norden and Werner Jaeger, now at Chicago) and Italy (Gentile, Pasquali, Bertoni).[431]

The talented young Jewish German scholar, fortunately for us, also included a full list of his twenty-one publications as well as eight others in preparation.[432] It permits us to date the letter written to the end of 1938 or even more likely some time in 1939.

Kristeller's biographical itinerary shows remarkable parallelism to that of another famous Jewish German student of Martin Heidegger, Hannah Arendt. It is quite probable that Arendt and Kristeller, two brilliant students, met during those years while serving as apprentices at the German universities where both Professors Heidegger and Jaspers taught. It's noteworthy, but not unexpected, that Kristeller does not include the name of Martin Heidegger in his list of academic referees, even though Heidegger was his first main professor, as well as his mentor.

[431] ASRS, AA.EE.SS., Ebrei 73, ff. 56r/v.
[432] ASRS, AA.EE.SS., Ebrei 73, ff. 57r/v.

So, what had happened? Heidegger, one of the world's most famous philosophers of metaphysics, became rector of the University of Freiburg in 1933. This was the same dark and fateful year Hitler became German chancellor. Heidegger did not seem to have any issues with the new chancellor or his hateful rhetoric, for he signed up and became a member of the National Socialist Party. It's known that from that day on, students of Jewish lineage no longer had Heidegger's support. The relationship between Heidegger and Nazism remains an ongoing debate.

The long typewritten curriculum vitae is all that Paul Kristeller's file contains. But it raises a curious question. Did Pius XII's office intervene? Or did Kristeller find help through other people in order to find safe passage out of the increasingly dangerous Germany, which would mean the Holy's See's intervention had become superfluous?[433]

Kristeller's biographers mostly indicate that it was the Italian senator Giovanni Gentile (mentioned in his letter) who helped him to escape, but it remains an open question if he might have had additional behind-the-scenes help from someone from the Vatican. His limited file in the Historical Archive of the Secretariat of State brings little information, but its existence is proof that Paul Oskar Kristeller, anxious to escape his personal and professional nightmare, put his trust in Pius XII and in his staff to help him.

Ironically, prior to the war and the anti-Semitic purge of the Nazis, both Germany and Italy had been at the forefront of studies of European Renaissance culture. Little did they know that their hateful dogma would cause one of the premier European medieval and Renaissance scholars to flee the continent. Europe's loss was America's gain. He became a naturalized U.S. citizen and taught at both Yale and Columbia universities.

*

*   *

Kristeller was not the only academic who found himself in danger during these turbulent years. Among the daily deluge of letters begging for help, one arrived in March 1939 on behalf of another well-known scholar, Professor Tullio Liebman, a Jewish man who had converted to Christianity. The letter was written by Msgr. Francesco Roberti, an expert in civil and canon law, and professor at the Pontifical Institute of St. Apollinare, and was addressed to substitute Montini.[434]

---

[433] It's also possible that traces of actions on his behalf may be found in other Vatican archives.
[434] ASRS, AA.EE.SS., Ebrei 82, ff. 61ʳ–62ᵛ.

Roberti explained:

> Although he had converted, Tullio Liebman had to leave the chair
> of Civil Processual Law at the University of Parma after the racial
> law was enacted in 1938. By the kind intervention of a friendly
> person he has the opportunity to get a post in the faculty of law
> at the University of Montevideo. But as his entrance to Uruguay
> is dependent on a special visa from the ministry of foreign affairs,
> he has directed himself to me, his old school friend, to obtain the
> protection of the Holy See to the desired aim.[435]

But the file made it brutally clear that paving Liebman's way to South American
liberty would be a challenge and would take a great deal of time. The Cabinet's
work on his behalf involved dealing with Cabinetcratic obstacles on opposite sides
of the world, South America and Italy. On March 25, 1939, Tardini sent a coded
cable to Msgr. Fietta, the nuncio of Buenos Aires in Argentina, ordering him to
take up the case from that end.[436]

In Rome, Msgr. Dell'Acqua went back to Msgr. Roberti in order to obtain the
usual and necessary background checks and information. Liebman, however, did
not know where exactly his visa application ended up: "The Professor has asked
me to express to his Excellency his great gratitude. He is, however, sorry he cannot
give more precise data than those already communicated, data that could make
the identification of his file easier. He would dare to hope that those already given
will be sufficient to his aims."[437]

On April 22, annotations in the file show that Roberti advised Dell'Acqua that
Liebman's application to Uruguay "was initiated by the Rector of the University of
Montevideo himself, and should be found at the Ministry of Foreign Affairs."[438] At
last, in possession of these critical details, Maglione sent a cable to Nuncio Fietta
in Buenos Aires with the updated information.[439]

[435] ASRS, AA.EE.SS., Ebrei 82, ff. 61ᵛ–62ʳ, letter from Msgr. Roberti to Msgr. Montini,
March 16, 1939.
[436] ASRS, AA.EE.SS., Ebrei 82, f. 65, draft of cable of Msgr. Tardini to Nuncio Fietta
[sent on May 25, 1939].
[437] ASRS, AA.EE.SS., Ebrei 82, ff. 68ʳ–69ᵛ, letter of Msgr. Roberti, April 10, 1939.
[438] ASRS, AA.EE.SS., Ebrei 82, f. 66, annotations by Msgr. Dell'Acqua.
[439] ASRS, AA.EE.SS., Ebrei 82, f. 67ʳ, cable signed by Card. Maglione, April 24, 1939.

Transcript of Msgr. Fietta's response to Msgr. Tardini and Msgr. Dell'Acqua's annotations, March 26, 1939.[440]

But in the meantime, Nuncio Fietta had made an additional appeal for help to the archbishop of Montevideo. The archbishop was clearly concerned regarding this matter and, not wanting to risk delay, had immediately made an official personal visit to the Ministry of Foreign Affairs of Uruguay. There he was told

[440] ASRS, AA.EE.SS., Ebrei 82, f. 66.

that Liebman had "to present himself in the Consulate of Uruguay in Rome or in Genoa (this last city would be better) to argue his case there. His request would then be, with a special recommendation, taken into account by the Ministry that would immediately grant the visa so that he could embark from that same city."[441] It seems the personal intervention of the archbishop hurried things along.[442] The secretary of state informed Liebman through his old friend Msgr. Roberti that his case was resolved.[443] Finally, a relieved Liebman climbed aboard a ship and set sail to a fresh new life in Uruguay, where he took up his post.

Professor Liebman's case is, in many respects, of outstanding importance. Following his time in Uruguay, he traveled to Argentina, then continued to Rio de Janeiro in Brazil where he accepted a professorship of civil process law. This gifted man would go on to become the founder of the "Brazilian processualistic school," a set of principles for process law that is still studied around the world today. The codex of Brazilian civil law still bears his name: "*O Código Liebman.*"

After Fascism collapsed and the war ended, Liebman came back to Italy, where he was able to teach at various universities without the constant threat of harassment or danger that he had faced earlier. His contributions to law and to education as well as the respect he gained led to a street in Rome being named after him. In saving his life, the Pius XII connection thus preserved a genius of juridical science for humanity.

An interesting sidenote: existing biographies on Enrico Tullio Liebman tell us he left Italy in 1938. But the documents in the archives of the Holy See indicate with certainty that he did not leave Italy before the end of May 1939. More importantly, these biographical accounts on Liebman make no mention whatsoever of any intervention by his old school friend Msgr. Roberti, the staff of Pius XII, nor the archbishop and the nuncio in Argentina — all of whom worked hard to ensure his escape to Uruguay.

Viktor van der Reis was a man whose interests and talents lay in the medical field. Prior to 1919, van der Reis studied at the universities of Würzburg, Leipzig,

---

[441] ASRS, AA.EE.SS., Ebrei 82, f. 71, copy of a letter of Msgr. Juan Francisco Aragone, archbishop of Montevideo, April 28, 1939.

[442] ASRS, AA.EE.SS., Ebrei 82, f. 70ʳ, letter of Nuncio Msgr. Giuseppe Fietta to Card. Maglione, May 3, 1939.

[443] ASRS, AA.EE.SS., Ebrei 82, f. 72, draft of letter of Msgr. Tardini to Msgr. Roberti, May 16, 1939.

and München and passed the German state exam with the highest distinction, earning his degree as a physician. When World War I broke out, he served Germany as a military doctor with skill and dedication, and he was wounded three times during the conflict. In 1918, he married Margarethe Ernst, one of the first women in Germany to obtain a medical degree. The couple had three children. The oldest son, Ernst, was born in 1922; their daughter, Annemarie, was born in 1925; and the youngest, Dierk, was born in 1928.[444]

Between the harsh years of the Great War and the time his youngest son was born, Viktor served as professor at the University of Greifswald. He then took up dual posts of both extraordinary professor and director of internal medicine at the public city hospital in Danzig, in East Prussia. Viktor found his unique medical passion and skill, becoming an expert in the fields of small intestine pathology and microbiology.

Viktor would have expected to lead the quiet and peaceful life of a respected medical specialist in Danzig, spending time with his wife and his children and enjoying the amenities and comforts of his position. However, this wasn't the case. He was an active member of the *Zentrumspartei*, sometimes called the "Catholic Centre Party." And although he was a baptized Catholic, he came from a Jewish lineage.

And so because of these two particular aspects of his life — his membership and his heritage — he found himself imprisoned for short periods from 1935 on. Then the Nazi noose began to tighten even more, and he had to give up his professional activities at the hospital in Danzig. For a short while he was allowed to briefly run a private clinic from his house. But under the heavy bootheel of Nazi control, that ended soon. Sensing that he and his family now faced a life-or-death situation, he encouraged Margarethe to take the children and escape from Danzig. They were successful and made it to Düsseldorf. This certainly had to have been a great relief to the doctor, but during his own attempt to flee, he was captured by the Gestapo and interred in a German concentration camp in Neufahrwasser near Gdańsk. Viktor was later transferred to a larger concentration camp in Stutthof, where in the autumn of 1939 he courageously found a way to escape.

Driven by fear and hope, and in possession of a Polish passport, Viktor managed to reach the border of Italy and cross over into the country. Details of this episode in his life have been, until now, unknown. But the Historical Archive shines a light

[444] ASRS, AA.EE.SS., Ebrei 154, f. 55.

on them. On May 11, 1940, Viktor van der Reis was hiding in Rome, in a house belonging to the Pallottine Fathers, located on the Via dei Pettinari 57. The same house also functioned as the central office in Rome for the Saint *Raphaelsverein*, the Catholic organization for German refugees. It's not clear how Viktor arrived in Rome or how he'd obtained the Polish passport.[445] Fr. Hecht, *Raphaelsverein*'s director, recommended the brave German medical researcher and doctor to the Holy See, describing him as "Catholic non Aryan, to obtain a visa to Brazil with the quota of the Vatican."[446]

Viktor also addressed a letter, written in French, "to the Secretary of State of His Holiness," recalling the events in Germany: "In consequence of the events in Germany I was forced to leave my homeland. I'm of Catholic religion but non-Aryan race. My family is Catholic, my wife of Aryan race." [447] He then requested visas to Brazil for his whole family.[448]

According to the archives, Viktor van der Reis delivered the letter to the Cabinet himself and gave it to Msgr. Dell'Acqua in person. This was quite a bold and brave step, keeping in mind that he was not only a fugitive but also one of Jewish lineage, moving through the hazards of Fascist Rome.

Dell'Acqua's annotations on May 11 read: "The other members of the family are still in Germany. In the meantime, I told Mr. van der Reis that they should contact the *Raphaelsverein*."[449] The clear, continued perils facing Viktor prompted the *minutante* Dell'Acqua to act quickly. A day later, on May 12, an *appunto* with request for his visa was sent to the embassy of Brazil to the Holy See. This all worked out perfectly, yet this embassy had warned that although he was given a visa, once in Brazil "it was absolutely forbidden" for him to practice as a medical doctor.[450]

Viktor's protector, Fr. Hecht of the *Raphaelsverein*, then suggested an alternative plan. On May 25, 1940, he sent the following proposition to Cardinal Maglione:

> Mr Professor Dr. Vittore [*sic*] van der Reis of Polish nationality had
> for a time been in a concentration camp but he has licence to go

[445] ASRS, AA.EE.SS., Ebrei 154, f. 58 (note of the office: "Maintenant passport polonais").
[446] ASRS, AA.EE.SS., Ebrei 154, f. 57.
[447] ASRS, AA.EE.SS., Ebrei 154, f. 55.
[448] ASRS, AA.EE.SS., Ebrei 154, f. 55.
[449] ASRS, AA.EE.SS., Ebrei 154, f. 56ᵛ.
[450] ASRS, AA.EE.SS., Ebrei 154, f. 60, letter of Fr. Francesco Saverio Hecht to Card. Maglione, May 27, 1940.

abroad. He would like to go to the United States as his name has been on the list for a visa for a few years. But now it seems that the given circumstances don't allow him going there until that visa is accepted. Therefore, he would like to go to Lisbon and wait there for the visa, asking your Eminence for a benign recommendation in order to obtain as soon as possible the Portuguese visa. The above-mentioned Professor is well known and recommended by His Eminence Cardinal Hlond and his Excellency Bishop Okoniewski.[451]

Perhaps somewhat impatiently, Fr. Hecht wrote again two days later. Once more, he emphasized that Viktor van der Reis had been on the list for a United States visa since 1938, a visa that could be granted him in a few months. He warned that

under the given circumstances, it seems he cannot stay [in Italy] for the time this necessitates, but he should go to Lisbon or Brazil in order to save himself (having been already in a concentration camp), where he will wait for the visa for the United States, with the belief that the visa for Portugal or Spain will be given him immediately. To shorten the waiting time for the American visa, I ask if Your Eminence would help by recommending him by Mr. Taylor [the U.S. special envoy to the Holy See], in order that Taylor would intervene in his favor.[452]

It appears that Dell'Acqua didn't appreciate the badgering and the stream of various suggestions. He had been working hard to get Viktor to Brazil as soon as possible. Dell'Acqua annotated, "I told Father Hecht that there is nothing that can be done about it,"[453] "that there are no possibilities for Portugal and that it would be good for Mr. van der Reis to depart immediately for Brazil."[454] Dell'Acqua certainly understood the frustration Viktor would experience in Brazil without having the right to practice medicine. Yet he would at least be safe and might be able to move on from there at some point in time.

[451] ASRS, AA.EE.SS., Ebrei 154, f. 61ʳ, letter of Fr. Francesco Saverio Hecht to Card. Maglione, May 25, 1940.
[452] ASRS, AA.EE.SS., Ebrei 154, f. 60, letter of Fr. Francesco Saverio Hecht to Card. Maglione, May 27, 1940.
[453] ASRS, AA.EE.SS., Ebrei 154, f. 60ᵛ, note of Msgr. Dell'Acqua, May 28, 1940.
[454] ASRS, AA.EE.SS., Ebrei 154, f. 61ᵛ, note of Msgr. Dell'Acqua, May 28, 1940.

And so Viktor van der Reis spent the next eighteen years in Brazil. He was never able to move on, however, and died in the city of São Paolo in 1957. What adds to the heartbreaking poignancy of his story is that not only was his professional career over, but it's unknown as to whether his wife and children were able to join him there. In spite of this sad ending, his work lives on and he is regarded today as the pioneer of gastrointestinal and microecology — what we call gut flora today.[455]

*

*   *

Leafing through these inspiring testimonies of attempts to help and save people facing real-life dangers tells us something of the "brain drain" — the loss of intellectuals from Europe to America and elsewhere. The relentless persecution of the Jews contributed to the impoverishment of postwar European culture and intellectual progress. It was a widespread and sweeping discrimination that went beyond religion to discriminate against those considered to be of a lesser "race."

Yet a few fortunate individuals would live on to become pillars of postwar society in their new homelands, and for the world, even if their biographies — until today — remained silent on how all this was made possible.

[455] Article by M. Knoke, "Viktor van der Reis — Wegbereiter der gastrointestinalen Mikroökologie des Menschen," *Food/Nahrung* 28 (1984), 6–7.

9

A Tale of Dark and Sinister Places toward the East . . . I

THERE WAS NOTHING new under the sun. The trains and convoys filled with people were once again heading "to the East."

During the First World War, Secretary of the Congregation for Extraordinary Church Affairs Eugenio Pacelli became very familiar with the dark and sinister slogan "to the East." In January 1918, three months before the ending of the hostilities in Eastern Europe and the establishment of peace with Russia through the Treaty of Brest-Litovsk on March 3, 1918, forty-one-year-old Pacelli, now recently appointed nuncio in Bavaria, wrote to Rome how "the German Government has found itself compelled to proceed with the announced reprisals. On the 6th of this month, 600 notable Frenchmen were transported to the occupied Russian territory. . . . In a few days will follow the transport of 400 women to the camp of Holzminden."[456] It already seemed as if, when at war, the German military saw the East the ideal place to ship and confine prisoners. Sending captives "to the East" also had a strong symbolic character. Those banished would disappear forever from the pleasant and comfortable West. They would be out of sight and out of mind in the cold, feared, far-away world of the Slavs, that other part of humanity that the Teutonics in 1914–1918 and later the Nazis held in contempt and animosity. Deportations would again become a reality throughout the 1930s, when the

---

[456] ASRS, AA.EE.SS., Francia 1282, fasc. 674 (1917–1918), f. 4, letter in code of Msgr. Pacelli to Card. Gasparri, January 16, 1918 (arrived January 19).

whole German territory was littered with concentration camps of various types. As secretary of state between 1930 and 1939, Eugenio Pacelli was perfectly aware of this reality.

*

*   *

The number of Jews targeted, and how they were treated, was beyond comparison; however, the clergy in Germany was also massively targeted by Nazi ferocity already before the war. The Polish embassy excerpts continued: "Almost thirty professors of the Cracovian University were imprisoned in camps in Germany, in particular in Dachau, Oranienburg, and in Mathausen."[457] In those 1940 reports, quite reliable as other documents preserved in the Historical Archive prove, certain sentences seemingly pop up off the page, sentences that make it clear that exiguous parts of the clergy had not been given a much better fate than the Jews. Not only were they prevented from celebrating Mass, notwithstanding the guarantees given before with a *note verbale* from the foreign ministry from Berlin,[458] but they were often treated as the worst criminals and submitted to incessant tortures.[459] Msgr. Cesare Orsenigo, the nuncio in Berlin, did everything in his power possible through diplomatic means to have the Polish priests incarcerated in concentration camps be expelled for neutral countries. This daring plan had produced "modest results" — as he reported to Rome. In April and June 1940, he had already protested to the State Department in Berlin about the brutal treatment in concentration camps, especially that of Sachsenhausen near Oranienburg, a nightmarish place where priests were routinely abused. In the same Sachsenhausen concentration camp, in addition to the Catholic priests, the Protestant pastor Niemöller was held in solitary confinement. He was later transferred to Dachau and would, surprisingly, survive the camp. After the war, he was very critical regarding the inaction of the Protestants during the persecution and horror that the Nazis meted out to the Jews. The nuncio in Switzerland, Msgr. Bernardini, pointed out that Niemöller asked himself in the

---

[457] ASRS, AA.EE.SS., Stati Ecclesiastici 688a, f. 455, "Extraits de plusieurs lettres ecrites de Pologne … (V. Lettre de Cracovie)," December 1940.

[458] ASRS, AA.EE.SS., Stati Ecclesiastici 688c, f. 336, *Note verbale* of the German Ministry of Foreign Affairs to the apostolic nunciature of November 23, 1940.

[459] ASRS, AA.EE.SS., Stati Ecclesiastici 630, f. 280, report on the situation in the camp in Silesia, dated January 29, 1940.

article he published in 1945: "How come, for instance, that in Dachau we were only 45 evangelical pastors against 450 German catholic priests?"[460]

Though the Nazi government refused to release the Polish priests, fearing they would stir anti-Nazi propaganda abroad, a small "concession" was made, and from then on all clergymen would be concentrated in the same camp at Dachau.[461] The Cabinet took the matter seriously, discussing various possibilities, but did not come up with a concrete plan.[462] By the end of December 1940, Nuncio Orsenigo informed the pope that twelve hundred clergymen would soon converge on Dachau.[463] The numbers of losses and deportation among the clergy were large: up to April 1941, twenty-five hundred to three thousand priests had been arrested in Poland, nine hundred of whom had already died and (only) seventy of whom had been released. All the others were in captivity.[464] And while, at the end of 1940, the nuncio in Berlin claimed that the concentration camp of Dachau "has the reputation of being less rigid in its control,"[465] it was only a matter of months before the Cabinet in Rome came to know that just the opposite was true. Reports arrived of two Jesuits who had been transferred to Dachau and had died quickly, one after the other: in February 1941, Fr. Kałuża and in March, Fr. Boleslao Szopiński.[466] Shortly afterwards, a *note verbale* from the Polish embassy informed the Holy See of the fate of a certain Polish priest named Prokopowicz. He had spent five years in prison under the Soviets before he was arrested by the Nazis, along with ten other priests, on August 27, 1940. He was first imprisoned in Oranienburg for several months, where, against the odds, he survived despite the high mortality of priests. He was then transferred to Dachau, which "seems for some categories of prisoners even harsher; he was there still in the month of May 1941, where he was wearing the number 22518,

---

[460] ASRS, AA.EE.SS., Germania 899, f. 362, Article "La responsabilité des chrétiens allemands. Une lettre du pasteur Niemöller," in *Tribune de Genève*, December 22, 1945.

[461] ASRS, AA.EE.SS., Stati Ecclesiastici 688c, f. 340ᵛ.

[462] ASRS, AA.EE.SS., Stati Ecclesiastici 688c, f. 343, dispatch of Card. Maglione to Msgr. Orsenigo, Roma, October 23, 1940.

[463] ASRS, AA.EE.SS., Stati Ecclesiastici 688c, f. 327.

[464] ASRS, AA.EE.SS., Polonia 208, f. 739.

[465] ASRS, AA.EE.SS., Stati Ecclesiastici 688c, f. 340ᵛ.

[466] ASRS, AA.EE.SS., Stati Ecclesiastici 688c, f. 355, copy of the report of Orsenigo to Card. Maglione, February 17, 1941; f. 359, letter of Father General Ledóchowski to Card. Maglione, March 2, 1941.

K/3, Block 28/3. His family asks us to save him."[467] *Minutante* Msgr. Samorè attempted to deal with the case, appealing to Nuncio Orsenigo to intervene, always bearing in mind the dubious promise of the Nazi Ministry that within a few months the priests in Dachau would be relieved of hard labor.[468]

That same year, in November 1941, the gruesome name of Oświęcim — Auschwitz — appeared once more in the Historical Archive, this time in a request from the embassy of Poland to the Holy See, which during those years was hosted within the Vatican walls. The request sought an intervention "that if done on time could save a life, most precious among all others." It was on behalf of the auxiliary bishop of Płock, Msgr. Wetmański, who was interred in Auschwitz and was "very ill and slowly dying."[469] Nuncio Orsenigo also made continuous, sustained interventions in favor of other Polish bishops and their auxiliaries who were barely surviving in various German concentration camps.[470] Excerpts of letters collected by the Polish embassy and sent to the Holy See as early as December 1940 mention that "there is, not far of Oswiecim [Auschwitz], a big concentration camp. Life over there is terrible. There is a big crematorium where each week 100 cadavers are burned."[471]

Distinct badge to be worn by Jews in Croatia (letter Ž stands for Židov or "Jew").[472]

[467] ASRS, AA.EE.SS., Stati Ecclesiastici 688c, f. 319, *Note verbale* of the Polish embassy to the Holy See to the Secretariat of State, June 4, 1941: "semble être, pour certaines cathégories de prissoniers [sic], encore plus dur; il y était encore au mois de Mai 1941, où il portait le n° 22518, K/3, Block 28/3. Sa famille demande qu'on le sécoure [sic]."

[468] ASRS, AA.EE.SS., Stati Ecclesiastici 688c, f. 320, note of the office (Msgr. Samorè); f. 321, draft of letter to Msgr. Orsenigo.

[469] ASRS, AA.EE.SS., Polonia 208, f. 696, letter of the ambassador to the Holy See to Card. Maglione, November 21, 1941.

[470] ASRS, AA.EE.SS., Polonia 208, f. 693, draft of letter of Card. Maglione to the Polish ambassador to the Holy See, November 30, 1941.

[471] ASRS, AA.EE.SS., Stati Ecclesiastici 688a, f. 455, "Extraits de plusieurs lettres ecrites de Pologne ... (V. Lettre de Cracovie)," December 1940.

[472] ASRS, AA.EE.SS., Jugoslavia 160, 231b.

*

*   *

The Cabinet also received information on the deportation and interment of Jews. Although these reports were sometimes less substantial and reliable than those on the Catholic clergy, the treatment of the Jewish population in Europe left no doubt as to the reality of their situation. During his visit to the Vatican, Msgr. Alojzije Stepinac, the archbishop of Zagreb, delivered on June 9, 1941, a "star of David" with underneath the letter Ž (*Židov* means "Jew" in Croatian), the distinctive badge to be worn by Jews in Croatia. With his intervention, the archbishop had only been able to avoid this treatment for the converted Jews, not for the others.[473]

In November of that same year, thanks to an account of a certain Dr. Schlefenberg, some details on the situation of the Jews in Romania became better known. He determined that of the three hundred thousand Jews in Bessarabia and Bukavina, only eighty to ninety thousand remained as of October 1941. It was assumed that during the "Operation Barbarossa" ninety thousand Jews had been immediately executed by the German army and others had escaped during the withdrawal of the Russian troops.[474] The documents preserved in the Historical Archive show that their fate under the Russians was definitely not more secure. A photo preserved elsewhere in the Historical Archive makes the horrific fate of these last ones, as well as many others under the Soviet army, visible today.

The informant, Dr. Schlefenberg, continued: "The survivors of Cernowits and Kishinew were huddled together in a small ghetto, surrounded by barbed wire, in the boroughs with ruins and without running water. They are not allowed to go out and cannot look for provisions elsewhere. Their properties are all confiscated and it is forbidden, on pain of forced labour, to come to their aid or to give them money etc. Diseases and suicides cause havoc; the young girls prostitute themselves for a piece of bread etc." Worse, if possible, was the situation of the Jews in other places, confined in the camps of Marculesti, Secureni, Edineti, and Vertujeni (in the latter, a population of twenty-two thousand Jews was crammed in 350 ruined houses). The report goes into more detail about the further eradication of the Jews on Romanian territory and concludes that

[473] ASRS, AA.EE.SS., Jugoslavia 160, 231a.
[474] ASRS, AA.EE.SS., Romania 149, f. 135, report on the Jews in Romenia, [November 11, 1941, signed by Dr. Schlefenberg].

"this entire policy has a very clear aim: complete spoliation and probably the physical extermination of all the Jews in Rumania. In Transnistria, one affirms that all the Jews are being executed."[475]

Deportation "towards the East." It is hardly a coincidence that exact same phrase was underlined by the Cabinet on an article cut out from the magazine *Deutschland*. In the article, the German journalist talked about the missed opportunity for amnesty for the political prisoners that Germany had offered. Because "nor the Belgians, nor the Poles, nor the Checks, nor the Slovenes, nor the Norwegians, nor the Dutch, reacted positively on the proposals. And therefore, the deportations are to be seen as a new and forced phase in the European cooperation. Already thousands of French, Norwegians, and Dutch find themselves as deported people in the Eastland. All male Poles between 18 and 60 years of age are compelled to serve in the '*Baudienstes*' [service of construction] that takes place under military discipline. 65,000 Slovenes were" already deported "in order to evacuate 40 kilometers

Prison in Lonski-L'viv. People murded by the Bolsheviks from June 15 to June 23–25, 1941.[476]

[475] Translation: "This whole politics have one clear aim; the total spoliation and probably the physical extermination of all Jews in Romania. One confirms that in Transnistria all the Jews have been executed." ASRS, AA.EE.SS., Romania 149, f. 136, report on the Jews in Romania, [November 11, 1941, signed by Dr. Schlefenberg].
[476] ASRS, AA.EE.SS., Russia 738, f. 485ᵛ.

of the German-Croatian border."[477] The article tackles the public opinion in some European countries that was upset about this "deportation to the East." In fact, the deportation of the Jews of Lyon and the vehement reaction of the French bishops to it occurred during the same month of July. And the arrest of twelve thousand Jews in Paris and their imprisonment in the Vélodrome d'Hiver at the end of July 1942 provoked great indignation among the Parisian population. The episcopacy wondered if it would be wise to raise a public protest against such treatments. A decision against that prevailed, however, in order "to avoid exposing the movements of the Catholic Action [that is] until now still tolerated." Instead, Cardinal Suhard would send a letter of disapproval to the head of state. Nuncio Valeri judged that letter to be "a rather platonic protest."[478] Also in Lyon, France, all Jews of foreign nationality who were living in France since 1936 were deported. During this time, Cardinal Gerlier rescued hundreds of children, who were separated from their parents, through the association Amitiés Chrétiennes, which was composed of Catholics and Protestants, and presided over by the cardinal himself.[479]

In August, news out of Slovakia was coming into the Cabinet:

> The deportation began on the 20th of March 1942, after numerous administrative measures were already in place: absolute prohibition on travelling, also a prohibition of transferring within the same village or city, curfew after 6 pm, marking of houses of Jews with the yellow star of David, lists of Jewish habitants on the house doors. The first transport of 25 March 1942 involved 8,500 persons, and the transports were separate for men and women. After 4 weeks it was announced that families should not be separated. At that moment began the "family-transports" in which there was no exception anymore for babies, old and sick people, or pregnant women. By the midst of July about 45,000 people were likewise deported.... The unimaginable suffering that the Jews in Poland experience, form the completion of a never ending tragic chapter of the history of suffering of the Jews.[480]

---

[477] ASRS, AA.EE.SS., Extracta, Germania 742, f. 83, article of *Deutschland*, July 31, 1942.

[478] ASRS, AA.EE.SS., Francia 892, f. 128ᵛ, letter of Msgr. Valeri to Card. Maglione, Vichy, July 29, 1942.

[479] ASRS, AA.EE.SS., Francia 892, ff. 137–139, "Quelques notes à propos des récentes évènements de Lyon," September 2, 1942.

[480] ASRS, AA.EE.SS., Cecoslovacchia 175, f. 535.

If there were still any existing doubts as to the devilish path Nazi Germany was paving, the letter of Msgr. Szeptykyi, Ruthenian Catholic metropolitan of L'viv, to the pope at the end of August 1942, cast them away:

Msgr. Andrej Szeptykyi's original letter to Pius XII, August 29–31, 1942.[481]

> Today, the whole country agrees that the German is at a higher degree than the Bolshevist regime, bad, almost diabolical. For at least a year, there is no day passing in which the most horrible crimes, murdering, thefts and robbery, seizures and concussions take place. The Jews are the first victims of all of this. The number of Jews killed in our little country passed certainly the number of

---

[481] ASRS, AA.EE.SS., Polonia 216, f. 444.

two hundred thousand. And while the army advanced towards
the East, the number of victims increased. In Kiev, in a few days,
130,000 men, women and children were executed. All the little
villages of Ukraine were victims of similar massacres.... In the
beginning, the [German] authorities were embarrassed by these
acts of inhuman injustice and made sure that documents would
prove that the citizens or enemy soldiers were the executors of
these killings. With the time passing by, however, they started
killing the Jews in the streets, in full view of the population and
without any shame. Naturally, multitudes of Christians, not only
baptized Jews, but "aryan" as they say, were likewise victims of
unjustified slayings.[482]

*

*   *

The titles of some files of that time that are preserved in the Historical Archive
betray the difficulty or even impossibility of obtaining reliable information on the
"non-Aryans" deported out of Germany.[483] The nuncio in Berlin, reporting in July
1942 on the search for news on these non-Arians, had to admit

with a heavy heart that unfortunately no one here is able to get
secure info about the non-Aryans, on the contrary, it is unadvis-
able to interest oneself in it, while it seems that here they ensure
to make loose traces of the deported. It is dangerous even to talk
with a non-Aryan person, bearing the star.... Lately the situation got even worse.... We are being forbidden to utter the most
simple question in favor of the non-Aryans.... Every intervention
also in favor of only non-Aryan Catholics was rejected, with the
common response that the baptismal water does not change the
non-Aryan race, and that the German Reich is defending itself

[482] ASRS, AA.EE.SS., Extracta, Germania 742, f. 11, excerpt from a letter of Msgr.
Andrej Szeptykyi to Pius XII, August 29–31, 1942. The original in ASRS, AA.EE.
SS., Polonia 216, f. 444.
[483] ASRS, AA.EE.SS., Extracta, Germania 742, f. 28, file "Impossibility of getting information on non-arians deported out of Germany" [in pencil (added later?): September–October 1942].

against the non-Arian race, and not against the religious confession of baptized Jews.[484]

The embassy of Poland, however, offered continuous and disturbing updates to the
Holy See on the situation of ghettos that were cleared out and "how the Jews are killed
in several cities. On the ghetto of Warsaw, methodologically emptied, . . . and each
day Jews are brought by train beyond Lublin, towards the East."[485] Someone in the
Cabinet was reminded of the information on Poland that was brought in earlier by
Count Giovanni Malvezzi, who spoke of "massacres of Jews that had taken terrifying
proportions and forms."[486] This uncertainty and, at the same time, impossibility of
the diplomatic representative to gather information compelled the Cabinet to seek
recourse from other sources in Switzerland, such as the direction of the Catholic
Mission in Switzerland, engaged in protective, proactive actions for Europe.[487]

It was in August and September 1942 that one of the major rescue operations overseen by the Cabinet occurred. As already indicated, during those days,
twenty thousand of the Jews living in the occupied zone in France were handed
over to the Nazis. The scenes of cruelty were devastating and indescribable. Msgr.
Louis Waeber, who was the vicar-general of the Diocese of Lausanne, Geneva,
and Fribourg, briefed the nuncio in Bern[488] about a meeting in which ten people
had taken part. These people were representatives of the Protestant and Jewish
faiths as well as neutrals and Swiss associations active in rescuing Jewish children,
particularly in France. "The meeting," so writes the Swiss informant, "was not
so much a very productive initiative in favor of the adults — it would have been
completely useless — but for the children. Those older than 16 have to follow their
parents; those less than 16 years of age can stay. And it is this group, about 3,500 in
number, which we dealt with during our meeting."[489] It was at that point, said Msgr.

[484] ASRS, AA.EE.SS., Extracta, Germania 742, f. 30, copy of a letter of Msgr. Orsenigo
to Msgr. Montini, July 28, 1942.

[485] ASRS, AA.EE.SS., Extracta, Germania 742, f. 35, Note verbale of the ambassador of
Poland to the Holy See to the secretary of state, Vatican, October 3, 1942.

[486] ASRS, AA.EE.SS., Extracta, Germania 742, f. 12.

[487] ASRS, AA.EE.SS., Extracta, Germania 742, f. 29, note of Tardini, October 11, 1942.

[488] ASRS, AA.EE.SS., Francia 892, f. 99, letter of Msgr. Bernardini to Card. Maglione,
September 1, 1942.

[489] ASRS, AA.EE.SS., Francia 892, f. 101, transcript of the letter of Rev. L. Waeber to
Msgr. Bernardini, August 31, 1942.

Waeber, "that I, as representative of the Catholic Church, was asked to request the Nonciature in Bern to write to the Holy See, in order that the Holy See would alert the Nonciatures in Portugal, Brazil, Uruguay, Argentina and maybe Venezuela and Chili, to ask to the bishops to prepare the catholic mileus. Portugal should accept on a temporary basis, and the other countries on a more permanent one, those poor Jewish children who were separated from their parents during heartbreaking scenes, parents whom, beyond any shadow of doubt, they will never see again." The only condition Waeber added was that "it is absolutely necessary to act very quickly: it is a question of days and almost of hours." Msgr. Tardini marked this last sentence with his blue pencil in the margin. With this, Vicar-General Waeber accepted the challenge. He would take up the charge to assure that, through the intermediation of the Catholic Church and especially of the Holy See, "the gates of oversea countries would be opened to these poor children. It is a Christian task, fulfilled by protestant, catholic and neutral circles towards the victims of Jewish race."[490] The Cabinet took notice of this all, and Cardinal Maglione added in his own handwriting: "The case is urgent. But what shall one be able to obtain? I beg you to refer to the Holy Father."[491]

At the end of August, a cable of the nunciature, almost indecipherable and therefore slow in being translated, arrived. It spoke of a letter of protest. That letter was written by Cardinal Gerlier, archbishop of Toulouse, regarding the growing tensions and the measures of the Vichy government in Lyon against the Jews. Bishops such as Msgr. Pierre-Marie Théas, in charge of the Diocese of Montauban, were writing letters to be read from the pulpit to the faithful in defense of the "respect of the human person."[492] This time Msgr. Valeri, the nuncio, did not consider these letters to be "platonic" — a term he had used earlier in the case of the official letter of Cardinal Suhard; on the contrary, they were more detailed, more challenging, and more straightforward than before.

Some Vichy government–aligned newspapers interpreted the attitude of the bishops as an effort to sabotage the work of Marshal Pétain, whose goal was to foster French unity. In fact, in another report sent by cable, the pope's representative, Nuncio Valeri,

[490] ASRS, AA.EE.SS., Francia 892, f. 102.
[491] ASRS, AA.EE.SS., Francia 892, f. 104, registration formular of the office, September 2, 1942.
[492] ASRS, AA.EE.SS., Francia 892, f. 152, "Lettre de Msgr. L'Evêque de Montauban sur le respect de la personne humaine," August 26, 1942.

informed the Cabinet that "those [bishops] who continue to take position against the Government are accused of being anglofiles, degaullists [sic] and saboteurs of the great work of Marschall Pétain."[493] This cable stated that different diplomats had transmitted the letter by Cardinal Gerlier to their respective governments.[494] In the meanwhile, Msgr. Barbetta, the *minutante,* did his homework in the office. In his opinion, the information from Vicar-General Waeber of Lausanne and the information sent in by Nuncio Valeri did not correspond with one another, not on the exact number of Jews nor on the fate of their children: "In fact the general-vicar spoke of '20,000 Jews already departed,' as of the 30th of August. This where Msgr. Valeri, on the 31st of August, mentions 4,500 Jews already departed and 12,000 still 'concentrated' in the Velodrome on the 24th of August."[495] Furthermore, the Swiss vicar-general stated that

> the children older than 16 "have to follow" their parents, and those under 16 "can" stay. However, Msgr. Valeri does not make this distinction but affirms without doubt that Mr. Laval has obtained from Mr. Hitler the instruction "that the children follow their parents" and this will be required for the occupied as well as for the free zone. It would be opportune to send a telegraph to Msgr. Valeri to know if it seems to him that 3 to 5 thousand Jewish children will be left abandoned and how the French episcopacy intends to proceed.[496]

The message from Msgr. Waeber was crystal clear "it is absolutely necessary to act very quickly" and that the tension in France between the episcopacy and the government of Pétain was ever increasing. Yet, as is very often the case, Cabinetcracy has its own rhythm. It took another ten days before a cable signed by Cardinal Maglione was sent out to Nuncio Valeri and his right-hand in Vichy, Msgr. Pacini, to check on the Jewish children.[497]

[493] ASRS, AA.EE.SS., Francia 892, f. 136ᵛ, report of Msgr. Valeri to Card. Maglione, September 8, 1942.
[494] ASRS, AA.EE.SS., Francia 892, f. 107, cable to the secretary of state, Vichy, September 5, 1942 (arrived September 6).
[495] ASRS, AA.EE.SS., Francia 892, f. 105, internal note of Msgr. Barbetta, September 11, 1942.
[496] ASRS, AA.EE.SS., Francia 892, f. 105, internal note of Msgr. Barbetta, September 11, 1942.
[497] ASRS, AA.EE.SS., Francia 892, f. 96, cable of Card. Maglione to nunciature in Vichy, September 17, 1942.

The discreet international diplomatic tam-tam made by the Vatican, however, had its intended effect. Already, on September 19, 1942, the nunciature in Haiti shared some good tidings with Cardinal Maglione:

> The newspapers of both republics [Dominican Republic and Haiti] reported on several occasions about the protests that the Holy See, through the Nuncio in Vichy, presented to the French Government in regard to the recent laws introduced in that country against the Jews. In that respect the President of the Dominican Republic, General Trujillo, has offered hospitality to 3,500 Jewish children, between 3 and 14 years old, that belong to the Jewish population of the free-zone. The same President would take charge of the organisation and the costs of the sea voyage.[498]

Some weeks later, a choir of well-disposed countries came forward. The United States would take one thousand children who had been threatened with deportation. The Dominican Republic would also take one thousand. At first Canada agreed to take five hundred and then another five hundred. There was hope that Switzerland would take some hundreds in, as well.[499] At least those thirty-five hundred children would depart to the West, not "to the East."

*

* *

On September 27, 1942, the personal envoy of President Roosevelt, Myron Taylor, went up into the Apostolic Palace to meet with Cardinal Maglione. In his leather suitcase he brought a document of most urgent importance. Maglione was absent, and so Taylor handed the envelope with its highly significant content over to someone of the Cabinet who immediately delivered it to Pius XII.[500] The pope opened the envelope and found two separate documents. The first one was a letter addressed to Cardinal Maglione. The second one was a kind of appendix, a memorandum. It mentioned two reliable Aryan eyewitnesses who had sent a report on recent events in Poland to the Geneva Office of the Jewish Agency for

---

[498] ASRS, AA.EE.SS., Francia 892, f. 109.

[499] ASRS, AA.EE.SS., Francia 892, f. 112, letter of Msgr. Waeber to Msgr. Bernardini, Genève, October 9, 1942.

[500] ASRS, AA.EE.SS., Extracta, Germania 742, f. 14, internal note.

Palestine. As the pope read, the far-away situation became shockingly and almost unbearably real, revealing itself as a film before his eyes: "Liquidation of the Warsaw Ghetto is taking place. Without any distinction all Jews, irrespective of age or sex, are being removed from the Ghetto in groups and shot. Their corpses are utilized for making fats and their bones for the manufacture of fertilizer. Corpses are even being exhumed for this purpose."[501] The pope turned over to the next leaf: "These mass executions take place, not in Warsaw, but in specially prepared camps for the purpose, one which is stated to be in Belzek. About 50,000 Jews have been executed in Lemberg [L'viv] itself on the spot during the past month. According to another report, 100,000 have been massacred in Warsaw. There is not one Jew left in the entire district east of Poland, including occupied Russia." Was such astonishing information credible? The eyewitnesses also identified "that the entire non-Jewish population of Sebastopol was murdered." A peculiarity in all this was that "so as not to attract the attention of foreign countries, the butchering of the Jewish population in Poland was not done at one single time."[502] The European tragedy continued: "Jews deported from Germany, Belgium, Holland, France, and Slovakia are sent to be butchered, while Aryans deported to the East from Holland and France are genuinely used for work." And then the old refrain, "deportation to the East," appeared with new, horrific significance: "Inasmuch as butchering of this kind would attract great attention in the west, they must first of all deport them to the East, where less opportunity is afforded to outsiders of knowing what is going on. During the last few weeks a large part of the Jewish population deported to Lithuania and Lublin has already been executed."

Now, it became obvious why Nuncio Orsenigo, in Berlin for months, was running from pillar to post, trying desperately and without success to find concrete answers to his questions regarding the destination of the trains that were departing "to the East." The report leaves no doubts on the mass executions: "Arrangements are made for new deportations as soon as space is made by executions. Caravans of such deportees being transported in cattle cars are often seen. There are about forty people in each cattle car. It is especially significant to note that Lithuanian non-Jews are entrusted with fetching the candidates from the death Ghetto in Warsaw." And

[501] ASRS, AA.EE.SS., Extracta, Germania 742, f. 16, letter of Myron Taylor to Card. Maglione, September 26, 1942.
[502] ASRS, AA.EE.SS., Extracta, Germania 742, f. 17, letter of Myron Taylor to Card. Maglione, September 26, 1942.

the report concluded by saying, "It is a tragedy that the Polish population is being incited by the Germans against the Jews and the relationship between the Poles and the Jews has been aggravated to the lowest degree."[503] The immense numbers of victims and brutal behavior of the Nazis would almost make one think that no one in Warsaw was doing anything to halt the deportations or killings, that no one cared or even noticed. Yet some documents, however small and easy to overlook, shed some light on heroic individuals who did not at all turn a blind eye in those moments. Such is the case with the scribble on a leaflet that was cut out regarding the verbal and written attempts of Archbishop Gall toward those in charge of the Warsaw ghetto in favor of Catholic Jews to be saved, but where he himself had to admit that everything remained without any result.[504]

With these facts now revealed, Myron Taylor, the American envoy, had a question for Cardinal Maglione, who was in that moment absent. He wanted to know "if Your Eminence could inform me whether the Vatican has any information that would tend to confirm the reports contained in this memorandum." In the case of a positive answer, "I should like to know whether the Holy Father has any suggestions as to any practical manner in which the forces of civilized public opinion could be utilized in order to prevent a continuation of these barbarities."[505] Two questions then: Do you have similar information? And if so, do you have suggestions on how to cope with the situation? The letter landed directly in the hands of Pius XII. The pope returned the letter to the office of his secretary of state, who would find it on his return.

Once Cardinal Maglione was able to read and absorb all the letter entailed, he annotated the following questions: "I don't think we have information that confirm, in particular, this grave news, isn't that so?" Someone of the Cabinet, probably Tardini, responded to this question on September 30, 1942, reminding, "There are those of Sig. Malvezzi,"[506] the Italian industrialist who had turned over his reports on the situation in Poland.

[503] ASRS, AA.EE.SS., Extracta, Germania 742, f. 18, letter of Myron Taylor to Card. Maglione, September 26, 1942.
[504] ASRS, AA.EE.SS., Extracta, Germania 742, f. 102, handwritten scribble handed over by Msgr. Adamski in 1943.
[505] ASRS, AA.EE.SS., Extracta, Germania 742, ff. 18–19, letter of Myron Taylor to Card. Maglione, September 26, 1942.
[506] ASRS, AA.EE.SS., Extracta, Germania 742, f. 14, internal note with handwritten comments.

An unexpected Mr. Tittmann, who was Myron Taylor's assistant, presented himself to the Cabinet with an impromptu visit on October 1. He insisted an answer be given to the memorandum that had been handed over a few days before by Myron Taylor. During his short visit, Tittmann let slip some circumstances and background on the document by saying that "the content of the memorandum was telegraphed by his Government to him, with the demand to talk about it with the Pope. But this order arrived two hours later than the audience, and therefore he no longer had the opportunity to refer it directly to the Pope." Tardini, who was clearly not impressed at all, suggested to the Cabinet: "Mister Tittmann should not be in such a hurry.... We are informing ourselves."[507] In other words, he was implying that impatient diplomats raise suspicion.

The file at last landed on Msgr. Dell'Acqua's desk. He began analyzing: "That the information in the letter of Ambassador Taylor is very grave, there is no doubt." But, as always, "one should assure oneself that they correspond to the truth, while exaggeration is easy also among the Jews." In his opinion, it was not sufficient to automatically base one's conclusions on the information given by the Ruthenian Catholic metropolitan in his personal handwritten letter to the pope ("also, the Orientals are not exactly an example when it comes to sincerity") nor those given by Count Malvezzi. It seems that Dell'Acqua was not just conducting an investigation here, but followed the established, rigorous procedure of the Cabinet. And we can summarize the procedure with the aphorism that Msgr. Cassulo, the nuncio in Bucharest, once noted in his diaries: "Never relate everything one says, and even when it is related, you don't have to believe it."[508] But even if the data proved to be true, one should still proceed with great prudence to confirm them to Mr. Tittmann,

> because I seem to also perceive a political aim (even if not purely political) in the move of the American government. This last one would not fail to seek publicity with an eventual confirmation by the Holy See. This could have very unpleasant consequences not only for the Holy See but for the Jews themselves who find themselves in

[507] ASRS, AA.EE.SS., Extracta, Germania 742, f. 24, internal note with handwritten note of Msgr. Tardini.

[508] ASRS, AA.EE.SS., Romania 186, vol. 32, p. 600.

the hands of the Germans, who would take advantage to aggravate the hateful and barbaric measures adopted towards them.[509]

One cannot deny that the impatient intervention of Mr. Tittmann to urgently seek a declaration of the Holy See was quite strange. Dell'Acqua's reservations toward the exaggeration among some Jews, who maintained that "corpses are utilized for making fats and their bones for the manufacture of fertilizer" and that "corpses are even being exhumed for this purpose," and his reservations regarding the lack of sincerity of "the Orientals," who affirmed that "there is not one Jew left in the entire district east of Poland, including occupied Russia" would later on prove themselves well founded. Likewise, his intuition on a possible instrumentalization or manipulation of the Jewish issue by the Americans is to be taken seriously. His comment also reflects the primary concern of the Holy See's agenda on the Jews: avoiding at any costs an even higher escalation of their suffering. "It convenes," so wrote Dell'Acqua, "to keep in mind that the recent protest of the French Bishops about the deportation of the Jews (a protest which is thought to be inspired by the Holy See) is sufficient to prove the disapproval of the Catholic Church for such inhumane acts. And the Anglo-Americans did not fail and will not fail to take advantage of such a protest." At the end he utters, almost desperately, "One could hear on this the Nuncio in Berlin: but what could he possibly say more with certainty, the poor man!"

Four days later, Pope Pius XII took notice of all this, and going slightly beyond the proposals of Dell'Acqua, he ordered an answer to the Americans and wrote:

> Prepare a short memo in which is communicated, in essence, that the Holy See has received information on the severe treatment of the Jews. That it had, however, not been able to verify the exactness of all the information received. The same Holy See did not fail, on the other hand, to intervene in favor of the Jews each time that the occasion did present itself.[510]

Dell'Acqua, as ordered by the pope, took a white sheet of paper, and without any protocol number or filigree, he reported the exact words as formulated by Pius

[509] ASRS, AA.EE.SS., Extracta, Germania 742, f. 25, internal note of Msgr. Dell'Acqua, October 2, 1942.
[510] ASRS, AA.EE.SS., Extracta, Germania 742, f. 25, internal note of Msgr. Dell'Acqua, October 2, 1942 (handwritten comments of Pope Pius XII, October 6, 1942).

XII himself. This document was handed over directly to Mr. Tittmann on October 10, 1942.[511] During the same month of October, the Cabinet continued to receive additional accounts on the terrible fate of the Jews. A written report from the Italian priest Don Scavizzi revealed:

> The elimination of the Jews, with the murdering in mass is almost totalitarian, without regard for children, not even for babies. All marked with a white bracelet the civil life for them is made impossible. They cannot go to the market, enter in a shop, jump on the tram or on a wheelchair, attend a theater, visit houses of non-Jews. Before being deported or killed they are condemned to forced hard-labour, even if they belong to the cultured class. The few Jews left over, appear serene, almost flaunting pride. One says that more than 2 million Jews have been killed.... The Poles are allowed to take over the houses in the Ghetto, that finally become empty due to the massacres of the Jews.[512]

Now, there are no surprises left in this world: exactly on that same October 10, when Tittmann got an answer from Pius XII, the Executive Committee of the League of Nations (the predecessor of the U.N.), with its honorary chairman Winston Churchill, handed over to the apostolic delegate in London a "resolution" that stated:

> The Executive Committee of the League of Nations Union has received with indignation the recent reports on the campaign of annihilation carried on in cold blood, and as a matter of policy, by the German Army Commanders and the Nazi officials in the countries occupied by them, and more particularly in Poland. It is of the utmost importance that those who can speak for all nations whose moral conscience is not dead should express their horror at this relapse into barbarism.[513]

---

[511] ASRS, AA.EE.SS., Extracta, Germania 742, f. 27, draft of note prepared by Msgr. Dell'Acqua, October 10, 1942.

[512] ASRS, AA.EE.SS., Extracta, Germania 742, f. 26, internal note of Msgr. Dell'Acqua, after October 7, 1942.

[513] ASRS, AA.EE.SS., Extracta, Germania 742, f. 63, copy of the letter of the chairman and text of resolution.

Dell'Acqua's and Tardini's intuition on the Anglo-Americans' possible attempt to manipulate the Holy See into making a declaration on the Nazi massacres becomes credible. However, the files in the Historical Archive seem to indicate that the Cabinet did not receive the letter from the apostolic delegate with the copy of the resolution's text before November 29, thus many weeks later.[514] An answer to it would not follow until January 7, signed by Cardinal Maglione. Relaying "the vivid impact all the pains the actual War has in the heart of the Holy Father," it reminded that "Your Excellency knows very well how the Pontiff, more than once, has publicly pointed out, in fact, the duties of the warring towards the populations of the occupied countries."[515]

*

*   *

At the end of October 1942, a thorough report on the situation of the Jews in Romania was sent by Mr. Saly Mayer, the president of the Israelian community in Switzerland. The report reached the Cabinet through the apostolic nunciature in Bern.[516] Mr. Mayer, asking for intervention that could in some way mitigate the brutal measures of the Nazis, warned that similar measures and actions against the Jews would soon been taken in Hungary and (even!) in Spain. Cardinal Maglione charged the Cabinet to read the report carefully and to annotate those things that were until then not known.[517] Msgr. Barbetta made a full analysis of the vexations, the measures, and the compilation of the Statute of the Jews[518] as he went through the report. He referred to a sort of

> psychosis [sic] in the rush to receive the baptism, in the hope to save oneself of the deportation, through a mitigation by the State and the protection of the Church. Therefore, the Jews of Romania plea for an intervention by the Red Cross, the Vatican, and other appropriate bodies. Such an intervention should come from a Commission

[514] ASRS, AA.EE.SS., Extracta, Germania 742, f. 61, note of the office, November 29, 1942.
[515] ASRS, AA.EE.SS., Extracta, Germania 742, f. 64, Draft of letter of Card. Maglione to Msgr. Godfrey, 7th of January 1943.
[516] ASRS, AA.EE.SS., Romania 149, f. 187, lettera di Msgr. Bernardini al Card. Maglione, 29th of October 1942.
[517] ASRS, AA.EE.SS., Romania 149, f. 191, Note of the office, with handwritten notes of Card. Maglione, 31st of October 1942.
[518] See A Tale of "Good That Makes No Noise", p. 124-125.

of the Red Cross, which is completely neutral, destined to bring
material and moral help, especially to the deported in Transnistria.[519]

At the end, Barbetta added that with the actions in favor of the Jews taken in Croatia
and Slovakia, it was his impression that the situation of the Jews in Romania "seems,
at least until that moment, somewhat less tragic than in the other two countries."[520]

In addition, on request of Pope Pius XII, Fr. Silvino Azzolini, the chaplain
of the Italian Labours in Vienna, described the continuing religious persecution
in Austria, Czechoslovakia, and Luxembourg. His account stated, for example,
that "in the Dachau concentration camp among the many priests there are also
4 Canons of the Cathedral of Prague. Last 14 September the former secretary of
the Nuncio was sent to the camp of Mauthausen.... In the camp of Mauthausen
there are ca. 42,000 persons. Among them Jews, priests, and convicts for political
reasons. It is a place of sufferance and very cruel and inhuman treatments, including asphyxiating gas."[521]

Msgr. Orsenigo, the nuncio in Berlin, repeatedly remarked in his reports that
with the deportations, the Nazis extinguished any trace of "those people they
hated," and surely a change of racial laws would follow. This time, deportations
would not only include non-Aryans divorced from a marriage with a Christian, but
it would be extended to all those married, be it illegally or with religious Christian
sacrament. The German episcopacy was anxiously pondering how to make a move
toward Hitler, and Orsenigo had already personally made his complaints to the
Nazi government.[522]

*
* *

The pope and his staff were continuously asked to intervene, to help, to mitigate
measures.

[519] ASRS, AA.EE.SS., Romania 149, f. 189^v, typewritten analysis of Msgr. Barbetta,
November 7, 1942.
[520] ASRS, AA.EE.SS., Romania 149, f. 190, typewritten analysis of Msgr. Barbetta,
November 7, 1942.
[521] ASRS, AA.EE.SS., Germania 854, f. 34, report about the actual religious situation
in Austria and Luxembourg, by F. Azzolini, October 11, 1942.
[522] ASRS, AA.EE.SS., Extracta, Germania 742, ff. 40$^{r/v}$, report of Msgr. Orsenigo to
Card. Maglione, November 7, 1942.

The brutality generated by the Nazis in Europe continued to grow and fester, an evil that seemed to laugh in the faces of those who were determined to protect the innocent. The Cabinet came to know about the most sinister fate that was reserved in those days for the Rev. Rab, of the Austrian Diocese of St. Poelten, who was beheaded, and for one of the Sisters of Charity of the Third Order of St. Francis, who was sentenced to death. A terrible lot also fell to other young priests, who were arrested and deported to Dachau merely because they were caught listening to foreign broadcasting.[523]

In the midst of all this cruelty and misery, one would almost forget that life was still going on, that fate also offers positive outcomes, and Providence enfolds its opaque design into human reality. This happened in the case of two young Polish priests of the Cracovian Seminary. These two were highly recommended by Cardinal Sapieha to continue their priestly formations in Rome. One of the priests asked the secretary of state to intervene with the Italian authorities to prepare papers that would allow them to depart from Poland and enter Italy to stay — first immediately after the war in the Belgian College — and later on in the Polish College in Rome.[524] Msgr. Antonio Samorè took up the matter and in less than two months resolved the case. The two young priests, however, would stay in the Belgian College in Rome right after the war. These two young priests were Stanislao Starowiejski and no one less than Karol Wojtyła, the future pope John Paul II. Neither the secretary of state nor Cardinal Maglione, Tardini, or Samorè were aware that they were giving support to a future pope and saint "coming from the East."

Typewritten leaflet of Karol Wojtyła, the future Pope John Paul II.[525]

[523] ASRS, AA.EE.SS., Germania 854, ff. 39[r/v], report of Msgr. Orsenigo to Card. Maglione, November 18, 1942.
[524] ASRS. AA.EE.SS., Polonia 210, ff. 7[r/v], draft of the *Note verbale* to the embassy of Italy to the Holy See, October 4, 1946.
[525] ASRS, AA.EE.SS., Polonia 210, f. 5.

While in Poland, the young Karol Wojtyła prepared for his travels to the Eternal City, and he witnessed the most terrible scenes inflicted on the Jewish population. In December 1942, the *note verbale* of the embassy of Poland to the Holy See stated categorically:

> The Germans are suppressing the entire Jewish population of Po-
> land. First the old men, the sick, the women and the children are
> brought away. A proof that it is not a deportation for labour, and
> which confirms the information indicating that the deported are
> put to death by different methods, in places especially prepared for
> this purpose. The young and valid men are often forced to labour
> until they die of exhaustion or malnutrition.[526]

And numbers don't lie. "One estimates that about more than a million Jews of Poland are exterminated. In the Ghetto of Warsaw alone in the midst of July there were living 400,000 Jews. During July and August 250,000 of them were deported to the east."

*

*   *

On November 30, 1942, the Vaad Leumi of Palestine — the "Elected Assembly" of the Jews of Palestine — appealed with a telegram to the governments of England, the United States, the Soviet Union, and the other Allied forces, as well as to the governments of the neutral nations and the heads of churches, to admonish the German National Socialist government regarding the severe punishments that the authors and executors of the atrocities against the Jews would face after the war.[527]

Just three days later, with a renewed appeal broadcast over the radio, Isaac Herzog, chief rabbi of Jerusalem and the personal acquaintance of Pope Pius XII and Cardinal Maglione, denounced the collective mass murders by the Nazis. These murders included some victims being burned alive while others were wrapped in sacks and then thrown into the river. The appeal of the rabbis

---

[526] ASRS, AA.EE.SS., Extracta, Germania 742, f. 42, *Note verbale* of the embassy of Poland to the Holy See, December 19, 1942.

[527] ASRS, AA.EE.SS., Extracta, Germania 742, ff. 85ᵛ–88, internal typewritten note of Msgr. Di Meglio, December 1942.

of Palestine, reunited in the Great Synagogue of Jerusalem, was directed to all the nations. Msgr. Tardini assigned to the *minutante*, Msgr. Di Meglio, the task of preparing a transcript of that public appeal in which the rabbis revealed "with pain that the Nations are not demonstrating an adequate interest in the condition of the Jews. They exhort all the Nations to use all means at their disposal to stop the destruction of the Jewish people."[528] Someone in the Cabinet marked with an arrow in the margin these few lines written by Rabbi Herzog: "Remember, however, that protests and warnings, important as they are, are not sufficient. With these there must come help, speedy and effective. Set up at once an international body charged with the task of finding ways and means of practical help." And with blue pencil Tardini underlined the sentence that followed: "Open the gates including those *of the Land of our Fathers*, to all who seek refuge from the Nazi tyranny."[529]

*

*   *

The friendship of Chief Rabbi Herzog with Pius XII and Cardinal Maglione as well as the easy communication with the Cabinet is most remarkable. It all started with a visit of the chief rabbi to Cardinal Maglione in March 1940. Not much later, in May 1940, the rabbi wrote on behalf of the Jews in Spain, those who had escaped from Germany in earlier years and who would be all arrested and returned to German hands if they could not obtain visas for other countries. Jewish children now living in Spain were no longer allowed in schools and the synagogue in Madrid was closed. Uncertain if all these tidings were true, Herzog still requested an urgent intervention toward the Spanish government to avoid worsening of the situation.[530] The second plea arrived a few days later through the Irish cardinal Joseph MacRory, archbishop of Armagh, who passed along a telegram from Chief Rabbi Herzog.

The reaction of Pius XII in that moment, keeping in mind that Vilnius was under Soviet occupation, was one of advice to his collaborators to act "with great

---

[528] ASRS, AA.EE.SS., Extracta, Germania 742, transcript of Chief Rabbi Herzog's broadcast of December 2, 1942, ff. 89–90.

[529] ASRS, AA.EE.SS., Extracta, Germania 742, transcript of Chief Rabbi Herzog's broadcast of December 2, 1942, f. 90.

[530] ASRS, AA.EE.SS., Spagna 969, ff. 3–4, letter of Chief Rabbi Isaac Herzog to Card. Maglione, May 8, 1940.

caution" and regarding the nuncio in Lithuania, Msgr. Luigi Centoz, he stated, "He would not be able to do much and it would be better not to take interest in the case."[531] However, the pope's replies did not discourage nor create bad feelings in the chief rabbi, who would write again with other pleas on other occasions. One of his most touching and significant letters was written in the last months of 1942 to Cardinal Luigi Maglione. It goes as follows:

Telegram of Chief Rabbi Herzog to Card. MacRory (passed to Pius XII), May 12, 1940.[532]

> Eminence, You will remember without doubt my visit in the month of February 1940. I will never forget the profound sympathy with which you talked to us about the terrible sufferance of our people and I hope His Holiness the Pope will do anything possible in this moment to save our unfortunate friends in Poland. The news that we receive is the most horrible that one can imagine. Over there one is doing systematic holocausts of thousands a day, especially of children and old people. Himmler

[531] ASRS, AA.EE.SS., Paesi Baltici 113, f. 35, internal note by Dell'Acqua, May 27, 1940.

[532] ASRS, AA.EE.SS., Paesi Baltici 113, f. 33, "Entreat you plead speedily for intervention Holy Father with Lithuanian government behalf Jewish refugees including many distinguished Rabbis now at Vilna threatened forcible repatriation to German and Russian occupation zones stop Jewish relief organisations ready provide their maintenance and arrange gradual emigration to Palestine and overseas. Thanks and greetings — Herzog chief Rabbi."

has ordered what he calls "Die Vernichtungskommission" [Commission of extermination], which is functioning unceasingly. His Excellence the Nuncio will transmit our petition to the Holy Father. In the name of God, in the name of humanity, I implore you, do all that is possible! Save!

With the benedictions of Sion and Jerusalem as with my most distinguished sentiments

Isaac Herzog
Chief Rabbi of Palestine

Letter of I. Herzog to Card. Maglione, Jerusalem, November 23, 1942.[533]

Again, during a personal visit to Angelo Giuseppe Roncalli, the apostolic delegate in Istanbul in February 1944, Isaac Herzog wanted to thank Pope Pius XII in an official way "for the many forms of charity used towards the Jews in those last years" and ask the interest of the Holy See on behalf of fifty-five thousand Jews in Transnistria (Romania). Maglione urged the apostolic delegate, Roncalli, to intervene and, with the cooperation of Msgr. Cassulo, the nuncio in Bucharest, to accomplish as much as possible regarding the Jews' evacuation to Palestine, which he did.[534]

Another urgent plea from Chief Rabbi Herzog would follow only a few months later in July 1944. He asked for an audience, to which the first reaction of the Cabinet was again very cautious. They avoided responding to his telegram with a written message and awaited Herzog's arrival in Rome. The details of how this matter ended up will be interesting material for historians.[535] With Isaac Herzog, the friendly relationship continued in the interest of the Jews of Hungary, Slovakia,

ASRS, AA.EE.SS., Extracta, Germania 742, f. 71.

[534] ASRS, AA.EE.SS., Romania 149, f. 75, report in code of Msgr. Roncalli to Maglione, February 28, 1944 (8:00 p.m.).

[535] ASRS, AA.EE.SS., Extracta, Germania 742, f. 247, internal note, April 18, 1944. The file with further evolution is kept in the Apostolic Archives.

and even for the rabbinic school of Shanghai in China. It is striking that with each interaction the chief rabbi of Jerusalem desired "to thank the Holy See for what has been attempted and achieved so far for the Jews in Europe."[536]

*

*   *

Let's turn back to the winter of 1942. The apostolic delegation, the diplomatic representation of the Holy See in Jerusalem, transmitted the appeal of the rabbis of Palestine "with which they exhorted all the Nations to use all means at their disposition to stop the destruction of the Jewish people" on December 10, 1942. The Cabinet received it with some delay, certainly after New Year's Day of 1943.[537]

On December 17, 1942, a Joint Declaration of the United Nations and the French National Committee on the mass extermination of Jews from German-occupied Europe was issued. They stated that "such events can only strengthen the resolve of all freedom-loving peoples to overthrow the barbarous Hitlerite tyranny," which beyond

> denying to persons of Jewish race in all territories over which their barbarous rule has been extended the most elementary human rights, are now carrying into effect Hitler's oft repeated intention to exterminate the Jewish people in Europe. . . . In Poland, which has been made the principal Nazi slaughter-house, the ghettos established by the German invaders are being systematically emptied of all Jews, except a few highly skilled workers required for war industries. None of those taken away is ever heard of again. The able unskilled are slowly worked to death in labour camps. The

---

[536] ASRS, AA.EE.SS., Asterisco, Stati Ecclesiastici 575, f. 2069, report of Msgr. Hughes to Msgr. Tardini, Cairo, September 12, 1944.

[537] In fact, a little tiny detail makes us wonder. The protocol number given by the Cabinet, number 1162/43, points to the Cabinet receiving this report long after New Year's Day 1943, when the protocol numbers start at 0001/43. Furthermore, the response to the apostolic delegation is dated on February 27, 1943 (ASRS, AA.EE.SS., Extracta, Germania 742, f. 91, draft of letter to the apostolic delegation in Jerusalem, February 27, 1943). Either the Cabinet received it in December but did not take it into account for a while, or it took a long time for the mail item to travel from Jerusalem to Rome and arrived, I would presume, in the midst of January. Given the reliability of the Tardini administration at that time, I would go for the second explanation.

infirm are left to die of exposure and starvation, or are deliberately massacred in mass executions. The number of victims of these bloody cruelties is reckoned in many hundreds of thousands of entirely innocent men, women and children.[538]

The declaration reaffirmed the determination of the United Nations to exact retribution for this crime against humanity and civilization.[539] But why was the official transcript of the text not handed over by the British ambassador to the Holy See, D'Arcy Osborne, until December 29, two weeks later?[540] December 29 was four days after the *Urbi et Orbi* Christmas radio message given by Pius XII. Had the Allies hoped that the pope would align with the joint declaration and in doing so he would have publicly aligned himself with the Allies? One thing is for sure, Msgr. Dell'Acqua, with his accurate intuition on the attempts of the Allies, shows he was born for Vatican diplomacy.

On December 24, 1942, a telegram to Pius XII from Chief Rabbi Horowitz and the Agudath Israel World Organization arrived[541]: "Respectfully beseech intervention by Your Holiness to save annihilation of Israel eastern Europe." The Union of Orthodox Rabbis of America and Canada

wish to express to His Holiness our profound appreciation for his effort in trying to save our persecuted brethren stop we take liberty to bring to His Holiness' attention that the tragedy of our co-religionists in Nazi dominated countries grew in magnitude to such extent that danger of complete anniholation [*sic*] of millions of our brethren is imminent stop hundreds of thousand innocent jews men women and children have been murdered in cold blood and the sword hangs

---

[538] ASRS, AA.EE.SS. Extracta, Germania 742, ff. 45–46, typewritten copy of the "Joint Declaration regarding the German persecution of the Jews," issued on December 17 in London, Washington, and Moscow.

[539] ASRS, AA.EE.SS. Extracta, Germania 742, ff. 45–46, typewritten copy of the "Joint Declaration regarding the German persecution of the Jews," issued on December 17 in London, Washington, and Moscow.

[540] ASRS, AA.EE.SS. Extracta, Germania 742, ff. 47–49, *Note verbale* of His Majesty's minister to the Holy See to the Secretariat of State, December 29, 1942. It contained possibly also a memorandum with a chronology on the latest German persecutions of the Jews of November 26th–December18th, 1942 (cfr. ff. 47-49).

[541] ASRS, AA.EE.SS., Extracta, Germania 742, f. 53a.

now over heads of millions more stop we realize how this affects your
noble heart stop we comme [sic] now to implore his holiness to use
his great influence and religious authority and raise his voice so that
it shall be said enough now stay thy hand stop we are convinced that
your voice will be heard all over the world and god the father of all
mankind will point the way for you to save those who can still be
saved — rabbis israel rosenberg eliezer silver ben levinthal presidum.[542]

In response to both Osborne and Horowitz, the pope charged the apostolic delegate "to give, if possible, a verbal response to assure that the Holy See has done
and is doing what it can."[543]

*

*   *

Before Christmas 1942, Nuncio Valeri in Vichy sent additional news. A Jew living
in Nice, and occasional correspondent under the pen name of "Jew" or "Persecuted,"
shared the dreadful circumstances of the Jews in France. His last letter told about
new threats to Jewish people following the recent occupation of the territory of
southern France by Axis troops. He asked "if the Holy Father would dignify himself to recommend the Italian authorities not to increase the suffering of the non
aryans who live in the territory occupied by them."[544]

In his report for the year, Msgr. de Meglio, *uditore* of the nunciature in Berlin,
mentioned the Jewish question and the German episcopacy. He observed: "Some
clergy and lay people noticed, to their surprise, how until now the German episcopacy had not given sign of any collective manifestation on the grave mistreatment
inflicted upon the Jews. This while the French episcopacy instead has taken immediate position against the racial legislation in France, introduced by Marshall
Pétain, as well as other voices of protest in other nations."[545]

[542] ASRS, AA.EE.SS., Extracta, Germania 742, ff. 56b–57.

[543] ASRS, AA.EE.SS., Extracta, Germania 742, f. 55, draft of a cable, December 26, 1942
(in handwriting: delivered to encryption office the morning of December 28, 1942).

[544] ASRS, AA.EE.SS., Extracta, Germania 742, f. 66, letter of Msgr. Valeri to Card.
Maglione, December 7, 1942.

[545] ASRS, AA.EE.SS., Germania 854, f. 136, report on "The religious, political and
military situation of Germany" by Msgr. de Meglio, December 9, 1942.

The Pope in his library in front of the microphone for his Christmas radio message in 1942.[546]

Pius XII and his staff chose to hold a steady course as they had done until now, keeping true to the pope's words that he "was doing, would do and continue to do what he could," and their plan would include making a public statement regarding this issue, in his own time and of his own accord. Pius XII had chosen not to align with the Allied forces, but that doesn't mean he decided to leave it all over to the others. He chose to make a historic gesture, something that

[546] ASRS, AA.EE.SS., Stati Ecclesiastici 740, ff. 34–34ᵛ, *L'Osservatore Romano*, December 25, 1942, pp. 1–2.

would be well perceived by the press and the diplomatic world all together. Such a move, the pope decided, should be executed in a twofold way. First: *ad internum*, a speech presented to the privileged audience of cardinals and the Roman Curia. Second: *ad externum*, a speech presented to the world at large. Coming out sequentially after the joint declaration of December 17, both his speeches were given on December 24, and they gave the pope the advantage to reinforce, echo, and amplify the voice of dissent and condemnation of the persecution and extermination of the Jews contained in the document of the Allies.

In his first address, given to the cardinals the morning of December 24,[547] the pope apologized and warned that he felt compelled to forego the age-old tradition of a speech dedicated to the Christmas Feast only for the cardinals, because "today's crisis, transformer of many things and customs, has partly modified this gentle custom too; because the obstacles, created by the war, to the normal contact between the Shepherd and the flock, have given rise to the need to give, in the solemn recurrence of the Christmas holidays, the faithful from all over the world the longed-for opportunity to hear the voice of the common Father." He encouraged all the cardinals and prelates of the Roman Curia not to give up on the defense of truth and virtue in a confused and chaotic world.

For his second Christmas message, given to the world, he chose instead the mighty microphone of the Vatican Radio.

> The watchwords "I have compassion on the multitude" is for Us a sacred trust which may not be abused; it remains strong and impelling in all times and in all human situations, as it was the distinguishing mark of Jesus, The Church would be untrue to herself, ceasing to be a mother, if she turned a deaf ear to children's anguished cries, which reach her from every class of the human family. She does not intend to take sides for either of the particular and concrete forms with which the single populations and states strive to solve the gigantic problems of domestic order or international collaboration, as long as these forms conform to the law of God. But, on the other hand, as the "pillar and ground of truth" (1 Tim. 3:15) and guardian, by the will of God and the mandate of Christ, of the natural and supernatural order, the Church cannot renounce her right to

---

[547] *L'Osservatore Romano*, December 28–29, 1942, p. 1.

proclaim to her sons and to the whole world the unchanging basic laws, saving them from every perversion, obfuscation, corruption, false interpretation and error.

And when the pope reached the portion of his public speech dealing with the "dignity and rights of the human person," it was profound and powerful:

He should uphold respect for and ... the practical realisation of the following fundamental personal rights: the right to maintain and develop one's corporal, intellectual and moral life and especially the right to religious formation and education; the right to the worship of God in private and public and to carry on religious works of charity; the right to marry and to achieve the aim of married life, the right to conjugal and domestic society; the right to work as the indispensable means towards the maintenance of family life; the right to free choice of a state of life, and hence too of the priesthood or religious life; the right to the use of material goods, in keeping with his duties and social limitations.

The careful studies and keen juridical analysis made by Msgr. Dell'Acqua, Msgr. Sigismondi, and other *minitanti* regarding the new racial laws on marriage were included and synthesized in the extended paragraphs regarding the "defense of social unity and especially of the family."

But the speech, given with bold oratorical vigor at the microphone, had not yet reached its climax. That came with the chanting of the horrors of contemporary reality. The pope's voice over the radio continued: Should mankind not

vow not to rest until in all peoples and all nations of the earth a vast legion shall be formed of those handfuls of men who, bent on bringing back Society to its centre of gravity which is the law of God, aspire to the service of the human person and of his common life ennobled in God?

Mankind owes that vow to the countless dead who lie buried on the field of battle: the sacrifice of their life in the fulfilment of their duty is a holocaust offered for a new and better social order.

Mankind owes that vow to the innumerable sorrowing host of mothers, widows and orphans who have seen the light, the solace and the support of their lives wrenched from them.

Mankind owes that vow to those numberless exiles whom the hurricane of war has torn from their native land and scattered in the land of the stranger; who can make their own the lament of the Prophet: "Our inheritance is turned to aliens: our house to strangers" (Jer. Lam. 5:2).

Mankind owes that vow to the hundreds of thousands of persons who, without any fault on their part, sometimes only because of their nationality or race, have been consigned to death or to a slow decline.

Mankind owes that vow to the many thousands of non-combatants, women, children, sick and aged from whom aerial warfare — whose horrors We have from the beginning frequently denounced — has, without discrimination or through inadequate precautions, taken life, goods, health, home, charitable refuge or house of prayer.

The citing of the Old Testament prophet Jeremiah and mankind was a clear and certain acknowledgment of the hundreds of thousands of persons who, without any fault on their part, and sometimes "only because of their nationality or race, had been consigned to death or to a slow decline."

*

*   *

The pope's radio message of Christmas 1942 had a tremendous international impact. It was a huge echo with the media worldwide.[548] The five points at the speech's conclusion were especially well received by news outlets, according to the hundreds of documents, newspapers, cables, and letters preserved in the Historical Archive.[549] The newspaper *L'Osservatore Romano* released an edition of two hundred thousand

[548] Madrid (ASRS, AA.EE.SS., Stati Ecclesiastici 740, ff. 142–229), London (ibid., f. 26), Roma (ibid., ff. 250–292), Bucharest (ibid., f. 27), Basel/Bern (ibid., ff. 356–362), Malines (ibid., ff. 363–395), Leopoldville (ibid., f. 30), Buenos Aires (ibid., ff. 239–242), and Ottawa (ibid., ff. 239–245).
[549] ASRS, AA.EE.SS., Stati Ecclesiastici 740, ff. 142–347.

copies, with the director calling the pope's address "an incredible undertaking."[550] A comment in one of the Canadian newspapers seemed to precisely and concisely share the meaning of the radio message:

> Tied impartially to all the people entangled in the war, Pope Pius occupies an unusual position. He does not — in the very nature of that position he cannot — speak as a political leader, nor as a martial leader of one host against the other. Yet as a spiritual leader, he did not hesitate to judge the issues, and the impartiality of his position lends mightily to the authority of his judgement.[551]

Now, one might question the effectiveness of words spoken into a microphone. The Nazis, for example, certainly were under no illusion as to the potential impact of this radio allocution. In fact, they tried hard as they could to get their hands on the text prior to its diffusion. The counselor of the German embassy to the Holy See, Karl-Gustav Wollenweber, came to the Cabinet asking for a copy on December 21, and called in on December 23 to repeat his request.[552] He asked (1) if "he could have the discourse of the Holy Father with some anticipation, before it was given out to the journalists," to which the Cabinet replied, "Immediately after the discourse"; (2) "at what time he could come to the Secretary of State to get the copies of it," to which the Cabinet replied, "At 12:30"; (3) "if he could have eight copies in German language and three in Italian," to which the Cabinet replied, "One hopes he will so, alerting Montini"; (4) "if he could have some copies of the discourse of the Pope to the cardinals," to which the Cabinet replied, "Unfortunately no; he will find it in the *L'Osservatore Romano.*"

But in Berlin everything kept still. Msgr. Orsenigo, the nuncio, had invited the Italian ambassador in Berlin, Michele Lanza, and his family, to gather in the nunciature on Christmas Eve to hear the radio allocution. The Italian ambassador listened with "devout attention and elevated interest." However, one week passed and with regret he reported, "I'm sorry to have to add that until now the German press did

---

[550] ASRS, AA.EE.SS., Stati Ecclesiatici 740, f. 25, letter of Dr. Festa of December 23, 1942.

[551] ASRS, AA.EE.SS., Stati Ecclesiastici 740, f. 244, excerpt of a letter from Msgr. Ildebrando Antoniutti, apostolic delegate in Canada and New World, to Msgr. Montini, January 30, 1943.

[552] ASRS, AA.EE.SS., Stati Ecclesiastici 740, f. 14, note of the office by one of the archivists, Msgr. Giovanni Belardo.

not once mention the message of the Pope."[553] Thus, for the Nazis, the message of Pope Pius XII had arrived, and it was easy to guess that it had not pleased them.

*

* *

In the last days of 1942, the British embassy handed over a *note verbale* to the Secretariat of State of the Holy See. It included a copy of the Joint Declaration of December 17 regarding the Nazi persecution of the Jews, "which was issued on behalf of the United Nations in London, Washington and Moscow on December 17th." And, once again, the *note verbale* played the same tune: "It has been suggested that his Holiness the Pope might endorse the Declaration in a public statement. Failing this, His Majesty's Government would strongly urge His Holiness to use his influence, either by means of a public statement or by action through the German Bishops, to encourage German Christians, and particularly German Protestants, to do all in their power to restrain these excesses."[554] The Allied powers of England, the United States, and Soviet Russia were anxious to get the pope in Rome on their side.

*

* *

A week or two later, the British ambassador to the Holy See, D'Arcy Osborne, came in to the Cabinet with a new *note verbale* but this time with no mention at all of a "public statement" of the pope. It only remarked that "it has been suggested that His Holiness might be able to use his influence in countries such as Italy, France and Hungary, where the Jewish persecution has not so far shown itself in a marked degree, to prevent any deterioration of the local situation and to strengthen local resistance to possible German pressure for increased anti-Semitic measures."[555] This reflects exactly the policy of Pius XII as it had been until then.

*

* *

[553] ASRS, AA.EE.SS., Stati Ecclesiastici 740, f. 397ᵛ.
[554] ASRS, AA.EE.SS., Extracta, Germania 742, f. 44, *Note verbale* of the embassy of Great Britain to the Holy See, December 29, 1942.
[555] ASRS, AA.EE.SS., Extracta, Germania 742, f. 51, *Note verbale* of the embassy of Great Britain to the Holy See, January 7, 1943.

New Year 1943 was not yet past, and news flashes on the persecution and extermination of Jews and others came pouring in. Two days after the *note verbale* from Osborne, a little typewritten note in French arrived, stating, "According to a statement on Radio London (of which I cannot guarantee the exactness) 77 percent of the Slovak Jewish population has been evacuated to unknown destiny — that means probably to death."[556]

From the Polish embassy to the Holy See, the Cabinet received numbers and facts regarding the unspeakable treatment of women and children by the Nazis and their associates. Part of the list detailed hundreds and thousands of women and young girls raped and mutilated by the Nazis. A single example is sufficient to set the tone of the atrocities told in this digest of reports from occupied countries: "Czekoslovakia. At Ruzyn a number of girl students taken from their hostel during a nocturnal raid, dragged to open spaces and violated by German soldiers in sight of bound male students, some by several in succession. The breasts of some of the girls were burned with cigarette ends — others forced to drink spittoons filled with urine. Some who protested were shot or bayonetted."[557] And then came graphic details on the secret eugenist experiments:

> An experimental camp "for the improvement of the Nordic Race" was set up in Helenowo, near Lodz. Over 500 boys and girls between the ages of 15 and 18 are accommodated there in huts each housing one pair — a boy and a girl — a German boy and a Polish girl of superior physique. Fine good food is supplied and the amenities are excellent. Sexual relations between the boys and girls are insisted on and checked by the camp doctor. When pregnant, the girls disappear from the camp, being sent to Germany for the birth of the child, their fate afterwards being to swell the numbers of "women of the Army."[558]

[556] ASRS, AA.EE.SS., Extracta, Germania 742, f. 50, typewritten note (in French) of January 9, 1943.

[557] ASRS, AA.EE.SS., Extracta, Germania 742, f. 76, "International Cabinet for the Suppression of Traffic in Women and Children, Digest of some reports from occupied countries."

[558] ASRS, AA.EE.SS., Extracta, Germania 742, f. 76ᵛ, "International Cabinet for the Suppression of Traffic in Women and Children, Digest of some reports from occupied countries."

The accounts on all these atrocities were seen and read by Pius XII.[559]

*

*   *

In February, new evidence on the ever-increasing persecutions in Czechoslovakia and Poland was transmitted by the "Swiss Ligue for Human and Civil Rights,"[560] through the nunciature in Switzerland, with the request "to continue to intervene in favor of the persecuted and oppressed Jews, which situation becomes ever more terrible, in order to protect and to save them."[561] The pope ordered a response: "The Holy See has done and does what is possible."[562] The same nunciature in Bern later added on a pro memoria, coming from the same Swiss League regarding the situation of the Jews in Germany and the occupied territories. The pro memoria depicted the situation: "The mass-executions in Poland are now confirmed by different sources. A report affirms that 6000 individuals are daily executed in one single place in Poland. Before the execution, the Jews have to take off their clothes that are sent to Germany." And then that now familiar, terrifying information: "A certain number of Polish Jews and the deported Jews of other countries are concentrated in labour camps in Poland and Silesia. News of these camps only rarely and occasionally comes through, as also is the case with Theresienstadt, whilst in general there is no news at all on the [55] ghetto-cities…. The reports coming in from Berlin and Prague confirm that by the end of the month of March, those two cities should be completely 'cleared' of Jews." The report ends with an accurate description of the inhumane conditions of the deported Jews in Romania.[563] What follows is a good example that can verify the reliability of the help and interventions of which the Cabinet always speaks in its responses: In February 1943, Pius XII sent to Msgr. Cassulo, the nuncio in Bucharest, a donation to be spent in favor of the imprisoned non-Aryans, Jews thus, but the

[559] On the original *Note verbale* is annotated: "Visto dal S. Padre, 6.II.1943." ASRS, AA.EE.SS., Extracta, Germania 742, f. 73, *Note verbale* of the Polish embassy to the Holy See to the secretary of state, Vatican City, February 2, 1943.
[560] ASRS, AA.EE.SS., Extracta, Germania 742, f. 93, letter of Msgr. Bernardini to Card. Maglione, Bern, February 24, 1943.
[561] ASRS, AA.EE.SS., Extracta, Germania 742, f. 95, copy of a letter of the "Ligue Suisse des Droits de l'Homme et du Citoyen" to the apostolic nunciature, February 19, 1943.
[562] ASRS, AA.EE.SS., Extracta, Germania 742, f. 93, letter of Msgr. Bernardini to Card. Maglione, February 24, 1943, annotation in handwriting: "28-2-1943."
[563] ASRS, AA.EE.SS., Extracta, Germania 742, ff. 98–98ᵛ, typewritten report of the "Ligue Suisse des Droits de l'Homme et du Citoyen" (N. 1333/43).

nuncio did have problems creating the right occasion for its distribution.[564] At the same time, Msgr. Cassulo took the opportunity to discuss the contents of the earlier mentioned pro memoria of the Swiss League with minister of foreign affairs Mihai Antonescu and Dr. Safran, the president of the Jewish community of Romania. The rabbi asked that his gratitude for the assistance and the protection of the Holy See be conveyed to the Holy Father.[565]

Now, in Slovakia, the fate of twenty thousand Jews, half of them baptized, was at stake. They were spared during the first waves of deportation, thanks to earlier interventions of the Holy See, but as Msgr. Rotta, the nuncio in Budapest, warned, "Now they find themselves in equal imminent danger, which equals to a martyrdom and death."[566] The nuncio's message betrays the near impossibility of the Holy See to attain results in matters of rescue operations at that level, as he writes:

> I know very well that it is certainly not the lacking of good will to come to the aid of those disgraced and without a doubt it [Holy See] will have already done what is possible on behalf of them. But I could neither refuse to send this Memoriale, to show to those who are interested in the fate of so many miserable people that the Nonciature is not deaf to their voice imploring for help from the Holy Father, of which one knows the goodness and the paternal charity towards those who suffer.[567]

Through the *memoriale*, one becomes aware of other details. First of all, the information collected on the deported Jews was obtained from spies. Secondly, the deportation of Jews out of Slovakia — eighty thousand in 1942 — went in the direction of Lublin, Poland. Once they disembarked the train cars, the victims had to walk forty kilometers to reach the concentration camp.[568]

[564] ASRS, AA.EE.SS., Romania 149, f. 247, copy of a letter of Msgr. Cassulo to Card. Maglione, Bucharest, March 2, 1943.

[565] ASRS, AA.EE.SS., Romania 149, ff. 249–249ᵛ, letter of Msgr. Cassulo to Card. Maglione, Bucharest, February 15, 1943.

[566] ASRS, AA.EE.SS., Cecoslovacchhia 175, f. 583, letter of Msgr. Rotta to Card. Maglione, Budapest, February 26, 1943.

[567] ASRS, AA.EE.SS., Cecoslovacchhia 175, ff. 583–583ᵛ, letter of Msgr. Rotta to Card. Maglione, Budapest, February 26, 1943.

[568] ASRS, AA.EE.SS., Cecoslovacchia 175, ff. 584–584ᵛ, "La demande d'un juif de Slovaquie" [1943].

But the worst was still to come. No one could imagine what devastating consequences the top-secret decision of the Wannsee Conference of 1942 — where the total extermination of the Jewish race once and for all was decided by the Nazi hierarchs — would have provoked on the largest scale possible.

10

A Tale of Dark and Sinister Places toward the East ... II

IT WAS NOT only Poland that was in the Nazis' crosshairs. The Cabinet was informed about the measures of extermination in place for Jews in Berlin. The account, written in English, said that "from Friday 26th of February to March 2nd a number of 15,000 Jews including partners of mixed marriages were fetched in their homes or working places and brought to 4 assembling centers in Berlin. Several hundred adults are said to have been shot. According to the same reliable source of information several hundreds of arrested children were separated from their parents and left without food."[569] The source seems to be very well informed because it stated that "the group of high S.S. Officials who have taken the initiative of this action are said to have decided that Berlin is to be rid of all Jews before the middle of March. 8,000 other Berlin Jews are said to be in hiding, sheltered by friends and sympathizers. Government instructions to abstain from measures against the mixed marriages and half Aryans are disregarded by the S.S."[570] In fact, due to the ever-solidifying German intransigence in all matters related to Jews, now the fate of the *Mischlinge*, the mixed marriages between Jews and Christians in addition to their children, became another huge and, unfortunately, unresolvable problem for the Catholic hierarchy within the German Reich and elsewhere.

[569] ASRS, AA.EE.SS., Extracta, Germania 742, f. 140, anonymous and undated account (in English) on the Jews of Berlin in 1943.
[570] ASRS, AA.EE.SS., Extracta, Germania 742, f. 140, anonymous and undated account (in English) on the Jews of Berlin in 1943.

Besides the reports of some of the nuncios on that issue, the cardinal archbishop of Vienna wrote to the Cabinet in Rome with more shocking figures: "In the years 1941 and 1942 altogether about 50,000 Jews were deported from Vienna to the east.... Among those were 1,600 Catholics. Nowadays about 7,000 non-aryans are still present in Vienna, of those 2,800 are Catholics. The majority of the non-aryans still living here are living in a racial mixed marriage."[571] With the new Nazi regulation in place, those married couples should now divorce. In that case, the non-Aryan partner would automatically be deported to the East. This threat caused enormous material and mental distress for the partners and their children. These families had already been under great duress during the previous months, having been economically hobbled by the exclusion of their non-Aryan partners from the employment market. Socially abused and officially neglected, they struggled to find ways to feed their children and keep them sheltered. The plea of Cardinal Innitzer, archbishop of Vienna, in the hope that at least mixed marriages with a Catholic partner would be spared by the Nazis, would ultimately prove pointless. Despite the energetic protest of Cardinal Archbishop Bertram in Breslau of December 1942, even those in mixed marriages of Jews with Christians without children would be separated.[572]

In 1943, as the tide turned and the military situation of the Reich started to crumble, the brutality of the Nazis worsened. They were ready to act on their threat of separating couples of mixed marriages and deporting the Jewish partner to a death camp. Immediately after a public speech given by Joseph Goebbels in the Berlin Sportpalast on January 30, 1943, the process started: "They were driven out by armed SS, put on cattle wagons and transported away. Everywhere heartbreaking scenes took place. In many cases the civilians took open defense of the Jews although in other cases also insults were heard."[573] Occasionally at first and then more rapidly, the "*Mischlinge* of the first degree" lost their somewhat-protected state and were captured. These were the children of a mixed Jewish-Christian marriage who had been raised with a Christian education. And although Adolf

---

[571] ASRS, AA.EE.SS., Extracta, Germania 742, ff. 110–111, letter of Card. Innitzer to Pope Pius XII, April 3, 1943.

[572] ASRS, AA.EE.SS., Extracta, Germania 742, f. 117, report "Die Lage der Mischlinge in Deutschland Mitte März 1943" by Gerhard Lehfeldt, March 16, 1943.

[573] ASRS, AA.EE.SS., Extracta, Germania 742, f. 118, report "Die Lage der Mischlinge in Deutschland Mitte März 1943" by Gerhard Lehfeldt, March 16, 1943.

Eichmann organized for those *Mischlinge* to be gathered in a separate collection
point of the city, giving rise to the hope that they would be served a better fate,
this hope would eventually be crashed, and they would eventually be carried away
together with all the other Jews, to the East ... and thus to their extermination.[574]
For Germany alone, the figures speak of three hundred thousand Christian descendants of mixed marriages.

The Cabinet took punctual notice of this important shift in the policy of the
Nazis toward Jews. On April 8, the *minutante* Msgr. Di Meglio created a comprehensible summary table for his superiors with a request for intervention for those
"*Mischlinge* of the first degree." In his note, Di Meglio suggested that one could
perhaps get the word out to the Italian government through the Jesuit Fr. Tacchi
Venturi, the Cabinet's go-between with Mussolini's circles, in the hope that Italy
might intervene with the German government in their favor. The hope and goal
was to offer as much protection as possible to the Jews and Christian Jews living in
the French territories occupied by the Italians. However, Cardinal Maglione wrote
two days later that "for this moment at least, nothing can be done."[575]

Written pleas and testimonies, addressed to the pope regarding the transports of
partners and children out of mixed marriages, followed. The pleas were filled with
desperation and hope, emotions that seemed to rise like heat from the very papers
on which they were written. Meanwhile, the nightmare continued. Unfortunate
people, condemned by the Nazis, were rounded up by the SS, any correspondence
they might have had with them fell out from coats or skirts or trousers, and within
days the victims disappeared forever. For a German woman who wrote to Pius
XII, "these measures are related to the planned annihilation of the Jewish race
and hundreds of thousands mixed marriages and Mischlinge could be involved,
it would be high time to put an end to it, otherwise a faceless misery will be upon
hundreds of thousands of mixed families or more."[576]

*
**

[574] ASRS, AA.EE.SS., Extracta, Germania 742, f. 118, report "Die Lage der Mischlinge
in Deutschland Mitte März 1943" by Gerhard Lehfeldt, March 16, 1943.
[575] ASRS, AA.EE.SS., Extracta, Germania 742, f. 133, internal note of Msgr. Di Meglio,
April 8,1943.
[576] ASRS, AA.EE.SS., Extracta, Germania 742, f. 137r/v, letter of Gertrude Einstein-
Winter, May 21, 1943.

A few weeks earlier, in March, telegrams from Jewish personalities had reached the pope. On March 16, for the second time, the Union of Orthodox Rabbis of the United States and Canada transmitted a cable that came via London from Warsaw. The cable's terrifying message sounded:

> January … Germans started liquidation of remnants Warsaw ghetto stop all over Poland liquidation of remnants warsaw ghtetto [*sic*] stop all over Poland liquidation proceeding stop liquidation of remnants planned for middle of February stop alarm the world stop apply to pope for official intervention stop we suffer terribly stop remaining a few hundred thousand threatened with immediate annihilation stop only you can rescue us responsibility towards history rests with you unquote as religios [*sic*] leaders of American jewry in solemn conviction we plead to his holiness in the name of humanity for positive action in this zero hour — union of orthodox rabbis of united states and Canada rabbis Israel Rosemberg Eliezer Silver Ben Levinthal precidium.[577]

The rabbis seemed to attribute to the pope the unique power to do something and, with that, to place the responsibility toward history and the fate of the tormented Jewish people squarely on his papal shoulders.

In late March, a cable came to the Vatican from Msgr. Cicognani, who was stationed in Washington, D.C. In the cable, he begged excuse from the pope: "I should not dare to present again another appeal." The cable tells how three rabbis, representing their various associations, "after alarming news coming especially from London about a fast and systematic extermination decreed by Hitler and ruthlessly started in Poland, came to me today with tears in their eyes begging the Pope to make a public appeal and a prayer to stop the massacre and deportation. I had to promise the transmission of this message."[578] Cardinal Maglione replied by cable, assuring Cicognani that "the Holy See continues to occupy itself in favor of the Jews."[579]

[577] ASRS, AA.EE.SS., Extracta, Germania 742, ff. 184b–185, cable of Union of Orthodox Rabbis of the United States and Canada, March 16, 1943.

[578] ASRS, AA.EE.SS., Extracta, Germania 742, f. 100, cable of Msgr. Cicognani to Card. Maglione, March 27, 1943.

[579] ASRS, AA.EE.SS., Extracta, Germania 742, f. 101, draft of cable of Card. Maglione to Msgr. Cicognani, April 3, 1943.

This plea from the three American rabbis was reviewed by the Cabinet. It seemed similar to another somewhat even more important appeal that was discussed months before and was administratively concluded by Msgr. Di Meglio. As early as January 1943, a proposal had been made by Dr. Temple, the Anglican archbishop of Canterbury, to Cardinal Arthur Hinsley, Catholic archbishop of Westminster, by which he suggested the Roman Catholic bishops in England be asked to approach the pope in favor of the Jews in Eastern Europe and in occupied countries.

Pius XII remembered very well how active and efficient Cardinal Hinsley had been before regarding the refugee policies of the Catholic Church. And their thinking on it was very much alike. Years earlier, in November 1938, Hinsley had written and insisted "for a public statement of the Pope [Pius XI] in which he would declare the principle by which in Christ there does not exist a discrimination by race and that the big human family should be united in peace by respect for the personality of each individual."[580] To this plea he had annexed a message written by Lord Rothschild who he introduced to Cardinal Pacelli, secretary of state, as "the best known and esteemed of the Jews of England." In his last paragraph, Lord Rothschild had shared his desire to receive a little word of sympathy from the Holy Father, Pius XI, and also alluded to the correspondence his grandfather had with the most distinguished members among Roman cardinals.[581] And while other proposals and pleas for assistance for the Jews had been addressed to the already sick Pope Pius XI — for instance, from the Irish Catholics — it had been Rothchild's addressee, Secretary of State Eugenio Pacelli, who, in January 1939, had set up and organized the worldwide project of a circular letter with appeal to all Catholics to help the Jews. The circular letter had been sent out with a dispatch to all cardinal archbishops of Westminster, Armagh, Quebec, Boston, Chicago, Philadelphia, and Buenos Aires, to all apostolic delegates in the world, and to all cardinal archbishops over the globe to call on them to help the Jews in whatever ways possible. While Hitler was secretly preparing his war, and just two months before being elected as Pope Pius XII, Cardinal Eugenio Pacelli had attacked the Nazi *Reichskanzler* (chancellor of the Reich), a move that had greatly irritated the Nazis, and issued the call for general mobilization of the whole Catholic world in defense of the Jews. Now three years later, Pius XII remembered very well his joint initiative with the English cardinal.

---

[580] ASRS, AA.EE.SS., Stati Ecclesiastici 575 P.O., 606 bis, ff. 3[r/v].
[581] ASRS, AA.EE.SS., Stati Ecclesiastici 575 P.O., 606 bis, ff. 4–5.

But today, in January 1943, things were different. The Anglican archbishop Dr. Temple "wondered whether it would be appropriate for the Roman Catholic bishops in England to make an approach to His Holiness the Pope" in favor of the Jews in Eastern Europe and in the countries under Nazi occupation. "No doubt the Pope is already doing very much but it may be that with assurance of support such as thus might be provided, he would feel able to take still stronger measures, for example recommending courses of action to the Roman Catholics in Germany."[582]

Cardinal Hinsley promised his Anglican interlocutor: "I will do all I can to carry out the suggestion.... At the same time I am quite sure that the Holy Father is already taking every possible practical measure to protect the Jews and other victims of Nazi persecution."[583]

To this request Msgr. Godfrey, the apostolic delegate in London, responded that "the Pope has done all that is possible, and he does this continuously to protect the suffering people of the whole world."

Afterwards, Dr. Temple "came to ask if it would be likely that the Holy Father would be disposed to accept the invitation, from different religious prominent leaders, to make a public appeal in favor of the persecuted people."

At the end of February 1943, Godfrey responded to him that "it seemed to me preferable to abstain for the moment of any formal step towards the Pope in order to avoid difficulties. I proposed instead" — so he said to Rome — "to bring it to your knowledge ... leaving the question to the enlightened judgment of the Holy See."[584]

Msgr. Di Meglio did not show the greatest haste in preparing the answer to Godfrey, the apostolic delegate. He sent it to Cardinal Maglione for signature and dispatch in early June only[585] — to the frustration of Maglione, who wrote: "This dispatch is written with a very considerable delay. I hope that this will not repeat itself again." The draft shows signs of pondering and overthinking. Initially, its central part included the following sentence: "It is well-known to Your Excellency [Msgr. Godfrey] that the Holy See is doing a multifaceted and large scale action, which, notwithstanding

[582] ASRS, AA.EE.SS., Extracta, Germania 742, f. 146, letter of Mr. Temple to Msgr. Godfrey, January 27, 1943.

[583] ASRS, AA.EE.SS., Extracta, Germania 742, f. 147, copy of the letter of Card. Hinsley to Dr. Temple, archbishop of Canterbury, January 29, 1943.

[584] ASRS, AA.EE.SS., Extracta, Germania 742, f. 144ᵛ, letter of Msgr. Godfrey to Card. Maglione, February 22, 1943.

[585] ASRS, AA.EE.SS., Extracta, Germania 742, f. 148, handwritten note of Card. Maglione, June 10, 1943.

the actual, arduous difficulties, has been crowned with successes. The Holy See will not desist to proceed in such work with all the interest and the solicitude that this grave problem merits." That Di Meglio put the words "which, notwithstanding the actual, arduous difficulties, has been crowned with successes the Holy See will not desist" between brackets, then canceled some of the words, and ultimately struck out the whole passage entirely, suggests he thought it sounded too much like self-glorification. Regarding the proposal for a common public plea, the final message was that, as Godfrey already had explained to Mr. Temple, "for obvious motives one does not see the opportunity of such a plea. The Holy See, as it has done until now, so it will not fail to do in the future, that is to vindicate the rights of the oppressed people with all means at its disposal and in the most convenient form."[586]

*
* *

Another telegram message came in from the United States in March 1943. This was from Generoso Pope, who served as the director of the newspaper *Il Progresso Italo-Americano*. It asked Pius XII:

> In the name of Christianity and human decency I humbly implore you to once again lift your sacred universal voice against intensified unchristian persecution being perpetrated by Nazi regime against Jewish people. Americans of all faiths and racial origin are filled with horror and shocked by brutalities against millions of Jews. The savage Nazi national cult is a cruel travesty on Christian conscience and human spirit. I particularly abhor barbaric antisemitism because Italy, the land of my birth, was until Hitler's intrusion free from all such beastly intolerance and endowed gentile and Jew alike with full freedom of worship and America, my adopted cherished land, has throughout its history been haven for victims of religious and racial intolerance and persecution. I pray and hope that intercession by the Holy See, ever a seat of racial spiritual tolerance and justice, will arouse world conscience and help halt the Nazis orgy of savagery.[587]

---

[586] ASRS, AA.EE.SS., Extracta, Germania 742, f. 149ᵛ, draft of dispatch to Msgr. Godfrey prepared by Msgr. Di Meglio, June 11, 1943.

[587] ASRS, AA.EE.SS., Extracta, Germania 742, 177b, telegram of Mr. Pope to Pius XII, March 5, 1943.

Three days later, Pius XII ordered an answer be sent by telegram through the apostolic delegate in Washington. The reply, in part, read, "The Holy See has done, is doing, and will do etc.... what is possible."[588]

Examining the many accounts on the dire situation of the Jews in Poland, Romania, and Transnistria that he received from Dr. A. Silberschein, president of the "Committee for Assistance to the Jewish Population Affected by War," Msgr. Bernardini in Switzerland pointed out a rare but positive note:[589] "In the one on Romania one confirms that over time the situation got better, probably after the steps undertaken by the Holy See." However, the account on Romania doesn't establish clearly whether this mitigation was due to the protest note sent by the United States government and then handled through intermediation by the Swiss legation, or if it happened due to the intervention of the papal nuncio to the government. A further explanation suggests that Marshal Antonescu, when he heard that the Jews of the first transports had been shot to death by the Nazis, had been so stunned that he, himself, started doubting and taking time on further deportations.[590]

The cables with pleas continued to flood into the offices of the secretary of state from around the world. Jews from Sydney, Australia, were alarmed at the atrocious actions of Germany and asked the Holy See to intervene. Cardinal Maglione responded to them: "The Holy See has done and will continue to do what is possible in favor of the Jews."[591]

*

*　　*

Is it coincidence that on April 12, 1943, a copy of the secret report sent by the Italian embassy in Berlin to the Italian Ministry of Foreign Affairs in Rome — dated October 30, 1942 — was brought back to the attention of Pope Pius XII and his staff? This particular report was based on the discourse of Nazi minister Goebbels "at the 'Feldherrnhalle' in which he had attacked the 'People of the Church' and the friends of the clergy, using no friendly word towards the Christian religion in general, when he spoke about the religious struggles that had torn Germany apart in the last centuries."

---

[588] ASRS, AA.EE.SS., Extracta, Germania 742, f. 177a, handwritten note of Pope Pius XII.

[589] ASRS, AA.EE.SS., Romania 149, f. 267, letter of Msgr. Bernardini to Card. Maglione, April 8, 1943.

[590] ASRS, AA.EE.SS., Romania 149, f. 272.

[591] ASRS, AA.EE.SS., Extracta, Germania 742, f. 182b, draft of message in code, April 16, 1943.

Originally it had been Mr. Luigi Petrucci, the Italian consul general in München, who had been interested "to know what would have been the reaction to Goebbels speech in Catholic circles of München."[592] The consul general's words left no doubt on how contacts with those of the Catholic hierarchy would dangerously compromise him and put him squarely on the Nazis' radar. He explained: "Not being able myself to make a visit to Cardinal Faulhaber [archbishop of Munich] for the obvious reasons of political opportunity, I sent my Counsellor adjoint, the Cavaliere Grillo to a private audience with the cardinal." A full account of the conversation between the Italian counselor Grillo and the German cardinal archbishop was compiled.

Petrucci's first important observation on the conversation between Cardinal Faulhaber and Grillo was that "the German police had refused to him [the cardinal] and all his fellow bishops in Germany a visa to Italy, breaking up in this way any personal contact between the high-ranking German clergy and the Holy Father in Rome."

In another paragraph Petrucci shared the words of Faulhaber, who was critical of Nuncio Orsenigo, for "his inactivity and lack of energy." That particular observation did not escape the attention of Cardinal Maglione. At one point, while discussing the conversation between Cavaliere Grillo and Cardinal Faulhaber, Petrucci addressed the following to his Italian minister of foreign affairs in Rome:

> But in Bavaria between National-socialism and Catholicism the bridges are broken, and by now very little hope is left that it could come to a "modus vivendi" between them. In the National-Socialist program, and in particular in its most active branches, there has been decreed the elimination of the "semitical" powers that have acted in Germany in the past, and no institution has had a bigger influence on the German historical evolution than Catholicism, and Christianity in general, considered by Rosenberg and his pupils as purely Semitic phenomenon ... The Nazi authorities, not being able to forcefully eradicate the religion in Bavaria, have already adopted a policy of encirclement, of exfoliation and of smoothing out by which, perhaps over a long term period, the fundaments of the catholic institution should be undermined, until its total extinction. The measures are

[592] ASRS, AA.EE.SS., Germania 854, f. 275, secret report of general consulate in München, by Mr. Petrucci, October 30, 1942.

notorious: (1) gradual reduction of the Clergy by closing seminars and theological courses; suppression of the convents, schools and colleges of religious orders and the "atheization" of the education of the new generations, a measure that already shows visible effects … (3) progressive distancing of the worker, male and female, of the Churches with all means, and not in the least by making the Sunday work obligatory; (4) gradual undermining of the religious orders …; (5) progressive alienation of the relation of the Catholic clergy with Rome, by not permitting the clergy, among other things, to go to the Capital of Catholicism; (6) to offer help and advantages to families that openly prove to abandon the religious practice and to adhere to the new conceptions proposed by the regime; (7) and finally the attempt to create a new religion.

The Italian diplomat pointed out that the Church authorities sought ways to resist, secretly bringing in new priests from clandestine seminaries. And he concluded that in spite of the war with all its horror and the inevitable discontent and threats, such anti-Catholic efforts appeared to foster and reinforce religious sentiment among the masses rather than squelch it. In fact, in the countryside, until now, the Catholic efficiency was unharmed. Yet he also noted, "And I have to add that, while some victorious resistance of the Catholic against the National-socialist action can be verified, none or almost no reaction is to be registered from the protestant element, that tends much easier to de-christianize itself. This makes the position of struggle of the Catholic Church even more difficult."[593]

Why was it so important for the Cabinet to dig up and reexamine this secret report of the Italian consul general and his *adjoint* in München from October 1942, so many months later in April 1943? The blue and red pencil lines in the margins and under significant parts of the text show that both Msgr. Tardini and Cardinal Maglione reflected throughout on the report, and annotations reveal that the two men also studied other available sources on the power that Nazism exerted over the Catholic Church in Germany. The report seemed to verify total defeat, the complete loss of the right to existence and the checkmate against the Catholic Church in Germany. Cardinal Archbishop Faulhaber was practically a

---

[593] ASRS, AA.EE.SS., Germania 854, f. 275, secret report of general consulate in München, by Mr. Petrucci, October 30, 1942.

prisoner, with little power to do anything but endure the attacks of the Nazi party bosses against the Church and himself. He was in a dire state of mind and heart in the face of the enemy with their tightening, aggressive fist. And yet he would not let his soul resign to such a fate. But most significantly is that this time it was an outsider, the Italian consul general Petrucci, a civil and Fascist observer out of the daily political and social realm in Germany, who detected and determined that the Nazis viewed the Catholic Church with the same hateful attitude as they did the Jewish people. On this point, Consul General Petrucci could not have been more correct. As for Tardini, Maglione, and Pius XII, Petrucci's analysis could only bring to mind again the words of Fr. Ledóchowski, the superior general of the Jesuits, who a year before had warned of

> the Nazis' clear intention, after having sent away all [religious clergy] from the military, to proceed with even more brutality against the religious houses, individuals and communities, in such a way that one notices a paralleling method as the one used for the Jews.... All this clearly reveals a persecution in place.... Well-informed men interpret these measures like this: after the communists, the free-masons, and the Jews, it will be the turn of the Jesuits, as if against the assault troops of the Pope and of the Catholic Church. In the schools they constantly launch accusations against us: that our religious vow could at anytime compel us to betray the fatherland [this is a reference to their vow of total submission to the pope]; the Nazis paint with the most ridiculous colors the obedience formula "perinde ac cadaver,"[594] declaring the Father General to be a Pole, which supposedly explains everything and claim the entire Company is dominated by the spirit and influence of Judaism. And this last one is the significant tag with which they try to justify each action, even the physical annihilation.[595]

This was the situation as early as 1941.

[594] *Perinde ac cadaver* is the formula adopted by the Jesuits to express, hyperbolically, absolute submission to the rule and the will of the superiors, with renunciation to one's own choices and desires.
[595] ASRS, AA.EE.SS., Germania 708, fasc. 305, f. 47–48, typewritten memo of December 18, 1941 from Fr. Ledóchowski, S.J., superior general of the Society of Jesus.

*

*   *

As if these cumulative tidings were not sinister enough, another informant came forward, adding more water to the overwhelmed, flooded boat of human misery. It was a woman, a Hungarian sister named Margherita Slachta. She was in charge of the relief work in Budapest. When in Rome, she was an occasional visitor to the apartments of the pope and his staff. Lately, she had dedicated herself to the fate of the Jews in Slovakia. To this end, she had traveled to Rome in March 1943 to meet with Francis Joseph Spellman, once in service as a desk officer in the Cabinet and at that time archbishop of New York and very close to Pius XII. It was Sr. Slachta's sincere hope and goal that her visit would generate the interest and sympathy of the United States and encourage them to help save twenty-five thousand Slovak Jews who — as the Cabinet annotated — "were menaced with deportation (= with horrible death)."[596] On March 8, after the meeting with Spellman, she handed over several documents and reports to Msgr. Di Meglio. Reviewing the documents, the Cabinet immediately instructed Msgr. Burzio, the chargé-d'affaires, to arrange an intervention and, if possible, a rescue operation; while "reports come in concerning imminent deportation of 20,000 Jews from Slovakia, would His Excellency question the government itself, and if the information is true, make moves that might make it possible to prevent the execution of the planned measure. I wait for further update."[597]

On her return to Hungary, Sr. Slachta put her efforts toward collecting additional information that she sent to the Cabinet. This information regarded the waves of persecution against the Jews in central Europe. Writing a letter directly to Msgr. Dell'Acqua on April 3, 1943, she shared with him her great joy over a joint circular letter of the Slovak bishops to the Catholics and the citizens of their country. In it, they reminded each other of the fundamental rights of all Slovaks: "Laws that grant to each citizen of Slovakia the complete equality with nothing whatsoever in regards to racial or religious considerations. The same circular letter brings up the point of view of the Church on natural human rights and applies this point of view of the Church to the Jewish question."

But at the same time, Sr. Slachta was dumbstruck that "Bulgaria has initiated a move, condemning its Israelite habitants for deportation. The first transport,

---

[596] ASRS, AA.EE.SS., Cecoslovacchia 175, f. 593, typewritten note of Msgr. Di Meglio.
[597] ASRS, AA.EE.SS., Cecoslovacchia 175, f. 588, cable of Card. Maglione, March 9, 1943.

consisting of four ships loaded with those unfortunates has passed across our Danube with destination of Bratislava where these poor deported should be put on trains for ... Poland."[598] She told how the Hungarian authorities would not even have been informed of this transit "and the unfortunate passed our country under the German banner." The sister correctly observed that until then, Bulgaria was the one to resist in its opposition against the German pressure in the matter of deportations, in spite of the occupation of the entire country. Therefore, she dared hope that "it would be possible for the Holy See, by submission of the high clergy, to assure the protection of these unfortunates. Filov and his 45 deputies will serve as support for this good action." Such support by Bulgarian prime minister Bogdan Filov and his fellow politicians might sound contradictory to us, given the general Germanophile policy of Filov and of the monarch, Tsar Boris III. But the facts on the deportation of Jews in Bulgaria put the hopeful words of Sr. Slachta in another surprising light. Msgr. Dell'Acqua suggested there be an "appeal to the Apostolic Delegate asking him for more information and to make those steps that he retains possible and opportune." The pope agreed, and Cardinal Maglione sent a cable to the Bulgarian capital city of Sofia:

> According to information received by the holy see deportation of Jews resident in Bulgaria would have started. If the news is true I beg your most reverend excellency to execute to the government steps that you consider possible and opportune in favor of so many unfortunates. I wait for precise information on this behalf.[599]

Five days later, Msgr. Giuseppe Mazzoli, the apostolic delegate in Sofia, replied:

> As a result of the request of the German Reich, from the 4th till the 24th of this month, this government has evacuated from the operating zones of Tracia Macedonia about 11,300 jews, ex Greek-Yugoslav-subjects, and handed 4,000 over at the Danube frontier, the others coming from Serbian territory were handed over to the German authorities that then deported them to Poland.... 20 March

---

[598] ASRS, AA.EE.SS., Bulgaria 29, f. 42, letter of Sr. Slachta to Msgr. Dell'Acqua, April 3, 1943.

[599] ASRS, AA.EE.SS., Bulgaria 29, f. 46, draft of cable of Card. Maglione to apostolic delegation in Sofia, April 7, 1943.

I had a conversation with the Minister of Internal Affairs who confessed (?) that ... the measure responds to the demands of internal
and external policy. The chamber of deputies discussed on the 24
of last month a motion by 40 members regarding the abolition
of restrictions against Israelis. After long discussion in which the
Government asked a vote of confidence the motion was rejected
but then the already-decided deportation of 6000 Jews resident in
Bulgaria was suspended. For now nothing new. [600]

Pope Pius XII was immediately alerted of Sr. Slachta's intervention. At the end of
her letter to Msgr. Dell'Acqua, she promised she would try to send a photo "that
would give a close idea of the infernal horror of the case in question." Some weeks
later this photo came through.

Corpses of Jews slaughtered by the Nazis in Kamianets-Podilskyi on December 22, 1941.[601]

The photo shows victims of a massacre that took place in Kamianets-Podilskyi,
Ukraine, months after the infamous Kamianets-Podilskyi massacre of August 1941

[600] ASRS, AA.EE.SS., Bulgaria 29, f. 47, cable from Msgr. Mazzoli to Card. Maglione,
April 12, 1943.
[601] ASRS, AA.EE.SS., Extracta, Germania 742, f. 151.

in which 23,600 Jews were killed at one time. The cadavers in the photo Sr. Slachta shared represent only 5 of the 150 people who were shot in December after four weeks of prison, a period of time during which others had suffered and died of sickness and starvation.

The case of Bulgaria would drag on over some months. For various and still uncertain reasons, the deportations in Bulgaria came to a stop. Was it because the Germans at that time were facing defeat? Was it by internal protest in the country? Was it by the insistence of Metropolitan Stefan I, the head of the Orthodox Church? Was it because the Allies started threatening those who committed war crimes? If one checks on the Internet there is no study or article to be found that suggests even a minor role of the Holy See.[602] In reality, however, other requests in favor of the Jews of Bulgaria continued to come into the Cabinet. In June, for instance, the Central Israeli Committee of Uruguay contacted them by both telegram[603] and by letter over the apostolic nunciature.[604] Pope Pius XII immediately reacted on June 27, 1943, deciding that the nuncio should first respond to the Central Israeli Committee of Uruguay, ensuring that "the Holy See did, was doing and would continue to do all that what was possible,"[605] and also to inform the apostolic delegate of Sofia about the matter and to involve them in a joint action. Regarding that last point, the Cabinet affirmed that it had been already done.[606] Could it be that those actions and interventions of the Holy See offer an additional explanation as to why the deportations were stopped?

But let's take up where we left off. During the first days of May 1943, the Cabinet compiled a bleak and troubling numerical balance, probably by the hand of Msgr. Di Meglio:

---

[602] See for instance: https://en.wikipedia.org/wiki/Rescue_of_the_Bulgarian_Jews; Nadège Ragaru, "Contrasting Destinies : The Plight of Bulgarian Jews and the Jews in Bulgarian-occupied Greek and Yugoslav Territories during World War Two," in *Sciences Po*, Violence de masse et Résistance-Réseau de recherche, [en ligne], publié le: 15 Mars, 2017, accéder le 17/02/2020, http://bo-k2s.sciences-po.fr/mass-violence-war-massacre-resistance/fr/, ISSN 1961-9898.

[603] ASRS, AA.EE.SS., Bulgaria 29, f. 53, telegram of the Central Jewish Committee of Uruguay, June 26, 1943.

[604] ASRS, AA.EE.SS., Bulgaria 29, f. 57, letter of Msgr. Alberto Levame to Card. Maglione, June 27, 1943.

[605] ASRS, AA.EE.SS., Bulgaria 29, f. 54, draft of telegram in code to nunciature in Montevideo, June 29, 1943.

[606] ASRS, AA.EE.SS., Bulgaria 29, f. 56, handwritten note with the decision of Pope Pius XII, June 27, 1943.

Before the war in Poland there were about 4,500,000 Jews. One cal-
culates now that there are actually (all together with those who came
in from other occupied countries) not more than 100,000 left. In
Warsaw a ghetto was created that originally contained about 65,000,
now there would be 20–25,000 left. Naturally many Jews might have
escaped control, but there is no doubt that the majority will be killed.
After months and months of transports of thousands and thousands
of persons, those have never been heard of again: a fact one cannot
explain otherwise than by (their) death, also taking into account the
enterprising character of the Jews, who in some way, when alive, make
their presence noticed. There are special death camps near to Lublin
(Treblinka) and near Brest Litowski. It is said that they get clogged
up with several hundred Jews at a time in big chambers, where they
are executed by poisonous gas. Then transported in cattle wagons,
closed hermetically with quicklime on the floor.[607]

The account dates from May 1943, and, even if those who read it remained incredu-
lous (as the conjugation of the verbs suggests), the reality of mass gas chambers
was, indeed, becoming a hard fact, at least to diplomatic circles.

The embassy of Poland to the Holy See warned the pope about injunctions
made by Germany to the Romanian government regarding Polish citizens living
on its territory. In particular Romania should send "to Germany Polish 'specialists'
[intellectuals and educated people] who had manifested a hostile attitude towards
the Germans and they would be put to forced labour, and those who were of the
Jewish race should be handed directly over to the German authorities."[608] The pope
took this seriously. During the usual audience with the Cabinet on June 26, 1943,
he decided the whole matter was "to be passed onto the 1st section (Race — Jew!)"
and thus to Dell'Acqua and his colleagues, to ensure it would be followed up.[609]
Immediately, the Cabinet insisted that Msgr. Cassulo in Bucharest investigate and
intervene. Nuncio Cassulo did so. On various occasions in the coming months,
he honored the Romanian authorities with his personal visits during which the

[607] ASRS, AA.EE.SS., Extracta, Germania 742, ff. 141r/v.
[608] ASRS, AA.EE.SS., Romania 149, f. 288.
[609] ASRS, AA.EE.SS., Romania 149, f. 291, handwritten note with decision taken on
June 26, 1943.

critical case of the concentrated Jews and eventual possible concessions in favor of them was on the agenda.

*

*   *

In the heat of the Roman summer of 1943, a member of the Capuchin Order, Fr. Marie-Benoît du Bourg d'Iré, delivered to Pope Pius XII a very extended note "on the situation of the Jews in France, on their conversions, on the sentiments of gratefulness they foster towards the Catholic Church for its charity towards them, and on some requests they would submit to the Pope."[610] The father's detailed document included appendixes with lists of those deported, information on the camps in Upper Silesia, and annotations on the camps and the deportations in France. He had lived for the last three years in the Capuchin convent of Marseille, France, and, moved by the spirit of compassion and mercy, had helped fifty-one Jews convert to Catholicism. The archbishop of Marseille had given Fr. du Bourg d'Iré the authorization to do so, and he had been assisted by the Sisters of Notre Dame of Sion. Most of the Baptisms had taken place in the sisters' chapel.[611] As a consequence of the persecutions of French and foreign Jews that plagued France, the friar informed the pope,

> this spiritual ministry brought me quite naturally to occupy myself of the protection in a thousand different ways of these unfortunate converted and not-converted Jews, as all of them are object of Christian charity. I did so in collaboration with other priests, religious sisters of Notre Dame de Sion, lay people of the Catholic Action and also, obviously, with the Israelian organisations, which display the greatest courage and the highest devotion in defense of their co-religionists.

These rescue operations had given him the opportunity to get in touch with the Italian authorities in the French zone occupied by their troops. "Italy performs over there a very humane action and is very protective towards the Jews, be it

---

[610] ASRS, AA.EE.SS., Francia 892, f. 56, letter of Fr. du Bourg d'Iré to Pope Pius XII, Rome, July 15, 1943.

[611] ASRS, AA.EE.SS., Francia 892, f. 57, "Note au sujet des Juifs" of Fr. du Bourg d'Iré, O.F.M. Cap.

against the German police, or even against the French police, for which it deserves all credit. To this end, I had to deal with Mister Lo Spinoso, the representative of the Italian government for Jewish affairs in Nice, whom I thanked for all this as a catholic and as a Frenchman." Fr. du Bourg d'Iré then told the pope that he could speak as a sort of delegate on behalf of French Judaism and of the other European Jews in France. His note, therefore, "expresses in a very discrete way, while waiting for the occasion to do this publicly and solemnly, the profound gratitude of all the Jews towards the Sovereign Pontiff and at the same time of their confidence in his goodness"[612] And so he went on, enumerating some of their pleas to the pope. The documents related to his letter show that about fifty thousand Jews were already deported out of France by the German police. Then he puts his questions to the pope: Would it be possible to get information about the deported that were on his lists? Would it be possible for the Holy See to intervene not only for better treatment in the camps but also in order to obtain permission for the international and French organizations to get access to the camps? In case of refusal by the Germans, would the Holy See be able to suggest to the Allied governments that they exercise pressure on the Nazis through the threat of a retaliation procedure?

Fr. du Bourg d'Iré's questions, included in his urgent and detailed report of July 1943, may seem like farfetched daydreaming. But as Cardinal Maglione sat in his office, poring over the writing, absorbing it all, a specific paragraph caught his attention. He signposted it with a red line in the margin, probably considering that this time there might be a minuscule possibility of success. The paragraph regarded a request to help facilitate the repatriation of Spanish Jews from France. Spain had promised to let them in, but the Cabinetcracy was slow, and the Spanish Jews were now at risk of being taken in by the German police. "Could the Holy See send a word on this to the Spanish government?" asked the Capuchin father. In addition to the frightening situation facing the Spanish Jews, another emergency loomed: What would become of the eight to ten thousand Jews now living under surveillance in the French zone under Italian authority once the Germans decided to also occupy that zone? Their situation would become immediately catastrophic. "As they live a few kilometres from the Italian border, would it not be possible" — so

[612] ASRS, AA.EE.SS., Francia 892, f. 58, "Note au sujet des Juifs" of Fr. du Bourg d'Iré, O.F.M. Cap.

suggested Fr. du Bourg d'Iré — "to allow them entry onto Italian territory? A suggestion of this kind to the Italian government, would that be possible?"[613] This last proposal was given serious consideration by someone of the Cabinet, as the marking in the margin indicates.

One falls silent and one's heart sinks when opening the "liste des internés de Nexon partis pour une destination inconnue (mars 1943),"[614] turning to the next "liste des internés à Drancy partis pour une destination inconnue ... 12 et 19-4-43,"[615] and to the list of names of those deported to Birkenau, Theresienstadt, and in the Arbeitslager of Trawinki, Tomaszow, Monowitz, Wlodawa, and Jawischowitz.[616] A very detailed description of the camps in France, followed by a list of persons deported "to an unknown destination" — but always pointing to the East — depicts the situation of the Jews in France during the previous three years. A list including information on the camps in Upper Silesia and the living conditions of women, men, and children closes this very arresting and devastating dossier brought in by Fr. du Bourg d'Iré.[617]

It's impossible to share here all the atrocities and sinister deeds preserved in the many files of the Historical Archive. One file in particular, and quite likely one of the most detailed of the eyewitness reports, includes two accounts. Although both date from November 1943,[618] the second one did not arrive in the Cabinet before April 1944.[619]

This last report was written by an unnamed twenty-four-year-old Polish Jew. Before the war he had studied medicine in Italy. The news of the Nazi invasion caught him by surprise on a sunny day of September 1939, while on a vacation at his mother's house in Poland. He first recounts how the Nazis used the Jews as

---

[613] ASRS, AA.EE.SS., Francia 892, f. 60, "Note au sujet des Juifs" of Fr. du Bourg d'Iré, O.F.M. Cap.

[614] ASRS, AA.EE.SS., Francia 892, f. 61. [Transl.: List of interned at Nexon departed for an unknown destination (March 1943).]

[615] ASRS, AA.EE.SS., Francia 892, ff. 62–63. [Transl.: List of interned at Drancy departed for an unknown destination.]

[616] ASRS, AA.EE.SS., Francia 892, ff. 64–69.

[617] ASRS, AA.EE.SS., Francia 892, ff. 76–78.

[618] ASRS, AA.EE.SS., Extracta, Germania 742, ff. 194–205, "Tears and blood in the tragedy of a circumcised Pole," November 1943.

[619] ASRS, AA.EE.SS., Extracta, Germania 742, f. 210–233, "L'extermination des Juifs Polonais racontée par un témoin oculaire," November 1, 1943.

hostages against the Russians and killed them afterwards.[620] A little later, the Jews, hunted by the Nazis, sought various ways to escape to the Russian zone. Some even tried to buy their freedom by offering considerable payouts to the Nazis. Needless to say, those payments were made in vain. Such desperate actions never saved any life. Our young Jewish man tells of his travels up and down from Warsaw under siege to the Russian front line again, of his three-week stay in a Russian prison, and how he was brought back to the German-occupied zone where he was arrested and held for a while by the Nazis. Having survived all these experiences of cruelty inflicted by the occupants, as well as frequent abuse by the local population, he managed, without permit and without wearing the mandatory yellow Star of David, to reach the city of Hrubieszow, near Lublin, Poland, in March 1940. There, he started to work in the Jewish organization for medical assistance (TOZ), under close surveillance of the Nazis, in the role of assistant surgeon.[621] The TOZ worked diligently to prepare and open a hospital of thirty-six beds, with twelve of them assigned to those who suffered from infectious diseases. However, this would soon show itself insufficient. The young assistant surgeon gave gut-wrenching, detailed descriptions of the mistreatment of the Jews in the concentration and extermination camp of Belzec. Later on, he was employed by the Nazis to safeguard the public order in the Jewish community.

At one point in his account, in which he titled the killings of the Jews as "the 'Actions,'" this brave, unnamed young Jewish surgeon stated that "the Germans called these murders: relocation to the East."[622] So the old refrain of the First World War, "to the East," has been passed on to the next military generation.

> In 1941 the German authorities obliged all Jews to leave the little villages and to gather together in the cities. In that way the Jews were easy to identify in the main cities of the provinces. It would become clear very soon that these relocations would facilitate the subsequent deportations to the camps of Belzec, Treblinka and Sobibor, places where Jews were killed in mass. The so-called "Actions" took place

[620] ASRS, AA.EE.SS., Extracta, Germania 742, f. 210, "L'extermination des Juifs Polonais racontée par un témoin oculaire," November 1, 1943.
[621] ASRS, AA.EE.SS., Extracta, Germania 742, f. 213, "L'extermination des Juifs Polonais racontée par un témoin oculaire," November 1, 1943.
[622] ASRS, AA.EE.SS., Extracta, Germania 742, f. 222, "L'extermination des Juifs Polonais racontée par un témoin oculaire," November 1, 1943.

step by step, in different time frames in those cities where the Jews were concentrated. In some cities these "Actions" took place repeatedly, in other cities the deportation was a one-time operation. The first "Action" took place in Lublin, on the 15th of March 1942. At that time the Jews had still the illusion that it really consisted of a mere departure "towards the east …" as the Germans told them. Other actions followed that first one; they lasted for six weeks and went like this: Of the 100,000 habitants of the Jewish "reservoir" of Lublin, first the Jews that were working for German households were separated. They were given the "Judenkarten" (cards of the Jews) that should protect them from deportation. Sometime later, however, the holders of the "Judenkarten" would suffer the same fate as the others. The massacre started at the Jewish hospital, where, under the pretext of being ill, the wealthiest Jews of the city had taken refuge. The sick were shot in their beds while helplessly lying there. The Gestapo, the Ukrainian and Lithuanian police, and also by order of the authorities the Jewish police, assembled or seized all the Jews who were hiding. Those who would not leave their place of shelter were killed on the spot. Those who were assembled were first brought together onto the court squares and then accompanied to the Jewish prayer houses. And last, from there, they were driven like cattle to the little railway stations to be sent away on wagons to Belzec. It happened frequently that some people resisted and refused to get on the wagons. In that case the Lithuanians and the Ukrainians, who were drunk with liquor and standing by, threw themselves on the Jews, beating them, torturing them, and finally killing them in an atrocious way and cutting the corpses of the Jews to pieces. In this way, each night thousands of people were killed, so that after six weeks, of the 100,000 Jews barely 4,000 remained. The Ghetto of Lublin presented an indescribable scene. The streets were covered with corpses, and the gutters literally flowed with blood. The screams of the deported were heartbreaking for the Christians who witnessed these horrible scenes. They said that they would never forget these bloody days. The route that leads to the railway junction near Lublin was also covered with corpses. The

Christian population was forced to remove them with the help of trucks. The 4,000 Jews of Lublin who were still alive, among them many women and children, were sent to Majdanek-Tatarski, 4 km. from Lublin, where a ghetto was created. Some months later this ghetto followed the same fate as that of Lublin.

On other pages, he described the killing of the Jews of the district of Lublin. After recounting the most horrible scenes of killing of children (taken by the legs and having their heads smashed against the wall of the cemetery) and men (shot in the back with machine guns), followed by the killing of the women, who had first to witness the murders of their beloveds, our eyewitness wrote: "I cannot describe the despair of those unfortunate women."[623]

Our Jewish witness does not shy away from a critical and burning question:

And what to say about my physical and moral status in all this? As part of my duties I was forced to assist these killings, and a gesture of protest would not have served anyone. Among 300 victims, some were my relatives.... We all knew that our days were counted, and we looked to the future with resignation. Besides, the Poles told us that, based on information they had, the rest of the Jews suffered the same fate in the 3 months that followed.[624]

It is not surprising that the conditions of desperation and the naivety of some people took an absurd turn. Some Jews, exhausted by famine, came to present themselves to the open location from which deportation "to the East …" started, begging the Nazis to send them also "towards the East …," but the Germans pushed them contemptuously back.[625]

These stories of deportations "towards the East," which stretch our minds beyond the limits of mental sanity, tell of the very narrow space for action that was left

[623] ASRS, AA.EE.SS., Extracta, Germania 742, f. 223, "L'extermination des Juifs Polonais racontée par un témoin oculaire," November 1, 1943.
[624] ASRS, AA.EE.SS., Extracta, Germania 742, f. 225, "L'extermination des Juifs Polonais racontée par un témoin oculaire," November 1, 1943.
[625] ASRS, AA.EE.SS., Extracta, Germania 742, f. 228, "L'extermination des Juifs Polonais racontée par un témoin oculaire," November 1, 1943.

in all the places where the Nazis took over command, first for all Jews and from 1941 onwards also for Christians. It was impossible for these people to escape the atrocities of the SS. They were unable to find a way to flee from the Gestapo and naïve to feel protected with hateful collaborators at their threshold. The reports continued to arrive, at times with months of delay, from the camps of Auschwitz and Birkenau,[626] with sketches of the gas chambers and crematorium in Birkenau.

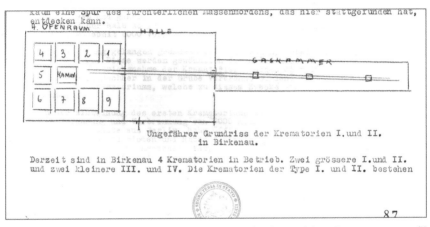

Sketch of the gas chambers and the Birkenau crematorium.[627]

Is it not surprising, though, that notwithstanding these shocking and bleak tidings arriving from dark and sinister places "towards the East," those in the Vatican and its outposts in different parts of the world continued to write, to analyze, to intervene, to strike back, to search for gateways of freedom and salvation? It can't be denied that, starting before the war, the number of people whom the pope and the Cabinet were able to save may seem mere drops in an immeasurable ocean of horror and misery. And yet against the plan of mass destruction of human beings, was it not the word of the gospel that still burned in the hearts and minds of different people who stood up against and obstructed this devilish plan, trying in silence to protect and to save every single treasure of human life?

[626] ASRS, AA.EE.SS., Extracta, Germania 742, ff. 75–108.
[627] ASRS, AA.EE.SS., Extracta, Germania 742, f. 261.

11

Short Story of a Mother and a Transit Visa

IN SEPTEMBER 1939, brothers David and Jakob Kutten were living and working safely in the bustling city of London. Yet they were sorely missing an important part of their family — their mother, Mina Kutten. She was stranded in Italy, and it was the brothers' great desire to have her join them. And so, they wrote to the English consulate in Milan on behalf of their mother, Mina Kutten, saying that she had been advised to apply to that consulate for a visa that would allow her to enter the United Kingdom. The request of these two young men was certified by a certain John Matthews, director of Matthews (Hosiery) Ltd. based in London (who was possibly their employer) and by the Jewish Aid Committee.[628]

Mina Kutten herself wrote to Pope Pius XII for the first time on February 29, 1940. In perfect German she explained her desperate situation. Mina's maiden name was Goldberg, and she had been born in 1869 in Poland. In June 1939, she and both her sons, David and Jakob, were expelled from Germany by the Nazi regime. The two sons had made it to London, where they now lived, but for reasons not made clear, the family had somehow been separated and Mina had ended up alone in Milan, Italy.

Mina Kutten.[629]

[628] ASRS, AA.EE.SS., Ebrei 74, f. 72.
[629] ASRS, AA.EE.SS., Ebrei 74, f. 73.

The request in her first letter was obvious — for assistance in getting out of Italy and traveling to London. She attached a character statement written on her behalf by Capuchin Fr. Giannantonio Romallo, who was the parish priest of Santa Tecla of the Dome of Milan. Fr. Romallo defined her as "of Polish nationality, of Israelian race and religion, a woman of high moral standards, foreign to any political question and an example as mother of her family." Mina's request was entrusted by the pope and the Cabinet to Msgr. Dell'Acqua.

That was February 1940. For the entire next year there is no mention in her file of what actions, if any, were taken on her behalf. It is also unclear as to why it took the Cabinet a year to respond. However, Mina was not one to sit around and wait for things to happen. Her file shows us that she used this time very actively and productively, gathering all the documents she could to support her case.

At last, Cardinal Maglione responded directly to Romallo's correspondence. His answer was disappointing, saying that unfortunately the Holy See felt "most hurt by the fact that it could not realize the good offices" request, because "the emigration of people of 'Jewish lineage' into England is regulated by peremptory norms of which they don't make exceptions."[630] Maglione was referring to the British quotas for Jewish refugees, which were very strict. As discouraging as it might seem, the Holy See wasn't in a position to wave a magic wand to get Mina, or any other refugees, into the United Kingdom unless the British government allowed it.

This did not deter Mina. On March 10, 1941, she again picked up her pen and sat down to compose a letter in hopes of securing the help she needed. This time she wrote to Cardinal Schuster, the archbishop of Milan. She complained that for more than a year she had been waiting to leave Italy in order to be reunited with her sons. Since then, David and Jakob had left London and had relocated to New York. Her life in Italy had most certainly become more difficult during the year she had waited, not in the least because of increasingly harsh racial laws. Mina confirmed that she had all the documentation needed in her possession, including an American visa. She was only waiting to hear back from Lisbon about a transit visa for Portugal, from where she would embark on a ship that was traveling to the United States. She appealed to Cardinal Schuster to intervene in order to help her get the necessary Portuguese transit visa.[631]

[630] ASRS, AA.EE.SS., Ebrei 74, f. 79ᵛ.
[631] ASRS, AA.EE.SS., Ebrei 74, f. 74.

Three days later, the personal secretary of Cardinal Schuster wrote to Cardinal Maglione, assuring him, just as Fr. Romallo had more than a year before, that "Miss Kutten has always had an exemplary conduct in morals and goodness; asking the intervention of the Secretary of State for her."[632]

Immediately, Msgr. Dell'Acqua prepared a note for the Portuguese embassy, stating that for her trip across the ocean, Ms. Kutten simply "needed only a 'transit-visa' for Portugal; we ask for a 'benevolent interest' in this case."[633]

Cardinal Schuster, archbishop of Milan, was notified about the steps that had been taken, and Mina was subsequently informed.[634] Ever the hopeful mother, she had already paid her full fare to New York for a ship departing from Lisbon, and the only thing left to do was to obtain the permission to travel. But time was running out for her to secure the transit visa. Her reservation was for a boat leaving the Lisbon harbor on April 15, although the ticket remained valid until May 15 — which suggests there may have been later boats. And so Mina wrote once more, pleading with the Holy See to try again with the Portuguese embassy on her behalf.[635] If this failed and all her efforts proved to be in vain, she might never be reunited with her two sons.

David and Jakob Kutten.[636]

[632] ASRS, AA.EE.SS., Ebrei 74, f. 75a.
[633] ASRS, AA.EE.SS., Ebrei 74, f. 80.
[634] ASRS, AA.EE.SS., Ebrei 74, f. 83.
[635] ASRS, AA.EE.SS., Ebrei 74, ff. 84$^{r/v}$.
[636] ASRS, AA.EE.SS., Ebrei 74, f. 73.

On April 11, only four days before her ship was to set sail, a frustrated Msgr. Tardini gave the Cabinet stern instructions to make one last attempt on Mina's behalf. With no time to waste, they ignored the usual slow diplomatic procedures. Tardini ordered his staff to pick up the phone immediately and call the embassy of Portugal to the Holy See directly. A move like this was unusual, for it could be seen as unnecessarily pushy, but for the desperate Mina every hour now mattered, and they were determined to help her.[637]

The urgent phone calls were to no avail. The boat left Lisbon for New York and poor Mina was not on it. One wonders the anguish Mina must have felt, knowing that her chance to be reunited with her beloved sons in the United States had just set sail and she had been left behind. Surely there were some tears of grief and frustration wept behind the closed doors of her room.

However, the Holy See didn't give up on the devastated mother. At the end of April, Cardinal Maglione assured Cardinal Schuster that "new steps have been taken regarding the Portuguese authorities."[638]

It may not have come in time for her to make the boat, but it seems the direct phone call of the secretary of state to the embassy of Portugal to the Holy See had, in fact, made a slight difference. There was relief all around when, on May 14, a copy of a telegraph message that the counselor of Portugal had sent to the international police in Lisbon came into the Cabinet's office. The counselor had asked his colleagues in Lisbon to hurry up with a response. He pointed out that he needed the answer urgently because without the Portuguese transit visa in place, he would not be able to request the additional transit visas Mina needed for Spain and France, as she would travel through those countries on her way to Portugal.[639]

At that point Fr. Romallo of Milan wrote yet again to Tardini. His letter of May 17 included the plea "that she is an old poor woman that has only to reach her children in America. It's true that she is Jewish, but we have good hopes that before departing the light of the Holy Gospel will illuminate her." In this letter, Romallo appears to wonder if the delays in helping her were because she was Jewish, and he seems to ignore completely that Tardini and the others had worked tirelessly to avoid the shipwreck that was her case.

---

[637] ASRS, AA.EE.SS., Ebrei 74, f. 85.
[638] ASRS, AA.EE.SS., Ebrei 74, f. 88, draft of letter to Card. Schuster (sent on April 29, 1941).
[639] ASRS, AA.EE.SS., Ebrei 74, f. 89.

Sadly, for Mina, being Jewish was indeed an issue in the eyes of the Portuguese and Italians. The power to allow her to travel rested squarely with them. Beyond making repeated requests for the transit visas on her behalf, there was nothing else the Holy See could do to help. Tardini wrote a note on Romallo's letter, to emphasize that "I responded to him that she was already recommended two times."[640]

Mina Kutten's file ends there. It is unlikely she ever reached her two beloved sons in the United States. What became of her is unknown.

---

[640] ASRS, AA.EE.SS., Ebrei 74, f. 90, May 28, 1941.

12

A Tale of Nine Wise Men around a Table

THE FILES ON Poland preserved in the Secretariat of State's Historical Archive speak loudly, from the very beginning of the war, of innumerable human tragedies. And, as the war progressed, the Archives start to murmur, often not with certainty, but with fearful, growing dread of the terrible picture that was slowly forming. Eyewitnesses wrote to Rome with tales of trains carrying SS convoys and cattle wagons packed with people moving toward some "unknown destination," as mentioned in more details in the chapter "A Tale of Dark and Sinister Places."

Under occupation, the country of Poland was intentionally and viciously abused by the Nazis, whose initial goal was the immediate, brutal annihilation of Polish Catholics — both clergy and laypeople — as well as the whole of the intellectual elite. The thousands of documents preserved in the Historical Archive tell us of this tragedy during the Nazi invasion. The second phase was the extermination of Jews from all across Europe with the culmination of Hitler's final solution. Millions were transported to Poland to be murdered within the gas chambers and ovens of the world's most notorious concentration and extermination camps — Auschwitz, Auschwitz II Birkenau, Sobibor, Majdanek, Belzec, and the two Treblinka camps.

The nation of Poland had a special place in the hearts of Pius XII and his Cabinet. It was a fervently devout Catholic nation with a long history of solid relations with the Roman Pontiff. The German invasion turned into an immediate attack on the populace based on two key Nazi principles: hatred of the Polish (who were considered their main Slav enemy) and hatred for the Catholic Faith practiced by the majority of Poland's population — a Faith that had long nourished the country's national sense of independency, be that against the Communist Russians or Nazi Germany. The Nazis did not see Poland as an occupied territory they could manipulate into becoming allies, as they did in some other countries. Rather, they saw it as an enemy that had to be viciously crushed.

The archives on Poland and the complex diplomatic activity undertaken by the Holy See in favor of this country would deserve a thorough academic study in the future. I have merely started to lift the veil. The world will benefit from this. The tale on these pages is of a single episode, a mere fragment in time. But it is a fragment that I hope will help shed a little light for readers as to how the Catholic hierarchy in Rome really stood regarding the Nazis.

*
* *

In January 1940, a few months after the German invasion of Poland, Rome was informed by an eyewitness that "crucifixes and portraits of saints of the schools, of the orphanages and hospitals were thrown away. All work was forbidden for religious sisters, taking away from them the orphanages and hospitals. Instead, in their place they have called in the 'Hitlerschwester' [Sisters of Hitler], whose shameful attitude provoked indignation, to no effect, from the sick, the doctors and the population.... The Convents are liquidated with no matter."[641]

Throughout the rest of 1940 and into 1941 this type of information was coming into the Cabinet thick and fast. One intelligence analysis report, seemingly prepared internally, summarized what happened in Reichsgau Wartheland, the annexed region of the provinces of West Poland. The report details the period there immediately after the German invasion of 1939 until the summer of 1942.[642]

Reichsgau Wartheland was also an archbishopric and primatial see of Poznan, with four million Catholics and at least two thousand priests. The Catholic Church was protected by the Concordat, the legally binding diplomatic agreement signed in 1925 between the Holy See and Poland.

[641] ASRS, AA.EE.SS., Stati Ecclesiastici 630, f. 281, document sent by Card. Hlond, January 29, 1940.
[642] ASRS, AA.EE.SS., Polania 208, ff. 576–582, internal report from Msgr. Samorè, February 20, 1940.

But the German invasion of 1939 changed everything. Almost overnight it was forbidden for the Polish Catholic Church to communicate with Rome. The Nazi occupation also made communications with the apostolic nunciature in Berlin impossible. Over the next two years there would be the total, orchestrated annihilation of the Catholic Church in the region. The Archives contain discussions about a thirteen-point Nazi plan that had circulated widely in Wartheland in the first months of 1940. The concluding statement of this diabolical plan was to say that Wartheland was an "'experimental camp': all of that applied and executed in this region would serve as the norm for the other territories annexed to Germany."[643]

This was all part of a broader plan that, had the war gone Hitler's way, would have been copied in other occupied territories. In Poland, the "experiment" was played out with ruthless efficiency. The thick cloud that hung over the nation was foul, dark, and shaped like a swastika.

Of the six bishops residing in Reichsgau Wartheland at the time of the invasion, perhaps only one remained. Two were forced to leave the region and forbidden to return. Two others were arrested and, in an attempt to degrade them, made to sweep the filthy floor of the train station. After that, they were exiled. A fifth was arrested in the autumn of 1939, imprisoned for two months, then transported to Dachau, the first and one of the most notorious of the Nazi concentration camps.[644]

In a different Polish region, an area known as Płock (East Prussia), the eighty-year-old bishop and his auxiliary bishop were arrested and deported. The bishop died two years later, in 1941, in the concentration camp of Soldau in northeast Poland. At least fifty priests across Płock were shot or put to death in other ways. Several hundred clergy were imprisoned and sentenced to hard labor, where daily humiliations included being forced to kneel and bow low on the ground, repeating, "We are Polish pigs."[645] The demand that the priests kneel and recite such a thing is just one of many sickening examples of the Nazis' desire to debase and attempt to crush the spirits of those they kept alive as slaves. A few priests managed to escape, but most perished in the concentration or work camps. Intermittent news

---

[643] ASRS, AA.EE.SS., Polonia 208, f. 582, internal report from Msgr. Samorè, February 20, 1940.

[644] ASRS, AA.EE.SS., Polonia 216, f. 532, statistics on the Catholic hierarchy and clergy in Poland, 1942.

[645] ASRS, AA.EE.SS., Polonia 208, f. 577.

of their deaths filtered into the Cabinet on various occasions. The archives contain lists of their names.

By October 1941, two years after the invasion, only one thousand of the original two thousand priests of the Reichsgau Wartheland region remained, over seven hundred of them having been detained in Dachau. At least four hundred Polish nuns were imprisoned in the slave labor camp of Bojanowo in western Poland.

Toward the end of 1941, there was yet another purge. Hundreds more clergy were arrested and either shot dead, imprisoned, or sent to concentration camps. In the city of Poznan, where there had been two hundred thousand Catholics, only four priests remained active. Many were shot or murdered in other ways.[646]

Bishops' residences and curia offices were confiscated, and all Church historical treasures were impounded. The Nazis stormed seminaries and houses of novices, throwing everyone onto the streets and locking the doors. Many buildings were destined for profane purposes: "stock houses for stolen furniture or banned books; or turned into theaters for Nazi-approved entertainment."[647] Some historic churches were destroyed entirely, blown sky-high with dynamite to make way for new buildings. Almost all convents were seized, along with the sometimes very valuable furniture. All diocesan museums and libraries were requisitioned too. The Catholic publishing houses were banned, and their printing equipment seized. The regular clergy of religious orders such as the Jesuits, the Franciscans, the Dominicans, and others suffered the same devastation.

Catholic schools, which over the years had educated countless Polish children, were declared forbidden, and those buildings were also taken over and then requisitioned for whatever purpose the Nazis deemed necessary. Any mention of the Catholic religion was abolished throughout the Polish education system. A decree of August 19, 1941, stated that the teaching of the Catholic religion "could only take place in the places of religious worship; for youngsters between 10 and 18 years old; only one hour a week, to be fixed between 3 and 5 pm (except on the days that were reserved for the exercises of the Hitlerjugend); the time, place and personnel for the teaching should be communicated previously to the police. The Movement of the Catholic Action is abolished. All Catholic associations for culture, beneficence and social activities are abolished."[648]

[646] ASRS, AA.EE.SS., Polonia 208, f. 578.
[647] ASRS, AA.EE.SS., Polonia 208, f. 580.
[648] ASRS, AA.EE.SS., Polonia, 208, f. 578.

Of course, the idea that people should inform the police of the time and place of meeting struck fear into hearts. Many easily saw through this as the trap it was.

Paying clergy any salary, previously agreed to by the Concordat of Poland, was banned. Any collection of money in favor of Catholic charity was forbidden.

In September 1941, the Cabinet received news that three religious fathers named Deszcz, Brandys, and Karcrmarcryk had been executed by firing squad and that a Fr. Butkowski had died of starvation. They also received the terrible report that the president of the Salesian Fathers, Fr. Kurak, had died in prison and the bishop of Łódź had been arrested.

And it was not only the Nazis doing the killing. After the rupture of the Molotov-Ribbentrop Pact in June 1941, Russian troops began retreating from Polish territory, and during that time they, too, murdered members of the clergy. In November 1941, the Holy See was informed of the massacre of a large number of priests of Greek-Ruthenian rites in the city of L'viv by Soviet troops.[649]

Illustration: *The Crucifixion by Jean-Louis Chancel (Paris, August 25, 1899–July 28, 1977), published in Match magazine on September 28, 1939.*[650]

These disturbing little bits of information continued to come to the Cabinet, often smuggled out through sources and go-betweens. One such example took place in January 1942, when Cardinal Maglione received a visit from an Italian lawyer named Adolfo Lucat. Lucat brought news on behalf of a Msgr. Adamski, the bishop of the Diocese of Katowice in Silesia, that

---

[649] ASRS, AA.EE.SS., Polonia 208, f. 742.

[650] ASRS, AA.EE.SS., Stati Ecclesiastici 630, f. 70.

a third part of the priests, about 130, had left the diocese. Only two thirds remained. The seminary was closed, the seminarians were distributed over seminaries in Germany. The occupying authorities know all this but act as if they don't. The priests who escaped from the diocese into the Governatorato [this refers to the general government, a part of Poland that was occupied but not directly annexed] are left in peace. The number of priests arrested across Poland until April 1941 were between 2500 to 3000. Of those 70 were liberated, 900 died. The others are still in captivity or on the run.[651]

By the start of 1942, the episcopate had been virtually eliminated. The clergy, secular and regular, had been reduced to the barest minimum. Hitler's plan was very well underway.

The Holy See was powerless to prevent any of it. Under the heavy thumb of the Nazis, the holy rights and fundamental prerogatives of the Catholic Church were no longer recognized. The Church's protests meant nothing to the cruel occupiers. In the Nazis' minds, what they had done was merely an important part of their established program of complete dechristianization of a region where Catholicism had flourished for centuries.[653]

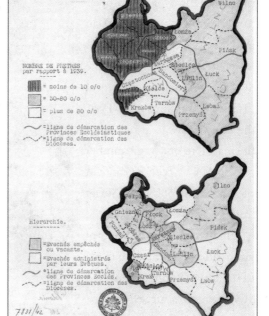

Two hand-drawn maps of Poland showing the number of priests present in Polish territory in 1942 in comparison with 1939, and the bishoprics suppressed, vacant, or still administered by a bishop.[652]

[651] ASRS, AA.EE.SS., Polonia 208, f. 739.
[652] ASRS, AA.EE.SS., Polonia 216, f. 532.
[653] ASRS, AA.EE.SS., Polonia 208, f. 581.

In short, what happened in Reichsgau Wartheland was a clear blueprint of the Catholic persecution under the Nazis, a blueprint they planned to continue following in the future. This was something of which Pius XII was painfully and keenly aware. Preventing it, and the strategic measures he could take to keep his flock safe, occupied his mind and the minds of those around him.

Many Poles living outside of Poland criticized the Holy See for not doing enough. The Polish ambassador to the Holy See made frequent visits to the Cabinet to express his displeasure in this regard. And within the occupied nation itself, the Nazis used all the propaganda tools at their disposal to convince the terrified population that the pope didn't care about them and had forgotten them. Even more diabolical, as Cardinal Hlond from his exile in Lourdes over the nunciature in France reported, "the Nazis spread the false news to the people that the Pope was about to issue a public statement instructing Catholics of invaded countries to renounce the resistance in name of peace and give up their liberty for the better of the whole of Europe, submitting themselves with evangelical mildness to the needs of the new order yearned for by the Axis."[654] But of course, none of this was true. There were endless, antagonized discussions by the members of the Cabinet about what to do.

The situation tormented Cabinet Secretary Tardini. He turned many ideas over in his mind, seeking some way to reach out to the Catholics in Poland. In May 1942, he asked if the Holy See could take further steps.[655] It would, in his opinion, "sustain the spirit of Cardinal Sapieha [the archbishop of Krakow] and encourage the Poles, to let them know that the Holy See steadfastly acts as avenger of all the most holy human and Christian rights."[656] But, whereas Tardini saw no harm in a letter to Sapieha, he did

> not consider it opportune to issue a public statement condemning and protesting so many injustices against the Polish people. Not that the *material* for it is lacking, and of course such a condemnation by the Holy See does belong to the rights and obligations of the Holy See. But for practical reasons that impose it seems wise to refrain

[654] ASRS, AA.EE.SS., Polonia 208, f. 751[r/v], copy of a letter of Card. Hlond to Msgr. Valeri, October 6, 1941.
[655] ASRS, AA.EE.SS., Polonia 236, f. 2.
[656] ASRS, AA.EE.SS., Polonia 236, f. 2[v].

from, at least for the moment, such a public manifestation. In fact, given the actual circumstances, a public condemnation by the Holy See would be exploited for political reasons by one of the parts in this conflict. Moreover, the German government, feeling attacked, would without doubt do two things: It would tighten the screws even more on the persecution of Catholicism in Poland, and would impede in all ways any contact between the Holy See and the Polish episcopacy. And also, it would obstruct that charitable work, that today both the episcopacy and the Holy See can achieve — even if in this present moment in a reduced form. Therefore, a public declaration by the Holy See would be distorted in itself; and exploited for governmental and further persecution.[657]

So, if Tardini's assessment was that a public declaration would make matters worse, what then did he see as an alternative? It was his view that the Holy See should prepare a beautiful diplomatic note addressed to the German government:

And when one says beautiful, it means high, noble, delicate in its form, however terrible in its substance, that is in its argument. One should depict a full picture of the situation and invoke the German government to put an end to this state of affairs. The Note should have the character of a sort of anxious appeal, more than that of a protest (the protest would be in the description of things themselves). Of course, all this is easier to suggest than to … execute.[658]

Tardini was well aware that the note was unlikely to have any impact on Nazi sensibility: "The Note (even the most … beautiful one) will not stop the Germans. But it will be a document that one day will come to light (and everything will come to light: delinquencies and condemnations!) — it will show the prudence and steadfastness of the Holy See."[659]

And so, Msgr. Samorè, the *minutante* of the Cabinet in charge of Poland, began the process of drafting the material and listing the evidence. It was a complex and time-consuming task that took many months. The drafts were prepared by Samorè,

[657] ASRS, AA.EE.SS., Polonia 236, f. 3.
[658] ASRS, AA.EE.SS., Polonia 236, f. 3.
[659] ASRS, AA.EE.SS., Polonia 236, f. 3ᵛ. The evidenciations in the text are Tardini's.

carefully weighing one word against the other, and then evaluated by Tardini — they fulfilled the task with *maestria*, creating thus a masterpiece of diplomacy:

> It is very clear and complete, and it gives a terrifying impression of the situation of Catholicism in Poland. It is the truth.... It would be opportune to reduce the tone of the sentences.... The ferocity of the facts stands out even more between the subtleness of words.... One should abbreviate,... reduce the tone.... By using the word Pole, I ask myself would it not give the impression that we take the defense of the Poles against the Germans?... Put in evidence that this is regards a religious question, and not a political one in the first degree of the Holy See ... etc etc.[660]

After Tardini's suggested revisions were implemented and after three stages of preparation, the final draft of the exceptionally large note was edited once again by Cardinal Maglione. The various drafts in the Archives prove what intense intellectual and administrative work was done by them on behalf of Poland alone in the months of December 1942 and January 1943.[661] On January 21, Tardini annotated some ideas and guidelines for the introduction and the conclusion of the note, reflecting on the diplomatic opportunities and risks of the note itself:

> With the intention to avoid the danger that the Embassy of Germany would not accept the Note, one should be sure that the document will be sent to the Ministry of Foreign Affairs in Berlin in its integrity. To seem to give more importance to the document itself makes it appear (in its external form) as an ultimate (or almost) diplomatic attempt of the Holy See.
>
> Would it not be opportune to give this Note in the form of a letter addressed to the Minister of Foreign Affairs? In that case maybe omitting the first part because I don't know if it would be ... tactical ... to begin the document with a protest against the response of the government [the latest document they had received from Germany and that excluded the Holy See from any authority toward the occupied zones in Poland] and then, immediately afterwards, to make observations — very

[660] ASRS, AA.EE.SS., Polonia 236, f. 6, handwritten notes of Msgr. Tardini, December 5, 1942.
[661] ASRS, AA.EE.SS., Polonia 236, ff. 97–98, handwritten notes of Tardini, January 21, 1943.

straightforward ones — regarding the very matter that, according to that response, we have no authority to discuss anymore.

In other terms: if the Ministry of Foreign Affairs accepts our Note, this would mean it annuls its latest document and implicitly acknowledges our authority on these Polish zones. Be aware that by criticizing them in the opening portion of the Note, [we] could dispose unfavourably the [German] government and obtain the opposite effect.

Because one of those two will be the case:

Either the German government accepts our Note and [implicitly acknowledges our authority] or the German government rejects our Note and confirms its latest document. Our protest at the beginning of this Note could rather push it to the second alternative.[662]

Tardini discussed this matter on January 23, 1943, with the pope, and Pius XII agreed with his ideas.[663] Just ten days earlier, on January 13, Hitler had signed his order for the total mobilization of the German army across Europe. Germany was starting to lose the war, and this was Hitler's attempt to turn the tide. His increasingly desperate actions ran parallel to increasing Nazi atrocities and racism, both in Germany and in the Nazi-occupied countries. Heavy military losses and the political uncertainty made the Nazi top level in Berlin ever more irritated and intransigent.

Msgr. Samorè was given the additional job of preparing different "beginnings" and "endings" for the note, in order to give choices to the senior cardinals who would soon take center stage on deciding the final contents.[664] He proposed the following two options. The first one, which was very optimistic, was written as if there was still hope appealing to the Germans to stop their terrible actions that were in contrast with natural and divine rights and that they would restabilize and reestablish religious liberty. The second option contained the same proposal but was presented in more direct and imperative terms, with an implicit threat that if Germany would not respond to the plea contained in the note, the Holy See would find it necessary to abandon its restraint.[665]

---

[662] ASRS, AA.EE.SS., Polonia 236, ff. 97ᵛ-98, handwritten notes of Msgr. Tardini, January 21, 1943.
[663] ASRS, AA.EE.SS., Polonia 236, ff. 97–98, handwritten note of Msgr. Tardini.
[664] ASRS, AA.EE.SS., Polonia 236, ff. 99–106.
[665] ASRS, AA.EE.SS., Polonia 236, ff. 100–103.

Now, from the early beginnings of the existence of the Holy Congregation for Extraordinary Ecclesiastical Affairs[666] in the year 1814, a group of senior cardinals gathered for a roundtable meeting every few months. The cardinals were chosen for their juridical, theological, and ecclesiastical expertise on issues with a specific international character. During their sessions they met in a private room of the Apostolic Palace to discuss the main problems of the day for the Catholic Church around the world. Prior to the *sessioni dei cardinali* (sessions of cardinals), all the participating cardinals received a printed briefing on the theme and important related documents in order to form his opinion and to prepare his personal intervention. During the meeting, the cardinals in attendance shared, one by one, their personal view on the matter, following a strict order. Depending on the circumstance, the order of who talked first might depend on their age, their seniority, or the importance of their dicastery or ministry.

These historic and important sessions continue to this very day and have always been presided over by the cardinal secretary of state, who in our case was Cardinal Maglione. The secretary of the meeting, responsible for taking minutes, is the minister of foreign affairs, who was at that time Msgr. Tardini. The group is akin to the pope's advisory board on the most burning political questions at stake, with the Holy See's key expertise gathered together. Imagine it as similar to a presidential briefing in a time of crisis.

On February 11, 1943, at 10:30 in the morning, these wise men made their way to the plenary session. They passed through the vast corridors, at last reaching the stately room where they took their places around the table. The item on the agenda of the cardinals that day was "Poland. Religious situation. Project of a Note to the Minister for Foreign Affairs of the Reich."[667]

The gray-haired cardinal Gennaro Granito Pignatelli di Belmonte — his name betrayed his high-society Neapolitan heritage — solemnly opened the session, with the following words:

> Unfortunately, the ever-long patience of the Holy See with the
> German Government has been poorly corresponded. I judge the
> response given by the government and his representative to the

---

[666] Nowadays known as the Section for Relations with States and International Organizations of the Secretariat of State.

[667] ASRS, AA.EE.SS., Rapporti delle Sessioni 100, Sessione 1428 (February 11, 1943), ff. 3–4.

Holy See tremendous and offensive. I believe that whatever Note
or proposal that will be given by the Holy See, for certain territories, will not even be taken into consideration. This is a moral slap,
and it doesn't look to me to be the case of offering the other cheek.

In Germany, and in other countries of the world, people ask
why the Holy See is not raising its voice in order that it would be
heard by the faithful, not only heard by Germans, but by all nations.
Knowledge of the facts by the public is the only way to worry the
German government. It would be necessary that the protest be
handed over directly to the head of the Government. Making them
understand that we dismiss the normal diplomatic praxis, because
some diplomatic representatives of Germany failed to show respect
to the diplomatic norms. I would ensure that the document would
discuss, in a veiled mode, about the fidelity of the Catholics towards
the State, a fidelity most necessary in this moment in which the
events generate in Germany a certain despondency.

The extremely well-respected Cardinal Enrico Gasparri, nephew of the famous
Cardinal Pietro Gasparri who had served as secretary of state during the First
World War, stood up next and said: "I agree fully with this opinion and proposal."[668]

The slight, bespectacled figure that was Cardinal Raffaele Carlo Rossi then
shared his views on the matter. He had a somewhat different opinion:

It's evident that the situation is very serious. It seems we find ourselves in front of the Antichrist and his satellites. One cannot doubt
that they do what their leader wants them to do. If the Russians
are more brutal, the Germans know how to persecute with more
perseverance, hiding themselves behind diverse faces and appear-
ances. The Holy See has given proof of its truly exceptional forbearance, inspired by its universal and superior charity. By now, the
patience — and fairly — has come to its end. This Note, dense in
its content and honourable in its form, is the last attempt.

There is no hope that one could in some way make the Polish
happy. Those, worth of all comprehension and compassion for so

---

[668] ASRS, AA.EE.SS., Rapporti delle Sessioni 100, Sessione 1428 (February 11, 1943), f. 5.

much sufferance that was unjustly inflicted on them, have however in their soul a hate that by disgrace becomes ever more vivid. On the side, even without pleasing the others, the Holy See does his duty. Thus, on the first question, that is, if we have to send the Note or not, I respond "Affirmative."

We send the Note, and quickly. Regarding the two possible conclusions, I prefer the second one — That if the German government would reject the Nota, we will see afterwards what to do.

There was much to absorb from Cardinal Rossi's comments. With due thoughtfulness, Cardinal Fumasoni Biondi, the prefect of the Congregation of the Propaganda Fide (missionary congregation), then stood to speak. He said: "I consider the Note perfect. As conclusion the second one is better. . . . However, I cannot, could not avoid asking, in this very delicate moment, if a public act of the Holy See would be opportune."

At this point Cardinal Rossi interrupted to observe: "There is always the possibility that the German government will reject the Note of the Holy See — waiting any longer before preparing a publication would make it seem as if that same publication would have the appearance of a stroke given to the vanquished. This would not benefit to the Holy See to make a bella figura (good appearance)."

The air in the room buzzed with tension as the cardinals — educated, rational, religious men — continued to deliberate the serious matter at hand. The floor was given next to Cardinal Federico Tedeschini, former substitute of the secretary of state during the First World War (the function now held by Msgr. Montini). He stated: "The situation is really of extreme gravity. The Holy See has given proof of all its patience and of all its forbearance. By now it should abandon its reserve. The Polish are agitated, while they ignore what the Holy See has done and is doing. But, could one not, by way of the Polish Ambassador, let know to that government what was and is actually the attitude of the Holy See?"

Tedeschini's suggestion that the Polish felt the Holy See wasn't doing anything remains an issue to this very day in some Polish circles. He continued: "The Note is very beautiful, and it is good that it would be sent as soon as possible."

After proposing a few small modifications to the text of the note, Tedeschini went on to say:

> If the German government would refuse to take in consideration the *Note*, I would suggest it most convenient that the Holy See

would break its silence. If the Holy Father would consider it digni-
fied to decide, he himself could speak out with that elevation that
is proper to Him.

Otherwise, one could think about writing a letter to Cardinal
Bertram,[669] about a publication in *L'Osservatore Romano*, about a
white book[670] [an official report of government affairs bound in white,
in this case of the Holy See], about something, in short, that would
enlighten the faithful and would safeguard the prestige of the Holy See.

Of the two proposed conclusions to the note Cardinal Tedeschini urged caution:

> Of the two schemes suggested for the conclusion of the Note, I
> prefer the first, because, although I am convinced that the Holy
> See should talk I don't find it opportune to say this openly in the
> diplomatic document, since this would equate to a menace and it
> could exacerbate the German government. The Holy See will, yes,
> come out of its reserve: but there is no need for it to declare that
> openly in the Note, in advance.[671]

Now it was the turn of the Roman-born Cardinal Francesco Marmaggi. He once
had been apostolic nuncio in Romania, in Czechoslovakia, and until the start of
the war in 1939, in Poland. Once back in Rome, he was appointed prefect of the
Congregation of the Council.[672] He offered this to the discussion: "We find ourselves in front of real tragic conditions. It is now more than three years that Poland
has experienced a massacre of the most holy rights of those poor Catholics. This
is particularly grave in Warthegau. The Holy See did everything that was possible
in respect to the German government: memos, conversations, notes. The Holy
Father himself deigned to speak with von Ribbentrop." There Cardinal Marmaggi
made a point. On March 11, 1940, von Ribbentrop, the minister of foreign affairs
of the Reich, had had a personal audience with the pope. The whole conversation
had been registered by the secretary of state in steno and in different transcriptions,

---

[669] Cardinal of Breslau, Poland.

[670] A publication of the war correspondence that evidences the position of the Holy See.

[671] ASRS, AA.EE.SS., Rapporti delle Sessioni 100, Sessione 1428 (February 11, 1943), f. 6.

[672] Nowadays the Congregation of the Clergy (a dicastery that deals with the discipline
of the secular clergy).

which proves, besides the extraordinary importance given to the meeting, that expectations and hopes for a change in Nazi policy were still high in 1940.[673]

> What has one obtained with all this? That the situation has been getting worse due to the tormenting will of the German government. The latter responded negatively to the document of the Holy See of last October. Now a Note has been prepared, complete in substance and elevated in form. It deserves praise, especially because it was able to condensate in very few words an immense material. I think it would be good to send this Note quickly. Even more, to make it more efficacious, I give some suggestions, in order to prevent the German government from getting away with a generic answer. But that it would, instead, be obliged to adopt some decision that would really demonstrate a little bit of good will. Therefore, the German government should be invited to free the imprisoned clergy, to reopen the churches in the coming Easter Time, when the faithful have to respond to particular religious obligations. In this way, one would have a way to judge *objectively* the dispositions of the German government. As far as the conclusion of the Note is concerned, I prefer the second scheme with some modifications and additions proposed by myself....
>
> In the hypothesis that the German government will reject the Note, the extent to which the Holy See should restrain its reaction will have to depend on the forms followed and motives raised by the German government.

Cardinal Ermenegildo Pellegrinetti, apostolic nuncio in both Poland and Yugoslavia during the interbellum, rose next.[674] Looking at all his cardinal brothers around the table, he sighed and said:

> We are in a situation that is almost as bas as a dead-end street. The German government has come to the extreme by forbidding to its Ambassador to the Holy See to receive the diplomatic documents of the latter, when those documents concern territories occupied by Germany. And this when the most simple and basic mission of an Embassy should be exactly that — of

---

[673] ASRS, AA.EE.SS., Germania 774.
[674] He died one month after this plenary session — on March 29, 1943.

transmitting diplomatic documents. On the other hand, the Holy See
did everything possible. It demonstrated a great patience. It conserved
an exemplary restraint, also because interventions and public declarations — most welcome to the Polish living far away from Poland — could
excite the mass murderer to torture his victim ever harder — in this case
the victim would be the Polish who remained in their homeland.

He continued: "The prepared Note is clear, complete, synthetical and serene.
Therefore, it has to be sent. Of the two prepared conclusions, I prefer the second
one. The names of places are in Latin or Polish. If the Note would be written in
German, one could, perhaps, think about using the German denominations."

Cardinal Giuseppe Pizzardo, prefect of the Congregation of Seminaries and
Universities, agreed with that tone:

> I am favorable on sending the Note, which I consider good, prepared
> and quite opportune. I do not suggest other modifications, after all
> those very wisely expressed by other Cardinals. Only towards the end,
> at page 22, where one suggests [at the second scheme of the conclusion,
> that Pizzardo prefers] that the Holy See should get out of its restraint
> to not fail its mission, I would add also the concept that the Holy See
> would be obliged to speak out for the preservation of its prestige.

Finally, the secretary of state, Cardinal Luigi Maglione, rose from his chair to thank
his colleagues for their well-considered words:

> Thank you all, your Eminencies, for your "wise" observations and
> your very high advice. I should observe that after all that was said,
> I can come to some brief conclusive observations. The Cardinals
> observed very well how different people are urging for a public word
> from the Holy Father.[675] In this request are particularly insistent the

[675] Not the least in a recent letter of German Bishop von Preysing of January 17, 1943,
in which he asked: "Your Holiness was already orientated on the situation of the
Jews in Germany and its neighbour countries. For mere information I would like to
inform that and of the side of the Catholics as of that of the Protestants I was asked,
if not the Holy See in this matter could do something, an appeal in favor of these
unhappy?" Von Preysing to Pius XII, Berlin, January 17, 1943. This letter in *Actes
et documents du Saint-Siège pendant la Seconde Guerre Mondiale*, vol. 9, pp. 82–83.

Polish who are far away from their homeland, and, thus, safe. The Ambassador of Poland to the Holy See did not do anything else but repeat such request and sometimes — as a matter of fact — with excessive petulance.

In such a way that I myself felt constrained to make him carefully consider how much it is easy to invoke a condemnation from the part of the Holy Father when one is a long distance away from Poland, where the German fury acts so cruelly.

For the rest, the cardinals present here know well that the Holy Father, in solemn circumstances, has spoken out, condemning the guilt of those who put themselves against the most holy rights of the citizens, and appealing to the superior norms of charity and of justice. But this is not sufficient for these Polish. They would like to hear explicit condemnations. Also recently, the Ambassador of Poland to the Holy See brought to His Holiness a message from the President of the Polish Republic in which was a request for the Pope to speak.[676] On the other hand, the Holy See must take into account the very painful situation in which the Polish who have remained in their homeland find themselves. The Holy Father has done and continues to do everything possible to help them, on the material and the moral levels. He searches, as much as possible, to stay in contact with those bishops, ensuring they receive his word. Now it is those very bishops — whose head is the zealous and courageous Monsignor Sapieha[677] — who make us know that they cannot make public the word of the Pope, for doing so would offer a pretext to the Germans a reason to pile on additional persecution. This confirms the wisdom and careful attitude of the Holy See.

But, at the same time, one cannot remain silent on another danger: in Poland itself among the population that suffers, very tendentious rumours are disseminated about the Holy See. These rumours say that the Pope is not interested in the Polish people, that he is not helping them and that he is in agreement with the Axis powers.

[676] ASRS, AA.EE.SS., Rapporti delle Sessioni 100, Sessione 1428 (February 11, 1943), f. 8.
[677] At that time bishop of Krakow. After the war Pope Pius XII elevated him to the cardinalate.

All slanderous assertions (diffused artfully by the Germans) tend to create a current of antipathy towards the Holy See and towards a movement for a national Polish church. In front of such a grave and complex situation, I witnessed with joy how all my colleague cardinals are agreeing in approving the sending of the Note that was put to their examination, and in its whole content.

As was said, the document gives a summarised, but complete, framework of the situation from the point of view of the Holy See. With this, the Holy See not only performs a duty, but safeguards his prestige and shows its will to come, as far possible, in aid of the poor Polish population.

And in his final comments, Cardinal Maglione, prophesized the very contents of this book:

One day the documents of the Holy See will become public, and then with the passions of the moment cooled down, one will see that the Holy See has followed the "providential" line of action and, at the same time, remained careful.

More or less one verified the same thing during the First World War, when the Belgians thought and said that the Holy See was disinterested by their fate. Now finished with that war, it has become known what the Holy See had done for Belgium. The accusations and the allegation fell away. It is, however, important to note that what the Germans are doing in Poland does not hold to comparison with what was previously done in Belgium. The injustice and the violence have now reached limits that before would have been considered far-fetched.[678]

Maglione went on:

Some of my colleague Cardinals have observed that if the war would turn out unfavorable for the Germans, it would be unfortunate that the Holy See would issue public acts exactly at the moment Germany was on its way to defeat. It would be wrong to give the

[678] ASRS, AA.EE.SS., Rapporti delle Sessioni 100, Sessione 1428 (February 11, 1943), f. 8ᵛ.

impression that the Holy See was silent when the Germans were strong and only talked afterwards, when they were weak.

I don't agree with such preoccupation. Now, the Holy See speaks out to the German government, with the needed clearness, through a diplomatic document. If that same government would show itself deaf and reluctant against this discreet and duty-bound intervention of the Holy See, it would not have anything but itself to blame if, one day or another, the Holy See would see itself forced to make its attitude public.[679]

At this point, the cardinals developed their clear diplomatic strategy. It was imperative, Maglione insisted, that it would be done in a proper, formal way. All other procedures had been exhausted, and there was no other option left. If this note succeeded with its goal, the Holy See would have the formal basis with which to publicly attack the German policy. While other cardinals at the table urged caution, Maglione insisted on moving forward. He was convinced that by putting the Germans in an either-or situation, the Holy See would have the possibility to strike back diplomatically. And even if they weren't very hopeful that they could sway Nazi policy, everything possible should be tried in order to keep open or create new corridors where at least some humanitarian action might be possible.

Maglione stated:

> Even so, I would have difficulty accepting the suggestion of Cardinal Marmaggi about an explicit invitation to the German government to liberate bishops and priests by next Easter. This could give the impression of an "ultimatum" and could possibly put the Holy See in difficulty if the Germans would not execute what we asked for.
>
> For the rest, the conclusion of the Note seems sufficiently clear, because one asks the German government to desist of the violence against the most holy human and divine rights and one reminds it to observe the superior norms of justice and liberty.

In conclusion, Cardinal Maglione, summarized all the main points discussed at the round table as follows:

---

[679] ASRS, AA.EE.SS., Rapporti delle Sessioni 100, Sessione 1428 (February 11, 1943), f. 8ᵛ.

(1) It is good that the Note would be sent without delay;

(2) In the text the modifications suggested by the cardinals will be introduced;

(3) For the future, we wait to see how things will develop.[680]

At that point, all the cardinals declared themselves to be in agreement. The meeting was adjourned.

The following day, on February 12, the minutes of this meeting were written up and handed over by Tardini[681] to Cardinal Maglione. Maglione delivered the minutes directly to Pius XII a day later.[682]

At that same time, in Berlin, Nuncio Orsenigo finished the umpteenth report on the arrest of priests, religious sisters, and lay Catholics in Germany and Poland. The overwhelming numbers could not numb the pain of the man who'd been tasked with recounting on paper, one by one, the stories of his brutalized Christian brothers and sisters. Surely his hands shook with both horror and anger as he typed each name, each place of arrest, each final destination. Among the seized were Msgr. Jakob Weinbacher, the secretary of Cardinal Innitzer, archbishop of Vienna, and the fervent anti-Nazi Austrian Msgr. Carl Lampert. Lampert's fate was particularly unimaginable. His Nazi captors, savoring the fact that they had yet another enemy at their mercy, methodically tortured him, isolated him in solitary confinement for months, and then, when they tired of that, marched him to a prison guillotine where he was beheaded.[683] Carl Lampert was beatified by Pope Benedict XVI in 2011.

The resolution from the session of cardinals sat on the desk of Pius XII for the next three days. One can presume that he talked it through at length with Tardini and Maglione, that he digested it and gave a great deal of deep thought to the proposed strategy. He made some final revisions and gave the order to send the note with the comment "that the efficacy of the document depends, not on

---

[680] ASRS, AA.EE.SS., Rapporti delle Sessioni 100, Sessione 1428 (February 11, 1943), f. 9.

[681] All this was signed by "Domenico Tardini, Segretario della S. Congregazione of the AA.EE.SS."

[682] ASRS, AA.EE.SS., Rapporti delle Sessioni 100, Sessione 1428 (February 11, 1943), f. 9.

[683] ASRS, AA.EE.SS., Germania 862, ff. 2–4, report from Msgr. Orsenigo to Card. Maglione, February 13, 1943.

the vivacity of the expressions, but on the gravity of the facts." He asked that the first option of the conclusion, which left open a possible dialogue, should be used.

By February 19, 1943, the last practical and formal details of the note were taken care of by the Cabinet.[684] The plan was for the note to be sent to Msgr. Orsenigo, the nuncio in Berlin, who would then carry the envelope to Mr. von Ribbentrop, the minister of foreign affairs of the Third Reich. In the note's final version, signed off by Cardinal Maglione, all quotations were translated into German, and where any city names were written in Italian, the equivalent German translation was added, in an effort to be as diplomatic and polite as possible under the circumstances.

Finally, Cardinal Maglione sat at his desk to make the final tweaks. He read over the text, now five pages long, one last time before declaring it ready and giving his order to print it in various languages[685] and send it immediately to Msgr. Orsenigo in Berlin with the order to get it to its destination — that is, to Minister von Ribbentrop.[686] One can only imagine the conflicting emotions Msgr. Orsenigo experienced when he went in person to the ministry with the aim of handing the note over to Baron von Weizsäcker, the German secretary of state. He might have felt a combination of both unease and hope — unease because he knew well the Nazi mindset yet hope because the note was so clear and to the point that it might make a difference. Von Weizsäcker accepted the note and assured Orsenigo that it would be transmitted to Minister von Ribbentrop on the fifteenth of that month.[687] Great was Orsenigo's surprise when, on March 17, he was unexpectedly summoned by von Weizsäcker to come immediately to his office. When he arrived, von Weizsäcker smiled, then dropped a bombshell: he had not passed the note on as he had said he would. Orsenigo later detailed the conversation to Rome. Von Weizsäcker had said:

> I believed I myself had to open the envelope that was addressed to Mr. von Ribbentrop. And I read the content. It deals only with "Warthegau" and the "General government" and you know what kind of reservations I already communicated to you in June last year regarding these territories that do not belong to the "Altreich" [the

[684] ASRS, AA.EE.SS., Polonia 236, ff. 118r/v.
[685] ASRS, AA.EE.SS. Germania 771, ff. 344–357, printed version of the note of Card. Maglione to Minister von Ribbentrop, March 2, 1943.
[686] ASRS, AA.EE.SS., Polonia 236, ff. 119ss; ibid., ff. 222–223.
[687] ASRS, AA.EE.SS., Polonia 236, ff. 224–225.

Altreich is the term for the original territories of Germany before the Nazi wartime invasions]. This is the original and the only territory for which you are accredited by the Holy See. And therefore, we are not able to accept this document.[688]

This was an enormous blow. But Orsenigo remained calm, stating:

I have received instructions to make sure that the document would be given personally to the hands of the Minister of Foreign Affairs. Therefore, I find myself now in the necessity not to accept back this document, which has not reached its intended addressee. Without being willing to criticise your boldness for reading it first, because that could be also the result of telephonic agreements [with von Ribbentrop], I permit myself to ask if you have measured the entire gravity of this gesture of yours and if you are willing to take the full responsibility for it?

Von Weizsäcker responded by saying he was indeed "sure of the responsibility and that he was not to say a word more."[689]

Orsenigo, however, continued to press the point:

Whether or not one can make a distinction between territories that are subject of credential letters [a formal document accrediting a diplomat to a foreign country or government] and other territories that are not, some inhabitants of all these territories are, in any case, Catholics. And in those territories, not by force of special diplomatic relationships, but by its divine mission the Holy See has the right to ensure that the religious liberty of its faithful is not harmed. And in case of violations, the Holy See has both the right and the duty to intervene with these authorities, with the obligation to contribute to the removal of the violations and the re-establishment of religious liberty. And therefore neither diplomatic relations nor Apostolic Nuncios are required. The Holy See can address itself directly to

[688] ASRS, AA.EE.SS., Polonia 236, f. 225ᵛ.
[689] ASRS, AA.EE.SS., Polonia 236, f. 226.

Heads of State, and as far as I can imagine it will have had previous occasion to do so, especially in missionary territories.[690]

His German interlocutor tried to point out that this was not a document from a head of state to another head of state, but that of a cardinal secretary of state to a minister of foreign affairs. Msgr. Orsenigo had a solid argument to back that one. He replied that it was the custom of the Holy See for all questions with every foreign state to be handled by the secretary of state, regardless of whether or not there were regular diplomatic relations between that country and the Holy See. "However," he concluded, "I brought you a written message, therefore I ask that you give a written message as an answer, feeling free to explain the motives of your non-acceptance."

Orsenigo's report to Rome explained what happened next in von Weizsäcker's office: "At that point Baron von Weiszaecker asked me not to insist any further. He pointed out on the good feelings he always had shown towards the Holy See (something I could not deny). He assured me that without written notification of this letter, from his side he would rigorously keep it secret."[691]

In spite of von Weizsäcker's comments, Orsenigo refused to back down. He risked further German anger by insisting yet again that he must inform the Holy See of the outcome of his mission. Baron von Weizsäcker warned in reply that this would compel him to send back officially, in a closed envelope, the document to the nunciature. Then came the veiled threat: "This will heighten tension. I propose to disguise the whole matter, in other words to act as though no one had spoken about the presentation of the document and of its acceptance, as if all of this never took place."[692]

The Nazis were using here their old tried-and-tested trick. By pretending this diplomatic encounter and the delivery of the note had never taken place, they intended to neutralize and bury the Holy See's protests about the horrors happening in Poland. And the suggestion was that this would somehow be a "win-win" for all.

By blatantly ignoring the official complaint from the Holy See, the Nazis had put the Holy See out of the diplomatic game — silencing them and telling them they had no legal right to interfere. Once again, soft diplomacy was all the Holy

[690] ASRS, AA.EE.SS., Polonia 236, f. 226ᵛ.
[691] ASRS, AA.EE.SS., Polonia 236, f. 226ᵛ.
[692] ASRS, AA.EE.SS., Polonia 236, f. 227.

See had at its disposal. At this point in the game, another country might have chosen to escalate militarily, economically, or through political allies. But, given the chosen and necessary policy of impartiality, none of these options were, or are, available for the Holy See.

It was clear to Orsenigo that — based on what von Weizsäcker had told him — minister of foreign affairs Ribbentrop, or possibly even the Führer himself, had indeed read the contents of the note. Orsenigo attributed the Nazis' determination to keep it silenced "to their intention to give little significance to the return of it."

Before he left the German foreign ministry, there was little else Orsenigo could do but restate what he had already said:

> I repeated that a power that is occupying a territory does not have the right to contest the Holy See's right to defend the religious interests of Catholics living on that territory, and to defend them by referring to the authorities that exercise a power on that territory. And that is exactly the case in "Warthegau" and in the "Generalgouvernement."[693]

But then Orsenigo, feeling the pressure of this most uncomfortable meeting, made a serious error of judgment. Instead of leaving the note with von Weizsäcker, he picked it up and took it away with him. Perhaps he realized instantly what an error he had made. Because in his report, which included a full release of all that had taken place, he immediately attempted to cover the tracks of his behavior by minimizing the importance of his action. When von Weizsäcker warned him that, if he refused to take back the note, it would only aggravate the situation, "to me [this] did not seem that bad at all," [694]wrote Orsenigo.

*

*   *

Back in Rome, Orsenigo's report made the hairs of many Cabinet members stand on end. What had happened was utterly unexpected. Msgr. Samorè rushed to his desk with a sheet of paper. He typed as quickly as possible, alerting the superiors

---

[693] ASRS, AA.EE.SS., Polonia 236, f. 227ᵛ. "Warthegau" and the "Generalgouvernement" were the two different zones of German-occupied Poland. One part invaded and then under direct SS command, the other under Wehrmacht (military) occupation.
[694] ASRS, AA.EE.SS., Polonia 236, f. 227.

of the secretary of state that in his latest report, Nuncio Orsenigo did not say it *expressis verbis* (expressly), but made it only surreptitiously appear in a sentence on the penultimate page, where he wrote "to the intention to give minor significance to the return of it." This left no doubt in Samorè's mind about what had happened: "Orsenigo had accepted back the Note."

Samorè continued to type furiously. There had been a terribly serious error of judgment and diplomatic practice on Orsenigo's part. He should have left the note there and not have taken it with him when he left: "He did so without being authorized by Rome! If the German Ministry of Foreign Affairs had been compelled to return the document in any other way, the Holy See would have had now in hand a firm official documental evidence to show that fact. And that would have been a most precious documentation for the Holy See."[695]

On March 21, 1943, the Cabinet played with the idea of immediately telegraphing Nuncio Orsenigo in Berlin with the following instruction: "Send the Note back to the Foreign Ministry (maybe by registered post?) and make it clear that, if the Holy See is no longer allowed to make known its complaints to the Government of the Reich through diplomatic documents, there will be no other way remaining than to speak out publicly."[696]

But the desk officer Samorè had begun to doubt what really happened — and he wondered whether or not he had judged the situation too quickly. Considering Orsenigo had received the note on March 10, Samorè presumed that the note had actually remained in the ministry for some days. This was an important consideration, for it meant the note must have been seen and read by top members of the Nazi government.

Pope Pius XII was briefed the very same day on this matter. He decided "the Cardinals should be given copies of all this. The question will be discussed again in the meeting of Cardinals of next 8th of April."[697]

It seems that Msgr. Samorè continued doubting the interpretation of Orsenigo's version of what had really happened in Berlin. But a lot now depended on being 100 percent certain.

A couple of days later, he wrote an internal memo:

---

[695] ASRS, AA.EE.SS., Polonia 236, f. 228, handwritten notes of Msgr. Tardini.
[696] ASRS, AA.EE.SS., Polonia 236, f. 228, handwritten notes of Msgr. Tardini.
[697] ASRS, AA.EE.SS., Polonia 236, f. 228, handwritten notes of Msgr. Tardini.

<![CDATA["

eliminating from the Courier service anything that can be sent by post, hoping to appease ... the suspicions of the Gestapo."[701]

Having your own diplomat living in a hostile country such as Nazi Germany, you must be very alert and careful not to let the enemy see any internal discord, perceived mistakes, or failures. If the Germans caught even a hint that Rome was displeased by Orsenigo's actions, it could be used as propaganda or extortion against them.

Therefore, Tardini's wise solution was to send a little message on a visiting card, asking simply, "Did you mean this or not?" It read:

Most reverend Excellence

Of the report of Your Excellency n. 2431 (51587) of 17th of this month, it does not appear clearly if the known document was given back to you. Here one desires to know if such return has taken place. With all the wishes. See me always as your servant in Christ.

Domenico Tardini[702]

Draft of the small personal note by Monsignor Tardini to Monsignor Orsenigo, Nuncio in Berlin, March 24, 1943.[703]

---

[701] ASRS, AA.EE.SS., Extracta, Germania, Pos. 600, fasc. 110, f. 28.
[702] ASRS, AA.EE.SS. Polonia 236, f. 230.
[703] ASRS, AA.EE.SS. Polonia 236, f. 230.

In this message, written cleverly, and intentionally with minimal details, Tardini didn't mention the note itself. He did make clear, though, that "here one wants to know," and that one was, of course, Pope Pius XII.

More than a week later, Orsenigo's reply arrived at the offices of the Cabinet. He confirmed, equally carefully, that "the document was given back to me. I did not believe it opportune to send it immediately and physically back to the Holy See. I preserved it in the Archives in expectation of …"[704]

As feared, he had indeed taken the note back. This was a disaster.

*

*   *

In spite of the earlier confusions, what happened next is clear. The cardinals were instructed to meet again in a plenary session on April 8, 1943. Each was provided in advance with all the documentation on the case: the final note of the cardinal secretary of state to the minister of foreign affairs of the Reich, the dispatch to Nuncio Orsenigo in which he was instructed to deliver the note to von Ribbentrop in person, and the report by Orsenigo detailing his conversation with von Weizsäcker.[705]

And so, at midday, nine cardinals gathered at the roundtable again to discuss the situation. The seat of the much-missed colleague Pellegrinetti was now occupied by Cardinal Canali. Msgr. Tardini was present as a secretary *a secretis*: he was under the absolute duty to keep secret everything he witnessed during the meeting.

Without ceremony or preamble, Cardinal Granito was first to speak. He was clearly angry: "The Nazi-government first accepted the Note (it cannot be that the Minister of Foreign Affairs would not have seen it) and then gave it back to the Nuncio. Oh, most deplorable."[706]

Cardinal Secretary of State Maglione attempted to calm the waters:

> Our meeting of today has a double aim: first, to inform you all of what has happened after the delivery of the Note that was examined by you in our previous meeting, and ask for your wise suggestions regarding what to do in the given circumstances. The behaviour of the German government is really offensive towards the Holy

---

[704] ASRS, AA.EE.SS., Polonia 236, f. 231, card of Orsenigo, Berlin, March 31, 1943.
[705] ASRS, AA.EE.SS., Polonia 236, f. 234.
[706] ASRS, AA.EE.SS., Rapporti delle Sessioni 100, Sessioni 1429 (April 8, 1943), f. 63.

See. The Holy See has incontestably the right and the obligation to defend the Catholic interests in whatever country. It is, as such, an injustice and offence towards the Holy See the fact that the German Government does not want to allow the intervention of that same Holy See when it comes to the territories occupied by the Germans, located outside the Old Reich. But that same German government does not fail to criticise and lament towards the Holy See when it comes to things, said or done by ecclesiastical authorities, that don't please it. In this actual case, the German government did not want to receive a Note of the Holy See, serene and polite in its form, concerning the religious interests of a Catholic nation actually subjected to German occupation.

The Nuncio has accepted the return of the document: that appears clearly in his report. But as he used in his report some sentences that were a little bit … long [by which he meant evasive], he was asked confidentially to specify on that point. The attitude of the Nuncio has made the situation, already a delicate one, much more difficult. Therefore, the suggestions of the Cardinals, who may express in all liberty their thoughts, will be even more necessary.[707]

It was abundantly clear that every single cardinal at the roundtable felt Orsenigo had made a huge error. Tension was heavy in the room.

Cardinal Granito spoke up again:

I can only recognize that the situation is grave and delicate. Making public all that has happened could certainly justify before the whole world the attitude of the Holy See. But it would provoke painful consequences, especially for the Catholics in Poland. I really do not know how to react and what to suggest. One could, perhaps, make public that the Holy See has done everything that was possible for the interests of the Catholics in Poland, even uttering protests. This in a general form. But where to make it public? I have no answer to this question: maybe [in a newspaper] in Switzerland? However, I am in favor of a generic and discreet publicity.

---

[707] ASRS, AA.EE.SS., Rapporti delle Sessioni 100, Sessione 1429 (April 8, 1943), ff. 63–64.

Cardinal Enrico Gasparri agreed: "I agree to publishing something, in the appropriate form and with the proper precautions."[708]

Cardinal Sibilia wanted to go further:

> In my opinion this would not be sufficient. I prefer to see the Holy
> See defending his honour. Therefore, I propose to publish the entire
> Note (which is a serene and objective text) on the *Acta Apostolicae
> Sedis* [the official bulletin of the Vatican], explaining in an introduc-
> tion the reason why the Holy See was constrained to publish the
> document. It would give a positive impression to all Catholics in
> the World. Nor does one have to fear the reprisals of the Germans.
> Worse than they are doing, regarding the religion, the Germans
> surely cannot do more. Notwithstanding that the Germans today
> are becoming ever less powerful.

Clearly, they were aware the tide of the war was already turning.

A worried Cardinal Rossi stated:

> The situation is grave: the gesture of the German Government is
> like a slap in the face of the Holy See. And yet, the same German
> government pretends to be heard and … revered by the Holy See.
> We cannot go on like this. One needs to undertake something, also
> so those who don't know what the Holy See did, will understand
> and not consider it impotent. But I fear for reprisals from the Ger-
> mans in case of publicity. The Nazis would possibly not only act
> cruelly on the Catholic population of Poland but could attempt
> also some hits against the Holy See and Vatican City State. There-
> fore, a release for the large public, no; but neither keep silent. So,
> I propose a diplomatic publicity: make the accredited diplomats
> to the Holy See aware that its Notes regarding the interests of the
> Catholics in occupied territories are simply rejected by the German
> government — as happened with this recent document of the Holy
> See. In this way, one would do something, without taking the risks
> of the consequences of a broader publicity.[709]

---

[708] ASRS, AA.EE.SS., Rapporti delle Sessioni 100, Sessione 1429 (April 8, 1943), f. 64.

[709] ASRS, AA.EE.SS., Rapporti delle Sessioni 100, Sessione 1429 (April 8, 1943), f. 65.

His colleague, Cardinal Fumasoni, agreed with him:

> I am quite of the same opinion: avoiding broader publicity — especially during the actual state of the war — but on the other hand, doing something. One should communicate to the German government that the Holy See, after careful consideration, regards the Note as received and read by its addressee. And at the same time, one could also examine if there is a case to recall the Nuncio of Berlin, leaving open however the question who would be capable of keeping the Nunciature open? Though on that matter of the Nuncio, a little bit of waiting would not cause harm at all, given that in a month the situation of the war could present some important changes.[710]

Cardinal Marmaggi was utterly furious with Orsenigo for allowing this to happen. His face was clouded with anger and his voice was full of righteous rage:

> The attitude of the German government is bullying and insulting. Furthermore, I deplore the action of the Nuncio Orsenigo. He should not have accepted the return of the Note! That the Holy See has to do something is obvious, while silence could be interpreted as tacit approval. But what to do? Not a public act, given the repercussions on the religious and political level in the actual delicate situation. I propose a leave for Nuncio Orsenigo, whose presence proved not to be useful and whose activity seems to be too weak. In the second place a memorandum or Note from the Secretary of State to the diplomatic representatives of the countries related to Germany and the neutrals. Such a document I would not put in the hands of the allied countries because they would use it against the enemy, be it in a military or political sense. In such a document one could:
>
> Reaffirm the right and the duty of the Holy See to take interest in all Catholics in all countries;
>
> Expose the principal facts that are to be reiterated to Germany, putting in evidence the forbearance and patience of the Holy See until this last episode. Beyond that I think it is necessary to, in some

---

[710] ASRS, AA.EE.SS., Rapporti delle Sessioni 100, Sessione 1429 (April 8, 1943), f. 65.

way or another, let the suffering populations know that the Holy See is following up the situation and doing anything possible for their advantage, making allusion also to this last step. In this way one would remain in between the lines of diplomacy, avoiding publications by the Holy See and delivering the Note to the representatives of the friendly countries of Germany or the neutrals. In that way the German government would not have a rational motivation to react.[711]

Marmaggi was not alone in his fierce criticism of the nuncio in Berlin. Even prior to his major blunder regarding the note, Orsenigo had created some serious divisions within the Church, causing some high-ranking German Catholics to openly question his person and his position. For instance, the bishop of Berlin, Msgr. von Preysing, had made complaints to Rome about Orsenigo several months earlier, suggesting the nuncio was not up to his task. Von Preysing had also made the point: "I ask myself if it is good that the high person of His Holiness in these days (of the Jewish question, persecution etc....) is still represented by an ambassador to the German government."[712]

Yet could Orsenigo's struggles and shortcomings have been a logical consequence of the constant, immeasurable, unmanageable pressure the German government had put on Church liberties as well as their devastating disrespect for human and Christian values? Was this not the same Orsenigo who, with a heavy heart, had written to Rome that it was now virtually impossible for any Jew to leave Germany or the occupied countries, who explained that those who were baptized Christians or who held a different nationality could, in some cases, still manage to get out, but it was becoming increasingly difficult even for them? Was it not also the same monsignor who advised, well before the troubles with the note, that his nunciature had not and would not give up trying to assist families searching for information on missing loved ones? And the one who explained that the harsh reality was that it was virtually impossible to get any information from the ministerial authorities in Berlin on any person of Jewish descent? All his enquiries were met by a Nazi wall of silence. He wrote that many German clergy continued to assist those in need by hiding them or, if they planned to flee, offering them financial assistance.

[711] ASRS, AA.EE.SS., Rapporti delle Sessioni 100, Sessione 1429 (April 8, 1943), f. 65.
[712] ASRS, AA.EE.SS., Germania scatole, 105, ff. 2–4ᵛ, letter of Msgr. von Preysing to Pio XII, January 23, 1943.

But such activities came with increasing risk. Orsenigo transmitted the sad tale of the imprisonment of the Franciscan father, Odilo Gerhard. At the request of Orsenigo, Gerhard had worked in Krakow, Poland, as a pastoral assistant on behalf of the German-speaking clergy and laity there. But in the summer of 1942, Fr. Gerhard was arrested and imprisoned in Dachau on charges of aiding and abetting non-Aryans, and specifically charged with providing them with money. Orsenigo had attempted to negotiate for the pastoral assistant's freedom but found German doors slammed firmly in his face.

While maintaining an embassy in Germany became almost unmanageable for the Vatican, the situation in countries occupied by the Nazis and their friends was going from bad to worse. This was especially true in Poland, which had become the scene of the worst and most persistent wholesale mass slaughter of its Catholic citizens as well as the deportation and annihilation of the entire Jewish population.

Back now to the room where the cardinals sat at the table, debating and discussing, determined to find a solution to the situation at hand. Cardinal Rossi felt the need to intervene again:

> If the silent and secret diplomatic action would still be valid, a public act might still be taken in consideration. If, for example, the Holy Father, in one of his magnificent discourses would emphasise that in some countries the Church is persecuted, and the Catholics are suffering. All that the Holy See has done, is doing and will continue to do. That its intervention unfortunately has not been well accepted and its actions were obstructed. Without citing names, everyone would understand, and the Catholic press could receive instructions to give particular attention to this pontifical statement.[713]

It's clear that Cardinal Maglione was a bit irked by Rossi at this point, interrupting with "What you are proposing, is exactly what the Pope did repeatedly and with such elevation and efficiency."

Cardinal Pizzardo agreed with Marmaggi that the nuncio of Berlin had made a big error: "I think it most opportune to recall the Nuncio for a leave and to give (and this should, in some way, be let known to the German government) information and explanations on circumstances of the withdrawal of the Note. It would

---

[713] ASRS, AA.EE.SS., Rapporti delle Sessioni 100, Sessione 1429 (April 8, 1943), f. 66.

be furthermore useful to inform all Nuncios about the attitude of Germany and its battle against religion and the Holy See."

Cardinal Canali also laid the blame firmly at the nuncio's door: "The Note of the Holy See was perfect. The German government did not have any reason to refuse it. But unfortunately, the Nuncio *took it back*. Thus, before anything else, one should let it be known that the Holy See disapproves the action of the Nuncio. I agree with his Eminence Pizzardo on calling back the Nuncio for a leave and to give explanations. Given the delicacy of the current situation [in Poland] I consider a public act of the Holy See most inopportune."

Cardinal Maglione listened to the comments of his fellow cardinals, considering each of them carefully and gathering his own thoughts. Then he, too, lambasted his own diplomat in Berlin:

> I agree with this last observation made by Cardinal Canali, who is saying that Nuncio Orsenigo, by accepting the return of the Note has compromised the whole situation. Monsignor Orsenigo should not have lent himself to this. It is true that the German government could have sent back the Note, but in that case the responsibility would have been totally theirs.
>
> Instead, the Nuncio, by ceding to the pressure of that government and letting himself be persuaded by invalid reasons, has regretfully agreed to retake the document, has burdened himself — to all the advantage of the German government — of a big responsibility! *Rebus sic stantibus* [given the state of matters] what can one do? The Eminences have observed all together, and justly, that it would not be prudent especially in the present moment, to publish the Note of the Holy See or any other public manifestations or protests. For the rest, including the diplomatic and secret documents of the Holy See — as this last Note is one — one day could become known to the public and they would demonstrate to the world that the Holy See herself was not tacit and has always done its duty.
>
> We heard Cardinal Pizzardo's suggestion to inform the Nuncios so they would in turn inform the different governments about the attitude of the German government towards religion and the Holy See. This was already done and can be continued. In particular, the

representatives of the Pope were given evidence of how much the Holy See did in favor of the Polish. In response, hence, to those who lament about the silence of the Holy See towards the poor Polish, it was shown to the Nuncios that the Holy Father has more than once, in public and solemn occasions, made his voice of comfort and lament heard. The Holy Father moreover has sent his precious personal letters to the bishops who are still present in Poland to encourage and bless them, together with their faithful. Such documents cannot now become known publicly while those same Polish bishops consider it most dangerous. All this has already been communicated to the Nuncios and we will not cease in keeping them posted, in accordance with the wise suggestions of the Cardinals here present.

Turning back to the sorry episode of the return of the Note, the Cardinals have shown one mind that one cannot simply drop the fact. It is necessary to take some measure. There was a proposal to call back the Nuncio. If it would be for a simple leave, I would be favorable. One could then let it be known, directly or indirectly, to the German government that the Nuncio was called in to give explanations about what happened. I consider, however, given the enormous difficulties and the great delicacy of the moment, we should not in this case do more.

Cardinal Marmaggi nodded. "I fully agree, but I would add to all this also a diplomatic communication to the governments."

As Cardinal Maglione pointed out, this had already happened:

The governments are already informed. I myself, during the conversations with diplomats, do not fail to mention the preoccupations of the Holy See for the religious situation in Germany. Particularly with the Ambassadors of Italy and Spain. In fact, during the Audience with the Holy Father some days ago the Spanish Ambassador remained quite impressed by the serene and firm words of the Holy Father, who, although convening with the Spanish Diplomat on the gravity of the communist danger, pointed out the equally grave danger that Nazism represents for the religion and for the Catholic

Church. Furthermore, the nuncios, according to the instructions received, have kept the different governments up to date on these arguments. Also, the Allies are more than informed on this.

Cardinal Marmaggi, however, did not want to back down. He proposed that another diplomatic communication be sent to the governments that would offer even more evidence regarding the gravity of the religious persecution. Cardinal Pizzardo tried to mediate, suggesting an oral communication would be preferable to a written one.[714]

Cardinal Maglione remained immovable. He refused both proposals. The other cardinals hemmed and hawed, but at last nodded and declared themselves in final agreement on what should be done. The nine wise men shuffled their papers together, stood up one by one, and left the table and the room.

Back at his desk, an exhausted Msgr. Tardini had not a moment to relax. He immediately prepared the written record of the meeting. The next day he delivered it by hand to Cardinal Maglione, who sat with the pope to discuss it.

On Sunday, April 11, the pope gave his orders to transmit the following instructions to Nuncio Orsenigo in Berlin. First: "With a written document he is to make it clear to the German Government that their gesture was not a friendly one towards the Holy See."

In diplomatic terms this was clear-cut. This was more than stating simple offense. For the Germans to refuse to accept a note was almost akin to declaring a war.

Second: "He has to add that the Holy See considers the Note as being submitted anyway."

As far as Pius XII was concerned, this note was submitted. And it was obvious to all in Rome that senior Nazi officials did indeed read it. So, as such, the pope's criticism regarding the religious persecution by the German government was affirmed and remain unchanged.

The above was a clear yet simple statement. Pope Pius XII was effectively saying to the Germans, "You can go on pretending you didn't see it if you like, but it still exists. We know you received it. We know you saw it. We know you read it."

And just as Cardinal Maglione prophesized, in the future people would find and read this note, and they would know that Rome did speak up to Germany. The contents and all the heavy discussions surrounding it are revealed here for the very first time.

---

[714] ASRS, AA.EE.SS., Rapporti delle Sessioni 100, Sessione 1429 (April 8, 1943), f. 67ᵛ.

But this second diplomatic attempt of the Holy See would also be squashed. Von Ribbentrop would once again assert that the religious situation in conquered territories was not the business of the Holy See.[715] As such, the Holy See had no means to continue any diplomatic discussions with Germany about Poland nor any other Nazi-occupied territory or country. In practical terms, there was nothing new under the sun, but the Holy See still clung to the belief — or a bit of hope — that the Nazis might be willing to maintain at least a veneer of official diplomatic discourse. Unfortunately, the Warthegau crisis made it brutally clear this wasn't the case.

However, as Pius XII concluded: "The response of von Ribbentrop confirmed that the document was received and read.... For the Holy See this is sufficient, given the gravity *of the facts,* to which the attention of the German government has been drawn."[716]

These events of April and May 1943 are key pieces of evidence in the perception of the pope by the Nazis. For the Nazi government to be able to implement their deceitful and diabolical plans, it was critical that all prying eyes be eliminated. Until that point in time, the Holy See had tried in every way to keep open a small window of diplomatic communication with the Nazis, to ask for the minimum of human understanding, with the hopes of remaining active, albeit in a very small way, on a humanitarian level.

The mistake made by Nuncio Orsenigo when he physically accepted back the note meant the official end of that narrow diplomatic corridor. And the illusion of a reasonable conversation with Nazi Germany was over.

The final words of Pius XII at the end of this diplomatic crisis, as revealed today by the exceptional archival series of the cardinal sessions, make it obvious that for the pope, when all was said and done, saving the diplomatic principle was the last thing they could hold on to: "[As long as] the document was received and read..."

For the Cabinet it was once and for all quite evident — the Nazis had declared war against the Catholic Church. And nothing the Church could say or do in the future would change even a modicum of Nazi policy or persecution. Not being able to acknowledge this could perhaps partly explain how deceptions on Pius XII and his actions and policies during World War II could proliferate for decades throughout the world.

---

[715] ASRS, AA.EE.SS., Poland 236, f. 266ss.
[716] ASRS, AA.EE.SS., Poland 236, f. 280.

13

A Tale of a Seller of Smoke

MR. FRANK VAN Gildemeester had made it to the top in the world of refugee and emigration aid. He could proudly put on his business card "Gildemeester Auswanderer Hilfsaktion," the Gildemeester Emigrants Help Action. The building where his offices were located in Vienna bore his name: the Gildemeesterhaus. The headings on his correspondence included the different titles he claimed, always followed by the name *Gildemeester*. He was quite fond of his rubber stamp with the bright red ink — "Gildemeester-Auswanderungshilfsaktion" — that he used to adorn all his correspondence because it looked so fine. As a respectable Dutchman, not only could he openly boast of his own personal status in society, but he could also refer to and rely on the stellar credentials of his family. His father, now deceased, had been the chaplain of Queen Wilhelmina's court. As a young man, Frank van Gildemeester had lived immersed in the high society of Den Haag.[717]

But for the founder and head of this Gildemeester Emigrants Help Action, which would act also under the name "The International Organization for Assistance of Jewish Refugees," new, challenging circumstances had arisen. Arriving in Rome in autumn 1939, he took a room in Pensione Ideale, a charming guesthouse with an almost musical name that was located at number 66 of the beautiful, central Via Nazionale. Yet there was no time to lose and no time to

---

[717] ASRS, AA.EE.SS., Asterisco, Stati Ecclesiastici 575, f. 62ᵛ, text of Hermann Furnberg, September 1939.

relax. He immediately got to work, writing and shaping the text of an article that he would submit for publication — and for publicity — in the newspaper of the pope, *L'Osservatore Romano*.[718]

Gildemeester delivered the article personally to the Secretariat of State on October 18, 1939, where he talked with the undersecretary of the Cabinet, Msgr. Giuseppe Malusardi. During that visit, Gildemeester also handed over letters of recommendation from the Viennese Archdiocesan Curia, all addressed to substitute Msgr. Montini.[719]

The aim of Gildemeester's visit was, of course, to ask the Holy See to endorse his activities.[720] But instead of being published, the article he'd given Msgr. Malusardi during their conversation was immediately transferred to the desk of Msgr. Dell'Acqua. Dell'Acqua took a long and careful look at all the information the man had claimed about himself and his organization:[721] "Mr. Frank van Gheel Gildemeester, founder and head of the Gildemeester Emigrants Help Action" had come to Rome to discuss with them a solution to the problem regarding the Jewish and non-Aryan transmigration. In the article, Gildemeester — referring to himself in third person — claimed that in the past he had helped about thirty thousand people out of Germany, spending at least 2,000,000 German marks to cover their traveling expenses. He stated that under his supervision and direction, everyone who was in need was helped, without distinction of religion or politics. Gildemeester also claimed that a reasonable solution to the European Jewish problem, which had become more severe due to the measures of Nazi Germany, could only be found by giving Jews the option of colonizing outside Palestine. The article Dell'Acqua was reading then became even more interesting: "For this reason, as of 1938, after the discourse of the Head of the Italian Government of 6th of October, Mr. Gildemeester gave the Italian Government his proposal to concede permits to the Jews and non-Aryans to settle in Ethiopia. The Italian Government has agreed the sending of a commission for a preliminary study by Gildemeester. That Commission was already on its way by the outbreak of the war." Next came the most

---

[718] ASRS, AA.EE.SS., Asterisco, Stati Ecclesiastici 575, f. 54.

[719] ASRS, AA.EE.SS., Asterisco, Stati Ecclesiastici 575, f. 59, internal note of Msgr. Dell'Acqua, October 18, 1939.

[720] ASRS, AA.EE.SS., Asterisco, Stati Ecclesiastici 575, f. 62ᵛ, text of Hermann Furnberg, September 1939; ASRS, AA.EE.SS., Asterisco, Stati Ecclesiastici 575, f. 60, draft of dispatch to Msgr. Orsenigo, prepared on October 19, 1939, sent out on October 21.

[721] ASRS, AA.EE.SS., Asterisco, Stati Ecclesiastici 575, f. 54.

intriguing part of his story: "Mr. Gildemeester had now come to Rome to transfer the central base of his organization out of Vienna to the neutral foreign, meaning here in Rome." Of course, Gildemeester said he planned on taking up the negotiations with the Italian government again, on behalf of the emigrants present in Italy and also on the issue of Jewish people colonizing a certain area in Ethiopia.

The last paragraph was certainly the most important one for Dell'Acqua: "Mr. Gildemeester's organization had its central house in Vienna, where he worked in very close contact with the Caritas of the Archdiocese and the Israelian community." After reading Gildemeester's self-congratulatory article, Dell'Acqua opened the little brochure that accompanied the article. Its content was translated into four languages and was the first issue of a *Mitteilungsblatt* (newsletter). On the newsletter's cover was the Star of David superimposed on the Cross of Christ as its symbol.

Gildemeester had had the newsletter printed in Rome. With his pencil, Dell'Acqua marked the paragraph of the Italian version that confirmed Gildemeester wanted "to get a concession for land in Abyssinia [Ethiopia]. The Italian Government has given its agreement to a preliminary investigation by a commission to study the question."

Mr. Gildemeester's newsletter.[722]

The archivists of the Cabinet were able to bring up correspondence of a year before, in 1938. These were letters sent to Msgr. Montini from Gildemeester, in which the latter told how he had discussed the immigration of Jews to Ethiopia with the Italian government.[723] The idea seemed very serious and credible. Immigration to Ethiopia for five hundred families with about four people each was something to keep an eye on.

[722] ASRS, AA.EE.SS., Asterisco, Stati Ecclesiastici 575, f. 46.
[723] ASRS, AA.EE.SS., Asterisco, Stati Ecclesiastici 575, ff. 43–47, letter of Gildemeester to Msgr. Montini (with alleged documents), October 30, 1938.

But first things first. Msgr. Dell'Acqua needed to investigate this intriguing visitor, a man whose personality and impressive appearance encouraged high expectations. Dell'Acqua quickly prepared a dispatch addressed to Msgr. Orsenigo, the apostolic nuncio in Berlin, to ask for "sure informations" regarding the poised and assertive Mr. Frank van Gheel Gildemeester.[724] Orsenigo's response came back very quickly. Nuncio Orsenigo had inquired of both Cardinal Innitzer, archbishop of Vienna, and Msgr. Tongelen, the director of Caritas in Vienna, and had the following to share: "Mr. Frank van Gheel Gildemeester, about 60 years old, son of a protestant pastor at the Court of Den Haag, is himself a protestant and director of the 'Gildemeester-Europaeische-Auswanderung-Hilfs-Aktion.'" The nuncio confirmed that Caritas had indeed collaborated with Gildemeester. But lately, while the costs for emigration had gone up, this collaboration had been reduced to only one Caritas member working with Gildemeester's organization, which now limited its action to converted Jews. The director of Caritas considered the work of Gildemeester to be valuable, but then he warned that "in case the Holy See would intend to grant subsidies, it would be opportune to pass them through Caritas to prevent the subsidies from being spent for other purposes."[725]

This last phrase was very disconcerting to Msgr. Dell'Acqua, and as the saying goes, "an informed man is worth two." Until that moment, the Cabinet had not done any additional research regarding the "Italian projects" of Gildemeester. And so, preparing a dispatch to the nuncio in Italy, Msgr. Borgongini Duca, the pope's diplomat in pole position to the Italian government, was the next step in the investigation. On November 19, this dispatch was signed by Cardinal Maglione and sent, with the necessary annexes, to the nunciature in Rome. Nuncio Borgongini Duca was briefed in detail on the steps already taken by the Cabinet. He was also informed of Gildemeester's presence in Rome and of his request to the Holy See to seek the endorsement of his activity. Maglione specifically asked Msgr. Borgongini Duca to gather more information about the projected colonization by Jews in Ethiopia and to report back to the cardinal what he discovered.[726]

[724] ASRS, AA.EE.SS., Asterisco, Stati Ecclesiastici 575, ff. 60$^{r/v}$, draft of dispatch to Msgr. Orsenigo, prepared on October 19, 1939, sent out on October 21.

[725] ASRS, AA.EE.SS., Asterisco, Stati Ecclesiastici 575, f. 64, report from Msgr. Orsenigo to Card. Maglione, November 6, 1939.

[726] ASRS, AA.EE.SS., Asterisco, Stati Ecclesiastici 575, ff. 65$^{r/v}$, dispatch of Card. Maglione to Msgr. Borgongini Duca, November 19, 1939.

Borgongini Duca went to see Ciano, the Italian minister of foreign affairs, to question him personally regarding the proposed plan to send Jews to Ethiopia and how successful such a scheme might be.[727]

Once seated in Minister Ciano's office, Msgr. Borgongini Duca immediately brought up the topic of the so-called emigration project. And according to Borgongini Duca's subsequent report: "The minister heightened his shoulders and interrupted me brusquely saying "nothing nothing"; it's a mere idea, of which we've talked a long time ago but without any follow-up." At that point, Borgongini Duca handed Ciano the newsletter and the correspondence the Cabinet had provided him which had been sent by Gildemeester himself. Gildemeester had informed the Cabinet that he had already sent thousands of copies of his newsletter to certain important personalities and interested authorities all over Italy. Minister Ciano glanced at the papers then gave them back to the nuncio. With an expression of disgust, he shook his head and mumbled between his teeth, "Sellers of smoke."

On his return from his high-ranking visit to the minister, Nuncio Borgongini Duca continued his report for Cardinal Maglione:

> Yesterday I was also walking in Rome and I met Monsignor Gustavo Testa, the Apostolic Delegate to Egypt, and I showed him the same manifest. To my surprise Testa left me the following note. "Mr. Gildemeester was in the Ruhr in 1923 and 24. He passed himself off as the head of a Dutch neutral organisation that was in favor of the Germans and that wanted to appear as a partner of the Holy See in its work for charity. He said he had a close relationship with Poincaré, the president of the French Republic and other personalities. I have heard the French authorities say that this man was 'a great crook' and that he would have been expelled in the near future from the occupied territories."[728]

Borgongini Duca assured Cardinal Maglione that "when he wrote this to me, Msgr. Testa didn't know anything about the words spoken by the Minister of Foreign Affairs just before. So these two versions of information confirm one another."

---

[727] ASRS, AA.EE.SS., Asterisco, Stati Ecclesiastici 575, f. 67, report from Msgr. Borgongini Duca to Card. Maglione, November 23, 1939.

[728] ASRS, AA.EE.SS., Asterisco, Stati Ecclesiastici 575, f. 67ᵛ, Report from Msgr. Borgongini Duca to Card. Maglione, November 23, 1939. The Ruhr in Germany was occupied by the French army from 1921 to 1925.

At last facts were coming together more clearly. How was it possible, wondered Dell'Acqua as he inserted a blank sheet of paper into his typewriter, that the Cabinet had lost valuable time with such a pompous windbag when they had to cope with questions of life and death over the whole of Europe. With a heavy sigh, the dutiful Dell'Acqua typed up his report. The memo for the Cabinet went like this:

26 November 1939

Note

Mr. FRANZ van GILDEMEESTER, of Vienna, last October, he came in visit to the Secretary of State with a letter of recommendation of the Archdiocesan Curia of Vienna

A) Affirming:

1) to be the head and the founder of the association "GILDE-MEESTER—EUROPAEISCHE AUSWANDERUNGS-HILFS AKTION" in favor of refugees of Jewish lineage;

2) to have worked in close contact with the work "CARITAS" of Vienna, for relief to catholic refugees

B) Asking:

The moral support of the Holy See for the activity that the association intends to carry out in Rome, especially with regards to the transfer to Ethiopia of people of Jewish descent.

The same Mr. Franz, or another person of his trust, has delivered to the editorial staff of "L'Osservatore Romano" a statement on the action which the "GILDEMEESTER" intends to carry out, asking to publish something on the matter.

The editorial staff of "L'Osservatore Romano", who reported the matter to the Secretariat of State, was told to wait for instructions before mentioning Gildemeester's activity in the newspaper.

Msgr. Orsenigo, Apostolic Nuncio in Berlin, and Borgongini Duca, Apostolic Nuncio in Italy were asked about the person of Mr. Franz and about the activity of his association.

Msgr. Orsenigo, on November 6 reported what he learned from Msgr. Tongelen, Director of the Caritas of Vienna and that is that the "Gildemeester" really works also in collaboration with the Catholic Caritasverband, which, however, limits his collaboration in favor of only converted Jews.

Currently, however, the work of the Caritasverband at the "Gilde-meester" has greatly diminished, reduced to only one of the secretaries of the "Caritas" who works there.[729]

The aforementioned Msgr. Tongelen concludes by saying that "he considers the activity that Gildemeester intends to develop worthy of consideration: he adds, however, that if the Holy See intends to contribute with subsidies, it would be appropriate to use the "Caritasverband" to prevent them from being donated to wider purposes."

The information given by His Exc. Msgr. Borgongini are 100% negative. (Report of 23 November)."

Among other things, he says that Minister Ciano regarding the planned colonization in Ethiopia stated:

"Nothing: nothing: it is an idea that was talked about long ago, but without any follow-up."

Minister Ciano himself called Mr. Franz and his collaborators: "smoke sellers."

The same Msgr. Borgongini adds in his report a note from H.E. Msgr. Gustavo Testa, Apostolic Delegate in Egypt who met Mr. Franz in the Ruhr. In it, it is said that the French authorities, of whom he obtained information, were told that Mr. Franz was "un grand escroc" and that he would be expelled from the occupied territories.

It would seem appropriate that:

1) The Holy See disregards the "GILDEMEESTER."

2) That the L'Osservatore Romano does not talk about it.

Mr. Franz Gildemeester gave me the impression of a money-maker who was also trying to get money from the Holy See

Dell'Acqua[730]

At the bottom of this memo, Cardinal Maglione wrote in ink: "I fully agree, the Holy See should disregard and L'Osservatore should remain silent."[731] The undersecretary Malusardi immediately alerted the redaction of the Vatican newspaper.

But the self-serving Gildemeester was a go-getter and would not accept no for an answer. He was determined to get what he wanted, regardless. So in December, he transmitted a copy of an appeal he wrote to the high commissioner for refugees

[729] ASRS, AA.EE.SS., Asterisco, Stati Ecclesiastici 575, f. 69.

[730] ASRS, AA.EE.SS., Asterisco, Stati Ecclesiastici 575, f. 69.

[731] ASRS, AA.EE.SS., Asterisco, Stati Ecclesiastici 575, f. 69ᵛ, internal note of Msgr. Dell'Acqua, November 26, 1939.

in London.[732] For the Cabinet it was immediately filed away and archived. He also came back in person on January 26, 1940, knocking at the door in hopes of seeing Cardinal Maglione, the secretary of state. This time, Mr. Frank van Gheel Gildemeester brought along a religious father of the Carmelite order. But rather than meeting with Maglione, Gildemeester and the Carmelite father met with the undersecretary Msgr. Malusardi. The two visitors were received and treated with appropriate courtesy, but Malusardi was acutely aware that both of them were *"very well known,* the first one as a seller of smoke and an authentic swindler as was referred by the Apostolic Nuncio after he talked with his Excellency Ciano, the Minister of Foreign Affairs. The man says that he occupies himself with immigration of Jews. The second one, the Carmelite father, is a poor deluded and no one knows why he lost his heart for such a cause which fails any principle."[733]

Both men wanted the Holy See to make a recommendation that would allow Gildemeester to have credit with the Italian banks, as he was in great need of funds to pay for necessities, bills that could not be postponed. The undersecretary replied simply that "the Secretariat of State cannot occupy itself of such financial recommendations." Then he added, "As you yourselves said, you have references all over, so you can present your case to our administrative offices competent for such matters."

When it was all over, and at long last the seller of smoke had vanished into thin air, Cardinal Maglione remarked, "Msgr. Malusardi has been far too good with them!"[734] He was right: the worse tragedies will always find their Gildemeesters, set to scavenge on the misery of other people.

[732] ASRS, AA.EE.SS., Asterisco, Stati Ecclesiastici 575, ff. 72–74.

[733] ASRS, AA.EE.SS., Asterisco, Stati Ecclesiastici 575, f. 75, internal report from Msgr. Malusardi, January 26, 1940.

[734] ASRS, AA.EE.SS., Asterisco, Stati Ecclesiastici 575, f. 75ᵛ.

14

A Short Story of Love and Lobsters

THE MAJORITY OF the names in the Ebrei Files are those of baptized Christians of Jewish lineage. The files reveal, sometimes in heartrending detail, their pleas for help. Yet the files also contain names of people of the Jewish faith who begged the Holy See for assistance and protection.

One such woman was Maria Adler. Her file states she was "Israelite," and German by birth. She lived for a while at the Piazza Cincinnati 1 in Milan with her Jewish husband, Simon, who at the time was sixty years old. Because of Simon's Jewish heritage, he was detained by the Italian Fascist government and sent to the concentration camp of Sforzacosta near Macerata.

A crowded concentration camp was a place of despair, deprivation, and anguish. Fulfillment of the most fundamental human needs was severely hindered. Hunger was a constant reminder that those interred were an afterthought, people without value. Prisoners didn't survive day by day but more often hour by hour. Knowing this, the request submitted by Maria Adler to the Ministry of Internal Affairs in Italy was very unusual. She wasn't begging to be released from jail or a concentration camp. Quite the opposite, she was asking to be sent to a camp. This loving wife begged to be permitted to join her husband, Simon, and to stay with him "to whatever destination."[735] It is quite an astonishing request, almost a contemporary Ovidian Philemon and Baucis saga.

---

[735] ASRS, AA.EE.SS., Ebrei 3, f. 5, letter of Canon Giuseppe Manio, charged for refugees in the Archdiocese of Milan, to Card. Maglione, September 4, 1940.

Not surprisingly, the Italian government, with its hardcore policies, ignored her request. So, in the beginning of September 1940, the resolute Maria turned to the Italian episcopacy for help. She contacted Cardinal Schuster, archbishop of Milan, asking if he could persuade the Holy See to sustain her case.

Cardinal Maglione was alerted by a letter from Fr. Giuseppe Maino, charged with the diocesan office for refugees in Milan. Within a few days, Maglione responded that they had taken care of the matter. He wrote that the secretary of state "did not fail to recommend to a person of authority the request of Maria Adler."[736]

Who was that "person of authority" they believed might help her? For some reason, Maglione intentionally did not give a name. This person's identity is not mentioned once, not even in the annotations and internal notes of the Cabinet's desk officers.

However, Cardinal Maglione went for the usual procedure and suggested an intervention by Fr. Tacchi-Venturi with the Italian Institutions.[737] The file makes clear that this was the right move, and the outcome of Maria's remarkable, selfless request was successful. A plain, typewritten message informed the Holy See of the "transfer of the German citizen of Hebrew race, Adler Simone, from the concentration camp of Urbisaglia to a town in the Province of Cosenza, where he could be joined by his wife."[738] Historical documents don't always tell us the exact truth: official Italian documents link Simon Adler to the camp of Urbisaglia, while the Vatican documents mention the nearby concentration camp of Sforzacosta, twelve miles from the town of Macerata. Further investigation will be necessary to remove this confusion.

And so Simon was transferred to this new location where his beloved wife was allowed to join him.

Still the question lingers as to the mysterious unnamed "person of authority" who approved this reuniting. Might this person remain anonymous forever?

On closer inspection, and with a little detective work, I discovered a clue to this person's identity. Indeed, the file also contains the transcription of a letter that was addressed to a "Most Reverend Father" from September 26, 1940. That letter had been passed on to Maglione. It is almost certain that "the Most Reverend Father"

---

[736] ASRS, AA.EE.SS., Ebrei 3, f. 6.

[737] ASRS, AA.EE.SS., Ebrei 3, f. 3, draft of letter of Card. Maglione to Fr. Tacchi Venturi, September 10, 1940.

[738] ASRS, AA.EE.SS., Ebrei 3, f. 7.

to whom the letter was written was the Jesuit Pietro Tacchi Venturi, Mussolini's private confessor and the key go-between for the Vatican and the Fascist government.

On that particular document, one notices that the approval for Simon's transfer was signed by a certain Bocchini.[739]

Risposta alla pratica per ADLER Simone
(Cfr. lett. 1U-IX-40 - N.7889/40)

Roma, lì 26 Settembre 1940-XVIII

Molto Reverendo Padre,

In relazione alle vostre premure, vi comunico di aver disposto il trasferimento del cittadino tedesco di razza ebraica ADLER Simone dal campo di concentramento di Urbisaglia in un comune della provincia di Cosenza, dove potrà essere raggiunto dalla moglie.

fto: Bocchini.

Copy of Mr. Bocchini's response to Father Tacchi Venturi, September 26, 1940.[740]

[739] ASRS, AA.EE.SS., Ebrei 3, f. 7.
[740] ASRS, AA.EE.SS., Ebrei 3, f. 7.

For experts in contemporary Italian history this last name sounds very familiar: Arturo Bocchini, also known as the vice duce, was a key player in the Fascist
regime and the most powerful man in Italy after Mussolini.[741] He began his career
as prefect of the Italian police. He became head of the police and served in that
capacity from 1926 to 1940. Beginning in 1933, he was head of the OVRA, the
secret police of the Fascist party, and was also in charge of the Italian secret services. This brought him in close contact on many occasions with the second most
powerful man in the Third Reich, Heinrich Himmler. Bocchini's biography states
that "he had a very strong sense of duty, together with a spirit of initiative," and,
maybe somewhat surprisingly, that "he was given the virtue of equilibrium and an
appreciable dosage of humanity and common sense, that helped in many cases to
mitigate the effects of the historical choices influenced by the ruthless decisions
made by the German allies."[742]

A bizarre postscript to all this is that Bocchini died unexpectedly on November
20, 1940, only two months after signing the decision that allowed Maria Adler to
join her husband. It is suspected that he died from indigestion after having a meal
in the very famous Ambasciatori Hotel at Via Veneto, where it is said he consumed
ten lobsters during that one dinner.

But, as a game of fate, in moving Simon Adler from be it Urbisaglia or
Sforzacosta to his new destination, Bocchini might have saved, at least for a
while, the lives of both Simon and his wife Maria. It is known that inmates at the
camps both at Urbisaglia and Sforzacosta were deported in 1943 to extermination camps in Germany, with few if any survivors.

This is a fascinating story that shows there were, among the Fascists, a few that
showed a little bit of heart. And that, when they could help someone, Cardinal
Maglione and the Cabinet were willing to use whatever contacts were at their
disposal, however unpalatable they might have been.

Above all else, this story of Maria and Simon is a story of enduring love. And
an elderly couple who simply wanted to stay together — in death as in life.

[741] Domizia Carafoli and Gustavo Bocchini Padiglione, *Il Viceduce: Arturo Bocchini, capo
della polizia fascista*, Milano, 2013.
[742] Pietro Zerella, *Arturo Bocchini e il mito della sicurezza (1926–1940)*, 2002.

15

A Tale of Secret Hiding Places

Basilica and Abbey of St. Paul Outside-the-Walls — February 3, 1944.

ROME SLEEPS, A city under the curfew of wartime occupation. No one, aside from the military, is permitted to move around the city freely during these hours.

11:30 p.m. A bell rings at the gate of the Benedictine Abbey of San Paolo Outside-the-Walls. It rings again, demanding, insistent.[743]

Fra Vittorino, the porter on duty, calls out: "Who is there?" A male Italian voice answers: "Ah, finally! We are two tired monks coming from a monastery near Florence. We have walked the city all evening trying to find you. Finally, we have made it here."

Fra Vittorino peers into the darkness. He is suspicious. Something doesn't feel right. He inquires further: "How could you walk the city all night? We are under strict curfew. It is forbidden to walk after 8:00 p.m." Fra Vittorino takes a step forward and studies the men more closely through the little window in the gate door. Even in the deep shadows of the night he can see that at least one of them wears a monk's habit. The two answer without hesitation: "The Abbot is expecting us."

His suspicion allayed, Fra Vittorino takes his key and unlocks the heavy wooden door of the gate. Suddenly several armed men catch him by surprise, running, pushing past him inside the gates, pistols in their hands. Shocked, Fra Vittorino tries his best to stop them, shouting: "This is Vatican territory! You have no right to enter."

---

[743] ASRS, AA.EE.SS., Stati Ecclesiastici 759B, f. 83, "Prima deposizione di Fr. Vittorino Carozzi, fratello converso."

One of the men responds mockingly: "We know this. We know everything."

The Palatine Guard, who oversee security on-site at the abbey, are taken by surprise, quickly overpowered, and rounded up. They are tied up and thrown to the ground, their weapons confiscated. Then the armed men cut the telephone wire to prevent anyone from attempting to raise the alarm. At the same time, an additional one hundred or so Italian policemen wearing civilian clothing storm the abbey. They run upstairs to the apartments where monks, students, and visitors are sleeping. They scream at everyone to get out of their beds. The armed men run the corridors, banging on doors, yelling at people to open them. If they don't, the door is kicked down. They start searching rooms, pulling out drawers, throwing clothing and possessions everywhere. Each inhabitant, whether monk or guest, is forced to go to the ground floor. They are divided by age, ordered into either the red or yellow grand salon. The members of the Palatine Guard are locked up in the little telephone room. All this lasts about two hours. As the armed men continue to search the abbey, they discover the parish complex close to the church. In one of the bigger rooms, guests — who knows how many of them refugees — are asleep. About forty-eight persons are lodged there.[744]

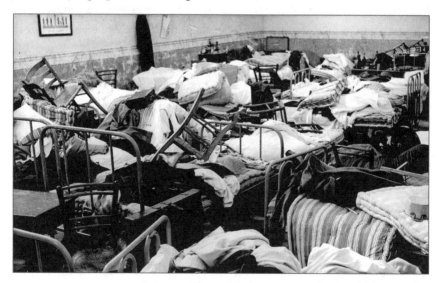

The common sleeping room, with bullet holes in the walls.[745]

---

[744] ASRS, Stati Ecclesiastici 759B, f. 572, handwritten report from the abbot, "Relazione intorno ai deplorevoli fatti avvenuti … 3 e 4 febbraio 1944."

[745] ASRS, AA.EE.SS., Stati Ecclesiastici 759B, f. 149ᵛ.

The intruders scream at everyone, shouting insults and threats, shooting into the air with revolvers to intimidate and scare people. There is panic, and people jump out of bed, trying to escape through the open *cortile* [courtyard]. The men give chase, smashing them down, beating and hitting them with pistols. Those who get caught are dragged into the salon with the monks and others. Many of them are badly injured, bleeding and crying.[746] An agent hits his baton into a man's stomach. They topple all the beds, throw the luggage and all the vestments and belongings of the people across the room. Anything they can find of value is taken to the *cortile*. The military gather all the gold and money there. The loot is confiscated and divided between different cars, which are driven away.[747]

Additional eyewitnesses share how the administration offices of the basilica were also raided. Drawers were thrown onto the floor and documents rifled through. An official Vatican report compiled after the event found that about fifteen eyewitnesses testified that among the armed intruders, there were at least two German-speaking men in uniform. These men appeared to be leading the raid. The climate of fear surrounding this violent invasion was so intense that some of the eyewitnesses, even the monks, did not want their names appearing in the official report. They only shared their accounts on a strict condition of anonymity.

Later, the Nazis would claim the purpose for the incursion had been to capture General Adriano Monti of the Italian army, a famous deserter who had been hiding out at the basilica. This might go some way to explaining the exceptionally large presence of Italian police who joined the Germans in the raid. Another eyewitness reported: "The monk Father Berardi was interrogated. They asked him repeatedly 'Where is Monti? Where is Monti?' Father Berardi answered that he did not know. Then they put a gun to his head."[748] Additional testimonies state that Fr. Berardi had tried to play for time, stalling the police as best he could. But after they threatened to kill him, he had no other choice but to tell them in which room General Monti

---

[746] ASRS, AA.EE.SS., Stati Ecclesiastici 759B, f. 309, "Relazione sui fatti accaduti la notte dal 3 al 4 febbraio 1944 nella zona extraterritoriale di San Paolo (p. 16)."

[747] ASRS, AA.EE.SS., Stati Ecclesiastici 759B, f. 192, "Deposizione di D. Bonifacio Bartolucci O.S.B., penitenziere della Basilica."

[748] ASRS, AA.EE.SS., Stati Ecclesiastici 759B, f. 308, "Relazione sui fatti accaduti la notte dal 3 al 4 febbraio 1944 nella zona extraterritoriale di San Paolo (p. 15)," and also ASRS, AA.EE.SS., Stati Ecclesiastici 759B, f. 195, "Seconda deposizione di D. Benedetto Berardi, economo del Monastero di S. Paolo."

was hiding. They smashed the door down to find him there, wearing the robes of a Benedictine monk. They dragged him out and took him prisoner.[749]

An eyewitness would report later: "He was beaten and called the whole time *Insignor* [Mister] Monti and not General. He was insulted, and they mocked him for wearing a monk's clothes." As the chaos continued, several monks attempted to argue with the Italian police. Just as Fra Vittorino the porter had done, they told the intruders they had no right to be on ecclesiastical property and that they were trespassing on what was clearly an extraterritorial zone. The agents responded several times very smoothly that they had permission from the pope and the government to be there.[750] This was, of course, a lie. They continued to interrogate and insult. They laughed and mocked all the people who were questioned. They started to eat and taunted the prisoners with the food.[751]

General Monti's apartment after the search.[752]

[749] ASRS, AA.EE.SS., Stati Ecclesiastici 759B, f. 195, second deposition of Fr. Berardi.
[750] ASRS, AA.EE.SS., Stati Ecclesiastici 759B, f. 132, deposition of Rev. Andrea Colombo, theology student.
[751] ASRS, AA.EE.SS., Stati Ecclesiastici 759B, f. 309 and 101.
[752] ASRS, AA.EE.SS., Stati Ecclesiastici 759B, f. 145ᵛ.

As it turned out, General Monti wasn't the only person hiding out in the abbey disguised as a monk. Many other individuals were too, a detail that the Fascist press in Italy would later stress.[753]

For the police, distinguishing who was a genuine monk and who was not proved difficult. To flush out the truth, they ordered the prisoners to pray the Ave Maria and the Pater Noster (Lord's Prayer). Those who couldn't recite gave themselves away as non-monks and non-Catholics. The police then demanded that the abbot, Don Ildebrando Vincenzo Vannucci, swear that all his guests were genuinely religious men, but he refused to do so, staying silent.[754] As the long night went on, more and more of those being hidden by the monks were discovered. When the agents found them, they started shouting, "Cowards! Traitors! Scoundrels! Rascals!" And they shouted to them: "While your compatriots are dying for your country you are hiding here. No one move, or he will be shot." Then they fired a few shots in the air.

A monk named Bartolucci, described:

> I looked out of my window overlooking the courtyard and I saw a group of youngsters. They ran out almost like mad men. Most were semi-naked. But at the door were 4 or 5 agents. They started to treat them very badly, beating them and hitting them with the truncheons. They forced them into the salons. The young men were uttering cries of pain. Their treatment was most brutal. Like beasts they were treated. The Italian and German agents shouted in vulgar terms using both obscene and blasphemous language.[755]

Another witness, a young Benedictine student of theology, also told of seeing savage scenes of violence:

> Shouting at poor people at one side, full of pain, the fury of the agents using words such as scoundrels, traitors etc. And after these insults follow the beatings, punches, kicking and cracks on the backbone. The various semi-nude youngsters in the salon attempt to

---

[753] See for instance the article in the *Tribuna* of February 10, 1944 (ASRS, AA.EE.SS., Stati Ecclesiastici 759B, f. 387; 391).

[754] ASRS, AA.EE.SS., Stati Ecclesiastici 759B, f. 661, testimony of Mr. Palmieri, Palatine Guard.

[755] ASRS, AA.EE.SS., Stati Ecclesiastici 759B, f. 192, testimony of Don Bartolucci.

escape. When they try to do so, revolvers are pointed on them. The scene in that nebulous obscurity, now and then lit up by the sinister light of the powerful battery-powered searchlights, is macabre and makes us realize at what point humanity has sunk downwards and below. Ten young Jews, and others, are bound, put on trucks and driven away.[756]

It shouldn't be a surprise to learn that the worst treatments were reserved for anyone suspected of being Jewish: "An agent said they were able to recognize any Jews by the fact that they are circumcised. They stripped them naked and checked." By the early hours of the morning, all the terrified prisoners had been rounded up. "To the abbot the Germans said in an irreverent way: 'You sullied your dignity as a priest by hiding in the monastery Jews and Italian deserters as well as permitting the distribution of subversive newspapers that we found in some monks' rooms.'"[757]

As a pink dawn heralded the new, late-winter day, a final contingent of sixty-six prisoners was forced onto trucks and taken to the Regina Coeli, Rome's central prison.[758] The fate of many of them remains unknown.

*

* *

It is still difficult to identify the exact number of persons who were hiding in the monastery the night of February 3 and into the morning of February 4, 1944. Not even the eyewitnesses were aware of how many there were, nor did they know all the secret hiding places in the abbey and its surroundings. Apparently, the guards, who had their own apartments or homes on-site, were also hiding people. Msgr. Giulio Fabbri, the secretary of the Pontifical Administration who lived in one of the buildings annexed to the monastery, can serve as an example. He was arrested in his home and forced to the monastery with a group of eighteen persons, all taken prisoner in the little wing where he had his apartment. He was able to categorize sixteen of those captured in this manner:

---

[756] ASRS, AA.EE.SS., Stati Ecclesiastici 759B, f. 611, deposition of Fr. Andrea Colombo, O.S.B., theology student.

[757] ASRS, AA.EE.SS., Stati Ecclesiastici 759B, 662, testimony of Mr. Palmieri, Palatine Guard.

[758] Among those there was also *un certo sig.* Ochetto, once secretary of the *questore* Caruso, who, from the prison, affirmed that during the raid there had been two German officials disguised as Italian police. Cfr. ASRS, AA.EE.SS., Stati Ecclesiastici 759B, f. 26.

A group of four, that were guests and of whom three managed to escape — all Christians, three others were guests of the Luzzi's [family], all Jews and one of them was later released. Then a group of four, guests of Torsani, all Jews, of which afterwards one was released. Three others, living with Pallotta, of which one was the brother of his wife, another was Jew who declared himself Christian, having changed his name also on his documents. And another two were family of the Rubinarca family and were staying with them.[759]

In the group of sixteen Fabbri described, we count eight Jews, of which one was "declaring himself" Christian.

However, Pietro Luzzi, who was head of the guardians of the basilica, had a different count from Fabbri. He referred to eleven Jews — "three Jews in his house,[760] four Jews by the family Torsani (of whom two were saved), two in the house of Olivieri (of which one was saved) and Pallotta kept two Jews in his house and was providing food for others."[761]

From Luzzi's testimony we learn furthermore that some of the Jews hidden in the buildings around St. Paul's Abbey had been previously sheltered in the Lombardian College, a seminary in the city of Rome, adjoined to the Basilica of Santa Maria Maggiore. Due to a raid in that college, they were transferred two months earlier to be sheltered in the Benedictine monastery. As to whose authorization allowed these Jews into the abbey, the witness answered: "Don Giulio Fabbri, the secretary of the Pontifical Administration. It was Mr. Rubimarca who brought in all these guests, asking permission for each one of them from Monsignor Fabbri."[762]

During his questioning later by the Papal Commission presided by Abbot von Stotzingen, O.S.B., Pietro Luzzi was asked who provided for the guests or if supplies for them were bought from the Vatican's store. Luzzi's answer was given reluctantly and,

[759] ASRS, AA.EE.SS., Stati Ecclesiastici 759B, ff. 625[r/v], first deposition of Msgr. Giulio Fabbri.
[760] That was the Spagnoletto family, father, son, and son-in-law. They were part of a group of seven Jews, guests of the Torsani family, another guardian of the basilica, that provided food for them, receiving 25 lire a day for this. Cfr. ASRS, AA.EE.SS., Stati Ecclesiastici 759B, f. 454, deposition of Pietro Luzzi, head of the guardians of the basilica. And see also the original in handwritten version: ibid., ff. 634–635[v].
[761] ASRS, AA.EE.SS., Stati Ecclesiastici 759B, f. 455, deposition of Pietro Luzzi, head of the guardians of the basilica.
[762] ASRS, AA.EE.SS., Stati Ecclesiastici 759B, f. 635[v].

at first, remained fairly vague: "I don't know. However, I have noticed that sometimes for instance the bill of meat for the Torsani and Rubimarca families is considerably higher than it should normally be. In fact, the family Torsani has 4 members, just as mine, and the Rubimarca has 3 members; yet their respective bills were much higher than mine. For 4 persons I paid 19 lire for meat; they 26 or 27 each."[763]

Luzzi went on to reveal that Torsani used the money of those he was sheltering to purchase many things on the black market. He then sold those items at higher prizes, thus making a tidy profit for himself. Luzzi and Rubimarca had only been asked to provide the Jewish refugees beds for the night, but clearly, they were taking advantage of them. Luzzi stated that he, himself, never asked for money from those he hid, though the Jews once gave a present of 400 lire to his young daughter. Luzzi angrily denounced his colleagues, Rubimarca and Torsani, for having profited from the Jews in their care. Then he cited another guard, Olivieri, who had sheltered four people and been paid by them: "He received 2000 lire a month from them for food and a bed. And from the others he received 50 to 60 lire a day from each of them. Torsani had first a guest that he made pay 55 lire a day. Later on, this guest moved over to the Monastery where he got food and bed for 900 lire a month."[764]

These little snippets are evidence of something that happened not just in Rome but across Europe. Whilst there were often good, altruistic people willing to hide those in need for the sake of Christian charity, some didn't hesitate to seek financial gain for their trouble.

At some point during the long night of the raid, the abbey's neighbors heard the commotion and managed to alert the Holy See. Frantic staff members ran down the corridors of the Vatican, knocking on doors and hurriedly waking up key people. A pontifical delegation was hastily put together to go find out what was happening.

The man chosen to head the delegation was Cavaliere di Gran Croce Enrico Pietro Galeazzi, delegate of the Pontifical Commission for the State of Vatican City. With him was Msgr. Ambrogio Marchionni, secretary of the apostolic nunciature in Italy, and Commandatore Adolfo Soleti, the superintendent of the Pontifical Gendarmeria.[765] The three men reached the abbey just after dawn. The Italian po-

---

[763] ASRS, AA.EE.SS., Stati Ecclesiastici 759B, f. 456, deposition of Pietro Luzzi, head of the guardians of the basilica.

[764] Cfr. ASRS, AA.EE.SS., Stati Ecclesiastici 759B, f. 454., deposition of Pietro Luzzi, head of the guardians of the Basilica. See also: ibid., f. 174.

[765] ASRS, AA.EE.SS., Stati Ecclesiastici 759B, f. 563, report from the Command of the Pontifical Gendarmeria, February 4, 1944.

lice had cordoned off the whole area and were in the red and yellow grand salons taking pictures of the terrified prisoners with flash photography. Galeazzi and his team were aghast to see that not only were monks and guests taken prisoner, but the abbey's supposed protectors, the Palatine Guards, were tied up and locked in the small telephone room.

Comandante Galeazzi, with the clear and confident determination of his station, indignantly demanded to speak to whoever was in charge. A lean, blond-haired man stepped forward and introduced himself as Lieutenant Koch of the German SS. He stared at Galeazzi with a haughty, arrogant expression, and before Galeazzi could say so much as a word, began to berate him. He accused the Vatican of hiding both "Jews and traitors of the State of Italy" in the abbey, and "even worse, dressing them as monks" to avoid detection. Koch also alleged his men had discovered a clandestine radio and piles of Communist journals and newspapers in the monks' cells. The monks would deny this, later claiming these things must have been planted there during the raid.

Galeazzi listened calmly to the flood of fabrications but refused to discuss the matter any further with Lieutenant Koch. Instead, he insisted on speaking to Comandante Caruzzo of the Italian police, whom he had been informed was there. Caruzzo stepped forward. With a quiet fury masked by curial politeness, Galeazzi reminded Caruzzo that entering the Vatican extraterritorial zone was a violation of international law. He demanded that Caruzzo explain the reason for his presence on Holy See property. He also insisted that Caruzzo disclose who gave him permission to enter such property. Was he in possession of a written mandate?[766]

Caruzzo crumbled in the face of these piercing questions. He had no permission. He had no valid, acceptable reason for being on Vatican property. All he could do was mumble a few weak answers and lame excuses.

In the hours that followed, news of the assault on the abbey was published in *L'Osservatore Romano*.[767] Very quickly the story of "the arrest of General Monti, numerous deserters, high level officials and Jews"[768] was broadcast all over the Italian and international press.[769]

---

[766] ASRS, AA.EE.SS., Stati Ecclesiastici 758B, f. 564, report by the headquarters of the Pontifical Gendarmeria.

[767] ASRS, AA.EE.SS., Stati Ecclesiastici 758B, f. 387.

[768] ASRS, AA.EE.SS., Stati Ecclesiastici 758B, f. 388.

[769] ASRS, AA.EE.SS., Stati Ecclesiastici 758B, ff. 32–41; 46–53.

Twenty-four hours later, the German denials began. Hauptman Mayer, the Reich Commander of Rome, sought to downplay German involvement with a statement, saying, "During the requisition of the monastery on the night of 3 to 4 February 1944, no German soldiers, nor German vehicles participated. Those who presume to have made such observation are mistaken."[770]

*

* *

Msgr. Tardini was extremely troubled by the coverage. He understood that most people would be shocked by the German aggression and intrusion onto Vatican territory. But suspicious that there was a backstabber in the abbey, he also worried about the consequences and how the Germans might try to spin this against the Holy See.

On February 7, Tardini gathered his thoughts and drafted advice on how the Holy See might best manage the fallout: "The publication of a protest in *L'Osservatore Romano* will make a terrific impression on all the honest ones (I don't know how many they are!). But one has to expect another reaction when everyone and everything that has been found in St. Paul's will come to be known." Tardini's intuition warned him that a public protest could easily turn out to be counterproductive and he reflected: "Here exists a great danger to end up on the side of the one who is wrong, because the ... simple people can be tricked by adverse propaganda." Although he had to admit

> that a general of the Italian aviation dressed like a monk is quite ... comical.
> Can one repair — at least in some way — things? I think indeed *yes*. And how? Well, this is what I humbly would think.
> On *L'Osservatore Romano* we should

> (1) Observe that, if the competent authorities would have had heard of something inconvenient inside the extraterritorial fence, they should have reported such matter to the Vatican authorities, and not violate the holy sacred rights of extraterritoriality.

In short, Tardini vigorously makes the point that, even if the Germans and Italians had concerns, they should have approached the Holy See first.

[770] ASRS, AA.EE.SS., Stati Ecclesiastici 759B, f. 738.

(2) Announce that the Holy See has already nominated a Commission to do an accurate investigation of all that happened (before and during the violation of the extraterritoriality).... Of course, this Commission would conclude *nothing* whatsoever regarding the effect of the ... invasion, but would be useful to show to everyone that the Holy See ... would have been diligent if it would have been informed in advance.

The Holy See can be seen as playing a little political game by setting up a commission and investigating witnesses, but a game it would remain, because, as Tardini's notes make clear, "Of course this Commission would conclude *nothing* whatsoever."

(3) Instead, for ecclesiastical purposes, the Commission could conclude a lot. (The Benedictines [of St. Paul] must have committed lots of imprudences (not to say stupidities!). Some friars have confessed ... astonishing things. For instance, one of the ... *invaders*, shortly before, had played football in the garden of that very monastery. Symptomatic — not to say otherwise — is the attached deposition of Don D'Amato. Who knows if among the friars themselves there might have been a ... traitor! Anyway, if the monastic discipline should have to be ... revived, then this would be a good occasion to do so.[771]

In the days that followed the raid on the Benedictine abbey, the Vatican set to interview dozens of eyewitnesses. The Holy See themselves had to determine if there was a traitor in their own midst. Tardini was convinced there must have been a spy informing the Italians and Germans as to the secret activities within the abbey and, in particular, as to the presence of high-ranked Italians living undercover.

Suspicions fell on a monk named Don Ildefonso Troia, who had arrived in the monastery from Florence only weeks earlier in January 1944.[772] Troia said he was a supporter of the Italian Fascist government, and during his stay in the monastery

---

[771] ASRS, AA.EE.SS., Stati Ecclesiastici 759B, ff. 12ʳ–13ᵛ.

[772] The Italian family name *Troia* would mean "slut or whore." With his typical cynical notes, Tardini sometimes makes a game of words with it, suggesting that with such a name the monk was predestined to "sell" himself out to others. ASRS, AA.EE.SS., Stati Ecclesiastici 759B, f. 22.

of San Paolo, he had never made any attempt to hide his political leanings. He did not attend Mass as often as he should have and was said to have no great capacity for preaching. But in wartime, things are rarely as they seem. What his fellow monks did not know was that prior to the event, Don Troia had actually been an active anti-Fascist. He had taken part in a political anti-Fascist meeting in Firenze and been arrested there. One can only assume that he was badly tortured. He was released only on the condition that he accept the nomination of Chaplain of the Republican Military, which meant he would be in service of the Fascist government.

Suspicion had grown among Troia's former superiors in Florence. They believed he had become a spy, a man blackmailed into working for the Republican Fascist police.[773] Eyewitnesses alleged that during the raid, he was heard to say, "*Il mio colpo e riuscito*" [My operation was a success]. A week later, when Don Troia was outside Rome in the town of Subiaco, another witness heard him say to a *brigadiere*, "I will show you who I am. I organized the assault against the Monastery of San Paolo: I have come to Subiaco to do the same at the monastery of Santa Scolastica, which is in the same situation as San Paolo."[774]

For the Benedictines of San Paolo, still reeling from their night of terror, the presence of Don Troia had become a serious problem. The superiors of the monastery came to the Apostolic Palace to meet with Tardini and discussed what needed to be done. Tardini reassured them that "the results of that Commission are not at all favorable to Don Troia," but he urged patience, saying they had to wait for the final report of the commission before deciding what course of action to take. It was decided that Troia, now living in a hotel, should immediately be brought to a monastery indicated by the superiors while they decided on his fate. His suspension was inevitable.[775]

At last, on May 12, 1944, the results of the inquiry were revealed, leaving no doubt as to the involvement of Troia.

(1) Don Ildefonso Troia had organized the assault against the Monastery of St. Paul (extraterritorial zone), as a principle agent of the police (*postestas laicalis*) [lay power]. During the attack, the

[773] ASRS, AA.EE.SS., Stati Ecclesiastici 759B, f. 643ᵛ, "Relazione del p. Emiliano Lucchesi per la Commissione d'Inchiesta."
[774] ASRS, AA.EE.SS., Stati Ecclesiastici 759B, f. 640, deposition of abbot general of the Benedictine Congregation "Sublacense," Emmanuele Caronti, O.S.B.
[775] ASRS, AA.EE.SS., Stati Ecclesiastici 759B, ff. 14ʳ/ᵛ, handwritten notes of Tardini on the visit (on April 13, 1944) of Placido Luchini, dated April 15, 1944.

jurisdiction of the Abbot of the Monastery was infringed, because the Abbot was locked up in a room together with other monks while the police searched all rooms and arrested the refugees and took away all that they wanted. Therefore, Don Troia has incurred the excommunication *latae sentantiae speciali modo Sedi Apostolicae reservata* (can. 2334 n° 2).

(2) Don Ildefonso Troia through his actions has caused a great scandal and grave damage to his Order, and to this is applicable the canon 668 [of Codex of Canon Law 1917] which infers the dismissal of the Order, of his religious habit, and requires him to leave on the spot.

In addition, Msgr. Dell'Acqua investigated the character of Troia for the superiors:

Certain elements bring to reflect even more on the person of the ... religious Don Troia. The report of the Commission of Investigation states he went to the Hotel Bernini where the famous Lieutenant Koch resides; and there is evidence as well that Don Troia did go to the town of Subiaco. But the physical descriptions don't coincide. In the report of the Commission one describes a male with black hair, in the newspaper article one talks of a priest with blond hair.... Therefore it would be useful to know where D. Troia had his lodgings, in the monastery or elsewhere.[776]

Tardini remarked underneath Dell'Acqua's text in handwriting, almost to indicate that this puzzle would never be resolved: "One has also heard of one disguised as a priest (but who wasn't one). D.T."

Although Tardini was personally in charge of settling Don Troia's case, the Historical Archive tells us that Pius XII had the final word on his fate.[777] "On explicit order of Pius XII,[778] on the 10th of September 1945, Don Ildefonso Troia was reduced to the lay status."[779]

---

[776] ASRS, AA.EE.SS., Stati Ecclesiastici 759B, f. 22, internal note of Msgr. Dell'Acqua, June 16, 1944.
[777] "Parlo al S. P. di D."
[778] ASRS, AA.EE.SS., Stati Ecclesiastici, 759B, f. 17.
[779] ASRS, AA.EE.SS., Stati Ecclesiastici, 759B, ff. 15–16.

The raid on the Abbey of St. Paul Outside-the-Walls is testament that eccle-siastical institutions acted as safe houses during the war, hiding places that were indeed secure so long as the Nazis did not trespass. For the Holy See, maintaining a veneer of official neutrality and diplomatic impartiality was key to preventing Nazi interference. But the case of the Benedictine Abbey of St. Paul shows that the veneer could be fragile. It makes clear that when the Nazis had no respect for Vatican boundaries, the Holy See was no longer capable of guaranteeing the protection of the refugees it tried to help.

From his exhaustive inquiries, Tardini learned that the original plan of the Italian police had been to lead additional raids on different Vatican properties the following week, including the papal Archbasilica of Saint John Lateran and the diocesan buildings throughout Rome. A German commander and the *questore* of Rome, Caruso, had opposed such a plot. Some high-ranking Italians turned their backs on their Nazi-supporting Fascist government, the deserter General Monti being one of them. That the Holy See and its network in Rome were prepared to offer Monti shelter should come as no surprise. When someone in need knocks at the door, doors will be opened. To actively take such a strong and consistent position is not just a consequence of faith or of diplomatic strategy. It is also a constant policy of the Holy See, both then and now. It is a policy that will always be the object of criticism for those who can't or won't understand it.

16

A Tale of Heroes, Rabbits, and Two Lions of Diplomacy

AFTER THE FEBRUARY 1944 raid on the Abbey of St. Paul Outside-the-Walls, a second *maioris momenti* of German intrusion on Vatican property took place, this time on the steps of the Basilica of Santa Maria Maggiore. This particular invasion in May of the same year was comparatively minor in scale but held potentially far more serious and dangerous consequences. The activities of the secret Roman Escape Line and Pius XII's covert involvement behind the scenes could have been blown wide open.

The active Escape Line maintained by people of the Vatican and led by the famous Msgr. Hugh O'Flaherty is today a well-documented fact. O'Flaherty was portrayed by Gregory Peck in the 1983 film *The Scarlet and the Black*, which dramatized the monsignor's dangerous and selfless exploits. The Irish monsignor was constantly under the SS radar, hence his many rumored disguises — one day a coalman, another day a nun. On at least three occasions, the SS set traps to catch him, all without success.

But O'Flaherty, who was based in the Vatican, did not work alone. He could count on a network of people spread all over the Eternal City. The network's clandestine activities were carried out under a pact of silence by brave women and men, a silence that would hold even when staring death in the face, as you will find out now.

Another key player in the rescue network in Rome, far less well known today but equally deserving of recognition, was Anselmus Musters, a Dutchman. He was an Augustinian father whose cover name, given by other members of the Roman

Escape Line, was "Dutchpa." Musters was an operative, risking his life daily to carry out the Escape Line's resistance activities across Rome. The Historical Archive of the Secretariat of State contain a fat folder revealing how Musters's bravery in the midst of grave danger led to a diplomatic conflict between the Nazi SS occupying Rome and the Holy See, a conflict that could have wrecked the entire Escape Line and everyone involved in it.

*
* *

It was May 1, 1944. The cobbled streets of Rome were revitalized with the warm air that heralds the coming of spring. The ruins of a grand and ancient empire awakened from winter's silent slumber into new life. Fresh green shoots pushed through crevices of ancient brickwork, exploding with blossoms. Rome is never more beautiful than in this glorious month of May.

Yet a dark and ominous shadow stretched long and low across the city streets. The centuries-old cacophony of a Roman springtime was driven into submission, deafened by the sound of jackboots marching across gracious piazzas. With it, a silent yet pervasive fear vibrated through the closed window shutters of the city's inhabitants.

On that balmy evening, two SS agents stalked their prey, a man in the robes of a monk. Unnoticed and dressed in civilian clothing, the agents silently, stealthily followed the "monk" through the streets of Rome. At first, the monk they were tracking wasn't aware he was being tailed. But as he turned a corner, he instinctively felt their presence. His gut lurched. Without looking back, he knew what was happening.

He tried to control his growing fear and to quickly come up with a plan.

He changed direction. His SS tails paused briefly. He held his breath — had they gone? But then they changed their direction, too, determined not to lose the man they were after. Hastening his pace now, the monk slipped through smaller, more narrow side streets, hoping to shake them off. But he could hear their footsteps getting louder, suggesting they were closing in and watching for their moment to strike.

The "monk" knew he had only a minute, if not seconds, to spare. Picking up speed, he walked across the busy square of the Basilica of Santa Maria Maggiore. Its symbolic *campanile*, (the highest one in Rome and built in 1377 to celebrate the return of the popes from Avignon) loomed over him as he broke into a run, darting through the crowds on the square. His predators kept up. The monk reached the far end of the square with the SS close behind, and then he dashed up onto the travertine steps of the basilica, knowing he was seconds away from losing his freedom and his life.

But then two strong hands grabbed him from behind and roughly pulled him down from the steps and onto the square. Angry voices shouted at him, demanding to see his papers. A gun waved in his face. With all his might, the captive struggled and was able to wrench free from his captors. He dashed past the guards, the Guardia Palatina,[780] at the basilica doors, shouting that he needed to seek safety inside.

The SS thugs tried to follow, but the Palatine Guards blocked their path. The "monk" was now on Vatican State property, an "extraterritorial zone" enjoying the same immunity as a foreign state or an embassy, and thus the Germans were denied permission to enter. Thwarted just as they were so close to catching their prey, the two SS men were furious. They stood by the paneled door, demanding that the guards "must hand over this religious man who has escaped us by entering the Basilica."[781]

The "monk" they were after was Dutchpa, Fr. Anselmus Musters.

*

*   *

There are different versions as to what happened next. The chronicles and poetry written by Musters and later published by his family are based on his personal diaries written after the war and therefore would be the most accurate account. In his writings, he states that he was physically grabbed by the men, who asked for his papers and then pointed a gun at him while attempting to arrest him, and that he ran inside the basilica to escape.

[780] The Guardia Palatina were made up of Roman citizens from high-ranking noble families who devoted themselves to defend the Holy See and the pope. Created in 1850 as a military corps, its role at that time in 1944 is best described as something between the Swiss Guard and the Italian Gendarmes. One should not confuse the Guardia Palatina with the Swiss Guard, the pope's force of bodyguards, which still exist today. The Palatine Guard became defunct under Pope Paul VI in 1970. It has continued to live on in the form of voluntary service to the pope and the Holy See through the Associazione Ss. Pietro e Paolo, under the command of the cardinal secretary of state.
[781] ASRS, AA.EE.SS., Stati Ecclesiastici 763, f. 7, draft of article for *L'Osservatore Romano* (unpublished).

The story, in Musters's own words, explains that a cardinal who was inside ushered him into his office "as no one could touch me there. But only a quarter of an hour later, I heard voices coming up the stairs, out of breath, panting and cursing. All of a sudden, the Cabinet of the Cardinal was filled with SS agents, armed to their teeth."[782]

The SS burst into the office and arrested Fr. Musters, dragging him out of the church and shoving him into a waiting car. He was taken to Via Tasso Prison, the headquarters of the Gestapo in Rome.

Musters's sixth sense that alerted him to the SS men following him had been honed over time. He knew that he was a Nazi target and had been expecting an arrest at any moment. At the beginning of 1944, the Germans had become aware of the Escape Line's activities, possibly through an informer. Msgr. O'Flaherty had warned Musters that the Gestapo were onto him personally and that he needed to be very alert. In his postwar diaries, Musters wrote of the warning: "Without taking the things too seriously I went on with my work, of course a little bit more careful with the moves I made and especially taking care that I never had names or addresses in my pockets that, if discovered, could cause harm to anyone."[783]

Until today, all that was known about what happened on that warm evening in May comes from the Musters family chronicles. The files of the Cabinet in the Historical Archive will now disclose the ramifications of the events in much greater detail, as well as the furious arguments that followed his arrest.

Once Musters had raced into the basilica, the Comandante della Guardia Palatina (the commander of the Palatine Guard), together with the Commissario of the Gendarmeria Pontificia (the Vatican police force), who were standing on a separate post outside the basilica, argued sternly with the SS, trying to stop them from entering the church and trespassing an international border. They reiterated to the SS men that they had absolutely no right to enter, because the basilica was part of the Vatican City State and as such had extraterritorial status since the Lateran Treaty with Italy in 1929. The Germans may well have occupied Italy, but they did not occupy the Vatican City State. For those unfamiliar with the Eternal City, one of its remarkable aspects is that many of the buildings, palaces, and churches dispersed all over the

---

[782] *Jonge Bloei: Gedichten van Anselmus Antoon Musters O.E.S.A.: Met een korte biografie en familieherinneringen*, 2016, 7.

[783] *Jonge Bloei: Gedichten van Anselmus Antoon Musters O.E.S.A.: Met een korte biografie en familieherinneringen*, 2016.

city are part of the Vatican territory. The border begins, ends, and begins again in the multiple locations where those buildings are located.

But listening was never a strong point for the SS. Arrogant power demands its own way. Following the heated argument, the SS stormed into the sacred building and dragged a petrified Fr. Musters outside toward inevitable torture and interrogation.

The bulging archival folders contain multiple typewritten eyewitness reports that were gathered after the incident. It is impossible to include them all here, but this is what a Palatine Guard named Filippo Cannizzaro said he saw that day:

> A Priest, (at least apparently, he seemed to be one), was in the sacristy under the protection of two guards. The Priest claimed to the two superiors of these guards that he had been followed, moreover, to quote his actual words he said, "was tailed" for more than a quarter of an hour already by some individuals. When those individuals arrived in the Piazza Santa Maria Maggiore they stopped him precisely between the obelisk and the entrance stairs. He was asked to show his personal documents. The Priest trying to avoid this told them to follow him into the Basilica if they wanted to, and he would show it them in there. And so, they did. Now the Priest, once coming into the Basilica, and I don't know for what motive at all, immediately sought a way to put himself under the protection of the guards.
>
> The guards, seeing the other individuals trying to take him out, thought it best to take him into the sacristy and to alert some of the Monsignors that were present in the sacristy. At that same time, an agent of the secret service of the SS ... insisted that the man be handed over, claiming that he was an English spy.
>
> But this SS agent was told by the Head of Inspection Mr. Ghergi to leave the Basilica immediately because he was on extraterritorial zone and it was not permitted for him to enter. In the meanwhile, they ensured that the Priest remained in the hands of the Palatine Guard and assured the SS agent that they would keep a scrupulous eye on him, in order that he would not escape.[784]

[784] ASRS, AA.EE.SS., Stati Ecclesiastici 763, ff. 42–43.

In the same file, there are at least seven equally highly detailed eyewitness statements like this one, by various guards on duty, all similar in content bar a few
inconsistencies on details of time of chronology — a classic occurrence in all
police investigations.

The very difficult job of attempting to piece together the facts from the various
statements was given to Cabinet Secretary Tardini.[785] Tardini, with his straightforward manner, wit, and sharp brain, needed every one of these skills to navigate
his way through the myriad of reports to determine what should and would be
done. Coming so soon after the German and Italian incursion into the Abbey of
San Paolo, it was of absolute importance that the Holy See did all they could to
defend their borders and the extraterritorial zone. If the Germans intended to make
regular invasions onto Vatican State property, the lives of thousands of people
hiding there were at risk, including hundreds of Jews. And Fr. Musters's life, too,
now depended on the Holy See's moves.

Tardini's reports and notes, detailing the furor as it unfolded, also show that
Pius XII himself was heavily concerned and involved, making key decisions about
how to handle the argument with the Germans. Perhaps it also goes some way to
helping understand why a quiet, prudent diplomacy and a language designed not
to inflame but to calm stormy waters might often yield the most effective results.

Bright blue pencil in hand, Tardini began writing his report.[786] It was May 3,
1944, a mere forty-eight hours after Musters was dragged out of the basilica. At
11:00 a.m., Cardinal Maglione called Tardini into his office and ordered him to
prepare a note of complaint to the German embassy to the Holy See. Dell'Acqua
would prepare the draft.

The almost hour-by-hour details Tardini provides us here are an indication
that the Cabinet worked around the clock when the need arose:[787]

> At 8:00 p.m. I sent the draft by Dell'Acqua to his Eminence [Maglione].
> The next day, 4th May, at 9:45 a.m. his Eminence returns the
> draft with some corrections, and orders that it should be submitted
> to the Holy Father.

[785] ASRS, AA.EE.SS., Stati Ecclesiastici 763, ff. 19–24ᵛ.
[786] ASRS, AA.EE.SS., Stati Ecclesiastici 763, f. 18. Tardini's long and comprehensive
report has a title page "S M Maggiore 1-V-44 Cattura del P. Muster[s] Agostiniano."
[787] ASRS, AA.EE.SS., Stati Ecclesiastici 763, ff. 19–23.

Between 9:45 a.m. and 10:00 a.m., substitute Monsignor Montini tells me that the Holy Father would also like to make something public on the *L'Osservatore Romano*. I charged Monsignor Dell'Acqua with this.

At 10:45 a.m. I sent the new draft of the Note of complaint to His Holiness.

At 11:00 a.m. His Holiness calls me by telephone to ... give me back the draft, which is approved....

At 11:30 a.m. the Note of complaint is approved by his Eminence and was sent to the Ambassador of Germany.

At 12:15 p.m. the German Ambassador comes to me in person. He claims that in Santa Maria Maggiore the Palatine Guard had ... *trespassed onto Italian territory, pulling Fr. Musters* out of the hands of the SS. And that they had done so while he was guilty of very serious crimes.

Thus, so he says, the SS didn't commit anything else other than a *constitutio in integrum* [that is, the restoration of the original rule of law altered by the occurrence of serious circumstances, or in common language: putting things back the way they were].

The ambassador added that he had personally made his own inquiries and visited the place of the incident. Finally, he said that ... he has testimonies to substantiate his version of events from both Italians and Germans.

Tardini was all too aware of the German ambassador's ability to use tricks and lies, fabrications of the type that the Nazis could easily twist into a pretext for a scandal to make the Holy See look bad. And so he responded carefully to the ambassador with thinly veiled sarcasm:

I responded to him that, even if I could accept this ... trespassing ... of the Palatine Guard, there would always remain a violation of the rights on extra territoriality in international law. And that it should be obligatory to try to resolve this with diplomacy.

I described to him that the facts according to what I know is that the religious Father Musters was *on the steps* (The Ambassador denies this).

> When it comes to regarding the ... Italian testimonies. I ask
> jokingly if those were not ... Republicans.

Republicans was another term for Mussolini's Fascists, who, of course, readily endorsed the Nazi version of the story. And this last line is classic Tardini. The use of the suspension points, three periods in a row, often appears in his thoughts, memos, and musings, either as a joke, a way of expressing his frustration, or as a wry way of indicating that he knows something someone said is a blatant lie. Reading his notes, I always have the sense that he was writing in part with the future reader in mind. He knew every word would be held for posterity and one day published, picked through, and analyzed as they are here. Of course, in internal memos he can't be blatant or call something an outright lie. But his use of the three suspension points makes it clear what he ... really ... feels. Of all the players whose voices speak clearly now from the folders of the archives, it is very often Tardini, this Roman son of a butcher, who articulated clearly what was ... actually ... happening between the written lines.

His report continued: "The Ambassador went away. I called the Holy Father to inform him of everything that was said. In the meanwhile, the Holy Father had already received the draft of the article for *L'Osservatore Romano* and approved it a little after midday. But following my telephone call to the Holy Father in which I communicated the ... version ... given by the ambassador, His Holiness decides to delay everything until tomorrow, including the communication about the bombardments of Castel Gandolfo."[788]

Castel Gandolfo was the papal summer residence just outside of Rome. By the end of 1943, many nearby locals had taken shelter there. This included a small number of Jewish refugees in hiding. Allied forces unexpectedly and inexplicably bombed it on February 10, 1944, causing considerable damage to the residence and killing more than five hundred innocent victims. For the Cabinet, the few days that followed shaped up to be very stressful and demanding. They were dealing with not one but two subsequent violent incidents on Vatican property, one by the Germans and one by the Allies.

With regard to the Basilica of Santa Maria Maggiore, after learning of the German ambassador's assertion that it was the Palatine Guards who first had trespassed onto Italian soil, Pius XII realized this could quickly turn into a sensitive

[788] ASRS, AA.EE.SS., Stati Ecclesiastici 763, ff. 20–21ᵛ.

international diplomatic incident involving claim and counterclaim. He changed his mind about publishing in *L'Osservatore Romano*, the Vatican newspaper, giving the order to wait a day and see how things transpired. During all this, Tardini went on with his investigations, determined to have on his desk by 6:00 p.m. the declarations from the guards that would pinpoint the exact spot where the Palatine Guard gathered Father Musters.[789]

Unfortunately, the inquiry would quickly dissolve into high farce. Comandante Soleti of the Vatican Gendarmeria suggested that Tardini speak with a man named Nocente, a Dominican father and a *penitenziere* (a religious position charged with hearing confessions in one of Rome's basilicas). Nocente claimed to have been there and to have seen everything. It was hoped that Nocente's recollections would be of great value to the investigation, and so Tardini told Soleti to bring him in. But when he heard Fr. Nocente's version of what had happened, Tardini could barely contain his amused astonishment at the obviously exaggerated story:

> 1:30 p.m. Father Nocente arrives. (This one, he must have been eating at midday!). He recounts a very long tale of which appears

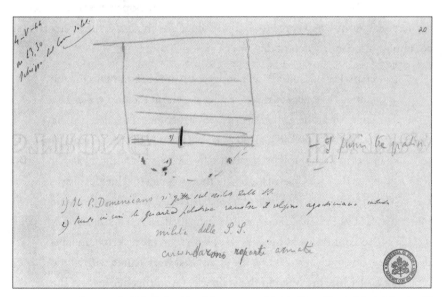

Commander Soleti's drawing of the entrance of the Basilica of Santa Maria Maggiore.[790]

---

[789] ASRS, AA.EE.SS., Stati Ecclesiastici 763, f. 21ᵛ.
[790] ASRS, AA.EE.SS., Stati Ecclesiastici 763, f. 20.

that he (who weighs less than 50 kilograms!) has jumped on the SS
dressed as civilians, between the *pillars* and the steps of the Basilica.
Then the Augustinian father [Musters] fell down on the first steps.
There the Palatine Guard took him with them.

Commandante Soleti, also present, made a drawing of the location, and on it Father Nocente indicated the spot of the first and
second acts of the drama.

We can only hope Tardini managed to restrain his laughter as Nocente embellished
his story further with a visual flourish, sketching a series of small pillars around the
edge of Comandante Soleti's drawing — pillars that don't even exist. He continued:
"I call Commandante Foggiani. He comes immediately and brings me annotations
of the Latheran treaty, with maps. On which are drawn the steps and not the pillars.
So ... these pillars are not to be found in the extra territorial zones."

But if Fr. Nocente's story was overblown by including pillars that do not exist, there was much more dangerous hyperbole to come from the German side.
Tardini's report gets even more gripping when it comes to the anecdote of how
Prince Carlo Pacelli, the well-connected nephew of the pope who also worked in
his personal service, had come to Tardini's office clutching a small piece of paper
containing a second, different drawing:

1:45 p.m. Prince Carlo Pacelli brings me a drawing and tells me the
story about it. It goes as this — Father Pancrazio Pfeiffer, [a German-
speaking Salvatorian father, also secretly a member of the Escape Line
and someone who often acted as go-between with the German authorities in Rome] had been called in by the SS, specifically by Signor
Kappler, the Vice Chief of the SS in Rome. Kappler told Pfeiffer he was
taking personal responsibility for what happened, and that the Palatine
Guard took Father Musters out of the hands of the SS on *Italian Territory*.

To confirm what he said, Kappler had made a sketch, in lapis
bleu, on which appears that the points that were signed with a little
cross by him are beyond the staircase. (And this because ... the
little piece of paper on which he drew his design has not permitted
bigger distance!)[791]

---

[791] ASRS, AA.EE.SS., Stati Ecclesiastici 763, f. 21ᵛ; f. 23.

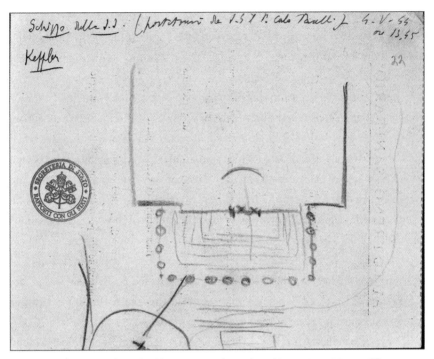

General Heribert Kappler's sketch of the entrance to the Basilica of Santa Maria Maggiore.[792]

Again, Tardini's dry wit and piercing intuition is on display. He noticed immediately that by creating a tiny drawing of reduced scale, Kappler was deliberately trying to make it appear as if the incorrect Germans' flawed version of events was correct.

Tardini went on to tell how Kappler's drawing had made a mini tour of Rome via various intermediaries before it finally landed on his desk.[793] "Father Pfeiffer brought this design from Kappler to Cardinal Canali, who then gave it to Prince Carlo Pacelli. Pacelli then brought it to me."

It's unclear why Kappler sent the drawing in such a roundabout way. In theory he could have had it delivered straight to the secretary of state's office. So why didn't he? Most likely because the office of the Holy See's Secretariat of State and the SS avoided direct communication.

Tardini's go-between, wily Fr. Pankratius Pfeiffer, had carefully cultivated contacts with the Italian Fascist government and the Nazis. He was, to a large extent, trusted by them all. But in reality, he, too, was a key member of the secret Roman Escape Line. That he was called in person by Kappler to be given the drawing makes it quite clear that the Gestapo didn't suspect him. Yet there he was right under Kappler's nose that whole time.

There were other occasions during which Herbert Kappler and Fr. Pankratius Pfeiffer met in person, with the brave Pfeiffer acting as an intermediary to negotiate for prisoner releases. One example of that had occurred a few months earlier, when the Cabinet sent an immediate plea by way of Pfeiffer, requesting the release of civil prisoners who had been arrested by the Nazis that very day, March 23, 1944. The arrests were a reprisal for the killing of some Nazi soldiers in Via Rasella in Rome. The plea went unheeded, however. As a punishment, all these Roman civilians were killed a day later during the infamous Fosse Ardeatine massacre.

The dangers Fr. Pfeiffer faced every time he went to Kappler's office cannot be understated. Had Kappler discovered that his trusted go-between was in fact a colleague of Msgr. O'Flaherty — the very man they were so desperate to capture — the consequences for the former are easy to imagine.

Cardinal Canali, the first man to have seen Kappler's drawing before it reached Tardini, was head of the Tribunal of the Apostolic Penitentiary [one of the three ordinary tribunals of the Holy See] and a Fascist-sympathizing conservative. It is easier to understand why he would receive the drawing and how he then came to pass it on to another noble, Carlo Pacelli, the nephew and trusted confidant of the pope. And finally, after winding its way around the city, Kappler's drawing sat on Tardini's desk. He appraised it with his cynical eye, comparing it to Fr. Nocente's. "2:15 p.m. At that moment Commandante Soleti and Father Nocente return to Santa Maggiore."

After this, Tardini's handwriting devolved into a hastily written scrawl that is very difficult to read. There are lots of annotated comments, underlines, and crossings out. He had worked nonstop without a break all day and couldn't help but make a little lighthearted comment about how hungry he was: "What luck that in between all this fuss I had a moment — just before 1:00 p.m. — to telephone home so that they would wait for my orders before ... putting the soup in the pot."[794]

In spite of the serious drama of this day, the down-to-earth Tardini was still able to joke that he knew he wouldn't be home in time for dinner and that his staff

[794] ASRS, AA.EE.SS., Stati Ecclesiastici, f. 23ᵛ.

should wait for him before cooking. It's as if he knew we'd be sitting here raising a wry smile alongside him.

He finally signed off his report: D. T. (Domenico Tardini).

As he wrote his initials, he was probably dreaming of that tasty bowl of hot soup. Yet additional notes, scrawled in ink underneath his initials, hint that yet more testimonies were coming in and that his long day was still not over. He didn't indicate what time he did finally make it home for dinner, or what flavor the soup was. But we can only assume he had a fitful night's sleep, his thoughts racing.

Early the next morning, May 5, he rose, returned to his office, and continued the intense investigation.

"9:25 a.m. Commandante Soleti arrives. He was charged by me yesterday to gather testimonies of others who had heard the official of the SS saying that the Vatican agreed to their operation. Naturally I didn't conclude anything from these words. And one of the two repeated again, having heard it said by the SS etc. etc." The claim that the Vatican agreed with the SS was a monstrous lie forged by the Nazis. Tardini did all he could to check and see if those who gave their testimonies were attempting to blur the facts and influence the public opinion in this sense.

> 9:57 a.m. The press release by Monsignor Dell Aqua for *L'Osservatore Romano* is ready.
>
> 10:02 a.m. Another draft of a communiqué prepared by me is ready.
>
> 10:08 a.m. I go to his Eminence [Cardinal Maglione] in the antechamber, and I give him in short explanations about all this.
>
> 10:12 a.m. His Eminence brings me before His Holiness. His Holiness concludes, agreeing with His Eminence, that it is better to *wait* before publishing on *L'Osservatore Romano*, given that facts are still contested by the Germans.
>
> His Holiness orders me to say to the Substitute [Montini] that nothing should be published — not even anything on Castel Gandolfo.[795]

Given the precarious situation in which the Germans were attempting to manipulate the Holy See in order to place the blame on them, Pius XII took control of the

---

[795] ASRS, AA.EE.SS., Stati Ecclesiastici 763, f. 24$^{r/v}$, handwritten notes of Msgr. Tardini, May 5, 1944.

situation. He decided that both incidents should be now subject to official public silence. This is a complete turnaround from his original wish to put out a press statement. His initial anger had given way to strategic management of the situation.

"10:30 a.m. I communicate to the substitute the orders of his Holiness."

And of course, while the investigation went on and the arguments raged, the unfortunate Fr. Musters was being tortured in an SS prison cell. Kappler himself personally interrogated him. Every hour he was incarcerated could well have been his last.

But what was the best way to help their imprisoned friend and associate? If the Holy See were to intervene on behalf of a simple monk, that would seem suspicious and give the game away as to who he really was. The following is from an internal memo of Msgr. Dell'Acqua: "Father Musters was violently arrested the 1st of May by the German police on the territory of the Basilica of Santa Maria Maggiore. The motives are not known. As Father Musters is a Dutch citizen and Sweden has taken over the charge to protect the interests of Holland and its citizens, would it not be useful and convenient that the Nunciature in Italy would ask the Swedish delegation in Rome to take interest in the matter?"[796]

The *minutante* Msgr. Dell'Acqua considered the proposal to ask the Swedes to intervene on Muster's behalf a positive one. But he posed the question as to why the Cabinet should always be responsible for these matters and why the good fellows of Augustinian fathers could not make appeals on Musters's behalf themselves. Dell'Acqua pointed out that it was important to be absolutely certain that Musters had Dutch citizenship, because he had heard other people suggest Musters was Maltese by birth. And if this was true, the Swedish would do nothing to help him.

Two days later, this internal memo was read by Pius XII. In scribbled handwriting at the bottom of the memo, Tardini wrote a single line: "His Holiness tells me that F[ather] M[usters] is of Dutch origin but is born in Malta."[797] As we already noticed, finding sentences handwritten personally by the pope in the Historical Archive of the Secretariat of State is a rare occurrence. But here and there his words, voiced during the audiences with his nearest collaborators — Cardinal Maglione, Msgr. Tardini, or Msgr. Montini — were immediately recorded and jotted down by them. This short mention at the bottom of the internal memo suggests more

---

[796] ASRS, AA.EE.SS., Stati Ecclesiastici 763, f. 78.
[797] ASRS, AA.EE.SS., Stati Ecclesiastici 763, f. 78.

than it was actually stating. How was Pius XII able to state with seeming certainty Fr. Musters's identity and origins? It could be an indication that he knew Fr. Musters personally. It poses an interesting theory, because if that were the case, then it means Pius XII very likely knew the same facts regarding other members of the Escape Line besides O' Flaherty and had probably even met them.[798]

*

* *

During these tense days, the other members of the Roman Escape Line lay low. One can imagine that they slept lightly, if at all, wondering as they awoke what the new day might bring. Each one was now more endangered than before, because if Musters was unable to withstand the agonies of torture, broke, and betrayed them, they were all dead men walking.

As if things were not already complicated enough, on May 9 a card written in elegant hand by Msgr. Marco Martini, the regent of the Apostolic Dataria,[799] reached the desk of Msgr. Dell'Acqua. On the card Msgr. Martini suggested it would be a good idea to question Mr. Eugenio Bussotti, the doorkeeper of the rectory of Santa Maria Maggiore. Msgr. Martini claims that Bussotti had left open the gate of the rectory "notwithstanding the order given by me to keep it closed."[800] It is obvious that Martini was throwing suspicion on Bussotti, perhaps even suggesting he might have been part of a plot.

Aware of the dangers of being sidetracked, Tardini thought this through:

> One could hear Mr. Bussotti, but without summoning him to come to the Secretariat of State. Someone could go over there.... But surely one should pay great attention to not fall into the gossip, in which Monsignor Martini could drag us. He says "I *ordered* (or better, *I had given him the order*) to close the gate." Now one asks: Why was it left open? One could also ask Martini: "And why did you not make sure your orders were obeyed?... Now, all of them ... are ... heroes: in this moment. But the thing lets itself easily be understood — that they were all *rabbits*!" [801]

[798] ASRS, AA.EE.SS., Stati Ecclesiastici 763, f. 81.

[799] A congregation now extinct that dealt with marriage cases.

[800] ASRS, AA.EE.SS., Stati Ecclesiastici 763, ff. 79r/v.

[801] ASRS, AA.EE.SS., Stati Ecclesiastici 763, f. 80.

Dell'Acqua eventually went and checked with Bussotti, concluding, as Tardini had suspected, that the gate story was "much ado about nothing."[802]

And while poor Fr. Musters languished at Via Tasso Prison, still suffering relentless torture at Kappler's brutal hands, on May 10 a courier arrived at the Apostolic Palace from the German embassy. He handed over a *note verbale*, a formal diplomatic document, to the Holy See.[803] The note boldly and arrogantly claimed that the whole incident was to be attributed to a trespassing by the Palatine Guards onto Italian territory. It pretended that the guards had dragged Musters back onto the basilica steps, leaving the German SS no choice but to go onto the steps and pull their rightful target back down into Italian territory in order to arrest the dangerous, wanted criminal.

The German ambassador to the Holy See, von Weizsäcker, then arrived in person to see Tardini, who noted: "12:15 p.m. The Germans, from their side, say they will not give publicity to the matter, as long as the Holy See will not publish."

This is blatant blackmail from the Germans; if the Holy See keeps quiet about the arrest, so will they. Pius XII may have suspected this would happen, which is why he had already made the decision not to go ahead and publish in the Vatican newspaper. The German claim continued:

> (1) That the arrested religious father has admitted his guilt — ("*un criminel*" — added the German Ambassador).

> (2) That in Rome there are many foreign priests that appertain to countries with which Germany is at war. The matter is very delicate. The Ambassador claims he has worked extremely hard ... sweating seven shirts to curb the military authorities. And he will continue to do so.... But ...

That's a veiled threat from Ambassador von Weizsäcker, with dark hints of measures that would be taken against foreign priests from countries at war with Germany. He was using a ploy, pretending he was trying his best to restrain the military whilst blaming the Holy See. Tardini noted the ambassador's words verbatim and included his own responses in parentheses:

---

[802] ASRS, AA.EE.SS., Stati Ecclesiastici 763, f. 102.
[803] ASRS, AA.EE.SS., Stati Ecclesiastici 763, f. 9.

(3) That this situation of the extra territorial zones in Rome presents some difficulties and it becomes always more "labile"[804] (He said it exactly like that). One has to proceed with a lot of "bon sens."[805] ... (I observe to him: "and with a respect of the rights.")[806]

The final exchange shows that Tardini replied quite frankly. With that, von Weizsäcker upped his attempts at intimidation:

The Ambassador hands over to me a written testimony. As if he did it on purpose, it was one exactly from a ... republican official! (The other time, when the Ambassador said to me that he had testimonies of Italians, I asked him if they were maybe ... republicans!).

To the Ambassador I said the following:

(1) Taking a look at his *Note*, I observed that the word *rückführung* [leading back] was quite an ... elegant term to describe the SS who actually entered with force, with machine guns in the Palace of Santa Maria Maggiore, and then with force and with beatings dragged away that poor friar, bleeding.

(2) According to the testimonies we received the Guardia Palatina picked up the Augustinian religious father on *the staircase* of the Basilica. The scuffle between the father and the agent of the SS (in civilian clothing) began earlier. But the Guardia Palatina did not ... trespass.

(3) Even supposed (and not conceded to) such ... trespassing, there would always remain *the violation* of extraterritoriality committed by the SS. Other ways for resolving this matter could and should have been followed.

(4) The religious father is unknown to the Secretary of State. We request that benevolence and mercy would be used. But the international question is different. The facts of Santa Maria Maggiore are by now known by the whole of Rome. The newspapers have already published the story and thus the Holy See also has to publish.

[804] Which means: volatile.
[805] Common sense.
[806] ASRS, AA.EE.SS., Stati Ecclesiastici 763, f. 8ᵛ.

On the presence of foreign priests of enemy states presently residing in Rome, Tardini responded:

> (5) That the foreign priests have always been respected in Rome, in part because many of them are in the service of the Holy See or working for the general direction of the different religious Orders.

On point 4, it was now Tardini who was telling a lie, or at least a half-truth. Not everyone in the Cabinet knew Musters's true identity, but the pope certainly did. And on his final point Tardini, subtly but pointedly, reminded the Germans that foreign priests had been a part of Roman life for a lot longer than the Nazis had occupied Italy. Having privately mocked Fr. Nocente's exaggerated bravery, Tardini was now able to twist it into a useful weapon:

> (6) The testimony of the republican lieutenant does not convince me, because he didn't see the Dominican friar (Father Nocente), who was the first to rush forward and who ... collaborated to drive the participants (the SS military and the Augustinian father) back towards the steps of the Basilica.

By raising the inconsistency on this small fact, Tardini immediately devalued the reliability of the Italian official's whole testimony.

And so it went on. Two lions of subtle diplomacy battling it out with polite language that masked their mutual antipathy. In an exchange like this, every word uttered, every nuance in tone, mattered. And whilst the words remained urbane, the tensions underneath were far from it. The Germans were one step away from publicly accusing the Vatican of covering for those on the Allied side. In order to retain the official stance of impartiality that allowed them to operate across countries at war with each other, the Vatican had to persuade the Germans to back down. By the end of the meeting, Tardini was the clear winner. The only thing left for him to do now was to establish the various testimonies and conclude his investigation.

He was helped with this effort by a new key witness who came forward. She was Miss Valeria Fabrizi, a member of the public who had been on the square, and who "saw everything happening, confirming our version, revealing all that was to reveal."[807] Having witnessed the entire dramatic incident unfold, this independent

---

[807] ASRS, AA.EE.SS., Stati Ecclesiastici 763, f. 10ᵛ, handwriting of Tardini, May 12, 1944.

witness said the fleeing Fr. Musters was gathered up by the Palatine Guard on the superior steps at the entrance to the cathedral forecourt — within church property and definitely *not* on Italian territory.[808]

The following day, a full nine days after Musters's arrest, Dell'Acqua was finally able to confirm that Musters did indeed hold a Dutch passport and that the Augustinian Fathers, the order to which he belonged, had already written to the embassy of Sweden — now responsible for Dutch citizens in Italy — with a plea for help. It's not clear why, but until that point it seems the Swedish embassy had done nothing.[809]

So now it was left to the Holy See to try to secure Musters's release. But to do so without arousing suspicion as to his importance would be a challenging and delicate undertaking. A meeting was arranged between the secretary of state, Cardinal Maglione, and the German ambassador for the following week.[810]

Prior to that, a pre-meeting had taken place between Mr. von Kessel, counselor of the German embassy, who was delegated by Ambassador von Weizsäcker and Tardini. The purpose of the pre-meeting was to define, ahead of time, the terms for the upcoming discussion between the ambassador and Cardinal Maglione.[811] From Tardini's handwritten notes, von Kessel had *"quelque inquiétude* [some unease] concerning the incident of Santa Maria Maggiore. The Embassy" — so said von Kessel — "had kept Berlin *à l'écart* [at bay], without transmitting the texts of the Notes that were exchanged."

That Berlin was initially kept out of the loop was important information for Tardini. Was that because the German embassy feared they had overstepped the mark? Tardini thought so, and believed he now had new leverage.

But now, as von Kessel went on, "Berlin had intervened with a certain vigor." There, Tardini notices that his "interlocutor uses very vague sentences: but he adds that the Embassy would not want to make to the Secretary of State some communications that were *désagréables* [unpleasant]. Thus" — von Kessel says — "it would be good that the Embassy could let Berlin know that the incident is settled."[812]

[808] ASRS, AA.EE.SS., Stati Ecclesiastici 763, f. 100.

[809] ASRS, AA.EE.SS., Stati Ecclesiastici 763, f. 103.

[810] ASRS, AA.EE.SS., Stati Ecclesiastici 763, f. 14.

[811] ASRS, AA.EE.SS., Stati Ecclesiastici 763, ff. 11$^{r/v}$–12$^{r/v}$, handwritten report from the conversation between M. von Kessel and Msgr. Tardini on May 13, 1944.

[812] ASRS, AA.EE.SS., Stati Ecclesiastici 763, ff. 11ss.

Tardini seized his opportunity.

I respond to him:

(1) That I don't understand this attitude of Berlin. . . . Mr. Von Kessel observes that to the government there is a *Jurisconsult* [legal adviser]. (And here he makes a gesture, as if he wants to say the adviser is terrible . . .). Well, if he is a real jurisconsult, I reply, he can understand the right of the Holy See, that is very clear. Mr. von Kessel looks at me and declares with another significant gesture that he is a *Nazista*, a word that was not pronounced . . . with any sympathy.

(2) That, in my opinion, the government of Berlin should now have other things to think about. Mr. von Kessel responds that these other things — heavier and more urgent — are *désagréables* [unpleasant] and, after several words, he says through his teeth: "They are fools!"

Von Kessel's frank — and unsubtle — outburst above may suggest that, on a personal level at least, he was uncomfortable with the Nazi agenda. Tardini internally assessed all this and made the Holy See's position clear:

(3) That the Secretary of State was ready to respond by letter to the document of the German Embassy. The Holy See (a) confirms that, according to the testimonies it gathered, the Palatine Guard . . . did not trespass (b) reaffirms that in no way one can justify the armed intrusion of the SS into an extra territorial edifice and (c) receives with satisfaction the assurances of the Embassy.

The whole conversation was a game of diplomatic one-upmanship. The rules of the game say you first attack on the points you are sure of and then leave the door open to compromise, and this is what happened. The real fight occurred during the pre-meeting between Tardini and von Kessel. The second meeting between Maglione and the ambassador was held essentially to formally "rubber-stamp" whatever was worked out during the pre-meeting.

"Mr. von Kessel says to me that the Embassy as well will stick to its version: what is certain was the fact that from the part of all the German authorities there was the intention to continue to respect the extraterritorial zones."

With that, Tardini had made another shrewd and clever move, making a distinction between the German embassy to the Holy See and the SS authorities — a sign to von Kessel that he heard and understood his disquiet. He then pushed that a bit farther, playing up a little bit of divide and conquer: "I show my doubts concerning the SS authorities. But Mr. von Kessel assures me *in camera caritatis* [as in a confessional] (so he said verbatim, and not ... *veritatis* [in truth]) that the SS authorities also have the same intention." All von Kessel could do now was try to wrap the matter up. From his words it's obvious he went into this meeting to prevent the Holy See from formally writing to Berlin. "Therefore, he insists on the opportunity that everything would be settled with an *oral* declaration."

The next day, during the meeting with the ambassador, Cardinal Maglione reiterated the same points as Tardini. These points included the fact that the incident took place on the steps of the basilica and that once in the basilica, the Palatine Guard refused to hand the religious father over because, in that instant, the Germans were trespassing on extraterritorial soil. And that was utterly unjustified.[813]

Cardinal Maglione demanded a formal assurance from the German embassy that extraterritorial property would be respected in future. Getting that assurance was key to protecting the souls currently hiding out on Vatican property.

What is perhaps surprising is that Maglione did not once refer to Fr. Musters by name or ask directly for his release, especially considered that securing his freedom was the reason why the Cabinet had called in the ambassador. It could be they had received new (but false) intelligence that Musters had already cracked under pressure. Incidentally, if the Germans had become suspicious as to why this one Augustinian father mattered so much, then the whole Roman Escape Line set up was at risk — not just the brave men organizing it but also those they were helping to flee. One of the brutal realities of war is that soldiers are often sacrificed to diplomacy. Perhaps it's as simple as that.

One month after his arrest, a battered, bruised, and bleeding Fr. Musters was dragged from his cell, driven to the railway station, and put on a train to a concentration camp in Germany.

The train on which he was being transported stopped in the city of Florence. The prisoners were ordered out at gunpoint and forced into the courtyard of an

---

[813] ASRS, AA.EE.SS., Stati Ecclesiastici 763, f. 13ʳ, handwritten note of Card. Maglione, May 15, 1944.

old *palazzo* to wait. With seconds to spare as the guards briefly turned their backs, the ever-determined and quick Musters made a daring escape. He fled to an Augustinian monastery outside of Florence, where he was hidden by the monks and had his injuries tended to.

With no accurate word about him since the day of his arrest, the Cabinet, his friends, and his fellow companions of the Roman Escape Line all assumed he had died at Kappler's hands during interrogation. A somber memorial service was held in his honor.

Much to their surprise, two months later, in July 1944, Fr. Musters — alias Dutchpa — turned up again in Rome — very much alive.[814] And very much a hero.

---

[814] ASRS, AA.EE.SS., Stati Ecclesiastici 763, f. 16, article "La Fuga dalla prigionia del sacerdote arrestato a S. Maria M," "*Il Quotidiano*," July 21, 1944.

17

A Short Story of a Common Man
and an Eight-Year-Old Girl

JUST WHAT CAN a self-described "ordinary and common man" like Dottore Mario Finzi do during wartime?[815]

Some men take sides to campaign or to fight. Others, like Finzi, turn their energies toward finding ways to help others in need. During the Second World War, his desire was to assist people in their desperate attempts to relocate in order to escape persecution, and so he served in Bologna, Italy, as the "representative of the Delegation for Assistance for Emigrants (DELASEM)." [816] Yet as the war grew in intensity and scope, he found doors were repeatedly slammed in the faces of the fleeing refugees. Perhaps that's why, in the autumn of 1942, Finzi wrote personally to Pius XII, imploring for the pope's direct help on a specific case: "I beg your pardon for taking the great liberty to address myself directly to You to ask You to want to intervene with Your highest authority and to fulfil an act of Christian charity, by saving a poor creature of eight years old, menaced by hate and by the ferocity of men."[817]

[815] ASRS, AA.EE.SS., ASRS, AA.EE.SS., Ebrei 76, f. 60, letter of Mario Finzi to Pio XII, no date (= September 1942).

[816] ASRS, AA.EE.SS., Ebrei 76, f. 60, letter of Mario Finzi to Pio XII, no date (= September 1942).

[817] ASRS, AA.EE.SS., Ebrei 76, f. 59, letter of Mario Finzi to Pio XII, no date (= September 1942).

The eight-year-old "poor creature" was a little Jewish girl from Yugoslavia named Maja Lang.

Maja's older brother Wladimir, who was seventeen, was living under what was assumed to be house arrest in the town of Sasso Marconi in the province of Bologna. Being apart from his family, in particular his young and helpless sister, was surely a great sorrow. And so it was the teenage Wladimir who had reached out in frantic hope that Dottore Mario Finzi would do everything in his power to save his precious Maja.

Maja and her parents had taken refuge in Croatia. Touched by the heartbreaking case, Finzi prepared his appeal. But, a few days before Finzi's call for papal intervention, the family of three was arrested and transferred to the Croatian island of Brac, located in the Adriatic Sea. In January of 1942, little Maja had already received a permit to go to Hungary to stay with her aunt who lived in Székesfehérvár in Rácóczi — street number 4, where she had resided for a number of months. Hungary was a nation in which Jews, at that time, were still moderately tolerated. But, as Finzi explained in his letter to Pius XII, "now her permit is set to expire, since it was extended for the last time and as it will expire, at the latest in the week of the 10th to 15th of October the little girl will have to be accompanied back to the Croatian border and leave Hungary."

Finzi made a powerful plea for little Maja: "Holy Father, you certainly know the violations against every human and divine law to which the Jews in Croatia are exposed. I am firmly convinced that the brother of the little girl is right when he says that returning to Croatia would mean a sure death: she will be sent into a concentration camp where hunger, epidemics and sadistic treatment make existence impossible."

Then he submitted his plan. The only way to save Maja was to bring her to Italy where she could stay with her brother, Wladimir. Of course, that was not at all an easy endeavor, given that Wladimir was confined in Sasso Marconi. A detail that should not escape the reader of his letter is that Mr. Finzi did not indicate exactly where and in what conditions the teenager was living. That Wladimir was able to contact the *dottore* is proof that he had a limited access to friends in the outside world.

Finzi's plan was to ask the Italian counselor in Budapest to give the little girl a permit to come to Italy. Of course, he was well aware this request would have to overcome a number of obstacles. The counselor would need to be given authorization by his Ministry of Internal Affairs through the Ministry of External Affairs in Rome. While the Italian authorities treated refugees "quite well" once they were on

Italian soil, "they certainly are not that sensitive to considerations of humanity when it comes to letting them enter their territory." Finzi was realistic, knowing that if he were to personally go to the Ministry of Internal Affairs, his efforts would fail. He knew his best chance — and the best chance for little Maja — was to ask the pope for help.

Maja's father was also desperate to help his young daughter reach safety. He had written a request letter asking permission from the Italian authorities to allow little Maja to join her brother in his confinement in Sasso Marconi. And with tentative hope he had also requested permission for himself and his wife to join with "his beloved children." Finzi explained all this in his appeal to Pius XII, concluding,

> There is needed an intervention of a high moral Authority and I could not think of someone else than You, who with fatherly love and with fraternal Christian charity loves all creatures, to whatever faith they belong, and are able to help the miserable who suffer. Holy Father, I know that what I'm asking is not small, but to operate in a Christian way in a world where so much seems the antithesis/negation of Christ, it is not a simple task for the common men. I am confident that You, instead will have a means to intervene effectively.[818]

The pope and his staff did not waste a minute. They knew there was only one contact at their disposal who might succeed in helping Maja. This was the Jesuit father Tacchi Venturi, who was their key go-between with the Fascist government. On September 23, 1942, Maglione wrote to Tacchi Venturi, imploring him "to judge, in his well-known prudence and charity, which steps would be possible and opportune to take regarding this proposal."[819] This request was made on behalf of Maja alone, and one might wonder why that was the case. What of the parents, who desired the best possible circumstance for their daughter but longed to be with their children, as well? The bottom line was this: adding the parents to the request at this stage might well have increased the risk of a negative answer by the authorities. And that could compromise the most important factor — saving little Maja.

Weeks passed. Then months. And then another long, agonizing wartime year had gone by. Finally, on January 17, 1943 (the twenty-first year of the Fascist era

---

[818] ASRS, AA.EE.SS., Ebrei 76, 60, letter of Mario Finzi to Pio XII, no date (= September 1942).

[819] ASRS, AA.EE.SS., Ebrei 76, f. 61, letter of Card. Maglione to Fr. Tacchi Venturi, S.J., September 23, 1942.

but also the last), Fr. Pietro Tacchi Venturi informed Cardinal Maglione that, "given the extreme difficulty to obtain such permits, he had thought to do well to call directly on the Minister of Internal Affairs himself, Mister Guido Buffarini Guidi." Guidi had given instructions to the director general of the state police "that they should allow the married couple Lang and their little daughter Maja to enter in the Kingdom and to stay at Sasso Marconi, with their family-member Wladimiro."[820] It had taken a very long time, but Tacchi Venturi had not only succeeded in gaining permission for the child, but he'd also managed to obtain the same for Maja's parents.

The final, most important question remains. Did the order given by the Italian minister of internal affairs come in time for Maja and her parents? Was the family reunited with each other? It seems they were. It is useless to look on the lists of the Jewish strangers interned in the Italian concentration camps, where the name of Maja's brother, Vladimir — or Wladimir — Lang, appears twice, but both those individuals do not correspond with the brother of Maja.[821] Neither Maja's name nor the names of her parents appear on those lists and they never will, for Wladimir was not living in a camp but surprisingly enough in a villa of the Canova family in Sasso Marconi.[822] He wrote memories of those years in Italy through which we learn that his parents were able to escape over Sarajevo to Spalato, slipping through the cracks just in time.

Of Maja, however, there is no mention in those autobiographical notes of her brother, and so at this point we do not know what happened to her. Her case, though, sheds an interesting light. The fact that Dottore Finzi of Bologna considered Pope Pius XII the only authority still capable of achieving a positive result in this complicated humanitarian case is striking. Finzi seemed very aware of Pius XII's interpretation of and dedication to the principals of active Christian charity and compassion. And yet Mario Finzi himself was a Jew. Wladimir described him in his dairy as a "very young lawyer and a talented musician" who regrettably would be arrested in March 1944, would be deported to Auschwitz, and would die of disease not long after the liberation of the concentration camp.[823] The Lang family was able to return to Yugoslavia in 1945, and from there they moved in 1948 to Israel.

---

[820] ASRS, AA.EE.SS., Ebrei 76, f. 62, letter of Fr. Tacchi Venturi, S.J., to Card. Maglione, January 17, 1943.

[821] See: annapizzuti.it/database.

[822] See: https://it.gariwo.net/giusti/biografie-dei-giusti/shoah-e-nazismo/giusti-tra-le-nazioni-di-yad-vashem/alfonso-canova-20507.html

[823] See: https://it.gariwo.net/giusti/biografie-dei-giusti/shoah-e-nazismo/giusti-tra-le-nazioni-di-yad-vashem/alfonso-canova-20507.html

Come la Paternità Vostra "ev·ma potrà
rilevare dall'acclusa supplica,che Le ri-
metto con preghiera di cortese restituzio-
ne,il Signor dottor Mario Finzi, implora
l'intervento del Santo Padre presso il
Regio Governo Italiano perchè alla bambina jugoslava MAJA IANG,non ariana,at-
tualmente residente a Budapest,sia accor-
dato il permesso di venire in Italia ove
già trovasi suo fratello.

Lascio alla Paternità Vostra di giudi-
care,nella ben nota Sua prudenza e carità,
quali passi sia possibile ed opportuno
compiere in proposito.

Profitto etc...

Reverendissimo Padre
Padre Pietro Tacchi Venturi S.J.
Roma
settembre 1942

Dell'Acqua

Letter from Fr. Tacchi Venturi S.J. to Cardinal Maglione, January 17, 1943.[824]

Together with the local heroes of Sasso Marconi, honored by Yad Vashem, and with the common Jewish man Mario Finzi (victim of the Nazi terror), Pius XII and his staff were able to save almost an entire family. Wladimir has never

[824] ASRS, AA.EE.SS., Ebrei 76, f. 62, letter of Fr. Tacchi Venturi, S.J., to Card. Maglione, January 17, 1943.

known — at least he never mentioned it — the silent force that had made all this possible for them. But unfortunately it was not possible for little Maja. As other historical sources reveal, she fell, despite all efforts done to save her, a victim of the Holocaust.[825]

---

[825] One might presume that little Maja Lang happens to be Maja Mia, born in Osijek in Yugoslavia in 1934, murdered in the extermination camp of Auschwitz, reported on the Yad Vashem digital collection: https://yvng.yadvashem.org/index.html?language=en&advancedSearch=true&sln_value=Lang&sln_type=synonyms&sfn_value=Roza&sfn_type=synonyms.

18

A Tale of a Controversial Word

APRIL 1940. MSGR. Paolo Giobbe, the apostolic internuncio in Holland, sent a letter to Cardinal Maglione in Rome. The members of the International Catholic Office for Refugee Affairs in the city of Utrecht in Holland[826] had learned that "the question ... of the Brazilian immigration visas for catholic refugees, that is the quota that the Holy Father has obtained, ... is now under examination of Your Eminence [Maglione] in collaboration with the Brazilian Ambassador to the Holy See, in order definitively to fix the procedure for their release." In cooperation with the Hamburg-based *St. Raphaelsverein*, the Catholic Association for Aid to Refugees in Germany, the Dutch Committee of Refugee Affairs had organized a first transit of German refugees through the port of Antwerp, with Brazil as their final destination. Anxious to make sure those refugees were successful, we learn from Giobbe's letter that many organizations were asking for information from Pope Pius XII regarding the procedures for obtaining visas for Brazil. One such organization was the "Germany Emergency Committee of the Society of Friends" (Quakers) in London. It had sought the information through its secretary, who had been appointed by Cardinal Hinsley.[827] The American "Friends Service Committee" in Rome and the High Commission for Refugees of the League of Nations were also interested in knowing more about the visas

[826] ASRS, AA.EE.SS., Olanda 77, f. 139, letter of the International Catholic Office for Refugee Affairs to Card. Maglione, April 4, 1940.
[827] See also "A Tale of Dark and Sinister Places II," p. 238; 256.

for Brazil. And so the "International Catholic Office for Refugee Affairs" wrote to Cardinal Maglione that "our recognition would be even bigger if it would be possible for catholic refugees in transit-countries of Europe (not only those in Holland and Belgium, but also those in Italy, England, France and other countries) to realize their emigration towards Brazil. It is known to us that the Catholic Committee of Utrecht, thanks to the lucky intervention of the Holy See, has obtained 217 visas for Brazil."[828]

The three thousand Brazilian visas for Catholic Jews, which were entrusted to Pope Pius XII, offered a window of hope to thousands of people living in countries under the threat of Nazi occupation. Yet within the span of a month, after the Nazi invasions of Holland, Belgium, and France, the granting of those visas would become a lot more difficult.

When it comes to operating in favor of refugees, the Catholic Church is bound by agreements and concordats that have been signed with each country. They allow the Holy See to protect and assist the Catholics in a country, provided it doesn't interfere with matters of internal political order. But the refugee aid also had its downside, especially for the staff of the Cabinet who had to deal with an enormous surplus of work. Allocating the visas and applications for immigrants all over Europe required a great deal of systematic effort and care. A strict tally of the number of applications had to be kept, identities and personal situations needed to be scrutinized and quotas checked for each country — not to mention having to manage the tensions between national committees, who were all too determined to get as many visas as possible for "their candidates." Last but not least, these efforts also had a major financial impact. To get two thousand families to Brazil, with each family consisting of an average of three members, one had to plan on a cost of at least $100,000.[829] The responsibility for it all fell upon Msgr. Dell'Acqua. He would be the one to break his head while dealing with this huge administrative and financial conundrum.

[828] ASRS, AA.EE.SS., Olanda 77, f. 140, letter of the International Catholic Office for Refugee Affairs to Card. Maglione, April 4, 1940.
[829] ASRS, AA.EE.SS., Olanda 77, f. 154ᵛ, report from Msgr. Giobbe to Card. Maglione, April 25, 1940.

ALLEGATO =A= al Rapporto 3064/40   156

KATHOLIEK COMITÉ VOOR VLUCHTELINGEN
KATHOLISCHES HILFSWERK FÜR FLÜCHTLINGE
COMITÉ CATHOLIQUE POUR LES RÉFUGIÉS · CATHOLIC COMMITTEE FOR REFUGEES · COMITÉ CATÓLICO PARA REFUGIADOS

Spreekuren: Drift 10-12   Sprechstunden: Drift 10-12
Iederen dag van 10-12 uur v.m.   täglich, von 10-12 Uhr. vorm.   UTRECHT,   le 20 avril 1940.
behalve op Zaterdag.   mit Ausnahme von Samstag.   Postbus 51 - Telefoon 16364 - Telegramcode: Catocom.
                                                                    Postgiro 320372

156
67
3
2
5
10
5
248

Gelieve in Uw antwoord te vermelden:
Bitte in Ihrer Antwort zu erwähnen: vW/3086.

CERTIFICAT DE BONNES MOEURS.

Par la présente nous déclarons que les 248 personnes
dans la liste ci-jointe sont des réfugiés catholiques
allemands confiés à nos soins. Ce sont des personnes
d'excellente réputation et leur conduite a été irré-
prochable.
Elles désirent se rendre au Brésil afin de se créer une
nouvelle existence.

Au nom du Comité,
Le Secrétaire:

Letter from H. Kuiper to Msgr. Giobbe, April 20, 1940.[830]

*

*   *

On April 20, 1940, Msgr. Dell'Acqua sat in his office and scrawled in pencil the numbers he had computed from the lists on his desk, totaling 248. Two hundred forty-eight refugees. Two hundred forty-eight lives. All of their names and addresses were listed on twenty-six pages that were attached to the letter. In a cover document, the secretary of the committee had assured Dell'Acqua that all persons on the list were "German Catholic refugees" of excellent reputation and irreproachable behavior, who "wanted all to go to Brazil in order to create for themselves a new existence."

[830] ASRS, AA.EE.SS., Olanda 77, f. 156.

Msgr. Dell'Acqua slid paper into his typewriter and began drafting a memo for the superiors with the title "Non-Aryan Catholic refugees in Holland," using the Nazis' sanctioned coded language "non-Aryan Catholic refugees," which of course stands for converted and baptized Jews, but in this case Germans who were no longer considered as such by the law. The purpose of the memo was to determine how many visas were left from the initial number of three thousand.[831] His memo explained that the internuncio in Holland wanted the 248 non-Aryan Catholic refugees, assisted by the National Catholic Committee of Holland, to be included in the number of the three thousand authorized to emigrate. He then summarized the repartition of the visas:

> (a) 1,000 of these visas that are put at disposal by the ambassador of Brazil to the Holy See and are assigned to non-Aryan Catholics who will be recommended by the secretary of state. Those people should be resident in European countries, except Germany or territories occupied by the Germans.

This large number also gave Msgr. Dell'Acqua some flexibility in his work assisting the people who wrote directly to Pius XII.

> (b) 2,000 visas are put at disposal to be issued by the Brazilian embassy in Berlin. They are to be assigned to non-Aryan Catholics who are resident in Germany or in territories occupied by the Germans. And that should be recommended by the Nuncio in Berlin or by the St. Raphaels-Verein of Hamburg.

These visas would be probably the most sought after and yearned for, Dell'Acqua thought. But regarding the above-mentioned two thousand visas, as he continued his memo:

> New difficulties arose, as the ambassador of Brazil in Berlin is reluctant to issue them. It seems that until now he hasn't given out any, or if he has, only a few. On that matter we wrote to the ambassador of Brazil to the Holy See, asking him to put his best work in order so that these visas would be immediately and without difficulty given out to non-Aryan Catholic persons who were recommended by the apostolic Nuncio in Berlin or by the St. Raphaels-Verein. But one is still waiting for a response.

[831] ASRS, AA.EE.SS., Olanda 77, f. 155.

With regard to those specific 248 refugees, for the 156 residing in Holland the office has prepared a note with which we ask that the minister-council of Brazil in Den Haag would be authorized to give out the visa. For the other persons who are not resident in Holland or Germany or territory that is occupied by the Germans we will make special notes to the Embassy of Brazil to the Holy See.

But for the moment, those who find themselves in Germany or in the occupied territories they should turn to the St. Raphaels-Verein of Hamburg or to the Apostolic Nunciature of Berlin. That is what the Brazilian Embassy to the Holy See has established. The 156 non-Aryan Catholic refugees in Holland surely can fit in the number of the one thousand while until today there were given out only 700 visas.[832]

Dell'Acqua's memo shows that the Cabinet was not only supportive of the Dutch efforts but they were also constantly ready to knock on diplomatic doors wherever there was a need. That they used the term *Catholic non-Aryans* is important. No government could criticize the Vatican or accuse it of interference in matters that did not belong to it, because, technically at least, these converts were now part of the flock of believers. And, for the Brazilian government, the distinctive term covered their requirement that only Catholics could apply. It is clear, then, that while individual priests and lay people risked their lives out there on a personal level, the Holy See — the headquarters, if you like — used all legal mechanisms at their disposal to save lives.

Lobbying for refugees was and is still a slow Cabinetcratic business involving soft diplomacy with ambassadors of different countries. But these internal reports prove the Cabinet was committed and very actively doing all they could.

*
*   *

In the following months things changed rapidly and dramatically, creating a completely different geo-military Europe. In August 1940 Msgr. Giobbe, the apostolic internuncio in Holland, wrote again to Rome detailing the precarious situation many people found themselves in after the invasion of his country. Earlier in the

---

[832] ASRS, AA.EE.SS., Olanda 77, ff. 155[r/v].

war, many Jewish refugees had fled from Germany to Holland only to have their sanctuary invaded, placing them in grave danger yet again. Msgr. Giobbe wrote: "After the occupation of Holland by the German Troops, the fate of the non-Aryan Catholic refugees who were welcomed with great hospitality in Holland, has become a situation that is very dangerous and precarious."[833]

The internuncio referred to a house search conducted by the Gestapo of the seats of the National Catholic Committee and of the International Catholic Cabinet in Utrecht, during which the president of the latter, Professor Schmutzer, and his wife were taken into custody by the Gestapo and detained in their offices for an entire day.

> And after a very rough and detailed interrogation, of which they had to sign afterwards the deposition, they were subjected to a full and intrusive body search like real delinquents. After all this they were set free but on the 12th of July Schmutzer was again put in prison, they said by order that came directly from Berlin. Prof. Schmutzer has been very generous towards the Spanish nationalist refugees who looked for shelter in Holland — fleeing the civil war, for which he had a document of recognition by General Franco who thanked him for it.
>
> I insisted immediately to the Charge D'Affaires of Spain in Holland that he should try by way of his government to do everything possible to get Schmutzer freed. But I don't know about the results of this intervention.
>
> In the beginning of June Schmutzer had come to the nunciature to tell me that given the new state of affairs they had decided, along with the archbishop of Utrecht, to close up the International Office for Refugees and to recommend the American Committee in New York to reconstitute it in that city.[834]

Msgr. Giobbe also forwarded to Rome a letter he had received some weeks later from the Catholic Cabinet for Refugees of New York. The undersigner was a certain

[833] ASRS, AA.EE.SS., Olanda 77, f. 210, report from Msgr. Giobbe to Card. Maglione, August 26, 1940.

[834] ASRS, AA.EE.SS., Olanda 77, ff. 210$^{r/v}$, report from Msgr. Giobbe to Card. Maglione, August 26, 1940.

Dr. F. W. Hess. After making clear the means and goals that we already know about this particular committee, Giobbe wrote:

> Dr. Hess asked if I would be willing to approach Your Eminence to see if you would help him facilitate some of the initiatives that the organisation for refugees has in mind. The first one — the International Cabinet would like to establish in the republics of Venezuela and Chile structures to help refugees. They have the goal of founding local committees in the capitals of these countries. And therefore, he asks if the Secretariat of State could take an interest in this and if the Pontifical Representation [the nunciatures and apostolic delegations] in these nations would help to give assistance and protection to these committees that are setting up.[835]

Clearly, Hess was asking for the direct support of the Holy See — both political and diplomatic — to gain assistance and protection for these committees. The fact that they asked for it means they knew the support was likely. Msgr. Giobbe continued: "The international Cabinet — Mr Hess — would also like to use the 3,000 visas that the Republic of Brazil has put at the disposal of the Holy Father, in order that a certain number of non-aryan Catholic refugees would be allowed to stay in the United States temporarily as visitors and could be then sent to those republics of Venezuela and Chile afterwards."

Then Giobbe asked: If what Hess said was indeed true, how many visas could be given out and what would be the procedures involved?

A handwritten internal memo, written by Msgr. Tardini and found in the Historical Archive,[836] reflects on this particular request. He noted:

> "Pay a lot of attention! We have to be aware.
>
> (1) This international committee for refugees with its headquarters in Holland was born in an equivocal way; it wanted to give itself an importance and a charge that was much higher than

[835] ASRS, AA.EE.SS., Olanda 77, f. 210ᵛ, report from Msgr. Giobbe to Card. Maglione, August 26, 1940.
[836] ASRS, AA.EE.SS., Olanda 77, f. 213, handwritten notes of Msgr. Tardini, September 3, 1940.

those that the Secretary of State sent in a letter at the beginning to Monsignor Godfrey.

(2) The American Committee is more dangerous than the one in Holland, as it [America] is the country of— disorder — and protest. And disorder and protest are both circumstances that would not be beneficial for the Holy See to enter into. Therefore, it would be opportune to have the Nuncio to respond to the letter of Mr Hess and then saying first, (1) That the committee of Utrecht only has a function for coordination, specifically for Europe. (2) And that therefore, given the recent events and the actual situation, Hess's duty is over.

(3) In the United States, where we have a committee that is presided by and depends on Bishops, it is not necessary and opportune to create another one, or to replace one with another. The one that exists there is sufficient to accomplish everything we need to have in process. In fact, it is evident that if the Bishops of the United States would contact Bishops of these South American nations they will find understanding, listening ears for help.

And therefore, we don't have to talk about this international committee anymore. And regarding all of this, we should additionally inform the apostolic delegation in Washington, and this is my opinion.

Tardini didn't see the need for any new committees. And so the request of Dr. Hess was immediately rejected. This does not mean, however, that Tardini was resistant to help. It means he didn't see the sense in setting up a new committee to do the same thing that one already existing was doing.

Strangely enough, although Tardini had exhausted the issue and had stated his decision, at the end of his annotations he offered a somewhat odd proposal: "But I ask however that Monsignor Lombardi, who knows the issue of the Jews better than I would also give his opinion on it."[837]

*

*   *

[837] ASRS, AA.EE.SS., Olanda 77, f. 213, handwritten notes of Msgr. Tardini, September 3, 1940.

So, at Tardini's request, desk officer Msgr. Armando Lombardi responded. He used a "curial style" that a friend of mine calls "Vaticanese," which is the typical language of the Roman Curia, or "Court of Rome": "I don't think I have this particular competence on the Jews that His Excellence the Secretary is attributing to me. It is a very difficult thing to get to know them well, the Jews. My experience of these past 40 days ... in their company has taught me that the Church is good and right to qualify them as the Holy Friday qualifies them."[838] Here, Lombardi pointed to a much-debated phrase that the Catholic Church recited during the liturgy on Holy Friday, a phrase in which the Christians prayed for God's mercy for the "perfidious" Jews who were responsible for the death of Christ. Lombardi defended the phrase and its theological background. However, he then went on to suggest that "the work of fatherly charity undertaken by the Holy Father in favor of them has something of the sublime and heroic." When I came across this document in the Archives, it struck me immediately: Lombardi's sentence betrayed a different view toward the Jews than that held by other colleagues and superiors. Msgr. Lombardi maintained the archaic theological viewpoint that Jews should be held accountable as those who delivered the Lord and sentenced Him to death. Yet Lombardi's comment that followed makes it clear he knew all too well that Pius XII held another opinion. Furthermore, it implicitly states that the pope assigned to himself a mission to help the Jews.

Lombardi did agree fully with Tardini's assessment that there was no need for a new committee. And he went further in criticizing the way the committee of Utrecht in Holland had operated until then. He referred to a recent controversy over some of the refugees sent to Brazil. Following that transfer, Brazil had immediately slammed shut its doors. Lombardi explained:

> Regarding the Cabinet in Utrecht, I'm taking the liberty to remind you of the very bad situation in which it has placed the Holy See and also the cause that it intended to serve. By making it possible for those 156 individuals (many of them non-Baptised and militants of the communist party) to depart for Brazil — an occurrence to which the nuncio of Rio de Janeiro referred in an open speech to the Embassy of Brazil — those particular refugees have made a painful, negative impression in their new country. A very bad service

[838] ASRS, AA.EE.SS., Olanda 77, f. 215, internal note by Msgr. Lombardi, September 6, 1940.

indeed given to the Holy See, because these individuals have been recommended by the same Holy See. It was, without any doubt, quite damaging to the cause of refugee-aid, because, due to this "very painful impression" the Brazilian government was induced to take restrictive measures, measures that have now paralyzed all practices of immigration, that were functioning regularly between the Embassy and the Holy See.[839]

Lombardi asserted that in the end,

> We can all be sure to have been victims of deception: the St. Raphaels-Verein, the Bishops, the Nuncios and the Secretariat of State. Some days ago Father Hecht of the St. Raphaels-Verein in Germany told me he believes that of those recommended to the Embassy of Brazil *more than 100* non-Aryans are not baptised. I have the impression that the diocese of Milan and Genova are the most deceived. Some of the cases were discovered by the Secretariat of State, but here we have neither the means nor the time to investigate fully the single cases that were given to us. And therefore, it gives some comfort reminding ourselves that *tutto è carità* — all is charity.

What can be said of Lombardi's concern? We can explain it in more than one way. Either he was an anti-Semite and deeply worried about the theological aspect of baptizing people he believed did not and could not belong to the Faith. Or perhaps he was simply worried that if the authorities in Brazil or other countries discover the refugees are not sincere Catholic, then that would cause diplomatic problems that might in turn compromise the lifeline set up by the Cabinet. Perhaps there is some truth to both explanations. It was clear that Lombardi had lost his patience. Yet although he was at odds with the pope's thinking regarding all this, he included the phrase *tutto è carità* — all is charity — which was obviously the central point on the agenda of Pius XII's magisterium. The inclusion of this phrase as a postscript seems to be an attempt by Lombardi to mask his dissatisfaction.

But then, as his reply continued, we are left with no doubt as to what Lombardi really thought. His anti-Semitism is revealed in a not-too-thinly veiled criticism of the pope:

[839] ASRS, AA.EE.SS., Olanda, 77, f. 216.

In so far as the gratitude in the heart of these Jews who were granted help is concerned, we know from a short examination that the percentage of those who really are thankful for the favor is only 5 per cent.... That's not even close to the percentage of gratitude that our Lord (Jesus) received after the healing of the ten lepers. One sees that in the last nineteen centuries the "race" has become worse.

But, all is charity: charity that, in this case, has something of the sublime and heroic.

No comment.

One should keep in mind that this was 1940, the first year of the war. Mass deportations to concentration camps of those whom the cold-blooded Nazis determined were unworthy were realities that would occur in the coming months. But what is clear from this exchange of views on a practical problem within the Cabinet is that some people in the Roman Curia — was it ever different and will it ever be? — were in serious disagreement with the pope's thinking and agenda. Pius XII's new way of viewing certain issues collided with the ideas of some conservatives in the Roman Curia who wanted to stick to the reviling of the Jewish people. Lombardi's sarcastic words make it quite clear that he knew the pope did not in the least embrace his anti-Semitic attitude. The pope's belief was that the Jewish people were our fellow brothers and friends. This view was astonishingly modern thinking for the time. But was it really that new?

In my discussions with my friends and colleagues, I often recommend they study the role of Pius XII in World War II in the light of his actions during the First World War, when he was minister of foreign affairs of the Holy See and head of the Cabinet, in the position held by Tardini during World War II.

One document in particular has remained completely unnoticed to his day in the context of Eugenio Pacelli's views on the Jewish people. It is an official letter of the secretary of state, Cardinal Pietro Gasparri, on February 9, 1916, in response to a petition by the American Jewish Committee in New York. The committee had asked for a public intervention of the Holy See in favor of the Jews that were persecuted and slaughtered in the Eastern War Zone, especially in Poland (those persecutions already took place during the First World War).[840] And here goes Cardinal Gasparri's reply:

---

[840] ASRS, AA.EE.SS., America 1915–1916, Pos. 195, fasc. 109, f. 7, letter of the American Jewish Committee to Pope Benedict XV, December 30, 1915.

The Supreme Pontiff is unable to express himself concerning the special facts referred to in the memorandum [of the American Jewish Committee], but in principle, as the Head of the Catholic Church, which, faithful to its divine doctrine and to its most glorious traditions, considers all men as brethren and teaches to love one another, he will not cease to inculcate the observance among individuals as among nations of the principles of natural right, and to reprove any violation of them. This right should be observed and respected in relation to the children of Israel as it should be as for all men, for it would not conform to justice and to religion itself to derogate therefrom solely because of a difference of religious faith.[841]

The impact of this message was not lost on the American Jewish Committee. They deemed it to be "a virtual encyclical."[842] And the *American Hebrew and Jewish Messenger* declared:

Among all the papal bulls ever issued with regard to Jews throughout the history of the Vatican there is no statement that equals this direct, unmistakable plea for equality for the Jews, and against prejudice upon religious grounds. The Bull issued by Innocent IV, declaring the Jews innocent of the charge of using Christian blood for ritual purposes, while a remarkable document, was, after all, merely a statement of fact, whereas the present statement by Pope Benedict XV is a plea against religious prejudice and persecution.[843]

Eugenio Pacelli was the co-inspirator (if not the main author) of Gasparri's letter: its file is preserved in his Historical Archive of that time. Is it possible that such a point of view, such a course of sailing with the compass fixed on considering that all men are brothers, teaching them to love one another regardless of a difference in religious faith would have changed radically over the next twenty-five years? I

[841] ASRS, AA.EE.SS., America 1915–1916, Pos. 195, fasc. 109, f. 8, typewritten copy of the letter of Card. Gasparri to Mr. Louis Marshall and the members of the Executive Committee of the American Jewish Committee, February 9, 1916.

[842] ASRS, AA.EE.SS., America 1915–1916, Pos. 195, fasc. 109, f. 6, press release prepared by the American Jewish Committee, April 17, 1916.

[843] ASRS, AA.EE.SS., America 1915–1916, Pos. 195, fasc. 109, f. 13, *The American Hebrew and Jewish Messenger*, April 21, 1916 — Nisan 18, 5676.

doubt it strongly, and I even believe it is quite the opposite. A close reading shows that it could be the preliminary text to the Second Vatican Council's *Nostra aetate*.

Nostra aetate, which is the Second Vatican Council's document on relations with non-Christian religions, with special attention given to the relation of the Catholic Church with the Jewish people, has to be seen in this light. The Second Vatican Council was announced in October 1959, only a year after the death of Pope Pius XII. And it was established in 1962 under John XXIII, the former diplomat of Pius XII, Angelo Roncalli. *Nostra aetate* itself was decreed in 1965 by his successor, Paul VI, who served as the former substitute of the secretary of state, Giovanni Battista Montini. This followed Pope Paul VI's historic visit to the Holy Land in 1964, during which the Vatican delegation, including Msgr. Dell'Acqua, who stood at the pope's side, lit six candles in memory of the six million Jews killed by the Nazis. Angelo Roncalli is also remembered for his activities as an apostolic delegate and nuncio under Pius XII's pontificate, dealing in hard times and in difficult regions throughout Europe, giving help to Jews. Later on, in 1965, the "all is charity" motto would be condensed into a theological statement as part of a major Church document. One should not be surprised by this; it is pure Catholic logic and progression. Church magisterium documents have a long period of development — over a matter of years and sometimes decades. In this case, these decades include the pontificate of Pius XII, which served as a most important and worthy workshop on how and what Catholic believers should think about the Jewish people.

Unfortunately, during the last half of the twentieth century there was an ongoing isolation and fragmentation of the Second Vatican Council, frequently caused by those who were most devoted to it. They often acted and spoke as if the evolved Church doctrine was a spur of the moment invention, a deus ex machina in the magisterium of the popes, a complete turning point in the history of the Church that had occurred all of a sudden. This is not true. The participants in the Second Vatican Council were men who had been members of the circles working for Pius XII. Throughout the tumultuous years of the terrible war and the years that followed, they had been greatly impressed and influenced by Pius XII's thinking regarding the Jews and how Christians should respect and help them in the name of God. And this is exactly what Msgr. Armando Lombardi did not want to accept or approve, together with the more than eighty bishops who voted against accepting this document during the Second Vatican Council.

In my opinion *Nostra aetate* is the official breakthrough, or better yet, the "fixation," of the thinking of Pope Pius XII — namely, charity above all. Roncalli, the former apostolic delegate and nuncio; Giovanni Battista Montini, the former substitute of the secretariat of state; Tardini, the former secretary of "the Cabinet"; and, oh yes, the former desk officer Dell'Acqua were all present to stand at the baptismal font of the magnificent *Nostra aetate*, a document that has an important place in the history of the Catholic Church, so sublime and heroic.

Biographical Outlines

BAFILE, CORRADO (born July 4, 1903, L'Aquila, Italy — died February 3, 2005, Rome, Italy) was a cardinal of the Roman Catholic Church. He was the youngest of twelve sons of a physician. At the age of twenty-three, he gained a doctorate in law at Sapienza University in Rome, then became legal procurator, and only at twenty-nine decided to pursue Holy Orders. He was a desk officer of the Secretariat of State and did pastoral work in Rome from 1939 to 1960, when he was ordained archbishop and appointed nuncio to Germany by John XXIII. From May 1975 to June 1980, he served as prefect of the Congregation for the Causes of Saints. He was elevated to the cardinalate in 1976, and at the time of his death at almost 102 years, he was the oldest member of the College of Cardinals.

BARBETTA, GIULIO (born May 13, 1890, Orbetello (Grosseto), Italy — died January 14, 1976) was a desk officer of the Congregation for Extraordinary Ecclesiastical Affairs (the equivalent of the Holy See's foreign ministry) in the Secretariat of State. In 1962 he was ordained titular bishop of Pharan.

Dell'Acqua, Angelo (born December 9, 1903, Milan, Italy — died August 27, 1972, Lourdes, France) entered the Roman Curia in 1938 to work as desk officer of the Secretariat of State, where he was charged with the coordination of the daily rescue operations by the Holy See of Jews all over Europe. Those efforts are particularly preserved in the Ebrei Files of the AA.EE.SS. fund in the Historical Archive of the Secretariat of State. On February 17, 1953, he was appointed substitute of the Secretariat of State (the equivalent to an interior minister) and on

June 26, 1967, he was elevated to cardinal. From the following year to death he served as vicar-general of Rome.

DI MEGLIO, GIUSEPPE (born August 15, 1907, Barano d'Ischia, Italy — died July 19, 1994, Rome) specialist in canon, civil, and international law. Ordained a priest on December 21, 1929, he entered the Secretariat of State as a "scriptor" in 1933. Pius XI sent him to the apostolic nunciature of Vienna during the delicate and difficult period of the annexation of Austria by Germany, and then to the nunciature of Germany under the religious persecution of the Third Reich. On the express assignment of Pius XII in May 1939, he participated with Apostolic Nuncio Msgr. Giovanni Cicognani in the meeting in Berchtesgaden with the German chancellor Hitler and Foreign Minister von Ribbentrop to suggest an international peace conference in order to avoid the invasion of Poland. During World War II, he served as a desk officer of the Congregation for Extraordinary Ecclesiastical Affairs in the Secretariat of State. Known for his juridical skills, classical culture, dedication, and spirit of service, he has received various honors and, due to glaucoma, was blind for the last twenty-seven years of his life.

LOMBARDI, ARMANDO (born May 12, 1905, Cercepiccola (Campobasso), Italy — died May 4, 1964, Rio de Janeiro, Brazil) entered the Pontifical Ecclesiastical Academy, the Vatican school for diplomacy, in 1934 and started his diplomatic career by joining the Secretariat of State as desk officer of the Congregation for Extraordinary Ecclesiastical Affairs (the equivalent of the Holy See's foreign ministry) in the Secretariat of State in 1940. After the war, in 1950, he was appointed apostolic nuncio to Venezuela and in 1954 apostolic nuncio to Brazil, carrying out diplomatic and pastoral activities throughout Latin America for almost fifteen years.

MAGLIONE, LUIGI (born March 2, 1877, Casoria (Naples), Italy — died August 22, 1944, Casoria, (Naples), Italy) became a cardinal of the Roman Catholic Church in 1935 and since March 10, 1939, served under Pope Pius XII. Having succeeded his schoolmate Eugenio Pacelli as secretary of state when the latter became Pope Pius XII, he was so close to him that Italian people joked, "Whenever the pope went out without his Maglione ["sweater" in Italian], he caught cold." On behalf of Pius XII, he took steps to oppose and to soften the racial laws and organized the help for persecuted Jews and baptized Jews. After his death in 1944, Pius XII did not replace Maglione and assumed the responsibilities of the office himself, with the assistance of both Msgr. Tardini, head of its foreign affairs section, and Msgr. Montini, head of the internal affairs section.

MONTINI, GIOVANNI BATTISTA (born September 26, 1897, Concesio (Brescia), Italy — died August 6, 1978, Castel Gandolfo (Rome), Italy; beatified October 19, 2014, and canonized October 14, 2018) was the future pope St. Paul VI (1963–1978). On December 13, 1937, he was appointed substitute of the Secretariat of State (the equivalent to an interior minister), and on December 15, 1958, he was elevated to the cardinalate. As one of the closest advisors of Pius XII, he had a key role in the Pontificia Commissione di Assistenza, the papal committee also known as "Vatican Relief," devoted to delivering prompt and direct aid to war refugees and prisoners (later changed into Caritas Italiana, the charitable arm of the Italian Bishops Conference). On June 21, 1963, he was elected pope and took the name Paul VI.

POGGI, LUIGI (born November 25, 1917, Piacenza, Italy — died May 4, 2010, Rome, Italy) was a diplomat and cardinal of the Roman Catholic Church. He was ordained a priest in his hometown at the age of twenty-three, and in 1944 he graduated in canonical and civil law in Rome. He then served in the diplomatic service of the Roman Curia at the Pontifical Ecclesiastical Academy until 1946, while also devoting himself to pastoral activities. In 1945, he joined the Secretariat of State in the Congregation for Extraordinary Ecclesiastical Affairs (the equivalent of the Holy See's foreign ministry). Twenty years later he was ordained archbishop. He served in various apostolic nunciatures (Central Africa, Cameroon, Gabon, Perù, Poland, and Italy) from 1965 to 1992. Through the 1970s and into the first half of the 1980s, Pope Paul VI and Pope John Paul II used Poggi's experience in Polish politics for their "Ostpolitik," which was aimed at improving Vatican relations with the Communist-ruled nations of the Warsaw Pact. In 1944 he was elevated to cardinal and appointed archivist and librarian of the Holy Roman Church. He retired in 1998 and died at the age of ninety-two as cardinal archivist emeritus of the Vatican Secret Archive.

PIUS XII, original name Eugenio Maria Giuseppe Giovanni Pacelli (born March 2, 1876, Rome Italy — died October 9, 1958, Castel Gandolfo (Rome), Italy), was born to a Roman family that was part of the papal nobility, with a long family tradition of jurists and lawyers in service to the Holy See and the city of Rome. Before his election to the papacy, he served as secretary of the Congregation of Extraordinary Ecclesiastical Affairs (the equivalent of the Holy See's foreign ministry). In 1917, he was appointed apostolic nuncio to Bavaria and then also to Germany in 1920. Under Pius XI, Pacelli was appointed cardinal secretary of state (February 9, 1930–February 10, 1939). He traveled widely on papal missions, visiting South America (1934) and North America (1936), where he was known as "the flying cardinal" because he traveled across the United States by airplane. He also visited France (1935, 1937) and Hungary (1937). In March 1939 he was elected pope, choosing the name of Pius XII. During his pontificate, the cautious and diplomatic pope confronted the ravages of World War II (1939–1945), the abuses of the Fascist and other totalitarian regimes, the horror of the Holocaust, the challenge of postwar reconstruction, and the threat of the Cold War.

SAMORÈ, ANTONIO (born December 4, 1905, Bardi (Piacenza), Italy — died February 3, 1983, Rome, Italy) was a diplomat and cardinal of the Roman Catholic Church. In 1938, after completing a six-year-long commitment to the Baltic, he was briefly called to the nunciature of Bern as chargé d'affaires, and then to the Secretariat of State by Msgr. Tardini, where he remained from 1938 to 1947. From 1947 to 1949 he collaborated with Msgr. Amleto Cicognani in the apostolic delegation of Washington, D.C. In 1950 he was ordained archbishop and appointed apostolic nuncio to Colombia. Three years later he was appointed secretary of the Congregation for Extraordinary Ecclesiastical Affairs (the equivalent of the Holy See's foreign ministry). In 1967, Paul VI elevated him to the rank of cardinal. One year later he was appointed prefect of the Congregation of the Discipline of the Sacraments and, in 1974, archivist and librarian of the Holy Roman Church.

SIGISMONDI, PIETRO (born February 23, 1908, Villa d'Almè (Bergamo), Italy — died May 25, 1967) served in the diplomatic service of the Holy See from 1934 to 1954. He was appointed archbishop and apostolic delegate to Congo and Rwanda in 1949 by Pius XII, who then appointed him secretary of the Congregation for the Propagation of the Faith: a role he held from 1954 until his death, at the age of fifty-nine.

TARDINI, DOMENICO (born February 29, 1888, Rome, Italy — died July 30, 1961, Rome, Italy) was born in Trastevere, in the heart of Rome, where his father was a butcher. Known for his charisma, feisty temper, and sense of justice, he headed the Congregation for Extraordinary Ecclesiastical Affairs (an equivalent of a ministry of foreign affairs). Tardini is known for his personal way of conducting diplomacy: blunt, keen, and full of typical Roman sarcasm. He had great authority among the members of the Roman Curia and was considered the confidant of Pope Pius XII. On November 17, 1958, John XXIII appointed him cardinal secretary of state.

Lexicon

ARYAN: in the Nazi party's definition of this term, it refers to an ideological concept based on the quest for biological purity of the German "race." The ideal Aryan was blond with blue eyes and light, Caucasian skin. Those considered to be "non-Aryan" individuals presented potential "biological" deficiencies: Jews, Roma, homosexuals, disabled people, psychiatric or hereditary patients, and so on.

CABLE: a message sent by electric signal

CANON: a religious man belonging to a chapter or congregation whose function is to devote himself to prayer and to advise a parish priest or bishop. He can also engage in teaching, charitable activities, and so forth.

CARDINAL: the highest dignitaries in the Roman Catholic Church, first collaborators of the pope. All cardinals assist the pope in the exercise of his functions. Nowadays, the cardinals under the age of seventy-five have the right to participate in his election.

CAVALIERE (A KNIGHT): title of honor bestowed by the pope on some distinguished members of the Catholic Church in recognition for their merits or also a secular noble title or honorific distinction.

CONGREGATION FOR EXTRAORDINARY ECCLESIASTICAL AFFAIRS: the congregation officially erected by Pius VII in 1814 that functioned as a ministry for foreign affairs of the Vatican Secretariat of State. During World War

II it was headed by Secretary Msgr. Tardini. It has changed name several times and is now called Section for Relations with States and International Organizations (Second Section).

CURIA/CURIALIST: The curia is the administrative apparatus of the Holy See that assists the pope in the day-to-day exercise of his jurisdiction over the Roman Catholic Church. A curialist is a member of the Roman Curia.

DICASTERY: a ministry or department of the Roman Curia (Congregation or Pontifical Council) through which the pope conducts the regular administration of the Catholic Church.

DISPATCH: an internal correspondence from the highest authorities of the Secretariat of State to the pontifical representatives abroad.

EBREI FILES: the archival series of incalculable historical value preserved in the Historical Archive of the Section for Relations with States and International Organizations of the Secretariat of State containing the pleas of Jews (*ebrei* in Italian), Christian baptized or not, from all over Europe to Pope Pius XII. They provide an invaluable historical testimony.

ENCYCLICAL: a magisterial document of the pope of the highest importance with commemorative, exhortative, or dogmatic character. An encyclical takes its name from the first two or three words of its text — for example, *Rerum novarum* (1891) and *Laudato si'* (2015). The encyclical letter is a rare form among the papal documents, used for a particular target group or argument. Normally written in Latin, the only exception was the encyclical letter *Mit brennender Sorge* (With burning concern) of 1937, issued by Pius XI during the Nazi era.

EXCELLENCY: honorific title of bishops, archbishops, princes, and ambassadors.

HOLY SEE: the body, endowed with juridical personality in international law, governed by the pope.

MEMORANDUM: a unilateral diplomatic document, similar to the pro memoria but more exhaustive.

METROPOLITAN: in the Orthodox Church, a bishop having authority over the bishops of a province, in particular one ranking above archbishop and below patriarch.

MINUTANTE: desk officer of the Secretariat of State, originally in charge of preparing the "minutes". He is generally a priest who has entered a diplomatic career, in charge of writing official notes, detailed reporting, drafts of public texts, and so on.

MONSIGNOR: honorary title for bishops, archbishops, and some selected priests with particular functions.

NUNCIATURE: the permanent diplomatic representation of the Holy See located in the capital of a foreign state. It is headed by an apostolic nuncio, an ambassador of the pope, and it exercises the dual function of representation to the foreign head of state and to the local Church.

POPE: the successor of St. Peter, prince of the apostles and vicar of Christ in the world. The pope, also called Roman Pontiff or Holy Father, embodies the supreme authority and is the visible head of the Catholic Church. He is also the bishop of Rome.

PRIMATE: ecclesiastical title attributed to bishops who have precedence over a number of other bishops, whose authority extends to entire regions or countries.

PRO MEMORIA (AIDE-MÉMOIRE): a unilateral diplomatic document, not undersigned, official but not binding.

RABBI: a doctor of Jewish law, often spiritual leader of a Jewish community and teacher on Judaism.

REPORT: internal correspondence from the pontifical diplomatic representatives to the superiors of the Secretariat of State.

ROMAN CURIA: the institutions and authorities that constitute the administrative apparatus of the Holy See. The Roman Curia assists the pope in the day-to-day exercise of his jurisdiction over the Roman Catholic Church.

SECRETARIAT OF STATE: the central body of the Holy See that assists the pope in his daily political-administrative activities and duties, and in the relations with the curial dicasteries, with apostolic nunciatures, with foreign states and international organizations. Head of the Secretariat of State is the cardinal secretary of state. During World War II it was divided into two Sections: the First Section was that for foreign policy and was headed by a secretary and an undersecretary.

The Second Section was in charge of general affairs. It was headed by the substitute and the assessor.

UDITORE (AUDITOR) OF THE NUNCIATURE: a diplomatic agent, collaborator of the apostolic nuncio. He ranks higher than secretary and lower than the counselor of the nunciature.

NOTE VERBALE: a written communication from institution to institution, short and written in the third person, without signature but with the stamp and initials of the superior.

SECOND VATICAN COUNCIL: a council is the assembly of all bishops convened and presided over by the pope to discuss doctrinal and disciplinary problems of the Catholic Church. The Second Vatican Council was formally opened under the pontificate of Pope John XXIII on October 11, 1962, and was closed under Pope Paul VI on December 8, 1965. It addressed in particular the relations between the Catholic Church and the modern world, the ecumenical dimension of the Catholic Faith, and interreligious dialogue.

Acknowledgments

I AM GRATEFUL for the many opportunities in my lifetime to meet and discuss with authors, scholars, specialists, and friends on Pius XII and World War II history. My masters of the Jesuit University in Rome merit a special mention. Among them, Fr. Paulius Rabikauskas, S.J., Fr. Pierre Blet, S.J., and Fr. Peter Gumpel, S.J., certainly crossed my path not accidentally. There are plenty of others I should mention, who helped me better understand Pius XII and his entourage, even when sometimes we disagreed. Some of them have sadly passed away and are fondly remembered. I thank all of them for their presence, inspiration, and vivid discussions during the past forty years: Cardinal Walter Brandmüller, Gisela Heidenreich, Jobst Knigge, Katrin Boeckh, Peter Pfister, Karl-Joseph Hummel, Michael Hesemann, Michael Feldkamp, Thomas Brechenmacher, Hubert Wolf, Dominik Burkhard, Msgr. Stefan Heid, Hartmut Benz, Gerd Vesper, Lutz Klinkhammer, Stefan Samerski, Philipp Weber, Horst H. von Wächter (Germany), Cardinal James Francis Stafford, Ron Rychlack, Susan Zuccotti, Fr. Gerald P. Fogarty, S.J., William Doino, Gary Krupp, Mark Riebling (United States), Robert Ventresca (Canada), Sr. Sabine Schratz, O.P. (Ireland), Guy Walters, Philippe Sands (Great Britain), Jean-Baptiste Amadieu, Marie Levant, Jean-Marie Ticchi, Jacques Prévotat, François-Xavier de Monts de Savasse (France), Robrecht Boudens, Lieve Gevers, Jean Puraye, Pierre Romain, Johan Van Canneyt, Dominiek Oversteyns, F.S.O., Lieven Saerens, Dries Vanysacker, Jan De Volder, Bruno Boute, Jean Cornet d'Elzius, Guy Deploige (Belgium), Jan Bank, Fr. Peter van Meijl, S.D.S., Stijn Fens, Rob Moscou, Cees van Nijnatten,

Paul van Geest, Victor Broers, Raphaël Hunsucker (Netherlands), Rupert Klieber, Andreas Gottsmann, Peter Rohrbacher, Stefaan Missine (Austria), Giorgia Pacelli, Sr. Margherita Marchione, Massimiliano Valente, Matteo Napolitano, Andrea Riccardi, Andrea Tornielli, Alberto Melloni, Martino Patti, Msgr. Francesco Maria Tasciotti, Giovanni Rizzardi, Giancarlo Caronello, Giovanni Coco, Alejandro Dieguez, Agostino Giovagnoli, Massimo de Leonardis, Emilio Artiglieri, Pier Luigi Guiducci, Andrea Pagano, Cristina Rossi, Alessandro Bellino, Fr. Livio Poloniato, O.F.M. Conv., Pietro Gaudenzi, Agostino Riccobelli (Italy), Phillippe Chenaux (Switzerland), Fr. Adam Somorjai, O.S.B., András Fejérdy (Hungary), Emília Hrabovec (Slovakia), Jure Krišto (Croatia), and Jeanine Burns (New Zealand).

In conclusion, I thank the publishers Elsa Lafon and Paul Van den Heuvel for their remarkable trust in this challenging initiative; Denis Bouchain and Honorine Dupuy d'Angeac for their continuous support along this project; Anne Maria Dube for the careful revision and editing of the manuscript; my superiors of the Secretariat of State, His Eminence Cardinal Pietro Parolin, His Excellency Msgr. Paul Richard Gallagher, and the Very Reverend Msgr. Mirosław Stanisław Wachowski, who without taking the slightest glimpse of the pages you are about to read, silently acknowledged my aspirations to write this book. I thank my colleagues of the Secretariat of State and the staff of the Historical Archive for the shared enthusiasm. Special thanks go to Katelijne Vandeputte, Felix and Lutgart Wolfs for their hospitality and the inspiring moments in the course of this endeavor and Lea Discart-Geukens and Rik and Gina Storms for their lively encouragement. To my wife and daughters for their daily patience, to my sisters and brother for their everlasting support, and to all friends worldwide I owe thanks and a profound gratitude.

About the Author

JOHAN ICKX EARNED a doctorate in Church history from the Pontificia Università Gregoriana and is the author of a book on the Vatican during World War I, *La guerre et le Vatican: Les secrets de la diplomatie du Saint Siège* (1914–1915). As head of the Historical Archive of the Secretariat of State of the Holy See, he orchestrated the digitization of the Vatican's World War II archives ahead of their official opening to researchers in March 2020.

Sophia Institute

Sophia Institute is a nonprofit institution that seeks to nurture the spiritual, moral, and cultural life of souls and to spread the Gospel of Christ in conformity with the authentic teachings of the Roman Catholic Church.

Sophia Institute Press fulfills this mission by offering translations, reprints, and new publications that afford readers a rich source of the enduring wisdom of mankind.

Sophia Institute also operates the popular online Catholic resource CatholicExchange.com. *Catholic Exchange* provides world news from a Catholic perspective as well as daily devotionals and articles that will help readers to grow in holiness and live a life consistent with the teachings of the Church.

In 2013, Sophia Institute launched Sophia Institute for Teachers to renew and rebuild Catholic culture through service to Catholic education. With the goal of nurturing the spiritual, moral, and cultural life of souls, and an abiding respect for the role and work of teachers, we strive to provide materials and programs that are at once enlightening to the mind and ennobling to the heart; faithful and complete, as well as useful and practical.

Sophia Institute gratefully recognizes the Solidarity Association for preserving and encouraging the growth of our apostolate over the course of many years. Without their generous and timely support, this book would not be in your hands.

www.SophiaInstitute.com
www.CatholicExchange.com
www.SophiaInstituteforTeachers.org

Sophia Institute Press' is a registered trademark of Sophia Institute.
Sophia Institute is a tax-exempt institution as defined by the
Internal Revenue Code, Section 501(c)(3). Tax I.D. 22-2548708.